· DIARY OF A · SURVIVOR

Nineteen Years in a Cuban
Women's Prison

Also by Glenn Garvin

Everybody Had His Own Gringo: The CIA and the Contras

· DIARY OF A · SURVIVOR

Nineteen Years in a Cuban Women's Prison

by

ANA RODRÍGUEZ
and GLENN GARVIN

St. Martin's Press ❧ New York

Design by Junie Lee

Library of Congress Cataloging-in-Publication Data

Rodríguez, Ana.
    Diary of a survivor : nineteen years in a Cuban women's prison / Ana Rodríguez and Glenn Garvin.
        p.   cm.
    ISBN 0-312-13050-3
    1. Rodríguez, Ana. 2. Political prisoners—Cuba—Biography.
    3. Women political prisoners—Cuba—Biography.
    I. Garvin, Glenn.   II. Title.
HV9557.5.R63A3   1995
365'.43'092—dc20
[B]   95-9861
                                                                       CIP

First Edition: June 1995
10   9   8   7   6   5   4   3   2   1

For the mothers—those whose bodies were inside the prison walls, and those who left only their hearts there. No one fought harder, or suffered more.

·TABLE OF
CONTENTS·

· ACKNOWLEDGMENTS ·

So many people helped to bring this book to publication that it's impossible to thank them all. But I'd like to mention a few.

My family members—especially my sister Milagros—for their sacrifice and dedication while I was in prison, without a word of complaint or criticism, despite the suffering and humiliation they endured.

All my fellow prisoners, witnesses to and part of the high price to pay for sustaining the concept of human dignity in a Communist dictatorship.

Griselda Noguera, Amelia Mederos, and Elena Zayas, whose encouragement and ideas led me to Jane Dystel, who brought all our efforts to conclusion.

Glenn Garvin, for his patience, his endless hours of silence, his brilliant interpretation of my ideas, and his accuracy when writing this story.

María Antonia Mier for her limitless tenacity and confidence, and her relentless pursuit of justice.

Miriam Ortega, who shared and endured countless severe punishments while fighting for the freedom of our country.

And all those who offered their lives in the name of freedom, liberty, and justice—those for whom the bells should have tolled, but haven't, because of a world's cruel indifference. Someday, they will.

ANA RODRÍGUEZ
Coral Gables, Florida
February, 1995

· ONE ·

"Don't Let the Sons of Bitches Get You Down"

FEBRUARY 26, 1961

I WAS STILL thinking about Audrey Hepburn as I closed the door, leaving the cool Sunday evening breeze behind me. We no longer got new Hollywood films in Cuba—one small casualty of Fidel Castro's escalating quarrel with Washington—but there were still plenty of prints of older American movies floating around the island. We could still root for Gregory Peck to win the heart of Audrey Hepburn, the runaway princess in *Roman Holiday*, although I wondered, as I took off my jacket, how much longer it would take the petty tyrants at the Ministry of Culture to ban the film as a sentimentalist bourgeois diversion from the important tasks of the Revolution. Silently I cursed them for intruding on my thoughts; it was supposed to be an evening without politics, a few hours to let the overwound mainsprings of my brain loosen themselves. As the Revolution careened into its third year, such opportunities were increasingly rare.

"Hello, dear," my mother said, glancing up at me from the couch, where she was watching television. "Your friends from the university should be here soon. They've already stopped by to see you two or three times tonight."

My smile of greeting froze on my face. "Friends?" I asked, keeping my voice casual. "Which friends?" None of my college friends would have been likely to make the thirty-minute trip, unannounced, from Havana out to Bejucal, the little town where I lived with my family.

"Oh, they didn't say their names," my mother replied as she threaded another needle. "But they were young men—several of them. I told them you'd be back after the movie."

Shit, they'll be here any minute, I thought. *They've probably been watching the house.* Carefully—I no longer felt completely in control of my arms and legs—I sat down in a chair across from my mother, who continued talking about something, though my brain had stopped processing the words. I knew I had documents that should be burned, papers that were dangerous not just to me but to so many others, and yet all I could think was: *Run.*

It would be so easy to walk upstairs, open the window in my room, and slip out, skipping across the neighbors' tile roofs as I had done a thousand times as a child. They'd never see me; in ten minutes I could reach the hills at the edge of town, lose myself in them, start making my way east to the Escambray Mountains where an army of peasant guerrillas still resisted Castro.

And who will take your place in prison then? asked a steely voice from the corner of my brain. *Mama? Papa? Your sisters? Do you suppose the police will ever believe that they didn't know what you've been doing?*

The sharp rapping of the knocker on the door cut through my muddled reverie. "There, that must be your friends," my mother declared cheerfully. I smiled at her again, a smile that felt bleak and grim, as I walked to the door and opened it.

There were seven of them outside, each holding his identification card in his left hand as his right hovered at his hip, prepared to draw his gun. They looked identical in their shortsleeve white shirts and tight black pants—all except one, who had on a black leather jacket. He stepped forward slightly. "We're from State Security," he announced. Like the others, his face was pale and his lips were set in a grim line. *They're scared,* I realized. *Finally I'm face-to-face with Castro's secret police, and they're scared.*

"Aren't you going to introduce me to your friends, dear?" my mother asked as we stood there at the door, silent and motionless. She walked toward us, then retreated in confusion as three of the men shoved past me and fanned out into the house.

"We're here to search your house," the one in the leather jacket informed her sternly. "Your daughter is an ally of North American imperialism. She's been engaged in counterrevolutionary acts of sabotage."

"Oh, no, there's been a mistake," my mother explained confidently. "She's not a counterrevolutionary. She's a medical student. But you're welcome to come in and look around. We're just working people here—"

"Gentlemen, my room is upstairs," I interrupted loudly. They were already starting to pull the cushions off the couch; there was no sense in letting them ransack the entire house. "Come with me and you can search it." Four of them headed up the stairs with me; behind, I could hear my mother continuing to explain my glorious academic record to the man in the leather jacket.

The upstairs was dark—my two sisters were out with friends, my father was at a Chamber of Commerce meeting—and all four of the men drew their pistols and pointed them at me. The glint of their guns in the moonlight streaming through the windows scattered the last wispy remnants of my thoughts of fleeing. Now I felt something much stronger: rage. Guns, with them it always came back to guns; they were right because they had guns and the rest of us didn't. It was sullen, cowardly little men like this, clutching big guns, who were crushing the life out of Cuba; and it was sullen, cowardly little men like this, clutching big guns, who would soon be ruling every detail of my life.

I stared at the closest man, computing how quickly I could spring across the room and grab his gun, calculating how many of them I could kill before they killed me. But even as my muscles coiled for a leap, I knew I couldn't do it, couldn't let them kill me in my parents' home as my mother listened. Instead, I reached over and flicked on the lights.

"This is my room," I said frostily. "Search all you like. But don't wreck the place." Then I sprawled indifferently across my bed to watch. I knew they wouldn't find anything of importance in the room. All my secret papers, including some that would give away the locations of weapons caches and the hideouts of fugitives, were in a nylon stocking tied around my waist under my dress. Somehow I had to destroy the documents before they thought to search me. And I also had to think of a way to get word to my friends Nelly and Ilia about what had happened. They might be arrested next.

The men edged forward. One began groping inside my dresser drawers with one hand while keeping his pistol trained on me with the other. Another man performed a similar, fumbling, one-handed inspection of my closet. The other two looked nervously around the room for something else to search, their eyes darting constantly back to me.

This is incredible, I thought. *I'm going to get killed not for fighting or trying to escape, but because a gun goes off when one of these idiots drops a drawer on his toe.* "I'm sure you have lots of experience," I said with exaggerated politeness, "but could I be so bold as to make a suggestion? Why doesn't one of you hold a gun on me while the others search? Wouldn't we all be more comfortable that way?" I smiled so broadly that I could feel cheek muscles tearing. The men glared back, but three of them replaced their guns in their holsters.

I lay back on the bed, watching them rifle through my underwear and pore over my medical books in bafflement. My mother's voice penetrated faintly from downstairs: "But I'm telling you, *señor*, it's impossible that she could be a counterrevolutionary. I can't even get her to help around the house. All she ever does is study and go to class." *Oh, Mama*, I thought, *you are so wrong.*

If the story had a beginning, perhaps it was in 1944, soon after my sixth birthday, when my grandfather came to live with us. He was a tall man, for a Cuban, with a long, straight Grecian nose and jet black hair. He was about sixty years old, but his illness had taken its toll and he looked much older. His face was very wrinkled.

Grandfather came to stay with us because he could no longer take care of himself; he had Parkinson's disease, which, in addition to causing tremors, made him nervous and fidgety. He was never quiet, always moving, but not normally: He ran, rather than walked, perpetually unbalanced, as though he were chasing his own center of gravity. In those days there were no drugs to treat Parkinson's disease. The only thing doctors could suggest was to keep him in bed.

And there—isolated, angry at a world that seemed interested only in confining him—Grandfather often lost the thread of reality. He babbled and shouted at phantoms from his past. Frequently his words were incomprehensible. But other times they were etched with a terrible clarity, and never more so than when he relived the Cuban War of Independence.

That war ended in victory in 1898, but not before Spain exacted an appalling price in Cuban lives. (The U.S. president, William McKinley, later observed that what Spain did "was not civilized warfare. It was extermination.") And though just a boy, Grandfather saw it all; at age twelve, he joined the rebel army of Antonio Maceo and rose to the rank of lieutenant by the war's end.

At first, I crouched around a corner in the hallway as I listened to him relive the war. Soon, though, I was creeping into his bedroom and pulling up a chair. Under the spell of his memories, I joined barefoot suicide attacks, armed with only a machete against a modern imperial army with heavy artillery. I looked into the eyes of starving children in the concentration camps where hundreds of thousands of Cuban civilians died. I rode in the secret funeral cortege after Antonio Maceo was killed in an ambush. I cried tears of rage as I gazed at the butchery and ruin left in the wake of Spain's scorched-earth warfare. Although most of the events Grandfather described took place five decades earlier, they were far more real to me than the news I heard on the radio of the world war that raged on every day in Europe and the Pacific.

Every single one of Grandfather's stories involved slaughter and bloodshed and pain and death. I didn't talk about them with my sisters, who were terrified of Grandfather, or my parents, who would never approve. But I kept repeating them to myself until they seemed like my memories rather than his. Later, when we studied the war in school, I listened as my teachers dryly recited the lessons, and thought to myself: *Oh, you don't know.*

Refighting the War of Independence with Grandfather, even on a battleground of hallucinations, always made me feel, even as a little girl, that I had an intensely personal stake in Cuba's fitful progress toward democracy. After independence, we had lurched between rigged elections and armed revolts, but since a 1933 coup by populist military men (the Revolt of the Sergeants, we called it) the political system had been evolving into something resembling democracy. Three peaceful and reasonably fair elections had been held. No civics textbooks would ever be written on the resulting governments—they all suffered from wild corruption—but at least they had been freely chosen, which is the bedrock definition of democracy.

But in 1952, a few months before a presidential election, one of the candidates and a handful of gunmen staged another coup, deposing President Carlos Prío. Fulgencio Batista had been the principal architect of the 1933 Revolt of the Sergeants. That coup, which ended a long period of government-by-goon, was a popular one. This one wasn't. Dozens of clandestine anti-Batista groups sprang up, particularly around the country's campuses. Just shy of my fourteenth birthday, I joined a small band of conspirators at my high school. After all, Grandfather had been even younger when he went off to war.

Our group varied in size over the years, but generally it hovered around sixteen to eighteen, mostly boys, and all teenagers. We performed dozens of minor tasks for the armed opponents of Batista: carrying messages, distributing propaganda leaflets, and raising money. Among my most important tasks was selling "bonds" for the one of the higher-profile anti-Batista groups, the 26th of July Movement. Founded by a young firebrand lawyer named Fidel Castro, the 26th of July Movement had carried out one full-scale military attack on an army barracks and scores of bombings. Castro himself was now in Mexico, raising an exile army to confront Batista.

At first, selling the bonds (for twenty pesos, the buyer got a written promise he'd be paid back with interest when the 26th of July Movement took over the government) was exciting. I was raising money, I thought, for an army like the one in which Grandfather fought. But as time passed, raising money for an army didn't seem enough; I wanted to *fight* in an army. I began thinking seriously of leaving home and running off to join one of the bands of armed rebels in the rugged Escambray Mountains. Maybe when Castro's army finally arrived, I could link up with it.

What changed my mind was a chance conversation with my friend Angel Pérez. Two years older than I, Angel was a prickly mix of keen intellect, racing hormones, and youthful rebellion. He was obviously sweet on me, which horrified my mother; he was not, in her view, good husband material. He knew practically everything about Russian literature, and practically nothing about anything that had to do with holding a job. He was always getting fired for trying to organize unions. In fact, my mother told me, town gossip had it that he was a secret member of the Young Communists.

At first I just assumed that was part of my mother's no-holds-barred campaign to discredit Angel in my eyes. (A campaign that was, incidentally, unnecessary; I liked discussing books with Angel—I shared his fascination for Dostoevsky and Tolstoy—but that was all.) But later I decided it was true. One day, when he wouldn't buy some of my bonds for Castro's group, I had gotten angry. "You talk all this bullshit about the rights of the worker, but when somebody wants to really do something about it, you won't help!" I shouted. "I think you're just a damned coward!"

It was an insult calculated to draw blood from any twenty-year-old boy, and coming from the girl he was courting, it cut Angel even deeper. "I'm not a coward!" he shouted back. "They won't let me buy those bonds!"

"Who's 'they'?" I asked.

"Nothing, no one," he replied, retreating. "I just meant, I don't want to." I let it drop and pretended to forget about it, but now I was certain my mother was right: Angel was under Communist Party discipline. Cuba's official Communist Party was, initially, very cool to Castro, believing him an impetuous adventurer rather than a disciplined Marxist.

A few months later, on a cloudless October afternoon, we were walking along a backstreet on the outskirts of town. Despite the glorious sunshine, Angel was glum and depressed. All of my attempts to draw him into a conversation about literature or music failed. Finally, as we perched upon one of the boulders lining the hills outside town, he blurted out: "I've got to be a pilot. After the Revolution, I'm going to be a pilot."

He said it with such distaste that I was startled, and immediately I had a thousand questions. I didn't ask any of them. I knew better than to interrupt. I knew what was coming was important, that it was going to reveal more than I wanted to know. And I knew I had to let it come, to let him talk without noticing.

"A pilot," I murmured. "Why, that's beautiful, to fly among the clouds."

"Yeah, yeah," he snapped, heedlessly. "But there's more to it than that. There's a lot more, and I don't want to do it."

"Well, if you don't want to, then why do it?" I asked.

"Because I'm physically fit, I have 20-20 eyesight, my reflexes are good. I just had a medical exam. I had one of the top scores."

Among whom? I wondered, but that was too direct. Instead, I asked: "Where will you go to train?"

"To Mexico," he replied, staring off into the distance.

"Oh, that will be nice," I said enthusiastically. "They have beautiful beaches, and the people are so friendly. You'll enjoy it." What I was really thinking about were Castro's intimate connections to the Mexican government.

"I'll only be there six months," he said.

"So you're just learning to fly small planes," I said carefully.

"No, jets," he answered. "There will be some training in Czechoslovakia when we're done in Mexico. I'm going to be a commander." He said it not with enthusiasm or pride, but with a heavy tone of inevitability.

I started talking about Dostoevsky then. I didn't want Angel to realize how much he had told me. But now I was the one who had trouble concealing my bleak depression. Without realizing it, Angel had made it plain that the Communist Party was not only working with Castro but preparing the officer corps of Cuba's post-Revolution armed forces. All Castro's claims that he wasn't a Communist were lies.

As we walked home, my heart felt as arid and desolate as the immense moon rising overhead. All that money I had raised selling bonds had gone to Communists. For more than four years, my friends and I had been working—without knowing it—to install a Communist government in Cuba. And we were not the only ones. There were a lot of organizations, some small, some big, cooperating with the 26th of July Movement. Most of them, I felt certain, did not know of Castro's plans.

I certainly didn't want to help install a Communist government. In studying Russian literature, I couldn't help but learn a good bit of Russian history and politics. I had read of Stalin's purges and the way he starved millions of his political opponents to death as he collectivized Soviet agriculture. I felt contempt for Marxist economics, and loathing for the way Leninists suppressed individual rights.

But . . . what about all my friends who had been beaten by Batista's hoodlum police? What about the ones who were sitting in his jails right now? Wouldn't I betray them by quitting? Besides, I couldn't stop the revolution against Batista; if I quit, it would just go on without me, with the anti-Communist forces weaker by one.

I also tried to convince myself—though I was only partially successful—that Communist domination of the post-revolutionary government was not inevitable. Castro's organization was not the only one, nor even the biggest one, fighting Batista. If one of the other groups delivered the decisive blow against the dictatorship, and if international forces moved quickly to recognize and support it, perhaps the Communists could be controlled.

This sounds like wishful thinking, but I still believe it was not without merit. Among Castro's early allies were several anti-Batista groups banded together in a coalition calling itself the Revolutionary Directorate. Mostly student organizations, they were all resolutely anti-Communist. In 1957, without Castro's knowledge, the Directorate launched a frontal assault on the presidential palace that was intended to kill Batista. The rebels came so close; they shot their way onto the second floor of the palace, but they just missed Batista, who was able to rally the army and crush them. If the Directorate's forces had been just five or ten minutes faster, they could have changed Cuban history.

So that was my decision: Despite my knowing now of the intimate Communist involvement in the anti-Batista movement, I would stay with it. I did, however, give up my plans to become a guerrilla myself. I never told Angel how close I had been to leaving for the mountains, nor that his inadvertent revelations changed my mind.

Two years after my talk with Angel, I graduated from high school and started my medical studies at the University of Havana. I had wanted to be a doctor since the first time I laid eyes on a biology book, when I was nine or ten years old. My parents, who were simple people—my father owned a small country store, my mother had worked in the fields cutting cane until their marriage—thought I was crazy: Everyone knew that doctors were *men*. They had difficulty conceiving of a girl going to college, much less becoming a doctor. But when I got into medical school, they went along with it, though skeptically.

All my friends were jubilant on January 1, 1959, when Castro arrived in Havana to take over the government a few hours after Batista flew into exile. I was hoping, without any real hope, that Angel had been wrong, that Castro would return Cuba to democracy. But within just a few weeks I could see what a dreadful mistake we had all made.

When my friends and I had talked of revolution, we were referring to the process of getting rid of Batista and his kleptocratic flunkies. But right from the beginning, it was apparent that Castro's Revolution (you could practically hear the capital R when he said it) was a living, breathing entity that would subsume all of Cuba. And what it wanted first was blood.

It was those terrible trials, more than anything, that turned me irrevocably against the Revolution. There were so many things to detest: the militarization of Cuban society, with tens of thousands of teenagers being swept up into the militia; the hateful Committees for the Defense of the Revolution, neighborhood watch groups that were turning us into a nation of informants.

But it was the trials in front of Castro's kangaroo-court revolutionary tribunals that repelled me the most. I had no sympathy for Batista's henchmen, but at least they had never tried to clothe their bloodlust in the robes of due process. The first trials were held in Havana's sports stadium, lurid Roman spectacles with mobs (mostly Castro's handpicked stooges) in the stands howling for blood—*Paredón!* To the wall!—on cue. Castro obliged them; although Cuban law prohibited capital punishment, the staccato retorts of firing squads could be heard nightly at La Cabaña, the old Havana fortress that had been converted into a prison.

Few voices were raised against those first trials, appalling though they were, because the defendants were the most notorious of Batista's torturers and killers. But as La Cabaña filled up with hundreds and then thousands of prisoners (many of them headed for the *paredón*), the definitions of both "crime" and "justice" were becoming more ephemeral.*

In March, a military tribunal tried forty-three pilots, bombardiers, and mechanics from Batista's air force. There was no evidence that the men were guilty of anything except wearing the uniforms of Castro's enemy; in fact, they hadn't even tried to flee Cuba when Batista's government collapsed. The tribunal acquitted them. Castro instantly created a right of appeal for prosecutors—something that neither Cuba, nor most other civilized countries, ever had before—and demanded a new trial. "Revolutionary justice is not based on legal precepts, but on moral conviction," he explained blandly. A second tribunal obediently convicted the airmen and sentenced them all to thirty years in prison. Seven months later, when one of Castro's guerrilla companions, Huber Matos, tried to resign from the

---

*By some estimates there were two thousand executions during the first year of the Revolution.

government to protest its increasingly obvious Communist bent, he was arrested, and Castro himself delivered a three-hour harangue in the court-room demanding Matos' conviction. Matos wasn't allowed to speak at all. He was sentenced to twenty years.

Many of those early trials were televised, and I watched several of them. Finally I couldn't stand any more. Nearly paralyzed with trepidation, I stopped by to see Beba Canabal, a friend from the anti-Batista group in my high school. "Beba," I said with studied nonchalance, "what do you think of the Revolution?" She laughed. "We were just getting ready to call you," she replied. We went back to work.

We worked against Castro much the same way we had worked against Batista, distributing propaganda, carrying messages, and doing other sup-port work for urban guerrilla groups. Sometimes a man would be "burned"—the police would be looking for him—and we would help hide him, carrying him around Havana to various safehouses. Women often got this assignment because we made it look like a couple carrying on a lovers' rendezvous. We also moved shipments of guns here and there.

I got pretty good at distributing propaganda. One of my tricks was to hold a stack of leaflets next to an open window on a bus, letting them be sucked out into the street as it drove along. Another of my favorite devices was to carry leaflets onto the roof of the medical school and leave them there on the edge where the blustery coastal wind would eventually scatter them across the city. Sometimes I'd pick up one of my own leaflets, go over to the student association offices, and read it angrily into the public address system as I shouted denunciations of the counterrevolutionary in-sect who had written it. Of course, in the process of condemning the leaflet, I broadcast it into every classroom on the campus.

But Castro was going to be a tougher, smarter opponent than Batista; leaflets were not going to be enough. Watching the trials on television, I was convinced that this man would never fly off into exile to enjoy his stolen millions, as Batista had. If Castro had to send half the island to prison or the *paredón* to break us, that's what he would do.

Yet it was hard to persuade my fellow conspirators. Like most Cubans who hated Castro, they were convinced that the United States would never tolerate a Soviet satellite ninety miles off the Florida coast. Most of them treated our clandestine activities like a game, something to annoy Castro until the Americans got around to kicking him out.

So, on my own, I became an arsonist. Someone had supplied us with sulphuric acid and some gelatin capsules. If you put the acid inside a capsule and then left it in a package of sugar, when the acid ate through the gelatin it would start a fire. The trick was to combine them in the right proportions, and to keep them from mixing until you'd had a chance to escape.

Since no one else in the group was interested, I began using the chemicals to start fires in stores that had been seized by the Revolution. I prepared packages and then left them in the pockets of clothing on display racks. I tried it hundreds of times. But the chemicals were too old, and I couldn't get the proportions right. My biggest success was scorching a few coats in a department store in downtown Havana.

But I didn't tell anyone in my resistance group what I was doing. I was certain there was a spy in our midst.

In a way, it would have been amazing if we hadn't been penetrated. When Castro took over, three members of the group had been rewarded for their work against Batista with positions in State Security, the secret police force that was supposed to sniff out counterrevolutionaries. They knew us, they knew all our tricks. It should have been obvious to everyone that they would be keeping an eye on us.

My worries, however, were based on more than supposition. In January 1961, we carried out our most important assignment yet. A renegade Cuban intelligence officer had agreed to supply the U.S. embassy with a piece of microfilm listing all of Castro's spies in the United States. But he could only remove the microfilm from the government vault for a few hours; it would have to be copied quickly and returned. To further complicate the problem, the intelligence officer's contact in the resistance was under surveillance. I would have to pick up the microfilm from him under the guise of borrowing a medical book. Then I had to take it to a lawyer who had a microfilm machine, wait while it was copied, and return the original to the man who gave it to me.

I picked up the package—a black plastic case about the size of an ashtray—in Old Havana and slipped it into my purse. On top of it I stuffed a bra, panties, and a Kotex; if I was stopped in a random search—they were getting depressingly common—I hoped the personal items might embarrass the policeman into cutting it short.

It was a sunny day, and if the stakes hadn't been so high, if the microfilm in my purse hadn't been so important, I might have truly enjoyed my zigzag stroll through the narrow streets of the old city. I doubled back several times; I entered a couple of stores through one entrance and then left through another; I deliberately walked for blocks through dirty, deserted alleyways. I wanted to make sure no one was following me. After an hour, I was satisfied that I was alone, and I headed for the high-rise building where the lawyer had his office.

"Hello, I have those real-estate documents you wanted notarized," I said as he opened the door. He nodded and ushered me inside where I handed him the plastic case. It took him half an hour to copy the film; as I waited, my anxiety began to melt away. If State Security had been onto us, we would already be chained up in an interrogation cell.

When the lawyer handed the plastic case to me, I replaced it in the bottom of my purse and sauntered almost merrily to the elevator. It would be like a kick in the stomach for Castro when the Americans started rolling up his spy networks. Better yet, he would suspect the presence of a traitor inside his security apparatus. With any luck at all, the investigations and recriminations would cripple the secret police for months or even years.

But when the elevator door opened, I had to stifle a gasp. The lobby was awash in a sea of olive green police uniforms. Here and there I could see pockets of civilians, their eyes a mixture of anger, resignation, and curiosity (for it was obvious this was no routine security check), obediently handing over purses and briefcases to be searched.

Trying to go back up the elevator would be a dead giveaway. There was nothing to do but forge ahead into the lobby. I didn't get two steps before a policeman aggressively blocked my way. "Your bag, señorita," he demanded. I offered it to him, carefully keeping my eyes on his face rather than his hands, and doing my best to look annoyed rather than frightened. He fumbled in the purse for a second, and then his young face dissolved into a fiery blush. The way he delicately held the Kotex between his thumb and forefinger, I was quite certain he had never seen one before. He dropped it back inside, handed me the purse, and—his eyes lowered, his face still beet red—told me: "You can go."

The rest of my journey was uneventful. But it was obvious there was a leak inside our organization. And as I mentally shuffled through the faces of our group, I always came back to the same one: Isis Nimo.

Isis, about a year younger than I, had joined our group late in the battle against Batista, when I had already departed for medical school. I didn't know her well. But when we reorganized to fight Castro, she seemed to be an intimate of almost everyone.

One reason for her popularity was that she was an apparently inexhaustible fountain of resources. Did you need to get a message across town in the middle of the night? Isis could find a car. Were you nervous about escorting a fugitive to a safehouse? Isis could get you a gun. Did you want to put out a new leaflet? Isis had access to a mimeograph machine. And she always had money to take us to lunch or dinner—even though her only formal employment, as far as I could tell, was as a volunteer in Castro's militia. Good cover, she called it.

Besides that, she talked too much. The first principle of clandestine activity is that everything is on a need-to-know basis; that limits the damage if a member of the group is arrested. For that reason, I was always trying to devise ways to minimize the amount of information I had to share with members of the group. I used code words instead of names, memorized phone numbers instead of writing them down. Isis, though, was just the opposite. She gossiped freely about anything she was involved in, and always snooped for details of everyone else's activities.

Thinking I might be imagining (or exaggerating) her nosiness, I tried an experiment: I casually mentioned, in front of Isis, an imaginary shipment of guns that I was helping to hide. "Really?" she said, fixing me with her balmiest smile. "Where are you going to put them? I know some good places if you need help." I declined, but three more times that week she asked about those guns.

Hardly anyone else, however, shared my suspicions. My friend Beba Canabal thought I was daft. "Nobody's worked harder for us than Isis," Beba insisted. "She's been involved in everything we do. Why would a spy help us so much?" Then, lowering her voice to nearly a whisper, she added: "There's something you don't know. Do you remember when we sent a group to break into the electric power plant at night and sabotage the generators? There was a guard there from the militia. They knocked him out and tied him up and were going to leave him that way. But Isis took out a gun and *shot* him, right in the head. She said it was better if there were no witnesses. Now, do you think a spy would do that, kill someone from her own side?"

"Absolutely," I replied. "Beba, *only* a spy would kill so ruthlessly when there was no need. What better way to convince us of her loyalty?"

"Oh, Ana," Beba sighed, "there's just no arguing with you. Once you get an idea, you won't let it go." Neither she nor anyone else in the group would budge.

The wise thing for me would have been to quit. Even before I started worrying about spies, I sometimes thought my life was coming apart at the seams. Juggling medical school and my job at the hospital had been difficult enough even before I added a part-time position as an urban guerrilla. And now I had a serious boyfriend, too.

His name was Carlos Pérez. Though he lived in my little town, he went to a Catholic college in Havana, and we didn't meet until we wound up in the same classes at medical school. I had always been attracted to boys with keen intellects, and Carlos certainly had that. But for the first time in my life, I found myself thinking about how a boy *looked*. Sometimes I daydreamed about the gentle curve of his mouth, or the depth of his black eyes. I wasn't the only one doing it; there was always a parade of girls following him around. But on the rare occasions when there was time for a date—an evening of dancing, or a Saturday afternoon at the movies— he always took me. The whirlwind of my life didn't offer me much opportunity to think about the future, but in a vague way I felt sure Carlos and I would be married.

So if I had dropped out of the anti-Castro movement, I would have had no trouble filling my days. But I didn't. In part, I suppose I felt some guilt over my role, however small, in putting Castro in power. And in part things were just happening too fast. I shared the popular belief that the United States would, sooner or later, squash Castro like a bug. But every day that we waited, there were more Cuban farms confiscated, more Cuban children sent off to school in the Soviet Union, more Cuban men dying at the *paredón*. I didn't think we could afford to wait until the Americans woke up.

So I stayed in the underground resistance and kept as far away from Isis Nimo as possible. Every time one of our operations failed—and it was happening more and more often; in November 1960, even my friend Beba was arrested—I wondered about her. But there was never a case where circumstances proved that Isis, and only Isis, must have betrayed us.

After the near disaster with the microfilm, though, I decided to lay a trap for her. I told her about another imaginary shipment of guns, only this time, I gave her an address where the weapons would be hidden. Although she didn't know it, the address was across the street from an apartment where a friend of mine lived. I went there to wait; sure enough, at nine P.M. a truckload of soldiers pulled up in front of the house. They burst inside and, holding the terrified occupants at gunpoint, rifled the place. They tore open mattresses, broke walls apart, and even drilled into the cement floor. This time there was no doubt; the only person in the world who could have directed the police to that house was Isis Nimo.

But when I called a group meeting the next day, no one believed me. "Your suspicions are getting a little tiresome, Ana," one of the men said. "Try to remember that our enemy is Castro, not one another." As the meeting broke up, I knew Isis would soon learn of it. I remembered one of my father's sayings: If you're going to attack a snake, don't just leave it wounded.

I had heard gossip around the university about a man who ran a medical lab in Havana's Vedado neighborhood. His brother had been a notorious gangster, and the doctor still had some connections with the underworld, they said. I went to the lab the next day on the bus; it was a big, boxy building that looked like a fortress. Guarding the door was a young thug with slicked-back hair and an ill-fitting sports jacket that barely concealed the pistol at his waist.

"My name is Ana Rodríguez and I'm a medical student," I told him. "I'm here to see the doctor."

"Do you have an appointment?" he asked.

"No," I said, shrugging my shoulders. He gave me a strange, perplexed look; it occurred to me that this was a building that few people approached casually. "Wait here," he finally said, and stepped inside. A few minutes later he reappeared and silently gestured me inside.

The doctor was sitting at a desk, gazing at me with a puzzled half-smile. "Do I know you, my dear?" he asked.

"No," I admitted.

"Well," he said, still smiling, "is there something I can do for you?"

"I need someone killed," I explained.

His smile vanished.

Before he could call for the guard, I started blurting out the whole story of Isis Nimo. As I continued, I saw him relax a bit and I knew he wasn't going to throw me out. But I couldn't read anything in his expression. When I finished, he asked: "So why do you come to me?"

"Because you have a reputation as a man who can do anything," I replied. "And I need help. Either I kill Isis Nimo, or she's going to kill me."

He laughed. "I don't kill people," he said. "I'm a doctor."

I jotted my name and address on a card and handed it to him. "I'll come back in a week," I said, and then I walked back out the way I had entered. I hoped he would do some checking on me and, perhaps, give me some advice. Certainly the gangsters had no use for Castro; though he had made little attempt to jail any of them, the Revolution had ended the stream of tourists who came to their casinos.

A week later I returned. The guard seemed to be expecting me; he showed me right in. The doctor was sitting behind his desk again, but this time there was no smile, no chatter. "Can you get this Isis Nimo to go to Guanabo Beach?" he asked.

"Of course," I said. "How about next Wednesday, say, around seven in the evening." He nodded. I left, and went straight to a pay telephone to call Isis. I have to pick up a load of guns, I told her, and I'll need your help. Let's meet at the beach, where no one will be around to bother us.

But the night before our meeting, my "friends from the university" came calling.

The State Security men looked frustrated. After three hours there wasn't anything left in the house to search. But so far all they had was a little tin box containing an enormous rat's skull that a teacher had given me as a curiosity (and, though they didn't know it, three hundred pesos that my sister Milagros had saved to buy a car and, for some reason, had hidden inside the skull), a couple of containers of prescription medicine, and a real human skeleton I had borrowed from one of the town doctors to study for a test. My mother was talking more confidently to the men now; if there was no evidence against me, she reasoned, then I couldn't be arrested. I knew that was not the logic of State Security, but I kept quiet.

"*Señora,*" the State Security man in the leather jacket said, finally managing to get a word in edgewise, "we have to take your daughter down town for a few minutes to clear up a few things. Then we'll bring her back."

My mother's smile faded. She looked uncertain for a moment, and then resolute. "This is a decent household," she informed him haughtily. "I don't permit my daughter to go out with strangers."

The State Security man took out his identification card and showed it to her. She inspected it for a few moments and then glared at the officer. "How do I know—"

"Mama," I interrupted quietly, "I'll go with them. It'll be all right." Worry and confusion flashed across her face. Then she brightened. "You can't go in those high heels," she insisted. "I'll go and get you some walking shoes." She darted upstairs. When she came back, she was carrying the shoes, a sheet of paper, and an inkpad.

"Now each one of you sign your name and your ID card number on this paper, and then you put your fingerprints under it," she ordered the State Security men. "And then remember that if anything happens to my daughter, you're going to have to cut off your fingers to hide from me."

To my utter astonishment, they obediently lined up to do as they were told. Mama watched with a look of prim satisfaction. I don't think I had ever loved my mother more than at that moment; she didn't know what was wrong, couldn't imagine what this was all about, but whatever it was, she would stall it with every means at her command, anything to keep me safe with her for one more minute.

When the officers finished signing, one of them moved toward me. But my mother stopped them again. "Just a minute," she snapped. She disappeared through the door that led into my father's store and came back a minute later with a carton of cigarettes.

"You think I don't know you smoke," she said, the same triumphant note in her voice I had heard a thousand times as a child when she outwitted me. "Ha! Go ahead, take them." As she paused, all the confusion and trickery drained from her face. Only anger remained. "Don't give in to them!" she shouted, tears welling in her eyes. "Kick them, bite them, but don't let the sons of bitches get you down!"

I hugged her tightly and whispered in her ear: "Call Nelly and Ilia and tell them I've been arrested." Then I kissed her cheek. In a moment I was inside the back of a State Security car, speeding toward my future.

· TWO ·

Behind Bars

FEBRUARY 27, 1961

IT WAS PAST midnight when we reached the headquarters compound of the Ministry of the Interior, which oversaw State Security, jails and prisons, and all the rest of the massive apparatus Castro had erected to stamp out his enemies. As the car fishtailed madly into the parking lot (State Security men always seemed to be practicing for a Grand Prix race) I reflected again on how abruptly, and totally, the Revolution had changed Cuba.

The building we were about to enter had been, until a few months ago, the home of a renowned writer named Jorge Mañach. A majestic colonial mansion within a stone's throw of the sea, at Fifth Avenue and Fourteenth Street in Havana's Miramar neighborhood, it was the nation's leading literary salon. Novelists, playwrights, poets, and editors gathered there to argue about art and politics in elegant revelries that were usually covered in Havana's newspapers, even after the Revolution. And why not? Mañach had led the campaign to get Castro out of prison during the Batista years. Who had less to fear from the Revolution?

And then, without warning or explanation, Mañach was out of fashion. He fled Cuba. The mansion was seized. And now the mention of the house at Fifth and Fourteenth connoted not erudition, but dread. Once you were summoned inside, the only exits led to prison or the *paredón*.

As two State Security officers walked me briskly down the corridors, the house's stately marble floors and mahogany doors seemed somehow forlorn, as though they missed the friendly wordplay of the writers. *Another achievement of the Revolution,* I thought to myself, *the most aesthetic secret police headquarters in the whole world.*

"Wait here," one of the officers said, gesturing to a chair in a small waiting room. As I sat down, my arm brushed against the nylon tied around my waist under my dress, stuffed with resistance documents. I knew my time to destroy them was running out; no one had bothered to search me yet—possibly because I still had on the evening dress I wore to the movies, too tight to conceal a gun—but that was bound to change. The documents inside the nylon would not only provide tangible proof of my part in the underground (which, judging from the frustration of the State Security men as they searched my house, they lacked), but would reveal the hiding places of several fugitives. I had to do something.

I walked over to the desk where a clerk was busily typing what I assumed were my arrest documents. "Where's the bathroom?" I asked casually. "Third door on the left," he answered mechanically without looking up. Before anyone realized what I was doing, I scurried through the door and latched it. An instant later a guard was hammering on it. "Goddamn it, come out of there!" he roared. I breathed a quick prayer of thanks to Mañach's interior decorator; it would take a battering ram to break through the thick mahogany door.

Slipping the stocking out of my dress, I used the book of matches the State Security men had left me for my cigarettes to light, one by one, the incriminating papers. As each one was reduced to a cinder, I crumpled it and dropped the pieces into the toilet. When they were all gone, I flushed the toilet, then washed my hands and face in the sink to give the smoke a chance to dissipate.

I opened the door quickly, hoping to have some fun, and I was rewarded; two State Security men stumbled into the bathroom like cartoon characters, thrust forward by the force of the blows they were aiming at the mahogany.

"What were you doing in here?" sputtered one of them. "You know you can't go to the bathroom by yourself."

"I was taking a shit," I replied acidly. "I didn't think I needed your help." The two men looked around the room suspiciously, but there was nothing to see. "All right, sit the fuck back down out there," one of them ordered me. "And if you move again before we tell you to, I hope your family can afford a wheelchair."

I did as he said without any backtalk. I was so pleased with myself I could hardly keep from smiling. I knew I was going to jail—to set me free would be to admit an error of the Revolution, which was inconceivable— but without any evidence, the sentence would be light, probably no more than a year.

After they photographed and fingerprinted me, they took me to the women's *galera*, as big dormitory-style cells were called. It must once have been a children's room; there were Disney characters painted on some of the walls. Otherwise, though, little trace of those days remained. The windows had been sealed with rough gray wooden planks and the only illumination came from a single faint lightbulb in the middle of the room that burned day and night. Nine or ten bunkbeds, stacked two-high, were lined up across the room, which had originally been much larger. A partition of wooden panels about seven feet high had been built across the front; a single guard sat at the entry, methodically clicking the bolt-action of his rifle every few minutes, reminding us who was boss.

In the surreal gloom of the *galera*, I drifted, without realizing it, into a depression. The perpetual twilight discouraged me from leaving my bed; and between the shouts echoing from other parts of the building, the periodic summons of women to the door for interrogation sessions, and the monotonous *click-click* of the guard's rifle, it was impossible to sleep.

Three times a day they brought us our food, but I wouldn't touch it. It was served on partitioned aluminum plates; the food was dished out in the kitchen, and a guard then stacked the plates on top of one another to deliver them to our *galera*. It was obvious that the bottoms of the plates were never washed—they were covered with a crust of black fungus and decaying bits of previous meals. To think something like that had been thrust into the food I was about to eat sent a wave of nausea rolling from my belly to my throat. After seeing it twice, I didn't even get off my bed when the food arrived.

For almost two days I lay there, never speaking, barely moving, listening to the sporadic clamor outside the *galera*. Occasionally I wondered why I hadn't been called to interrogation, but mostly my mind was a blank. It was the bathroom that brought me back to life.

There were seven toilets in a room off to the side. And when I shuffled in, on the evening of my second day at State Security, the stench jolted me into full and annoyed consciousness. All seven were filled to the brim with urine. I whirled and stomped out into the *galera*, slamming the door behind me.

"Damn it!" I bellowed. "This may be a prison, but we aren't pigs! Can't everybody flush the toilet when they're finished? And let's take turns cleaning them."

Several of the women stared at me. One, chuckling, shook her head, making her long honey-colored hair shimmer. "Look, child, we already take turns cleaning them every day. And of course we flush the toilet. It's the guards who are pigs, not us."

"What guards?" I asked sharply, wondering if I were the butt of a joke. It would have taken that single guard at the door a week to fill up all those toilets.

"There's a disciplinary unit on the other side of the partition, for guards who have been caught sleeping and things like that," she replied. "But they don't have a bathroom, so they use ours."

"Well, how come I've never seen them?" I said, still skeptical.

"Because you lie on your back staring at the ceiling all day and all night," she said, still smiling. "We've been wondering if we should water you. By the way, my name is Milagros Bermúdez."

Now I smiled, too. "I'm Ana Rodríguez," I said, extending my hand. "It's nice to meet you. Or it would be, anyway, if we were somewhere else."

"Ahhh, Ana Rodríguez, my coconspirator," Milagros nodded. "I had been wondering if we would meet before we were convicted of plotting together."

Unlike me, Milagros had been shown a copy of the indictment listing charges against her. It accused us of working together, even though we had never met. It was another indication that they didn't have much evidence against me.

Arguing with the guards gave me something to do. I spent the rest of the night standing at the entrance to the *galera*, turning away guards who wanted to use the bathroom. There were furious arguments and threats, but when they tried to put me in solitary confinement, they discovered all the punishment cells were already filled with men. And other women were joining me at my post; the guards would have had to find punishment cells for a dozen women. They decided it was easier to use another bathroom.

On the third day, my friends Ilia Herrera, Nelly Urtiaga, and Olga González—all members of my resistance group—joined us in jail. Nelly said she thought some of the boys had been arrested, too; it looked like they were rolling up the whole group. "Funny, isn't it, that the only woman in our group who hasn't been arrested is Isis Nimo," I noted. "*Now* do you believe me?" Olga, the only person in the group who had agreed with me that Isis Nimo was a spy, smiled bitterly; the others shrugged. I let it drop. Rearguing the past, wasting our energy on old fights, would only help State Security.

That afternoon, inspecting the planks that sealed our windows, I discovered a small chip of wood that could be removed from one at the end of the *galera*. We could see down onto Fifth Avenue, the Miramar neighborhood's main thoroughfare. Crowding the sidewalk on the corner across from our compound were dozens of men and women who were obviously relatives of prisoners, hoping to catch a glimpse of a loved one being carried to or from the courthouse. Shoulders slumped in dejection, they were almost too sad a spectacle to bear.

I was about to let someone else look when my eyes latched on to a familiar figure: Papa! Like the others, he was scanning the building's entrance, hoping for a familiar face. Remorse, delight, and then fury gripped my heart in quick turns. How many hours had he been out there? How many *days* had he been out there? How many humiliating insults had he endured from the guards lounging insolently against the front wall?

"Papa!" I screamed. "*Papa!*" The din of an argument in the *galera* masked the sound of my voice from the guard at the front. But my father heard me; a smile brightened his face like a beacon. He waved in the direction of the building, though there was no way he could spot the little hole through which I was shouting.

"Papa, don't try to talk," I shouted. "Just nod yes or no." His head bobbed up and down, nodding yes.

"Have you been there long?" Yes. "All day?" Yes. "Were you there yesterday?" Yes. "And the day before?" Yes. "Did you ask them if you could visit?" Hesitation. . . . Suddenly I was sure what had happened. "Did they admit I was here?" No. *Fuckers,* I cursed mentally, *you vile, base fuckers, leaving him out there, lying to him, letting him wonder if his daughter was dead.*

For the first time it occurred to me that this might be harder on my family than on me.

We continued our lopsided conversation until I was too hoarse to go on. I asked him to try to get me a case for my contact lenses—I had been wearing them for four full days now—and some clothes; all I had was the same black evening dress I had on when I was arrested. My father was grinning broadly when he hurried away, and I knew he would get a package to me. A lifetime of running a store in Batista's Cuba had made him adept at spotting the right person to bribe and guessing the price within a few pennies.

That afternoon they finally called me in for interrogation. A guard showed me into a large, soundproof room; the only noise was the hum of a powerful air-conditioning unit mounted high on the wall. I wandered around the room, but it was completely empty except for a desk with locked drawers and several chairs. After a few minutes, I sat down. The hush of the room, probably intended to unnerve me, had the opposite effect; after the cacophony of the *galera*, the quiet seemed luxurious to me. The air chilled and grew heavier. At last I put my feet up on another chair and closed my eyes. . . .

"Wake up, damn it!" A gruff voice sounded in my ear as someone yanked the chair out from under my feet. "This is not a resort!"

My eyes, aching from three days without changing contact lenses, were blurry. So was my brain. Where, exactly, was I? As my eyes focused on a line of seven men—all dressed in identical black chinos, black leather jackets, and black gloves—arrayed in a semicircle around me, the pieces slipped into place.

The one I took to be the leader sat down at the desk. The other six stood off to the side. The man at the desk fixed me with a theatrically threatening glare. "Where is Isis Nimo?" he barked.

"I don't know anyone by that name," I answered mildly.

"She says she knows you."

"Well," I replied, "if she says she knows me, it must mean you're talking with her. And if you're talking with her, then why are you asking me where she is? Bring her in to identify me, and I'll see if I know her." *Oh, yes, bring her in here,* I begged silently. *I'll tear her throat out before you can stop me.*

"No, you misunderstand," the State Security man replied. "We want to arrest her. Tell us where the counterrevolutionary bitch is, and we'll pick her up right away." We continued like this for another ten minutes, until I started feeling insulted. How stupid did they think I was? Every question was about Isis Nimo. They were trying so desperately to convince me that she wasn't one of their spies that they might as well have put up a flashing neon sign: WARNING: TRICKERY AT WORK. I decided it was time to change the subject.

"Hey," I said, turning to the line of men along the wall, "is this guy your boss?" Several of them nodded. "Well, your organization has some serious deficiencies," I continued. "Anybody can see that all six of you are smarter than he is. This guy's barely human. I'll bet if you took him to a meadow, he'd drop to his hands and knees and start grazing."

Several of the State Security men couldn't hide their smirks; a couple of others were making a visible effort not to laugh. *I wouldn't want to be at your staff meeting when this is over,* I thought. The interrogator, his face flushed, was banging a sheaf of papers on the desk. "Go ahead, be funny!" he shouted. "But I'll be laughing later! Because I've already got the papers—you're going to rot in prison for thirty years!"

"Oh, sure," I snorted at this absurd bluff. "And what's the crime?"

He rifled through the papers in his hand, pulled one out, and read from it: "Sabotage and other counterrevolutionary actions."

I kept my expression blank, but I was stunned—this was no bluff. He already had the verdict and the sentence in his hand. I had known the trial would be just a formality, but I was expecting a sentence of five or six years at the absolute worst.

Slightly calmer, he went back to questioning me about Isis Nimo. For twenty minutes I mechanically denied everything without really hearing a word he said. In my brain I was doing multiplication: 30 years times 365 days times 24 hours times 60 minutes . . .

My clandestine group was not the only one that had been busted. There had evidently been a major crackdown on the anti-Castro underground, and new prisoners were streaming into our *galera* around the clock. Even though some women had been transferred to prison, there weren't enough beds to go around. And male prisoners were shuffled through the halls like herds of cattle.

I started pulling a chair up to the wooden partition at the front of the *galera* and standing on it to observe the activity at the booking desk just outside. The guards threatened to shoot me a few times, but I kept quiet, and eventually they forgot I was there.

One morning I watched as they brought in three handcuffed prisoners. The one in front was a thin old man with white hair, but the firm set of his shoulders and his steady pace radiated an unexpected virility. Behind him were two glum men in their mid-twenties. As they got closer, it was plain that they were his sons. One guard edgily trained his rifle on the old man while two others conferred on the paperwork. The old man observed it all with a serene expression that intrigued me.

"What are you here for?" I asked quietly. He glanced upward in faint surprise, then smiled when he saw I was a prisoner. "I'm afraid they discovered a barn full of weapons on my farm in Güira de Melena," he replied. "There's no hope for me."

He turned to his two sons. "Listen to me," he commanded them in a low voice that was somehow gentle and steely at the same time. "They're going to separate us in a minute, and you won't see me again. But I want you to remember this: The problem for a man isn't dying, but how he dies. A man dies in silence. Do you understand me?

"Those guns were mine. I'm the only one who knows how they got there, when they came, and what they were for. No matter what they say to you, no matter what they threaten you with, that's what you tell them— to ask me. Anyone who says anything different, I'll damn for a traitor. Anyone who says anything different, he's not my son."

One of the guards looked up from his papers. "Shut up, you fucking *gusano*," he snarled, using Castro's favorite epithet—worm—for enemies of the Revolution. The old man ignored him. He raised his handcuffed wrists slightly, then dropped them. I had the powerful feeling he wanted to hug his sons a last time. "A man has to be above fear," he said, even more quietly. "And when he can't be above it, he must bear it." A guard grabbed his arm, pulling him off down the corridor, and he didn't look back.

"Let's go, the car is waiting," the guard said impatiently. "And we've got to stop in the property room." I quickly tied my shoes. After eight days at

State Security, they had given up on interrogating me, and I was being transferred to Guanabacoa Prison just outside Havana. But I had no idea why we had to stop in the property room—all I had here was the grimy evening dress still on my back.

When we walked into the property room, a guard handed me a canvas bag. Inside were two blouses, a skirt, pajamas, my contact lens case, and a box of talcum powder. My father had come through. I was turning to go to the bathroom to change when something caught my eye: the tin box they took from my room, which contained a rat's skull and—maybe— the three hundred pesos my sister had saved for a car. "That box is mine, too," I said innocently, and the guard handed it to me.

In all, six of us were being transferred, and they split us into two cars. I was in the middle of the backseat, between my friends Ilia Herrera and Nelly Urtiaga. A guard sat in front with the driver.

Both cars, as usual, sped out of the parking lot in a cacophonous burst of squealing tires and howling engines. The lead driver, though, was a nut case even by the liberal standards of State Security. After his car skidded wildly through a right turn and nearly wound up on the sidewalk, our driver got on the radio.

"Hey, Juan, remember what the boss said about all the car wrecks," he cautioned the lead driver. "The next guy to crack up a car has to pay for it himself." The reply seemed like an inaudible burst of static to me, but our driver seemed satisfied.

We continued racing through the city's serpentine streets until we reached the Malecón, the broad boulevard that winds along Havana Bay. It was filled with a crowd of dancers rehearsing for Carnaval, the week-long celebration that precedes Lent. The lead car braked sharply to avoid the throng and we slammed into it from behind. Our driver stopped immediately; the other car continued for about a block before slowing to a halt.

"Now I'm completely fucked!" exclaimed our seething driver. "Look at that fender! I'm going to be paying for it for months." He jerked the door open and jumped out, followed by the guard. They paused briefly to inspect the front of the car before marching up the street, yelling at the other driver. Nelly and Ilia watched with amusement; I opened my talcum powder and patted some on a rash on my neck. Then I pried open my tin box and looked inside the rat's skull. It was still there—three hundred pesos. I glanced up the street to see the State Security men arguing vehemently about who was at fault.

"Nelly," I said excitedly, "let me out! I'm leaving!"

"Are you crazy?" she demanded in alarm. "They'll kill you on the spot!"

"All I've got to do is walk into that crowd over there and lose myself in it," I said, my fists clenched in urgency. "Look at them yelling at each other—by the time they notice I'm gone I'll have disappeared. With three hundred pesos, I'll have no trouble getting out of Havana!"

Nelly shook her head stubbornly. "I'm not going to let you kill yourself," she insisted. I turned to Ilia, but her head was going back and forth, too. "She's right, Ana," Ilia said. "They'll shoot you like a dog."

I looked from Ilia to Nelly and back again, incredulous. There was freedom, two hundred feet away inside the gay Carnaval crowd, and it was not State Security but my own friends who were stopping me. An avalanche of despair crushed me back against the seat, and there I sat, mute, as my chance to run melted away.

Grinning like an imbecile, our driver strutted back to the car, the guard trotting behind him. He must have won the argument. "What's going on here, ladies?" he inquired, leaning jauntily into the open window. In his smiling, stupid eyes I saw gates closing behind me; I saw thirty gray years stretching out across a dim horizon. I jerked my elbow, and half a pound of talcum powder flew into his face.

The startled driver banged his head on the roof of the car as he jerked away. Outside he unleashed a flood of curses as he wiped frantically at his face and hair. When he climbed back into the car, the look he gave me was murderous. "I ought to kill you right here," he snarled, and for a moment he seemed to be considering just that. Then he turned back to the steering wheel, twisted the keys in the ignition, and slammed his foot on the gas pedal. "Goddamn, what a day," he lamented as we lurched forward.

"Look at that," exclaimed Yara Borges, one of our fellow prisoners, as we waited outside Guanabacoa Prison for guards to escort us into our new home. She pointed at a large poster mounted above the prison entrance, an immense gate of iron bars. *When these bars are no longer necessary, the*

Revolution will have triumphed—Fidel Castro, the poster proclaimed in garish red letters. "In that case, we may be here a long time," Yara cackled as the gate swung open.

Despite a warm sun overhead, I felt a chill as we entered Guanabacoa. Unlike State Security headquarters, where the leftover amenities of its days as a mansion softened the edges, Guanabacoa was unmistakably a prison. Its whitewashed stone walls and red barrel-tile roof bespoke its origins from the Spanish colonial days nearly a century ago.

A towering wall topped with broken glass ran through the interior of the prison, dividing it roughly in half. The right wing, in a state of crumbling disrepair, was occupied by about forty women who were imprisoned for common crimes.

The left wing was for the political prisoners. It consisted of five *galeras* that opened onto a common courtyard or patio, as we called it. The *galeras* lay to the left; to the right was an ancient stone well (a wooden pulley atop it, though there was no bucket) and, beyond that, nine industrial-size stone sinks for doing laundry.

We were assigned to *Galera 1*, closest to the entrance. As I entered the room, I heard someone shout "Ana!" from behind me. Beba Canabal, my high school friend and underground collaborator, raced across the patio to hug me. It was the first time we'd seen each other since her arrest, five months earlier.

"I guess you were right about Isis Nimo," she said apologetically as we walked back to the *galera.* "Do you know, she actually came to visit me here after I was arrested? She was commiserating with me, promising me I'd be out of here soon, telling me we've got Castro on the run." Beba laughed. "I wish she'd come visit *now.* There are a few things I'd like to say to her. Or do to her."

Galera 1 was a single room, about twenty feet deep and thirty feet wide, containing two toilets, two showers, and two sinks. It was probably designed to hold ten prisoners, but there were thirty-nine of us. Double-decker iron bunkbeds were tightly lined up at right angles to each side wall, with another row arranged head-to-toe in the middle of the room.

The beds were so closely crammed together that we could walk between them only by turning sideways. Just before the lights were turned out at eleven P.M. we opened three folding cots and put them in the aisles to accommodate those without beds. The women on the cots rarely got a full night's sleep; they were awakened every few hours by someone climbing over them on the way to the bathroom. After a few weeks, more prisoners arrived and there were always two or three sleeping in chairs and on the stone floor.

Even so, I preferred Guanabacoa to the strange twilight existence of State Security headquarters. There, counterrevolutionary prisoners hadn't been permitted any contact with the outside world. But Guanabacoa was so hectic, with a steady stream of new prisoners arriving every day at the same time the guards were scrambling to make security arrangements for a dozen or so women going off to trial, that no one had any time to think about drawing up new rules for political prisoners. So we lived by the relatively liberal regulations of the Batista era. We were permitted visits once a week, and our families could bring us twenty-five pounds of gifts on each visit. So we had fruit, candy, crackers, and powdered milk to supplement a prison diet that, if not exactly appetizing, was at least edible. (And the food at Guanabacoa was served on clean plates, too.)

My parents brought some of my medical books the first time they visited. After that I gave up my bed at night to one of the women on cots. Instead, when the *galera* lights went out, I moved to a chair at the cell door and waited for the incessant chatter of three dozen voices to die away. Then, in the tranquility of the night, I read.

It wasn't easy. I had to lean my forehead against the upper bars of the door and extend my arms out through the lower bars in the patio, holding the heavy textbook almost at arms' length to catch the illumination from the large outside security lights. By dawn my wrists were numb, but it was worth it: Reading was my best defense against the worst part of prison life—the boredom. I ate breakfast with the rest of the women, then slept four or five hours when they went to the patio.

When I awoke around noon, the *galera* was usually empty, except for a single lonely figure hunched in the corner. Squeezed into a tiny pocket between the wall and a sink, she knelt in a semicircle of pygmy candles arrayed around a small makeshift altar topped with a picture of Jesus torn from a book. She never spoke to me, but whenever I passed her, I could hear a low, racing stream of prayers. Her name, the other women told me, was Gladys Hernández. In an attempt to make her confess to membership in the anti-Castro underground, State Security had executed her mentally retarded brother, even though he had the mind of a twelve-year-old. Gladys hadn't spoken a word, except to God, since.

She was not the only woman in Guanabacoa teetering on the ragged edge of sanity. Her story was replayed, with variations, every day when prisoners returned from trial.

The State Security interrogators couldn't credibly threaten us with death; they knew the world's uneasy acceptance of Castro's firing squads would end instantly if he started marching women to the *paredón*.

But they *could* threaten us with the lives of our fathers, brothers, sons, husbands, and sweethearts. And who could doubt the veracity of that threat? Every night at the men's prison at La Cabaña, the guards called out names at the cells along Death Row. As the men came out, their shoes were taken away, to be given to the prison's population of common criminals. The next stop often was the prison infirmary where several pints of their blood were removed to be given to hospitals. Their hands were tied behind them and they were gagged; Castro ordered that after he tired of hearing unrepentant shouts of *"Viva Cristo Rey!"* and *"Abajo comunismo!"*—long live Christ the king, down with Communism. Then they were herded down into the old dry moats of the fortress, tied to wooden stakes in front of a wall, and shot by a firing squad of soldiers who got three pesos apiece for every execution. The pay was low, but the work was steady; some nights as many as twelve men went to the *paredón*.*

The women with loved ones in La Cabaña—and there were many— were all eventually confronted with the same choice that faced Gladys Hernández: *Talk, or he dies.* Some stayed silent, and their men were shot. Others talked, and their men were shot anyway.

It was the stuff of nightmares, and I listened to them every evening as I read my medical books at the *galera* door. Some women moaned and thrashed in their sleep; occasionally they howled with grief. Awakening them brought silence, but no relief—this nightmare was round the clock.

The bunk next to the chair where I studied my medical book at night belonged to a woman named Zelma Hazim. During the day, she rarely

---

*Outside Cuba, the stories of forced blood donations by prisoners on the way to the firing squad have often been scorned as propaganda. But Castro himself spoke of the grotesque practice in a speech on February 6, 1961.

joined the small talk when we grumbled about the food, the guards, or Guanabacoa's large and canny population of rats.

But one night as I sat there reading after the *galera* was dark, Zelma rose on one elbow and glanced around to make sure no one was listening. Then she leaned toward me. "It's coming," she whispered. "The Night of the Hundred Bombs. All over Havana they'll hear it, and they'll know that no matter how many of us they put in jail, Cuba will keep fighting Communism." Every night for a week she repeated her warning in that same confidential whisper.

It started shortly after the lights went out at eleven P.M. Some of the explosions rumbled like distant thunder; others were sharp reports, close to the prison. Outside, the guards, near panic, scurried from one wall to the other in a futile attempt to learn what was happening. With every new blast, Zelma leaned over and asked in a low voice, "Did you hear it?" Each time I nodded yes, she put her head back on her pillow. When I quit counting, after two hours, there had been fifty-five.

Near dawn, after the explosions had stopped, I heard a burst of machine-gun fire answered by the crackle of small arms, deciding a life, maybe one of ours.

· THREE ·

The Trial

"ANA RODRÍGUEZ," THE guard bellowed from the patio gate. Making no effort to hurry—the first rule of prison life we learned was that no news was good news—I ambled in his direction. "You're only wasting your own time," the guard called. "Your defense attorney is here."

I hastened my pace, but at the same time I shook my head. I'd told my father, during our last visit, not to waste the money, that my trial would be a sham like all the rest. But he didn't believe me. And I hadn't had the courage to tell him that I'd already been sentenced to thirty years.

The lawyer was waiting at a table in the visiting room. He was a black man in his mid-thirties with a friendly face and steady eyes that occupied me so completely that it took me a minute or two to realize that his left arm was atrophied, with a tiny, clawlike hand dangling useless at the end of it.

"My name is Lázaro Ginebra," he said. "I'm glad to have this opportunity to work with you."

"I'm sure you'll pardon me if I don't feel the same way," I replied, winning a chuckle in return. "Look, Lázaro, no offense, but I think my father would get more value out of his money by using it for firewood than he will by paying you. There's nothing anyone can do in my defense."

"We're going to see about that," the lawyer said. "Now, since your father is going to pay me whether you like it or not, you might as well talk to me. All I know is that they searched your home and they took a few things away. Tell me about it."

I recited the tale of the search and gave him a few details of what other evidence State Security might have based on my conversations with the other women in my group who had been arrested. I was careful, however, to skirt the issue of whether I had really been involved in the underground. The principle of attorney-client privilege was an outmoded one since the Revolution, and the knowledge that I was an arsonist and gunrunner would be as dangerous to him as to me. From the quick glances he gave me at certain points in my story, I was certain Lázaro understood.

"That's all?" he said in disbelief when I finished. "That's all they took? Some bones? It sounds like they don't have any evidence at all. Plus, you're a medical student with an excellent academic record. They don't have a case—I'm amazed they're even taking it to court."

Again I found myself shaking my head. Lázaro, like my father, didn't understand that the rules had changed. Under Batista, the police might take you into a dark alley and beat the hell out of you. And if you fought back, you might even get killed. But the judicial system itself had remained more or less intact. Many, probably most, judges remained independent of Batista. If the government couldn't produce evidence against a defendant, he walked away free. It happened many times.

Under Castro, however, the task of the judicial system was not to judge right or wrong, not to sift evidence in an attempt to find the truth; it was to vindicate the Revolution's decisions. That was why Cuba's court system had been abolished in favor of revolutionary tribunals where legal niceties had no place.

"Lázaro," I said in exasperation, "you're talking like it's going to be a real trial. But it's just a show. Every one of us who will be in that courtroom has already been convicted and sentenced. Even if you prove that I'm the Virgin Mary, I'm still going to prison for thirty years."

His face fell. "I know I can't do much," he admitted. "But maybe I can help just a little. And I can certainly demonstrate for history that they condemned you without evidence, that they sent you to prison not because you were proven guilty of anything but simply because they felt like it. Will you allow me that much?"

I nodded, a little shamed. He was attempting, in the only way he knew, to fight them. Was it any more futile a gesture than scattering propaganda leaflets from buses as I had done?

He smiled again. "Then I must go," he said. "I've got to get to work on my arguments. The trial is the day after tomorrow."

It was a little after seven-thirty A.M. when the six of us from Guanabacoa arrived at La Cabaña for the trial. Our driver raced through the giant iron gates and pulled over at one of the administration buildings. Even though we were already inside a maximum-security prison, several dozen guards were deployed around the building. *If only we had ever done anything to deserve this kind of precaution,* I thought sadly.

The guards ushered us through a door into a large meeting room inside the building. The front of the room was covered by a platform about eighteen inches high with three long tables arrayed on top. We sat just in front of it, at the kind of desks that schoolchildren use.

The nineteen male defendants arrived a few minutes later. Although we were all supposed to be part of one vast underground group, I didn't know most of them. But I smiled and raised a hand in greeting as my friends Alejandro Marchese and Roberto Núñez walked in. They both smiled weakly in return as they sat on either side of me.

"What's wrong?" I whispered to Alejandro. "Don't tell me you're not enjoying the accommodations."

"Haven't you heard?" Alejandro replied soberly. "They're asking the death penalty for Roberto and me. And for José Linares, too," he said, gesturing to a middle-aged man on his left whom I knew only vaguely.

I was stunned. Alejandro was just seventeen, and Roberto only sixteen. Neither of them had been major figures in our group. "What happened?" I finally stammered. "What could they possibly have on you that's so serious?"

"It was that goddamn Isis Nimo," Alejandro said bitterly. "I wish we had listened to you when you warned us about her. She gave us a bomb and asked us to drive it across town. State Security picked us up before we had gone a block."

I must have looked stricken, because he summoned a faint smile from somewhere. "We've still got a chance," he assured me. "You know my mother is a Mexican citizen. She's trying to get the Mexican ambassador to come here and intercede for us. Castro still listens to him, sometimes, because of all the favors the Mexicans did for him when he was an exile. But the ambassador is flying in from Mexico today—I don't know if he'll get here in time."

Just then a man in an olive green military uniform strolled to the front of the room, stepped onto the platform, and sat down at a table right in front of us. When he turned slightly, Alejandro's face paled and a wave of nausea rolled through my stomach. We both recognized him: Fernando Flores Ibarra, the most infamous of Castro's inquistors, whose single-minded pursuit of the death penalty had won him the nickname "Bloodbath." The prosecutor who had filled entire cemeteries with his legal handiwork, the prosecutor who sent Gladys Hernández's retarded brother to a firing squad. Silently I prayed for good weather between Mexico and Cuba.

A few minutes after the prosecutor's arrival, about three dozen of our family members crowded into the back of the room. There were no chairs, so they all had to stand behind a wooden barricade. Though I tried not to look—I knew it would only make me feel worse—I caught myself peering back into the sea of faces. I caught glimpses of both my father and my mother, and though I didn't see him, I felt certain my boyfriend Carlos was there somewhere.

For the thousandth time I wondered what he must be thinking. He hadn't been allowed to visit me at the prison. My parents said he was fine, but I knew my arrest must have come as a dreadful shock to him. Carlos didn't care about politics at all, and we never discussed it. Now he had learned, in a stupefying and terrible way, that there was an entire side of me that he knew nothing about.

The defense lawyers—twelve in all—arrived and took seats at a table on the other side of the platform. Right after that the men who supposedly would decide our fate, the president of the tribunal and its four other members, took their places at the table in the middle. Their attire, the same olive green uniforms worn by the guards and the prosecutor, laid to rest any lingering delusions about their allegiance.

The president of the tribunal bustled about officiously, conferring with Flores Ibarra and assorted Interior Ministry bureaucrats, while the other members cackled at one another's jokes. It was past ten A.M. when the president called everyone to order. The first speaker was Flores Ibarra.

"For one hundred fifty years the workers and peasants of Cuba have been robbed, raped, cheated, and exploited by North American imperialism," he began as he paced the platform a few feet away from us. I leaned back in my chair; it sounded just like one of Castro's speeches, and I knew that, like Castro's, it would go on for hours.

And it did. Flores Ibarra talked until past noon, barely pausing for breath. He talked about casinos and prostitution. He talked about sugar prices. He talked about Puerto Rico and the Philippines, which he said were American colonies, and he talked about the Platt Amendment, the American law that led to the establishment of the U.S. naval base at Guantánamo Bay. Apparently we were charged with all this and more.

Of course, the trial wasn't really about us, as Flores Ibarra made clear during the few times he actually mentioned any of our names. The trial was to reaffirm once again that the Revolution was just, the Revolution was all-knowing and all-seeing, the Revolution represented the highest development of mankind, the Revolution was a historical imperative. The way Flores Ibarra talked, we weren't even human beings, merely bits of chaff that had momentarily gummed the gears of the Revolution and had to be cleaned away.

My mind wandering, I gazed out one of the doors that had been left open in hopes of catching a breeze. Except for the cordon of guards in the distance, I couldn't see any people. But an emaciated stray dog, ribs poking through its mangy skin, watched us curiously from just a few feet outside.

At noon a guard had passed silently among the defendants, handing out sandwiches wrapped in waxed paper as Flores Ibarra railed away. Hardly anyone had touched them. Now I opened mine and removed a scrap of pork. I could see the stray's nose twitch. Unobtrusively I lowered my hand beneath my desk and let the meat fall to the floor.

The dog, leery of all the people in the room but tantalized by the pork, crept through the door. His eyes swiveled to and fro as he came slinking under my desk, but Flores Ibarra's oratory had lulled the room into a torpor, and no one took any notice of the stray as he huddled in front of me.

The prosecutor's voice started climbing as he prepared to make what he thought was a particularly damning point against us. "And we," he proclaimed, "we, the revolutionary combatants, shouting in a single voice—" I swung the pointed toe of my high-heeled shoe into the spot just below the dog's tail. His howl of canine outrage filled the room. Two members of the tribunal banged their knees on the table as they jumped in surprise. Flores Ibarra dropped a sheaf of papers. And startled gasps came from every corner of the room.

The dog flung me a wounded and accusatory look before bolting to the rear of the room to evade the guards who were closing in on him. He evaded them with the ease of a practiced escape artist, darting beneath desks and squirting between their legs as he barked his defiance. The guards, all fat, lumbering men carrying rifles, looked like circus clowns as they reeled into one another in pursuit of their nimble prey.

When they nearly had him cornered, the dog dashed into the crowd of spectators at the back of the room. They acted as passive allies, blocking the way and responding with stupid *Who, me?* looks whenever a guard shouted at them to move. It was all I could do to keep from applauding as the dog confounded them again and again. Finally he spotted an open lane and dashed the length of the room and out the same door he entered. The huffing, puffing guards made no attempt to pursue him, and they didn't close the door behind him, either.

When I lured the stray into the courtroom, my only plan had been to make him howl to annoy Flores Ibarra. But his helter-skelter pursuit by the guards had taken more than twenty minutes. The outline of a plan began to assemble inside my head. I leaned over to Alejandro Marchese. "Give me your sandwich," I whispered. "That dog will be back, and every time he comes in here, we're going to stop the trial. It'll give the Mexican ambassador more time to get here." There was doubt in Alejandro's eyes, but he pushed his sandwich across the desk to me.

When Flores Ibarra finally ran out of things to blame on us—I was relieved that we were not held responsible for any hurricanes or volcanoes—a parade of witnesses began. Most of them were State Security officers who lumped together hearsay with surmise, conjecture, and outright falsehood around what was at best a small kernel of truth. One notable absence was that of Isis Nimo; State Security apparently still believed that her cover could be preserved so that she could spy some more.

With the appearance of witnesses, the defense attorneys at last were able to go to work. Several of them were very good, catching witnesses in contradictions and fabrications at every turn. I watched my own attorney, Lázaro, with a mixture of admiration and sympathy; he was undeniably skilled at cross-examination, but it was only getting him in trouble.

"So," he asked the State Security officer who led the search of my house, "did you confiscate anything you found there? Or were you just having fun poking around in a woman's closet?"

"Sarcasm to a servant of the state is not permitted," the president of the tribunal intoned. "You are hereby fined fifty pesos, Counselor."

"We seized some things," the State Security officer replied defensively. "Searches are hard work. We search for evidence, not for pleasure."

"Well, what did you find, then?" Lázaro asked.

"Those things to the right," the officer replied, gesturing at a pile of evidence heaped on the platform.

"Ahhh," Lázaro said, picking up the medical school skeleton that they'd found in my room. "These bones. Now, let me get this straight— you're saying she *killed* this poor man?"

Muffled laughter rippled through the room. "Your insults are intolerable," the tribunal president thundered. "You are hereby fined another one hundred pesos." Lázaro's fines continued to mount until the tribunal president shouted for him to sit down and shut up before they packed him off to one of La Cabaña's cells. He had charged my father two hundred pesos for a job that wound up costing him five hundred.

The efforts of the defense attorneys infuriated Flores Ibarra, who launched into several more long speeches, his blue eyes icier and his face more contorted with every one. He hadn't mentioned the death penalty during the morning, but now he brought it up every time he spoke. And each time, it seemed to me that Alejandro's eyes sank a little further into his head. There was still no sign of the Mexican ambassador.

Throughout the day Flores Ibarra had filled me, by turns, with loathing and boredom. Now, though, he was making me angry. It was bad enough that he wanted to kill Alejandro and Roberto; he didn't need to bully them, too. The next time the prosecutor turned toward us, I gave a theatric, drawn-out yawn. His eyes narrowed. I waited a moment, then said loudly to Alejandro: "Man, doesn't he have anything new to say? This is *boring*."

I kept needling the prosecutor at regular intervals with yawns, whispers, and snoring noises. By the time I took the witness stand, he was overflowing with venom.

"What justification do you have for fighting against something as beautiful as the Revolution?" he demanded. I sat there, silent, matching his angry glare with one of my own. He slapped some papers on his table and wheeled toward the tribunal. "Honorable President," he growled, "there are times when I deeply regret the compassion and benevolence of the Revolution. It is a great mistake, in my judgment, that Cuba has no death penalty for women." That was the end of my testimony.

As I returned to my desk, from the corner of my eye I saw something move outside. When I sat down, I stole a quick glance toward the door. The stray dog was back, his brown eyes a mixture of reproach and hope. Casually I pulled a piece of pork from a sandwich. *I know I'm making you work hard for this meat,* I thought. *But it's for a good cause.* I dropped it on the floor.

The dog performed almost as well the second time around. Later he made a third, briefer, visit, but the combination of smaller pieces of meat and stiffer kicks had worn thin; he disappeared and didn't come back.

Meanwhile, the lengthy speeches of Flores Ibarra were taking their toll on the tribunal, too. When defense attorneys had the floor, the members of the tribunal sometimes chatted among themselves or read newspapers. But when the prosecutor spoke, they tried to at least feign attention (though I saw one of them doze off a couple of times). As the afternoon wore on, the tribunal began calling recesses. At first they lasted just a few minutes, but then they lengthened until the final one was more than an hour.

"Look at those idiots," Alejandro said bitterly as another break began. "This is all a damn joke to them." I clucked sympathetically, then added: "But the more time they waste, the better for you." He nodded gloomily and scanned the crowd once more. Still no sign of the Mexican ambassador.

Actually, I could almost sympathize with the tribunal members. From their swarthy, suntanned skin and calloused hands, I was certain they were peasants who had been drafted for the job, the customary practice for these tribunals. Sometimes a law student or someone else with at least cursory knowledge of the law was chosen to be president, but the other members were selected for their malleability rather than their intellect. Their only real function here was to read the verdicts and sentences that Flores Ibarra would give them later in a sealed envelope.

It was three A.M. when Flores Ibarra began his final, and by now dismally familiar, speech. An hour later, the tribunal followed the prosecutor into a back room. *No real jury would convict any of us,* I thought. Even though I knew several of the defendants were guilty, the evidence had been fragmented and confusing. And because Flores Ibarra made no attempt to call witnesses and unfold his case against us in an orderly way, there were times when even I was confused about who among us was supposed to have done what.

Unfortunately, we didn't have a real jury, just five flesh-and-blood scarecrows who probably wanted to get Flores Ibarra's instructions as quickly as possible so they could go home to bed. I couldn't bear to look at either Alejandro or Roberto. There had never been any sign of the ambassador. Did he miss his plane? Did Alejandro's mother fail to convince him? The useless questions gnawed at my brain as the minutes ticked away.

The sound of the door opening echoed like a shot in the tense stillness of the room. The tribunal members filed in, inching their way forward as if they were in a slow-motion movie. Gradually they lowered themselves into their chairs as they beamed broad smiles to one another. *Oh, Alejandro, I'm so sorry,* I thought as a curtain of despair dropped across my brain. When Flores Ibarra got to his feet and started speaking, the words seemed to fade in and out of my ears.

"To commit violence against the Revolution is the ultimate crime," he declared, "and it deserves the ultimate punishment. Those who bear arms against the people—because the Revolution *is* the people—in the service of reactionary forces should expect no mercy when the people judge them." He paused. "But the Revolution is also capable of magnanimity . . ." The next words were lost in the loudest sigh I have ever heard in my life, the collective expulsion of seventy-five breaths throughout the room. The Mexican ambassador, from somewhere, had pulled a string.

I reached out on both sides to squeeze the hands of Alejandro and Roberto, who were wearing real smiles for the first time that day. Meanwhile, Flores Ibarra was reading off the sentences: thirty years for Alejandro, Roberto, and José Linares, nine years for a couple of the women, twelve years for everyone else. Then Flores Ibarra's taut lips curled into a malicious smile. "And for Ana Rodríguez, thirty years in prison, followed by thirty years of house arrest," he proclaimed ebulliently. I kept my eyes straight ahead; I was afraid of what I might see if I looked into my parents' faces.

When we arrived back at Guanabacoa shortly after dawn, it looked like an olive green anthill. Soldiers were scurrying all over the prison, including the roof. I joined a mystified crowd of prisoners on the patio to watch as the troops rigged cranes and pulleys around the roof.

"What's going on?" I asked a passing guard.

"We're putting anti-aircraft guns on top of the prison," he replied smugly. "The Americans are about to invade, and when they do, we're going to shoot down their planes. And then," he added, chortling, "we're going to point the guns lower and shoot *you*."

"That is, if those old roofs don't collapse the first time the guns fire," I rejoined. The guard's laughter halted abruptly and he walked away. "Well, that explains all that weird stuff we've been hearing on Radio Swan," Isabel Molgado said as he disappeared into the offices.

Radio Swan was a station that had gone on the air about a year earlier. Based somewhere outside Cuba, it usually broadcast virulent anti-Castro diatribes by Cuban exiles from Miami. We often listened to it on a small portable radio that one of the prisoners had been given by her family. But for the past week, the regular programs had been interspersed with nonsensical little nuggets: "Look well to the rainbow. The fish will rise very soon. Chico is in the house. The sky is blue. The fish is red." Now we understood: The gibberish must be coded messages to underground groups signaling an invasion.*

As the news that the government expected a U.S. invasion raced

---

*Years later I learned that Radio Swan was indeed operated by the CIA on Swan Island, a tiny island 150 miles off the coast of Honduras. But the "coded messages" were disinformation, intended to make Castro think that the CIA was coordinating its invasion plans with the underground. There was no serious cooperation. Radio Swan disappeared soon after the invasion fell apart, but the CIA must have liked Swan Island, because later the agency planes that supplied the American-backed Contras in their war against Nicaragua's Marxist Sandinista regime during the 1980s were based there.

around the prison, the patio filled up with armchair generals, breathlessly trying to guess where and when the strike would come and how long Castro could withstand American might. The overall consensus was that the Revolution was about to enter the history books as nothing more than an unpleasant footnote. But there were a few skeptics, including me.

"I don't have much faith that the United States has the resolve to do this," I insisted. "Castro is a fanatic—he'll make them destroy the whole island before he gives up."

"Are you crazy?" demanded Isabel Alonso, one of the other prisoners. "There's no bigger problem in the whole world for the United States than Cuba. They can't let the Communists create a giant military base ninety miles from their border." Several women nodded in agreement. Before anyone else could say anything, the guards appeared, shooing us inside the *galeras* and locking the doors. "You're not coming out until it's over," one of the guards informed us.

Although I hadn't said it aloud, something else was troubling me. If an invasion *was* on the way, Castro obviously knew about it. How carefully had the Americans prepared this thing?

It was three days later, on April 15, that the guttural roar reverberated through the inky predawn sky. "Airplanes!" shouted someone from the back of the *galera*. The noise of soldiers sprinting across the roof above us confirmed it. A moment later, the anti-aircraft cannons located atop the roofs on all four sides of the prison thundered to life. The heavy crash of the guns sent dust and chunks of plaster falling onto our heads from the ceiling, and the roof beams squealed in protest.

"Under the beds! Under the beds!" somebody screamed needlessly; the floor was already filled with women scrambling for cover. Stumbling over them in the darkness, I ran to the *galera* door. Climbing the iron crossbars like a ladder, I scanned the skies, hoping to get a clue about what was happening.

The sky was an eerie palette of darkness and illumination. Some of the anti-aircraft guns were heavy cannons that gave off bright flashes as they fired. Others were small-caliber weapons firing streams of red tracer bullets that curved gracefully into the horizon. And through it all glowed the orange flames of the gas burners at the Bellot petroleum refinery down the road from the prison.

In the herky-jerky light of the muzzle flashes, I could clearly see bombs tumbling into the sea, throwing up geysers of foam, glistening stalagmites of an instant's duration. *What are you doing?* I screamed mentally. *Why are you bombing fish?* Surely those bombs were intended for the refinery. And just as surely, the continued glow of the gas burners must have told the pilots their aim was way off. Either they were incompetent, or the Americans thought they could scare Castro away with a flimsy bit of psychological warfare. *Whichever it is, we're doomed,* I realized. Between the bursts of gunfire, I could hear the shouts of the other prisoners yelling at me to get down. But I hung there on the bars, watching the bombs kick plumes of seawater high into the sky, and crying tears of frustration.

It took four days for the defeat I read in the steady flames of those gas burners to unfold. We learned the details as we huddled around the radio in a corner of the *galera*, interrupted only occasionally by the taunting threats of the guards. About 1,400 Cuban exiles (not, as many expected, American troops), armed and trained by the CIA, had landed on a beach near the Bay of Pigs, about one hundred miles southeast of Havana. The U.S. withdrew air support from the invasion at the last minute, leaving the task to exile pilots in ancient B-26 bombers, which were cut to pieces by Castro's jets. Then the dictator's air force turned its attention to the landing party. Only a few dozen of the exile soldiers escaped; 114 were killed and 1,189 were captured.

For the Cuban underground the toll was even worse. Immediately after the April 15 air raid, State Security began rounding up anyone even vaguely suspected of disloyalty to the Revolution. When the prisoners filled all the available jails, they were herded into theaters, hotels, even stadiums. Most of them were released within a few days of the invasion's defeat, but State Security gleaned enough information from its interrogations to launch a terminal crackdown on the anti-Castro resistance.

A pall descended over the *galera* in the wake of the invasion's defeat. But a few nights later the Voice of America broadcast the news of a new speech by President Kennedy. The invasion wasn't "the final episode," he said. "Cuba must not be abandoned to the Communists. And we do not intend to abandon it, either."

Among many of the women there was renewed optimism. "The next time, the Americans will get it right," someone said to murmurs of assent. Silently I withdrew from the group around the radio, picked up my medical book, and went to my regular nighttime perch at the *galera* door. But once seated, I left the book in my lap, unopened, and stared into the darkness. There wouldn't be a next time, I knew; the Americans wouldn't try it twice. They weren't coming. *Thirty years,* I thought in wonder, *I'm going to be here thirty years.*

· FOUR ·

Mother's Day

I YAWNED LAZILY as I swung my feet from the bunk to the floor. My morning sleep was over; time to head outside, wash some clothes in the big stone sinks on the patio and catch up on the gossip. Several women had returned late the night before from a trial at La Cabaña. They would have news of recent arrivals among the men, as well as the latest grim tidings of executions. But before I could find my shoes, Beba Canabal burst into the empty *galera*.

"Ana, come quickly!" she exclaimed breathlessly. "There's a captain outside from the Interior Ministry, and I think they're going to transfer some of us to Guanajay."

I shuddered and then started grabbing clothes. Guanajay! Like school girls at a slumber party terrorizing each other with ghost stories, we sometimes talked about the place at night.

About fifteen miles west of Havana, Guanajay was the largest women's prison in Cuba. Most of the prisoners there were common criminals: thieves, prostitutes, drug addicts, and the occasional murderer. But in the first weeks of the Revolution, when Castro was jailing tens of thousands of accused Batista sympathizers, he sent the women to Guanajay. The misery of the *Batistianas*, as they were called, was legendary. The prison director was a woman named Carmelina Guanche, a holdover from the Batista days. She had been retained because of her kindness to female friends of Castro who were jailed before the triumph of the Revolution. (At times she even let them leave the prison for an evening at the local movie theater.) Guanche, determined to prove her loyalty to Castro, made Guanajay a living hell for the *Batistianas*.

Visits were rarely permitted and had to be conducted through a double-mesh screen that didn't permit prisoners to even kiss their loved ones hello. Packages from outside were allowed only infrequently, and then had to be small. But what really made our skin crawl were the stories of how Guanche used the common criminals at Guanajay to bully the *Batistianas*. In Guanabacoa, the common criminals were confined in the prison's old right wing, separated from us by a tall, thick wall, and we had virtually no contact with them. But at Guanajay, they lived in the same cellblock as the *Batistianas* and the guards encouraged them to torment the Batista women at every opportunity.

The worst of it came at mealtimes. The *Batistianas* had to walk a gauntlet the length of two city blocks to reach their dining room. Every foot of the path was lined with common criminals screaming threats and insults, spitting on them, and sometimes even darting out to punch and kick them. Once the *Batistianas* reached the dubious shelter of the dining room, they often found worms, cockroaches, and even fragments of glass inside their food, which was prepared by cooks drawn from the common criminal population.

As I raced outside, still wrestling with the top button of my blouse, I could hear the booming voice of the captain. "The following prisoners should gather their belongings and report to the prison offices," he announced, reading from a list. "Martha O'Neal—"

"But didn't you hear a word I said?" Beba interrupted, evidently continuing an earlier plea. "I know we're prisoners, and I know that we can't pick and choose our prison like tourists on a vacation. But Guanajay— Guanajay is *subhuman*. If we can talk to some officials from the Interior Ministry, if they take some steps to improve the conditions, then we'll cooperate. Otherwise, we're not going."

The captain looked at her woodenly, then resumed reading: "Martha O'Neal—"

This time he was drowned out by a chorus of shouts of "We're not going!" and "We're political prisoners, not common criminals!" The captain regarded us sourly for a few moments while the jeers grew louder, then walked away.

"That was almost too easy," Beba said as we watched him disappear back into the offices.

"I'm not sure we've heard the end of it," I replied. "This place is full to the brim. They've got to do something or pretty soon we'll be able to escape just by standing on each other's shoulders."

"Maybe Castro will declare a general amnesty," Beba deadpanned.

Our laughter was chilly.

Whatever tension we felt over the near transfer to Guanajay faded as May 13 approached. Every Sunday was special because it was visiting day, but this one was also Mother's Day. Even prisoners from distant towns knew their mothers would find a way to visit. All week long the *galeras* bustled with activity as we fussed and fretted with our clothes, our shoes, our hair, our nails. We couldn't buy our mothers presents or cards or flowers or candy, couldn't do any of the things that once had been so routine and now seemed so marvelous. All we could do to honor them was try, for a few hours at least, to hold the drabness of the prison at bay.

At breakfast that morning, a guard explained the logistics of the visit to us.

"We're dividing your *galera* into three groups," he said. "The first one will go for a visit of one hour, and when it returns the second group will go out, and so forth. We'll call the first group at eight A.M."

Our *galera* now contained sixty women and just two showers, which meant that even those of us in the third group, with three hours to prepare for the visit, had only a few minutes each to bathe. Scarcely did a woman step inside the shower before the cries of "Hurry up, hurry up!" were echoing around the room. A cloud of free-floating anxiety hovered over the room, turning us taut and shrill.

Shortly after nine, the women from the first group started streaming back. The rest of us crowded around to ask how the visit had gone. "We hardly got to see our families at all," one complained. "First they searched us before letting us into the room, then they searched our families before letting them in. Finally we were all in there together, but five minutes later they told us to line up to be counted before bringing us back inside." Still, she added, she had gotten to kiss her mother on Mother's Day; that counted for something.

When the second group of prisoners returned just after ten, they were nervous. "Something's up," one woman told me. "My mother says there are so many guards outside that it looks like a forest out there. And there are three *jaulas* out there, too." We called the sealed, windowless trucks they used to transport us *jaulas*, the word for the vehicles driven by dog-catchers before the Revolution. Ordinarily their presence would mean some prisoners were going to court, but trials weren't held on Sundays.

Tense and fidgeting, those of us in the third group waited for them to call us. But an hour passed without any word. Silently I walked back to my bunk and started exchanging my skirt and high heels for blue jeans and walking shoes. Beba Canabal looked at me, eyebrows raised. "If something happens, I want to be ready for it," I shrugged. I didn't say anything else—I didn't know what I was expecting, or even if I really expected anything at all—but other women began changing clothes, too.

"Could this have something to do with Guanajay?" asked a woman changing nearby.

"No, no," said another voice. "They're evil, but not stupid. They're not going to pick a fight with us while our families are watching."

"Then what *is* it all about?" someone else asked, a question that was answered with silence.

It was nearly noon when a guard appeared on the patio and read off a list of the names of the women in our group. By then nearly all of us had taken off the dresses we had worked so hard to clean and press. All that preparation, and now we looked like we were going to pick coffee rather than to celebrate Mother's Day with our families. I smiled at Gladys Hernández and pointed at her jeans; she smiled back—something she was just recently learning to do again—and pointed at mine. We were wearing the same distinctive aquamarine shade of blue.

As we trudged across the patio to the visiting room, Luisa Pérez called to some prisoners from another *galera*. "If anything happens to us," she promised, "I'll scream as loud as I can." They nodded solemnly as we disappeared through the door to the offices.

What we called the visiting room was really nothing more than a screened-off corner of the open-air courtyard just inside the prison's main gate.

About twenty feet wide and sixty feet long, it was divided from the rest of the courtyard by a gray wooden partition topped with wire mesh. Inside were half a dozen narrow, low-slung, wooden benches. There were two doors: one near the prison offices, which we used, and one at the other end of the room, near the main gate, which visitors used.

We entered the room one by one after a search. When we were all inside, our visitors began arriving in clumps of two or three. The guards seemed edgy and preoccupied as they directed us inside, adding to the nervous atmosphere.

"Mama!" I shouted as my mother entered with my sister Milagros trailing behind. We embraced frantically. I had dreaded the first visit with my parents after my trial, dreaded the bruises I might see deep in their eyes. Instead, they bubbled with the popular certainty that the Americans were preparing to avenge the Bay of Pigs defeat. I hadn't the heart to tell them of my own conviction that Cuba was on its own.

Today my mother was chattering again about how angry Kennedy was. But her words came in jittery bursts. "It's very strange outside," she confessed after a few minutes. "The guards are acting peculiar, like they know something we don't."

"I'm sure it's just the large number of visitors for Mother's Day," I said, trying to soothe her. The look she gave me said plainly that she was not convinced, and I didn't blame her. All around us I could hear the same doubts being expressed by other visitors.

But my mother, deciding to make the best of it, dropped the subject. "Carlos comes to visit every evening and asks about you," my mother said. "It kills him that he can't see you." I nodded, but my thoughts about Carlos were such a tangle of contradictions and confusion that I didn't know what to say. Every time I tried to sort them out, the words *thirty years* sent them tumbling in all directions again.

We bounced from subject to subject that way, saying too much and too little, until a guard shoved his way to the center of the visiting room and announced loudly: "The visit is over! Form up for recount!" We began slowly lining up at our door so the guards could count us. Some of the visitors drifted toward the door at the other end. Like all visits, this one was ending slowly, with tearful embraces and drawn-out good-byes, while guards shouted for us to move along.

Then the door at the other end of the room swung open and a crowd of men in civilian clothes spilled inside. *Who the hell are they?* I wondered. A couple of them were shouting unintelligibly. "The visit is over!" insisted one of the guards a final time, and then both the guards and the men in civilian clothes started shoving our family members back toward their door. Several of the mothers stood fast, and the pushing got rougher. Then, as we watched with mouths agape, one of the men cocked his fist and punched an old lady in the chin, dropping her in a heap.

"You bastard!" a prisoner yelled, and we surged toward them. "Attack them! Attack them!" someone among the guards yelled, and the men without uniforms sprang toward us snarling. Even more men pushed into the room, a few uniformed guards with rifles among them.

The room was a kaleidoscope of flying fists and swinging feet. Except for a few sharp curses, there were no words, only thuds, grunts, and cries of pain as blows landed. I jumped on a bench at the side of the room and used it as a staging area, jumping down into the crowd to land a few kicks on a surprised male target, then leaping back out to look for another opportunity.

Casualties were falling on both sides. On the far side of the room, I could see a lieutenant crawling away, one hand clutched to his face. One of the men in civilian clothes had vomited from a kick in the stomach, and a pungent odor of stale alcohol filled the air.

But the men had the advantage of size, numbers, and weapons— several guards were using their rifle butts to administer fearful beatings— and we were taking the worst of it. The mothers had mostly been pushed out the door near the gate, where I could see some of them scratching and clawing at guards in an unsuccessful attempt to get back in.

In one corner I saw several men had separated a prisoner named Julia González Rosquete from the crowd and were battering her. Curled into a ball, she could do nothing but grunt as their heavy boots pounded her body from all sides. I jumped down from my bench to go to her aid, but strong arms seized me from behind and I was dragged out of the room, kicking wildly at an assailant I couldn't even see. The last thing I saw in the room was Luisa Pérez mounted on a bench, the veins in her neck standing out like thick cords as she screamed a warning back toward the patio: "They're taking us! They're taking us!"

I was dragged through the open prison gate toward the three *jaulas* parked outside. There were men on every side of me, kicking and punching me. With my arms pinned back, I couldn't even ward off their blows, much less do any damage of my own. A guard opened the double doors at the back of one of the *jaulas* and trained a gun inside. "The first one of you who tries to come out, I'll shoot you like a dog!" he threatened, and I could see several prisoners huddled against the interior walls of the vehicle.

I let my body go slack as though all the resistance had been beaten out of me, and four men picked me up and tossed me toward the back of the *jaula*. But I caught the top edge of the door with my feet and bounced back like a spring, knocking the men to the pavement like bowling pins. I jumped back to my feet and started swinging at them again. More men ran forward to pin me; again I went slack; and again I used my feet to bounce off the top of the *jaula* and knock them down. We repeated the process over and over for what felt like an eternity.

At last two broad-shouldered State Security men shoved aside the staggering men in civilian clothes. One grabbed me by the hair and yanked me almost completely off my feet. The other snatched my legs and shoved them under his arm as though I were a package. Together they carried me into the *jaula* and threw me violently to the floor. I tried to sit up, but the man who had grabbed my hair pulled back his arm and smashed his fist into the side of my head like a battering ram. My whole body flew into the metal bench at the side of the *jaula* and then dropped to the floor.

"Murderer! You've killed her!" screamed Zelma Hazim, crouching beside me, but her voice receded as I moved rapidly down a long dark tunnel. Tiny colored stars peeked through the ceiling, marking my progress. *This is just like in the comic books,* I thought. *I'm about to go un-conscious.* On the smooth side of the tunnel, I clawed for a grip, and the stars slowed. Then I was moving the other way, and I felt myself pop out the mouth of the tunnel.

"Murderer! Murderer!" Zelma's voice returned. I cracked open an eye and saw that I was lying on the floor of the *jaula*. The State Security man was standing over me, one leg on either side, with his back to my head. Two prisoners were swinging at him ineffectually, and he was cocking his fist again.

With my eye I measured the distance. Then without a sound, I grabbed both his legs and used them to propel myself upward, launching my right knee into his exposed crotch like a rocket. His howl of pain was cut off almost immediately as he banged his head hard against the low roof of the *jaula*. As he stood there, stunned, I did it again. This time the only sound he made was a hoarse croaking noise.

I was completely conscious now, the rage coursing through me like molten steel. No one had hit me since the last time my mother spanked me ten years ago. What gave them the *right*? They were like schoolyard bullies with uniforms: *We're doing it because we* can. *We're doing it because no one can* stop *us.* My fury shot through my body and exited from my right knee, slamming again and again into his balls. Half-crazed with pain, penned into the *jaula* by the women in front of him and by guards trying to push inside to stop me, the State Security man was a deliciously defenseless target.

Somehow they managed to pull him out of the *jaula* and slam the doors shut. I climbed uncertainly to my feet. From outside we could still hear the sounds of blows and the screams of "Murderers!" from our mothers and a growing crowd of townspeople. "Does anybody know who those bastards in civilian clothes were?" I asked my companions. "They were common criminals from one of the men's prisons," a woman answered. "Do you know who was with them? Ramiro Valdés, the Minister of the Interior. He was the one who yelled, 'Attack!' And just before they started hitting us, I heard him say to a couple of them, 'Remember, do a good job and you'll be walking the streets of Havana tonight.'"

Then the *jaula*'s engine roared to life and we had to brace ourselves as the truck peeled out from the prison like a race car. Just as suddenly, it stopped again with a piercing shriek of brakes. After creeping forward for a minute or two, it sped off once more.

We learned later that Gladys Hernández' mother had thrown herself into the street in front of our *jaula*. Miraculously, it passed right over her without harming her. Gladys' mother was distraught because, watching from afar, she'd seen a woman dragged kicking and struggling into the *jaula* and then hit in the head so hard that it surely killed her. She couldn't see the woman's face, but there was no mistaking the bright aquamarine blue of her jeans—it had to be her daughter Gladys.

Of course, the woman she had seen was me. Gladys had somehow been separated from us inside the prison and retreated to the patio, where she found events had taken a bizarre twist: The prison was in the hands of the inmates.

It started when the women in *Galera 2*, alerted by the screams of

Luisa Pérez, brought out an iron bar that they had somehow stolen and hidden away for an emergency. Using it as a crowbar, they broke open the padlock on the *galera* door. Once outside, they broke the locks on the other *galeras* and even the one on the door to the offices.

They burst into the offices, guarded by a single desk sergeant—everyone else was outside, beating us—and tore out the telephone to prevent him from calling for reinforcements. The terrified sergeant bolted out the gate, screaming, "They're loose! They're loose!"

Luckily for the guards, several fire trucks—summoned earlier, when the guards thought they might need help forcing us into the *jaulas*—pulled up at the prison just then. Using their ladders, firemen scaled the prison walls from outside, climbed onto the *galera* roofs, and turned two of their powerful hoses on the prisoners in the patio.

Women were flying everywhere, like flower petals caught in a rushing river. The firemen deliberately aimed the high-pressure streams of water at the prisoners' breasts, and their screams of pain mingled with the roar of the hoses. When the firemen caught sight of Raquel Romero, seven months pregnant, they turned the hoses on her belly and sent her sprawling twenty feet against a wall. Meanwhile, guards joined the firemen on the roof and were lobbing bottles down into the patio. One shattered right behind my friend Ilia Herrera, filling her buttocks with glass fragments. Several other women suffered less serious cuts.

Soon most of the women were caught in the spray of the hoses, buffeted against the wall in the center of the patio by the torrents of water. The only one who somehow managed to defy the hoses was a tall, wiry young prisoner named Emelina Hernández. Inch by inch, clutching furiously to tiny toeholds on the patio floor, she crawled straight into the stream. Finally she was beneath the angle of the hoses, and she dived to safety under the short overhanging roof that sheltered the *galera* doors.

To get as close as possible to their targets on the patio, the firemen had climbed down onto those overhanging roofs, which were only eight feet or so off the ground. Emelina, looking up, could see the blunt snouts of the firehose nozzles extending just beyond the overhang as they blasted water at the women trapped on the patio.

Dragging a bench out of a *galera*, Emelina placed it just at the edge of the overhang where the firemen couldn't see it, and climbed atop. With a quick leap she grabbed one of the nozzles from the surprised firemen and dragged it to the ground. With the stream of water temporarily diverted, several more prisoners ran over to hold the hose, which was bucking and twitching like an angry snake, while Emelina unscrewed the nozzle. Seconds later a team of firemen, with a mighty heave, jerked the hose back to the roof—but without the nozzle, the water just traveled a few feet before harmlessly tumbling to the ground.

"Come on!" Emelina shouted to the other women. "They can't control us with one hose—let's climb onto the roof and kill them!" As the prisoners rushed forward, the firemen beat a panicky retreat, climbing from the low overhangs back onto the main roof and then scurrying back down their ladders into their waiting trucks.

The women were milling around the patio arguing their next move when a battalion of female anti-riot police walked into the prison and massed at the gate to the patio. "Advance!" an officer shouted somewhere from the rear, and the police began stalking through the gate. They carried rifles with bayonets fixed to the barrels, flashing in the afternoon sun. The prisoners just stood there, frozen in a tableau of confusion and fear.

The only one who moved was Gladys Hernández. She stooped to pick up a bottle of mineral water at her feet, miraculously unbroken when the guards hurled it down from the roof. Taking a few running steps, she flung it upward in a long, looping arc that ended at the feet of the first few police. The bottle exploded in a shower of glass that sent the police stumbling backward.

It broke the spell. Prisoners scurried across the patio, scooping up shards of glass. The police watched reluctantly from the gate. What had started out as a simple mop-up operation was shaping up as a bloody hand-to-hand combat.

An Interior Ministry captain emerged from the knot of police around the gate and took a few steps onto the patio. "This makes no sense," he called out. "You've proven you can fight. Why don't we stop now, before someone gets hurt?"

"We're not stopping anything until you understand that we all stand together," one of the prisoners shouted back. "When you attacked the women from *Galera 1*, you attacked us all."

"Yeah, if you want peace, bring them back here," chimed in another.

The captain put his hands forward in a gesture of supplication. "I can't bring them back, you know that," he said. "They're at Guanajay and they're staying there. What I can do is transfer any of you who want to join them. And I'll let you pack up the things they left behind and take them with you."

The prisoners looked at one another. The ferocity of their anger was slowly dissolving into realism. Ultimately, the Interior Ministry would retake the prison regardless of the cost. And whatever casualties they would inflict on the police would be returned tenfold. Joining us at Guanajay would at least keep together a large bloc of political prisoners; the bigger the numbers, the more difficult to push us around.

"I'll go," announced Gladys. "Me, too," echoed dozens of others. The captain nodded. "We'll transfer you on Tuesday," he said. "Use tomorrow to pack." He walked out, the police trailing behind him.

About the time that an exhausted peace was descending on Guanabacoa, my *jaula* arrived at Guanajay. The guard at the front gate waved us through and the *jaula* continued on to our assigned pavilion, as cellblocks were called there, followed by the same State Security patrol car that had been tailing us since we left Guanabacoa.

When the *jaula* doors opened, I climbed stiffly out. We were parked in front of a long two-story building. "Welcome to Guanajay!" someone shouted, and I looked up to see several women waving through the bars of upstairs windows. *At least the neighbors are friendly,* I thought dryly as I waved back. A guard in civilian clothing strutted officiously toward us. "I'm in charge here," he announced, "and—"

"Hey, cunt!" a rasping voice cut him off. "Bitch with the long hair!" I turned to see the tall State Security man, the one whose crotch I had battered. He was clinging to the open door of the patrol car with his left hand while his right leveled a .45 automatic pistol at my chest.

"Yeah, bitch, I'm talking to you," he continued as our eyes met. "You really fucked me over. And now you're going to die for it." His pale, sickly face pulsed with hatred.

I didn't move as I glanced around. There was a small pile of what looked like construction debris at my feet, and beside it was a broken chunk from a two-by-four wooden beam. Fixing my gaze on the State Security man, I slowly knelt to pick it up. "Go ahead, shoot," I said. "But you better not miss. Because if you do, I'm going to do to your head what

I've already done to your balls." He hissed and clicked the safety off his pistol.

"Drop the gun!" a voice boomed from my right. I glanced over to see one of the uniformed policemen who patrolled Guanajay's fences. He was sighting down the barrel of his own .45, which was trained on the State Security man.

The State Security man was staring at him in disbelief, but the policeman's aim never wavered. "I know how to use this thing," he barked, "and I'll do it! This is the last time I'll say it: Drop your gun." Whatever the State Security man saw in his eyes, it was enough; he lowered his gun and tossed it inside his car. Painfully he bent down and climbed into the seat.

The policeman quickly moved to the other side of the car, picked up the gun from the seat, and ejected the clip, dropping it onto the floor in the back. "Whose side are you on, anyway?" the State Security man asked angrily.

The policeman shook his head back and forth. "I'm sorry, comrade, but what happens inside this prison is my responsibility," he replied. "And you're not killing anybody in here."

The State Security man gave him a baleful look, then turned to me. "This isn't finished, bitch," he snarled. "You'll be seeing me again." He waved at the driver, and the car sped off, tires squealing defiantly.

The policeman watched as the car disappeared behind a building. "Now I'm really fucked," he exclaimed, turning to me. "You've spoiled everything. I've got to get out of here." He put his pistol in his holster and then started trotting in the opposite direction. He, too, disappeared around a building.

I looked around for the guard who, it seemed like hours ago, had come out to escort us to our cells. He was still rooted in the same spot, eyes bulging. "Hey, I thought you were in charge here," I told him. "What do we do now?" Wordlessly, he turned and led us into the pavilion.

The State Security man was wrong; I never saw him again. And I never saw the policeman again, either. His mother, who was a guard, told us later that he climbed the prison's fence after dark and made his way to a foreign embassy in Havana, where he received political asylum. Eventually he was allowed to leave Cuba. I think he must have secretly been a member of the resistance. If so, it was quite a loss for our side—but well worth it, as far as I'm concerned. I never had the slightest doubt that the State Security man was about to pull the trigger.

We were assigned to the first floor of D Pavilion—D Lower, in prison shorthand. After the guard showed us to our cells, about a dozen political prisoners approached us.

"Hello, I'm Sinesia Drake," said the one at the head of the group, a buxom woman with skin the color of obsidian.

"Ana Rodríguez," I replied, shaking her hand. Though I tried not to let it show, I was surprised. Nearly all the political prisoners—among the women, anyway—were white. Castro was still successfully courting the black population, promising that the Revolution would repudiate the racism of Cuba's past, although I never saw any black faces among his own coterie.

"You're just in time to join our hunger strike," Sinesia continued. "We can't stand their shitty food anymore, and for the past three days, we've been refusing to eat it."

"Now that there are more of us here, maybe it would be worth expanding the strike into a *toque de lata*," I said. "That might work faster." In a *toque de lata*—literally, "playing the cans"—we grabbed anything metal we could find and beat it against the cell bars, creating a deafening racket. After a few hours, the guards were usually so sick of it that they would agree to our demand.

"Yeah, let's a do a *toque*," agreed one of the other prisoners who had just arrived from Guanabacoa. Several others spoke up in agreement, and—making no effort to keep our voices down—we began planning. But Sinesia looked aghast. She put an arm around my shoulder and walked me away from the group.

"Look, you have to be careful what you say here," she said in a low voice. "They keep a woman guard in here at all times, watching and listening. She even sleeps in a cell here."

"The same woman all the time?" I asked in amazement. The poor woman might as well be in prison herself.

"No, they work in twenty-four-hour shifts," Sinesia said. "Today it's Ramona. See her over there? The one with skin even darker than mine?"

She pointed to a mild-looking matronly woman who appeared to be in her early sixties.

"Don't worry," I said. "In just a minute she's going to lock herself in her cell and you won't see her again."

Putting on a grim expression, I walked briskly toward the old woman. "Excuse me," I said. "They tell me one of the guards lives in here. Can you point her out to me?"

"Why are you looking for her?" the woman asked, warily eyeing the tight set of my lips.

"Because I'm going to hang the bitch," I snapped, pounding my fist in my hand.

"I'll go get her for you," she nodded. She took a few small, nervous steps, then broke into a run. She dived into her cell and quickly turned a key in the lock from inside.

One by one the other *jaulas* arrived and the welcome rituals were repeated. But it was getting harder for me to concentrate. Numb when I arrived, I was starting to feel the pain of the beating. "Why don't you take a hot bath?" Beba suggested. "There's a bruise on your right cheek where that State Security man hit you, and I'll bet you've got some others. We can plot Castro's downfall in the morning; he'll still be there."

Wearily, I trudged to the bathroom and peeled off my blouse and jeans. I groaned at the sight. It looked like the entire front of my body had been painted purple. *How many times did I get hit, anyway?* I wondered. It was my last thought as I toppled over backward.

"Unfortunately—or maybe fortunately, I'm not sure—I don't have a mirror here," the prison doctor told me when I regained consciousness on a bed in one of the cells. "So I can't show you your back. But take my word for it, it's worse. Between your shoulder blades, your skin is black as coal. I've never seen anything like it." He shook his head. "There's nothing I can really do for you, except give you some aspirin. Keep cold compresses on your back as much as you can, and try not to run into any more fists." By the morning, I could hardly move and it was weeks before I could walk normally.

Luckily, the Interior Ministry seemed somewhat taken aback by the violence surrounding the transfer. The food improved, and the Ministry offered to allow more frequent visits.

But deciding to press our advantage, we refused to accept any visits at all until the hateful screen that kept us from touching our family members was removed. Though we had no way of knowing it, we couldn't have picked a better tactic. The Interior Ministry offices in Havana were under daily siege by our family members demanding visits. Many of them thought some of us had been killed or maimed during the transfer, and they refused to believe it when the Ministry said that *we* were the ones refusing visits. The Ministry ran off our male relatives by threatening to shoot them, but our mothers continued to show up every day, shouting and crying and generally making the lives of the officials miserable.

The Ministry tried everything it could think of to trick or manipulate us into accepting visits. They forwarded desperate letters from our mothers asking if we were dead. When that didn't work, they tried phony telegrams advising us of the deaths of relatives. We would be allowed to attend their funerals, we were told, if only we would agree to visits. Cruel as that tactic was—for we could never be certain the telegrams were fake—it didn't work, either.

On June 22, after a six-week standoff, we heard the sound of hammering and tearing from the visiting room. Beba Canabal came racing in from a chat with a friendly guard.

"We've won, we've won!" she laughed, dancing around the pavilion corridor. "They're tearing down the screen. And listen to this: There's a rumor that they've fired Sanjurjo, the national director of prisons, because he couldn't make us back down."

"Who's replacing him?" Sinesia asked.

"I don't know," Beba replied, "but what difference does it make? Anybody's got to be an improvement."

Two weeks later, as we ate our meager lunch in the D Pavilion dining room, a tall, gangly stranger walked in. At first he just stood against the back wall, but after a few minutes he started slowly pacing the edge of the room. His skinny limbs squirmed this way and that, like they were struggling to get free of his body, but his piercing blue eyes moved deliberately, taking in every detail. As he neared our table, his body stiffened. He had spotted the place on the wall where someone had scrawled in chalk, *O liberty! What crimes are committed in thy name!*

"Who wrote this?" he demanded.

"That was written by a lady during the French Revolution," replied Luisa Pérez, eyes wide with mock innocence.

"No, damn it," the man said. "I mean, who wrote it right here on this wall."

"Ahh," I said, imitating Luisa's expression. "That was written by another lady, during the Communist Castro dictatorship."

The women around the table could no longer stifle their laughter. The stranger's blue eyes flashed.

"Allow me to introduce myself," he said. "My name is Manuel Martínez. I'm a veteran of the Spanish Civil War."

"Don't worry," cracked Emma Rodríguez, repeating a slogan the Communists had used during the war. "From Madrid they shall not pass!"

Now we were collapsing with laughter.

"Laugh now," the stranger said, his voice ominously low. "I assure you that, later in our acquaintance, you'll have lost your sense of humor." He walked away.

"Who was that, anyway?" I asked a guard.

"The new national director of prisons," he answered with a smirk. "And I don't think you made a very good impression."

· FIVE ·

The Littlest Gusanos

I LOOKED UP from my book as Beba Canabal entered my cell, two metal cups in her hands. "One of the women made limeade, and I thought you might like some," she said, handing me one of the cups as she sat at the foot of my bunk. I sipped the cool drink and thought, as I often did these days, how prison made you appreciate the simple things.

Outside, a glass of limeade was nothing. You flipped a ten-centavo piece on the counter of any lunch stand and then gulped it down without thinking while you flipped through the pages of a newspaper or argued with your mother.

In here, it was a major production. Just tracking down a pitcher to mix it in probably took an hour or more. The limes and sugar required to make it must have amounted to half the contents of one of the packages our families were permitted to bring us once a month. And it could only be made during the erratic hours that the guards turned on our water in D Pavilion. To call the limeade a miracle would be too strong (a piece of chicken at dinner, now *that* was a miracle, proof of the existence of a Supreme Being), but I thought the word *marvel* might be appropriate as I swirled it around my tongue.

Beba, too, looked thoughtful as she sat in the patch of afternoon sunlight at the end of the bed, the bright beams turning her black hair silver. But her mind was not on the theology of limeade.

"You know, Ana, when we got here I expected to hate the *Batistianas*," she said reflectively. "But I don't, not at all. In fact, I'm a little ashamed of the way we used to talk about them."

I knew the feeling. Like Beba and I, most of the political prisoners from Guanabacoa had fought against Batista before falling out with the Revolution. And as much as we hated Castro, we still thought of Batista as the embodiment of corruption and sleaze. We had nothing but contempt for his supporters; unlike us, they *belonged* in prison.

That was what we thought, anyway, before we arrived at Guanajay. But seeing the *Batistianas* at close range, it was impossible to feel anything for them but pity. The beatings they absorbed from guards and the prison's common criminals, coupled with their starvation diet, had nearly erased them; they moved through the pavilion like ghosts, barely clinging to the corporeal world. On the rare occasions when you could catch their eyes, it was easy to read both the fear and the resignation there. They had learned to expect scorn and abuse from anyone they encountered.

Worse yet, these women weren't even true *Batistianas* in the way most people understood the term. The real Batista supporters, the ones who grew fat and rich gorging themselves at the trough of corruption, had either fled to their beachfront homes in Miami or had changed their spots and convinced Castro they were indispensable.

The women in Guanajay—there were about thirty of them, all with two years or more in prison—had neither money nor political connections. They were mostly wives and daughters of enlisted men in Batista's army. In most cases, their only crime was being related to someone who fought on the losing side, although a few of them had worked actively against the Revolution after their men were imprisoned. Even the richest among them were dirt poor; often their relatives couldn't visit because they couldn't afford bus fare.

There were a couple of exceptions. The most notable was a young woman who had been used as a sort of sexual bait by Batista's police. Her assignment was to sleep with men from the anti-Batista underground and then report any secrets they gave away during pillow talk. It would have been easy to despise her if she wasn't so hopelessly crazy. A twisted masochist, she sported a new self-inflicted bruise or cut almost every morning. Her most exquisite form of self-punishment, saved for special occasions, was to scrub her own breasts with a stiff wire brush.

Just as our wariness of the *Batistianas* had been proven unwarranted, our fears about sharing a prison with common criminals seemed—at least for now—to be needless. Guanajay Women's Penitentiary consisted of four large two-story pavilions arranged in a roughly rectangular pattern around an immense yard. Pavilions A and B were home to two hundred or so common criminals; C and D held political prisoners, 130 of us counting the *Batistianas*. But there was little contact between the pavilions, which limited friction between the criminal and political groups.

About the only trouble revolved around meals. Guanajay's kitchen was staffed by common criminals, who sometimes—intentionally or carelessly—contaminated our food with insects or broken glass. And even that was probably done on instructions of the ill-tempered kitchen supervisor, a prison employee.

D Pavilion, where I lived, was a long L-shaped building. (Another wing, which would make it into a T shape, was under construction, though it didn't look like there was any hurry.) We were overcrowded—between two and four of us assigned to cells built for one—but the doors were almost always unlocked, giving us access to the broad, clean corridors, and we didn't feel nearly as squeezed as we had in Guanabacoa's teeming *galeras*.

Each morning began with the ritual of the count, to make certain none of us had escaped during the night. Our count wasn't until seven-thirty A.M., but we were usually awakened by the count in A Pavilion at seven A.M. We didn't mind; although most of the routine business inside the prison was attended to by female staffers known as *llaveras*—literally, the ones with the keys—the morning count was conducted by male guards.* The half-hour head start gave us a chance to get dressed before they arrived.

Breakfast was served in the D Pavilion dining room (downstairs, at the corner of the L formed by the building) at eight A.M. As far as I was concerned, it barely counted as a meal. They served us only weak,

---

Llavera is pronounced yah-vay-ra.

sugary coffee, which we sometimes fortified with powdered milk from our packages, and a crust of bread.

After that, there was nothing to do until lunch. At Guanabacoa, with women shuttling in and out to trials all the time and new prisoners arriving every day, we hadn't tried to organize any activities. But as our situation stabilized at Guanajay, we set up classes.

Most of them were elementary-school-level lessons in basics: reading, writing, grammar, mathematics, and geography. A lot of the women (including nearly all of the *Batistianas*) had only attended a year or two of school, if that. We had a few books that our families had been permitted to bring us openly, and pencils, which they had to smuggle. For paper we used the backs of cigarette packages and tampon boxes.

The classes were not at all political; any attempt at ideological coloring would have threatened the still-fragile reconciliation between the *Batistianas* and the rest of us. (Politics did sometimes surface unexpectedly in a couple of the advanced literature classes, however. One day the reading assignment was an essay that included the observation that "no matter the place or the circumstance, a man is always free to choose to be a traitor, or not." It launched a venomous argument about informers—a subject that, for most of us, was anything but academic.) But the prison authorities, inevitably, were suspicious, and stopped us from meeting in the dining room. So each morning we dragged the bunks from a few of the cells and turned them into classrooms.

At noon we had a quick lunch: usually *harina*, a thick cornmeal soup, and (on good days) an egg. Then we had two hours of free time for laundry and other chores. Classes resumed at two-thirty and ran until five-thirty, when dinner—rice, a watery portion of beans, a piece of bread, and sometimes a cold baked potato—was served.

To call the food unappetizing does not do it justice. At the best of times it was bland; the cooks never used any spices, not even a pinch of salt. And the beans usually arrived with a thin white scum on top. "Don't eat that!" Sinesia Drake exclaimed the first time I lowered a spoon into it. "Those are worms." In tropical climates, dried beans are often infested with tiny worms; you can get rid of them by soaking the beans in water for a few hours before cooking them, but the prison kitchen didn't bother.

We got accustomed to the quality of the food. The quantity,

though, was another matter. The portions wouldn't feed a canary. In most Cuban families, a pound of beans made a single meal for six people. In D Pavilion, it had to feed sixty women. We stopped asking our families for little luxury items in our packages like cookies and candy and begged them for crackers, fruit, sugar, and salt to make our regular meals palatable and filling.

Since dinner often arrived cold and half-cooked anyway, most of us took it to our cells rather than eating it right away. Later we reheated it on hot plates supplied by our families; that way, we weren't starving to death before bedtime. Our only dining utensils were a single aluminum plate and spoon each. At first we had to turn them in after every meal. But we complained so much about the haphazard way they were cleaned that the *llaveras* started letting us keep them. After every meal, someone went to the pavilion gate and called out: "D Lower *llavera*, turn on the water please, we have dishes to wash." Then we had ten minutes or so to clean everything before they cut it off again.

At seven-thirty P.M. we started up a final round of classes. They ended at ten P.M. and we broke out our single deck of cards for our nightly canasta tournament. Only four women could play at a time; the rest stood close by, kibitzing and waiting their turn. Some nights, the *llaveras* arrived at eleven to lock us inside our cells; more often, they didn't want to face our jeers and protests, and the game went on until midnight. Then everyone else went to bed. I sat in the corridor, alone with my medical books and— unwelcome though they were—my thoughts.

My nighttime reading had been my solace since my arrest, a daily opportunity to slip out of prison and back into my old life, if only for a few hours.

But lately my mind had been wandering; sometimes I realized with a jolt I had been gazing at the same page for half an hour or more. And always the cause was the same: my boyfriend Carlos.

At Guanajay, the restrictions on visitors were much looser and, when our standoff with the prison ended in late June, he came to see me along with my family. It was torment to sit there across from him, hands primly folded in our laps, like characters in some colorless Victorian novel. My mother and sisters, still reeling from the Mother's Day riot, galloped excitedly from subject to subject like hopped-up racehorses until it was little more than static flickering across my brain: "Oh, Ana, your bruises, you should have seen the way those guards shoved us, we thought Gladys' mother was going to die, oh did I mention the González boy down the street has been drafted, oh, Ana, your *bruises*." I tried to keep track, at least enough to smile and frown at the right times, while Carlos and I tried to say secret things with our eyes.

Even during the minute or two when my family walked across the room to say hello to Beba and a few others, we couldn't talk, not really. Carlos leaned across the counter that separated us (oh, if it were only a counter that separated us) and whispered, "I'm going to wait for you, no matter how long." It was both a promise and a question. "I'm going to wait for *you*, no matter how long," I answered, because I believed it, or wanted to, or wished I could, and because what else can you possibly answer?

Then my family was back, and we went back to the script. "How are things at the university?" I said, asking the stupidest question I could think of. "Oh, they're fine," he said, giving the dullest reply he could imagine.

My father was always outmatched by the females in his family when it came to these chatter-thons, but toward the end of the visit he worked in a few words, reassuring me that I wouldn't have to serve thirty years; the Americans would get this straightened out. My mother and sisters enthusiastically shook their heads in agreement. "Papa," I interjected gently, trying to speak to Carlos through him, "I don't think you can count on the Americans. It might take longer than you think."

"No, no, the Americans can't tolerate this," he said confidently. There were nods of assent from everyone, and then they changed the subject. What I was saying was unthinkable, and they wouldn't think it.

The visit ended a few minutes later. I braced myself for an inquisition when I got back to the pavilion—most of our husbands and boyfriends were in prison, and the presence of a tall, dark stranger had not gone unnoticed. "Oooooooh, *Aaaaaaaa-na*, why didn't you tell us about him?" someone brayed the minute we were inside. "Hey, Ana, my sentence is only twelve years," called out another. "Can I borrow him when I get out, just to warm him up for you?"

"Ladies, I don't think there's any point in this discussion," I replied. "By the time any of us get out of here, our ovaries will be ready for the museum."

Everyone laughed. But later that night, for the first time, my mind strayed from my medical books. I knew that decisions were going to have to be made.

"I'm not going to class this afternoon," Japonesa proclaimed one day at lunch. "There are other things in life besides school."

"Oh, yeah, like hanging around your cell in case Fidel sends you a pardon," someone scoffed.

"No, I think it's time we did something just for fun," Japonesa insisted.

"Like what?"

"I think we should organize a baseball league," she replied.

There was muffled laughter from around the tables. Japonesa's world often seemed to spin on an axis two or three degrees different than ours. Her real name was Dora Delgado, though no one ever used it. The irrepressible daughter of a Cuban-Japanese mother and a Spanish father, Japonesa was an exotic tropical hybrid: thick black hair that fell straight to her shoulders as though it had been ironed; almond-shaped green eyes; silky olive skin. She was in her mid-thirties, though her delicate features and tiny stature—she was barely five feet tall—made her look like a teenager. That hadn't stopped her from fighting as a guerrilla in the Sierra Maestra mountains, one of a very few women to do so, against both Batista and Castro.

A number of us were baseball fans, at least casually. It was Cuba's national sport. We had our own professional team, the Havana Sugar Kings, that played in one of the American minor leagues. (Or had, anyway, until the Revolution.) And several Cubans were stars in the U.S. major leagues, including Minnie Minoso and Camilo Pascual.

Playing baseball was another matter. I suppose a Cuban mother of the 1950s would have preferred her daughter playing baseball to having sex with a motorcycle gang, but that's about as much as they would concede. It just wasn't proper.

Of course, as prison inmates, we had a certain immunity to popular conceptions of femininity. But there were practical problems, too. We didn't have a single ball or glove. And I had a sneaking suspicion that the guards would look down on the idea of equipping us with bats.

"Oh, come on," Japonesa taunted us. "Some of us were building bombs just a couple of months ago. Improvising a little baseball equipment should be easy compared to that."

So we went to work. Someone stole a board from the construction on the new wing of D Pavilion, and, with some knives we had hidden away, we trimmed it into something approximating a bat. For a ball we used a round stone, also lifted from the construction site, wrapped tightly in a scrap of bedsheet. And Japonesa herself contributed our only glove, a catcher's mitt pieced together from strips of blanket. A couple of days later, we canceled afternoon classes and went out to the patio. With the shout of "Play ball!" (in English, just like we had heard it at Sugar Kings games), the official Cuban Female Political Prisoners' World Series began.

Our play had more to do with Minnie Mouse than Minnie Minoso. Some of the women were natural athletes who showed some real talent for the game, but they were wildly outnumbered by the lame and the spastic. A lot of women got hit in the face by almost any ball that came their way. And even those who could play a little soon realized it was better to let the ball hit the ground and bounce before trying to catch it barehanded.

Then there was the matter of umpiring. A woman named Esperanza Oliva, who loved baseball but was dangerously uncoordinated even by our generous standards, was appointed permanent umpire. The problem was that she was also a big fan of my team, and in the late innings of close games, her calls on balls and strikes became increasingly creative. If anyone argued, she just made up a rule on the spot.

"The rulebook says that for anyone under five foot two, the strike zone goes up to the eyebrows," she said once to a batter complaining about a call.

"Really?" the batter asked, intimidated by the authority in her voice. "That doesn't seem fair."

"It's a special rule to keep the owners from hiring midgets," Esperanza explained solemnly. The batter, duly impressed with her encyclopedic knowledge of the rulebook, returned to the plate.

We had spent two or three of our weekly afternoons on the patio playing baseball when Manuel Martínez—or Manolo, as everyone called him—came down from his office to watch us. First he stood back against the pavilion wall, well away from the field. But as the game continued, he kept creeping closer. Finally he was standing right beside the umpire, leaning forward with every pitch. I was playing catcher, and from the corner of my eye I had seen him slinking around, but I ignored him. Even when he ostentatiously cleared his throat a couple of times, I refused to turn around.

"I was watching you from my office with a telescope," he finally said. The thought made my flesh crawl, but I didn't say anything.

"It looked like you were having fun, so I decided to get a closer look," he added. I silently returned a throw to the pitcher.

"Let me play!" he burst out. "Let me be the catcher! I'm really good at it."

"Go to hell," I snapped, keeping my back to him.

"Come on" he begged. "Let me be the catcher. Please, please let me be the catcher."

"Are you crazy?" I shouted, finally turning around to face him. "You can't come down here and *play* with us! You're our enemy! You torture us! We hate you! Get the hell out of here!"

"Aww, come on," he pled. "Don't be like that."

"Ana, don't let that son of a bitch touch my mitt!" yelled Japonesa, who was standing on first base. From the other infielders came hoots of derision. Manolo, his face twisted in a childish pout, stormed off. Esperanza, elated to have home plate to herself again, celebrated by shouting "Strike!" at a pitch three feet over the batter's head.

We were playing the next week when Manolo pulled up at the field in a Ministry pickup truck. The game stopped as we watched him get out of the cab, walk to the rear of the truck, and drop the tailgate open. My jaw dropped. The truck was filled with gloves, bats, and balls.

"There's enough for two teams," Manolo said proudly. "I bought it with my own money. Now you'll let me play, won't you?"

"Manolo," said Japonesa in a calm voice, "get the fuck out of here."

His face fell. He looked around at us for a moment; then, mumbling curses, he got into the truck, slammed the door, and drove away.

"He just wanted to give us the stuff so that he could take it away later to punish us," Isabel Molgado said as we walked back to our positions. I nodded in agreement, but I thought there might be more to it than that. Manolo visited D Pavilion a lot more often than his duties required. He wandered the corridors with no apparent purpose. If he encountered a conversation, he always tried to join it. Sometimes he would stick his head into a cell and ask: "If we met outside the prison, would you go dancing with me?"

We feared Manolo might retaliate by stopping our baseball games. But although he stopped coming to watch us, he didn't try to interfere. We ended the games ourselves after about a month. They had become too competitive; fielders insisted on catching balls in the air, before they bounced, and we were afraid someone was going to break a finger if not a whole hand. Japonesa, heartbroken, hung her catcher's mitt at the end of her bed like a shroud.

"Ana, I'm really worried," Raquel Romero told me one morning in late July as we sat in the corridor outside our cells. I looked at her with concern. Raquel looked like she had swallowed a beach ball; her pregnancy was in its final stages.

"What's wrong?" I asked. "Has the baby stopped moving?" Though I had never voiced my fears to Raquel, I had been worried about an injury to the baby ever since Mother's Day, when the firemen trained their hoses on her belly.

"No, no, that's the problem. He's kicking all the time, and I know he wants to be born." From the day she learned she was pregnant, Raquel had referred to the baby as "he," regardless of what we told her about random selection of chromosomes. "And it feels like he wants to be born on July 26. What am I going to do?"

I couldn't help laughing despite the grave expression on her face. Raquel's only worry about this child, it seemed, was that he would be born on the day from which Fidel Castro's 26th of July Movement took its name. To me, that was the least of the problems.

So many things could go wrong in here, where the diet was inadequate even for those of us who weren't carrying children, and where prenatal medical care was unknown. Just a couple of months earlier, a prisoner named Lydia Pérez León began hemorrhaging uncontrollably about thirty days before she was due to give birth. The Ministry refused to supply plasma for a transfusion—"The blood in Cuba's hospitals is for the Revolution's combatants, it cannot be dispensed to *gusanas*"—and she died, along with the baby.

But if that was on Raquel's mind as we sat there in the corridor, she kept it well hidden as she frowned at her mountainous belly. "I don't want to have to throw a party every year on July 26," she said gloomily. "Can't the baby understand that?"

"Look at the bright side," I counseled. "Think how much it will annoy Manolo and everyone at the Ministry to have a counterrevolutionary born on their special day. In fact, to *really* annoy them, I think you should name the baby Fidelito." Raquel laughed despite herself. "It would be too much for the baby's ego," she said, shaking her head. "Every time those ass-kissers in the plaza started chanting, 'For sure, Fidel, give the Yankees hell,' he'd think it was for him."

Two days later, Raquel packed some clothes in a canvas bag and called to a *llavera*: "It's time." Within an hour, she was on her way to the hospital. She went into labor on the evening of July 26, but the baby—a boy, as Raquel had predicted—put up a ferocious fight and stayed put until the next morning. Raquel was in bliss.

Ordinarily the baby would have gone to live with his father. But that wasn't an option. The father was a man Raquel had met in her underground group. If she sent Fernandito to him, he would immediately fall under suspicion by the police and would probably be arrested.

So Fernandito, a week old, went to prison.

He was the joy of D Pavilion, that boy, the contented object of the thwarted maternal instincts of sixty women. Sometimes Raquel had to stand in line to cuddle her own baby. We cared for him in shifts. Since I was up all night anyway, I picked him up on the rare occasions when he awoke from a nightmare. I fixed his milk in the morning while Carmen García, an early riser, bathed him. Later she handed him off to someone else for a walk.

Fernandito repaid us by being a model baby. He rarely cried (perhaps because, with sixty women watching him round the clock, incipient hunger pangs and wet diapers were detected within moments) and slept without complaint through the considerable racket of our late-night canasta games and bull sessions. The only thing that upset him was the cry of *"Requisa!"* —Search!—that the guards gave when they came to shake down our cells. The mere word started him crying inconsolably.

If anything, Fernandito thrived on the prison environment. He grew like a weed. Raquel's visits were often suspended for two or three weeks at a time because of the cutting remarks she constantly directed at the *llaveras.* When her relatives could finally get in to see her, Fernandito inevitably would have outgrown the clothing they brought. He was eight months old before he got a pair of shoes he could wear.

When he was six months old, Fernandito got a playmate. *The Revolution is certainly making our children precocious,* I thought. Fernandito, who had been fingerprinted and posed for a prison mug shot when he was a week old, could now trade reminiscences with Natacha Valdés, who at two and a half was already under a psychiatrist's care. She had been home the day State Security came to arrest her mother. The police let her watch as Onelia Valdés was handcuffed; as they ripped open the sofa, the mattresses, and the armchairs with bayonets, searching for weapons; as her mother was marched away at gunpoint, forbidden to kiss her daughter goodbye. Natacha stopped screaming only when she fell unconscious after a seizure. After two more weeks of constant tantrums, often followed by seizures, a frazzled State Security psychiatrist suggested she be allowed to join her mother in prison.

She was a tiny little girl, barely bigger than an infant, with fine brown hair that hung to her shoulders without a hint of a curl. Her button nose and lilliputian mouth were in marked contrast to her enormous brown eyes, which took in everything around her. We watched with amusement and, sometimes, heartache, as Natacha made herself at home in the prison.

For some reason, the only plaything she had brought with her to Guanajay was a toy kitchen, complete with little pots, pans, and dishes. Japonesa built living and dining room furniture to go with it from discarded cigarette boxes. Then she made two rag dolls, one white and one black, and two dresses apiece. Natacha played with them for hours at a time.

One evening while I was holding Fernandito, I watched Natacha cook a pretend dinner (including, I noted wryly, steak; she remembered some things from outside) in her toy kitchen. She seated her dolls at their dining room table, fed them, and chatted with them about her day. She put the dolls to bed, then gathered up her miniature plates and casserole dishes and put them in one of the pavilion's big washbasins. Carrying it to the gate, she wrapped her tiny hands around the bars and shouted: "D Lower *llavera,* turn on the water please, I have dishes to wash." I put my head in my hands, not sure whether to laugh or to cry.

Everyone in D Lower had household chores, and Natacha was no exception. Her job was to deliver coffee to the cells each morning. A number of us had asked our families to smuggle ground coffee in during the visits (for some inexplicable reason, we weren't permitted to get it in our monthly packages) and we pooled it. Onelia, Natacha's mother, brewed the coffee, and the little girl carried the steaming metal cups from cell to cell on a tray, watching closely as we sniffed it delicately and then swished a little in our mouths, like we were tasting a fine wine.

Coffee, real black coffee and not hot sugar-water, in our cells as we blearily prepared for another day—it felt so luxuriant that, for a moment as we savored the rich fumes rising from the cups, we could almost believe we were the pampered plutocrats that Castro called us.

So imagine our disappointment one morning when Natacha arrived with the coffee and there was only half a cup apiece. We moaned like thwarted junkies. We cursed our own mothers for their indolence; what did they *mean*, their bras would only hold a quarter of a pound, we were their *daughters*, how could they *betray* us like this?

"I can't believe we're already running out," Sinesia Drake lamented to Onelia as we gathered in the dining room.

"Running out of what?" Onelia asked absently.

"Coffee. Do we have any left at all?"

"What are you talking about?"

"The *coffee*, damn it," Sinesia said impatiently. "The coffee that we only got half a cup of this morning."

"Half a cup?" replied Onelia in confusion. "But I made everyone a full cup, just like usual." Then stormclouds gathered at her brow. "Natacha!" she roared, and stamped out of the dining room in search of the culprit. The little girl, however, was unrepentant as she bustled about her kitchen, frying pretend eggs for her dolls. "I just can't face the morning without a cup of coffee," she explained in the gravest three-year-old voice I had ever heard.

Poor Onelia! She was constantly having to explain to Natacha why she couldn't do all the same things the rest of us did. I didn't fully understand the hardships in raising a child in a prison cellblock until one afternoon I found Natacha packing all her things in a canvas bag. "I'm getting a transfer to another pavilion," she said, a pugnacious scowl on her face.

"My mother won't let me do anything!" Onelia, it seems, had told Natacha she couldn't gamble with us during our late-night card games.

Sometimes Natacha went out on the patio by herself while the rest of us did laundry or other housekeeping tasks. We never paid much attention to what she was doing until one morning when she asked to wear her prettiest dress some mornings "because I'm going to visit my *amigas* in the other pavilions."

A few days later, one of the *llaveras* came to D Lower to perform the weekly ritual of the report. In the report were the names of everyone who had broken a prison rule during the past week, their offenses, and their punishments, which could range from loss of patio time to suspension of visits, mail, and monthly packages.

In her regular monotone, the *llavera* read off the names of half a dozen women for the usual crimes against the Revolution: stealing bread from the kitchen, insulting a guard, possessing a pencil. Then she added: "Natacha Valdés, for the offense of passing unauthorized information between pavilions, your patio privileges are suspended for twenty days in the name of the Revolution."

The rest of us laughed, thinking the *llavera* was flashing an unexpected sense of humor. Natacha, however, was outraged. "You can't take away my patio time!" she shouted, stamping her right foot furiously on the floor just the way she had seen us do it. "This is an infamy! This is an *injustice!*" She broke into tears of anger.

The joke was on us. The suspension was real, and it stood.

"Somebody remember to bring a bucket of water!" someone yelled from the back of the corridor as we lined up for the visiting room. "We might need it in case Ana and that boy burst into flames." If anyone noticed that my smile was arctic, they didn't say anything.

Four months had passed since my first agonizing visit with Carlos. He had been to the prison half a dozen times. Each visit was the same, and each one was worse: wooden conversations followed by frantic vows followed by breezy assurances that everything would be all right.

After every visit, my depression grew. Carlos seemed less and less real to me every time I saw him, a hazy tropical mirage that disappeared if I blinked. The gray walls of my cell, the rust-flecked iron bars of my window, the dim lightbulb dangling above my bed: Those were reality. Those were my world.

What weighed on my heart most of all was that Carlos really had no idea what this was about. He had never cared about politics; all he wanted to do was practice medicine, to make sick people feel better. He didn't care if the country was run by Batista or Castro or Genghis Khan. He entered this maze not because he wanted to, but because he was following me. Somehow, I had to show him the way out.

My father was ill and hadn't made the trip that day. But my mother was there, and Carlos had brought his mother, too. The three of them smiled as I entered the room, but I could tell my mother was nervous about something. She told me the usual stories about people in our neighborhood, little things that had happened at the store, my father's aches and pains. But she was skittish and preoccupied.

Finally she interrupted one of her own stories. "I'm sorry, Ana, but I'm worried," she confessed. "Some of the other mothers were talking while we waited outside the prison. One of them is smuggling in a bottle of holy water from the cathedral in Havana. It's so big, and you know if she gets caught they'll suspend the visits for all of us."

"I'm sure they'll manage it," I said.

"Probably, but it just makes me so, so nervous. I wish—"

"I wish you would be quiet about it," I snarled. "When you don't understand something, mind your own business."

My mother recoiled like she'd been slapped. Mrs. Pérez looked like she was about to faint.

"Ana," Carlos said quietly, leaning across the counter, "don't treat your mother like that. If she's doing something wrong, take her aside, speak to her privately. Be gentle with her—it's not easy, having a daughter in prison." I heard the disappointment in his soft voice.

"You're the one who went to Catholic schools, not me," I snapped, "and you don't understand how important that holy water is to a woman in here, separated from her church. You make me sick with your false piety. Don't come here again." My voice was rising, and conversations paused all over the room. "Don't come here ever again."

"Wait, Ana—" his mother began.

"Mind your own damn business." I cut her off.

"What are you doing?" my mother cried. "What are you *doing*?"

"I don't want to see him anymore," I told her, my voice cold. "Don't bring him again." I got up and walked out without looking back.

I didn't come out of my cell for dinner, or for the card game. At midnight, when the other women got ready for bed, I took one of my medical books out into the hall. It was a long time until dawn.

· S I X ·

Fight or Flight

JANUARY 4, 1962

THEY JUMPED WHEN I walked into the cell, Beba stammering incoherently while Isabel Rodríguez furtively tried to stuff something down her pants. Then a look of relief flashed across Beba's face, followed by one of annoyance.

"Damn it, Ana, you scared the shit out of us," she lectured me while Isabel slumped back down onto her bunk. "Quit sneaking around like a cat."

"Sorry, sorry," I repeated, although in truth their guilty looks had been quite comical. But I knew everyone got a little touchy just before a visit. We had one scheduled the next day, the first in a few months, and everyone—including Beba and Isabel—was busy writing clandestine letters that would be passed to our families for smuggling out of the prison.

Technically we had the right to regular correspondence, but almost no one bothered trying to write letters openly. First you had to ask the *llaveras* for paper and pencils (we weren't allowed to keep either one on a regular basis) and it could take weeks to get them.

Then the *llaveras* had to screen your letter before it could be mailed. If they found even the mildest criticism of the prison or the Revolution, the letter was confiscated and you were placed on report. And if the letter contained a word the *llaveras* didn't understand—a common occurrence, since most of them had grade-school educations or less—they assumed it was a code, which also meant confiscation and punishment.

So we opted for clandestine letters, despite all the difficulty and risk they entailed.

We wrote them on any little scrap of paper we could find, usually the back of a discarded package of cigarettes or tampons. Pencils were even more scarce, and, strictly speaking, they weren't pencils at all, just pencil leads. Because pencils were difficult to conceal against the frequent searches of our cells, whenever we got one we broke the eraser off and then pulled the lead out the back; it could be hidden in our hair, a place that the *llaveras* usually overlooked when patting us down during searches.

To conserve paper and to keep the size of the clandestine package smaller and easier to pass, we wrote in minuscule letters about an eighth of a inch tall. It was a maddening process, cramping your handwriting down to that size, gripping that fragile pencil lead tightly but gently as you squeezed in the lines. It made me feel like a monk in some obscure catacomb, engraving verses of the Bible on the head of a pin. Some women couldn't do it at all. For help, they went to letter-writing specialists like Isabel, who had been an anesthesiologist outside and had deft, supple hands.

Once the letter was finished, it had be prepared for the pass. At first we folded and refolded them into tiny bullet-like packages, concerned only about size, but as time passed we realized that comfort had to be considered.

Each letter would be concealed on an intimate spot of one of our bodies for at least twenty-four hours (we kept them on us at all times after they were written), and then on the body of a family member for several more hours. A sharp edge pressed against your lower abdomen for that amount of time could raise a blister, even break the skin, leaving a cut and inviting infection, no small matter considering the lack of medical care in the prison.

So we started rolling the letters into tight little cylinders and using our hot plates to seal them in bits of plastic, which protected them from our sweat. You wrapped each letter separately, then combined them all into a small package so you could pass several at once.

Inside the visiting room, pretending to scratch, you removed the package from wherever you were carrying it—usually your crotch, sometimes your hair. Once it was in your hand, you started talking to the person who was receiving the pass. "I've got a package of letters here in my hand," you said in a voice that was low but calm. "I'd like you to take it, but if you don't want to, you don't have to." They were always nervous about it and you had to talk them down gently, like a spooked horse.

Because concealment was a way of life for prisoners, we were expert at it. Our families were clumsy at first, and it was a wonder that we didn't get caught more often, but with practice, most of them developed some skill. It was rewarding for them, too, to put something over on the same *llaveras* who humiliated them every time they entered the prison. First the canvas duffel bags they were bringing to us would be tipped over so that everything spilled onto the floor where the *llavera* could inspect it. Then everyone had to strip, and women were required to jump up and down a few times to jar loose anything they might be trying to smuggle inside their vaginas.

A few women did smuggle things inside their vaginas (and one or two even used their anuses, though the idea made me shudder). More often, though, they sewed the goods in between two pairs of panties and then wore them. And heftier women could almost always conceal things in the rolls of fat at their lower abdomen.

Sometimes they put larger clandestine objects in the duffel bags they were carrying and gambled that they could distract the *llavera* during the search. My younger sister Magda was a virtuoso at this technique.

Magda would walk to the front of the line of visitors waiting to have their bags searched and begin cooing revolutionary slogans at the *llavera*. "Oh, comrade, you work so hard at this, and don't think we're ungrateful," she'd say. "We know that without your labor, we couldn't have these visits. Here, let me assist you, we'll get this line moving faster and then you can rest."

Then Magda would help lift the bags and tip them over—but she would unobtrusively keep one side tilted slightly up, stopping the clandestine object from falling out. She also encouraged the visitors to chatter like parrots. The din created by three hundred women in full gossip mode was a powerful distraction.

I didn't realize just how good my family had become until one visit when my mother somehow produced five pairs of socks she had slipped by the *llaveras*. (Prison rules said our families could give us just one new pair every six months.) "I never thought I could be so good at tricking people," my mother said proudly.

I knew how she felt. It was the same way inside the prison; we spent every day getting used to things we had never imagined we would—or, in many cases, *refusing* to get used to them.

Using the toilet, for instance. The majority of us had grown up in middle-class homes where privacy in the bathroom was taken for granted. Now we had to use a toilet in the middle of a cell while three or four other women looked on. A lot of women simply couldn't do it and became hopelessly constipated. Without any discussion, a code of behavior evolved. If someone headed for the toilet, everyone else left the cell if possible. If we were locked up, the rest of us wandered over to the windows and looked out, for five minutes, ten minutes, an hour, whatever it took.

The toilet was really just one element—though for many it was by far the most disturbing—of the problem of privacy. Being suddenly thrust into a small, overcrowded space with hundreds of strangers had reminded all of us, in different ways, how much we valued our solitude. It was hard to go to sleep when the little coughs, sniffles, and snores of so many others echoed through the corridor. It was unpleasant to wake up in the morning amidst other people, without a few minutes to arrange yourself physically and mentally. It was discomfiting to undress in front of others.

Most of all, it was hard to be tested on so many different things at once. Everything, *everything*, was different than it had been at home: the smell of the pillows, the shape of the mattress, the way the beans were cooked. We had to adjust to all that while learning the tasks necessary to cope with this new environment.

In some ways it was hardest on the *campesinas*, the peasant women. Coming from small country towns where everyone knew each other, they had little practice in dealing with strangers and even less in settling disputes in large groups. Those of us who had gone to high school or college had plenty of classroom experience in arguing about something without getting angry about it. But the *campesinas* tended to take disagreements (over, say, the best way to protest a prison policy) personally.

On the other hand, the *campesinas* knew how to *do* things. They showed us how to build primitive coffee pots from the heating elements of broken hot plates and how to turn a torn scrap of bedsheet into a pair of panties. They had a hundred skills that had long since been lost in our middle-class homes.

In my house, for instance, we always had a maid who did the laundry, and I didn't know how to clean things by hand. I tore a hole in my only pair of jeans from scrubbing them too hard. "Your mother never taught you how to clean clothes?" said a disgusted peasant woman working at the sink next to mine. "In a *campesino* family, we would have been ashamed of a daughter so stupid. Get out of here, I'll do the rest! I can't stand watching you." I *was* ashamed, not because I had made a mistake, but because I didn't even know what the mistake was.

Even after I learned how to wash clothes, I was much slower than the *campesinas*. And that was much more than a matter of inconvenience; we had a limited amount of time at the sinks where we did our laundry, and soap and water were strictly rationed.

The water rations were an open sore in our relations with the prison staff. The *llaveras* were supposed to turn on the water in D Lower at various times throughout the day for a total of about four hours. But almost from the day we arrived, the four hours had been shrinking as Guanajay's antiquated pipes and pumps, built to serve a prison population one-third our size, gave out.

First the *llaveras* cut off a few minutes here and there; then they removed entire days from the schedule. After a couple of months, the water never came on at all. The only source of water for the entire prison was a single faucet located outside C Pavilion.

We stood in long lines at the faucet for two or three hours every afternoon in the searing midday sun, dragging as many buckets as we could hold. When we finally reached the faucet, we filled every bucket right to the brim. Then we had to inch our way back a quarter of a mile to D Pavilion, babying those buckets along so that we didn't spill a drop. With what we carried we had to brush our teeth, clean the pavilion, launder our clothes, wash our dishes, bathe, and fill cans and jars with drinking water.

The water lines were cranky and irritable places where fistfights sometimes broke out between prisoners arguing about who was first. One day an ordinarily mild woman named Gladys Suárez accused another prisoner of cutting in front of her. Their argument quickly escalated into a vitriolic shouting match that threatened to go further. A passing State Security lieutenant came over to break it up.

"What's wrong?" he asked as he stepped between them. "What are you fighting about?"

Gladys, still snarling, meant to reply, *"Cola de cubos"*—the line of buckets. But the words that popped out of her mouth were, *"Cola de culos"*—the line of butts. Everyone around her roared with laughter, including the lieutenant. Gladys whirled around, her face reddening as she glared at us, which only made everyone laugh harder. She spun back on the lieutenant. "What are *you* laughing at?" she demanded, poking a finger in his chest. "What's so funny?" She followed him back to the prison offices, shouting "What's so funny?" all the way.

The well that supplied the prison's water was not only hopelessly inadequate, it was also contaminated. It was uncovered twenty-four hours a day, and the water wasn't treated with chloride or anything else. The result was an epidemic of vaginal parasites followed by two waves of severe diarrhea that sent several prisoners to the infirmary near death from dehydration.

As if that wasn't bad enough, one morning we spotted a group of common criminals bathing in the well. One of them, Luz Marina, was a prostitute with an advanced case of syphilis. Because the well lay outside the walled compound formed by the pavilions, they could only have been out there with the permission of the guards.

Our protests about the water were our loudest, but by no means our only, complaints. Every day brought some pointless new act of petty tyranny by the prison staff.

The worst things were the searches, which took place at all hours of the day and night. Almost daily, the male prison guards would rampage through our cells, supposedly searching for weapons. In reality, they seized anything that struck their fancy: wristwatches, cooking utensils, even our underwear. (Bras and panties were among the many items starting to fall into short supply outside the prison as Castro dismantled Cuba's market economy in favor of Marxist central planning.) By the time they left, the cells were wrecks, with mattresses and clothing scattered everywhere.

We didn't resist the searches until November, when they tried to take our hot plates. Hot plates weren't contraband—our relatives had delivered them to us openly at visits—and to seize them was simply an act of theft. When the guards started to grab them, we fought back. Most of the hot plates were smashed to pieces in the melee that followed.

Much as we hated it, we could at least understand when the guards took things of value. But their next move was incomprehensible, except as a display of pure malice. They took our books—all of them: trashy paperback romances, basic reading primers, my dozen medical textbooks, even scholarly volumes on Marxism published by the government's own press. At the same time, they seized all our letters from our families, and most of our photographs. Then they piled it all in the middle of the patio and burned it as we screamed curses from our windows.

Our protests over the lack of uncontaminated water and the searches and confiscations had heightened tensions at Guanajay . . . and led to the loss of most of our privileges as well. We hadn't been able to see our families in nearly three months.

But in mid-December, the *llaveras* told us we would be permitted a visit on January 5. Telegrams had already been delivered to our families. The promise of that visit had sustained us through a gloomy Christmas behind bars. Now, with less than twenty-four hours until the visit, we were edgy: too much loud talk, too much prowling the corridor. Tonight's card game, I knew, would last past midnight. No one could sleep.

The morning of a visit was always frantic, an endless parade of women seeking reassurance about the way they looked. Since we had no mirrors, we had to rely on each other—just as well, since mirrors wouldn't lie but we could.

"What do you think of my dress?" Gladys asked me anxiously, twirling around so that I could inspect her blue cotton shift. I knew she had left it under her mattress last night. If you lay down just right, and didn't move very much, and then didn't look very closely in the morning, a garment might give the impression it had been ironed. I winced at the deep creases in the back, then recomposed my face an instant before she turned around.

"It's beautiful," I said. "Your mother is going to think the *llaveras* have opened a dry cleaner for us." She left beaming. My next visitor was Beba. "How did my hair turn out?" she asked. I had seen her earlier in the morning, her hair tightly strapped to the cardboard cylinders that come in the middle of toilet paper rolls—the closest thing any of us had to curlers. The lopsided loops in her hair looked like the work of a beauty school dropout.

"You could be in a magazine," I assured Beba, biting the inside of my cheek hard. There was a new bounce in her step as she walked out. I finished combing my hair, then headed down the corridor to find someone to lie to *me*.

The visit was scheduled for two P.M. Just after eleven, our families started gathering outside the prison gate. The prisoners on the second floor of C Pavilion, who could see the gate from their cells, shouted to us every time they recognized someone: "Nelly Urtiaga's father is here! Ilia Herrera's sister just arrived!" The shouted news bulletins only made us fidget more.

They always escorted us to the visiting room in little groups of three or four, a monotonous process that usually took about two hours. And, sure enough, just after noon a *llavera* appeared at the pavilion gate. But we knew something was up. She was wearing a broad grin instead of the pinched look of annoyance that the extra work of a visit usually gave the *llaveras*.

"I have a communiqué to read to you from the Interior Ministry," the *llavera* said, giggling. Crowded behind the gate, just inside the pavilion, we looked at one another uneasily as she pulled out a piece of paper.

"Today, January 5, 1962, we commemorate the first anniversary of the treacherous and cowardly assassination, by bandits supplied by the American CIA, of the heroic educator and revolutionary combatant Conrado Benítez," she read. Snorts of derision echoed through the pavilion. Conrado Benítez was an army captain who used Castro's rural literacy campaign as cover to spy on anti-Communist guerrillas in the Escambray Mountains. He was killed by survivors of a guerrilla band that he betrayed.

The *llavera* shot us an annoyed look, then continued reading. "To honor the revolutionary labors of our comrade Conrado, we declare a recess in the labors of this Ministry. For that reason, visits to counterrevolutionary prisoners are suspended."

"What?" sputtered a prisoner somewhere behind me. "What did she say?" The rest of us silently turned and walked back to our cells to change clothes. We were strangling on our own rage. They had lain in wait nearly an entire month to play this trick on us. They had lured some of our families hundreds of miles for this phony visit, and they had teased our expectations only to crush them.

Before I even reached my cell, I could hear the hammering. Water buckets, cracker tins, metal plates, even the large aluminum containers they brought our food in: anything that would make noise, someone was hitting it. There was no rhythm to it, just a continuous, frenzied scream of metal on metal as women pounded out their fury.

As soon as I pulled on some jeans I ran to the dining room to find something to beat against the bars of my cell. But Fidelina Suárez, who had been expecting a visit from her two children, grabbed my arm.

"I think we can tear down the dining room gate!" she shouted into my ear, struggling to make herself heard over the deafening crash of metal. "But I need some help." She pointed at the gate on one wall that divided the two wings of the pavilion. It was open at the moment—the *llaveras* rarely locked it during the day—but they would be here to close it any minute, the first step in returning order to the pavilion.

I nodded and followed Fidelina to the gate. She pointed at the hinges, and I instantly understood; they were mounted in a narrow strip of wall only about a foot wide, and the mortar around them was crumbling. By banging the gate backward, we could use the wall as a lever to tear the hinges out.

I hopped up and clung to the bars of the gate to put as much weight on the hinges as possible. I was joined a few moments later by another passing prisoner. Meanwhile, Fidelina, her adrenaline surging, flung it backward into the wall as if she were an Amazon warrior. There was so much noise that we couldn't hear the gate when it hit the wall, but each collision sent a mighty jolt reverberating through my entire body. The mortar was disintegrating before our eyes and finally, with a puff of dust, the upper hinges ripped out of the wall. We steadied the gate until we could climb free; then we pushed it over, the lower hinges coming free as it slammed into the floor.

We were standing over the gate like hunters over dead prey, a little awed at what we had done, when I realized the clanging had died almost completely away. "I think someone's outside," Fidelina said. We ran to the windows where we could see the chief of the guards, a man named López, signaling for silence. The last dinner plate stopped beating the bars as we waited to see what he had to say.

"I've been sent to tell you to stop this protest at once, or drastic measures will be taken," he barked.

"That's *it?*" shouted one woman. "You walked all the way over here to tell us *that?* You wasted your breath." There was a chorus of jeers followed by a ragged clatter of banging dinner plates.

"You think you can defy me?" López shouted. "I'll hang up my uniform the day I can't make a bunch of silly cows like you shut up!" He peered through one of the windows. "Matilde!" he called, and a woman with curly brown hair stepped to the bars. We were startled—Matilde Martínez was the *llavera* assigned to stay inside the pavilion that day. But the *llaveras* always fled at the first sign of trouble, and everybody just assumed that she had left.

"Matilde," López continued, "every time one of these bitches destroys something or breaks a rule, I want you to write it down so we can settle with them later. I'll be back in an hour and you can tell me what they're doing." He spun on his heel and walked briskly back toward the offices.

Matilde's pretty face, always pale, was now downright ghostly. Her hazel eyes were full of panic. López had practically signed her death warrant. It was a betrayal of stupefying proportions—they were not only colleagues, but lovers.

"Matilde," I said gently, "I think the best thing for you to do is give us your keys, and we'll lock you inside one of the cells." Wordlessly, Matilde pulled the keyring from her pocket and handed it to me, then followed me down the corridor.

We assigned a few women to keep banging the bars just to let the guards know we hadn't backed down. But most of us spent the afternoon preparing for the attack that we knew was inevitable.

We managed to break three iron bars out of the giant gate we had toppled; they would come in handy as weapons. Then we picked up the gate itself—it took ten of us—and propped it against the pavilion's only entry door. We tied it to the bars of nearby windows with some piano wire we found in the *llavera*'s cell, and we braced it with two heavy water tanks, each measuring about three feet by five feet.

Meanwhile, other women were assembling a small arsenal. They found a rope somewhere and were swinging it out a window on the side of the pavilion by the construction site, using it to lasso bricks and drag them within reach. Then they broke the bricks in two, the better to fit our hands. We also pooled our individual stashes of salt—we planned to throw it into the guards' eyes as they came at us.

Late in the afternoon, the women in C Pavilion began shouting warnings to us from their vantage point overlooking the main prison gate. "They're bringing in soldiers," someone yelled. "And they don't look very happy." Each time a new truckful of troops arrived, our lookouts advised us. Eventually the trucks numbered a dozen. Then, a few minutes after six P.M., we got a final warning: "They're coming inside. . . . Give them hell."

We hustled the two children, Natacha and Fernandito, into a cell at the back of the pavilion and strapped a mattress across the door to protect it and muffle the noise. Then we turned off the pavilion's interior lights. The advancing troops were plainly silhouetted by the prison's bright outdoor security lights.

Gladys, Emelina, and I—armed with the iron bars broken from the toppled gate—stood immediately behind the barricaded door, watching as the soldiers stopped about a hundred feet away. Three of them broke away from the main group and cautiously approached the door. "Do they look funny to you?" Gladys whispered, and I muttered my agreement. There was something bulky and alien about their silhouettes. I held a finger to my lips, signaling Gladys and Emelina to stay calm; I was certain the soldiers couldn't see us in the darkened pavilion, and I wanted to find out what they were up to before jumping them.

When the soldiers reached the gate they bent down to examine the lock. Then we heard a short, low *whoomp* and a blue flame shot from one man's hand. Seconds later, there were flames from the other two. *Blowtorches,* I realized. *They're going to cut the lock out with blowtorches.* The *llavera* was ordinarily in charge of locking and unlocking the pavilion door, but we had her keys; apparently they couldn't find a spare.

"Get away, you son of a bitch!" I shouted as I jabbed my iron bar through the gate like a lance, hitting one of the soldiers a solid shot to the chest. He staggered backward with a cry of surprise and pain. Gladys and Emelina were shouting and thrusting, too, and all three soldiers retreated. "They've got some kind of spears," shouted one. "We need some help."

A dozen men dashed to the gate, reaching in to grab us. We parried them, landing several vicious blows on hands and shoulders. We jumped back and forth with them like wrestlers, grunting in pain and exertion, while shouts of encouragement rang out from both sides of the door.

Gladys was the first to lose her bar; a soldier snatched it from the side with a perfectly timed grab, then used Gladys' own momentum to help pull her violently into the door. Stunned, she let go of the bar. Within moments, Emelina and I lost our bars, too—there were just too many hands out there. As the soldiers went back to work with their blowtorches, we retreated a few feet and began throwing bricks at the door. Each time one hit the iron bars, it shattered, hurling a cloud of sharp rock fragments outside into the faces of the men and igniting a flurry of curses.

It took them twenty minutes to cut the lock out, and another ten minutes to figure out that we had wired the door to the toppled gate. After they reached in with bayonets and cut the wires, they massed against the door and managed to shove it open a couple of feet, allowing them to slip inside one by one.

The prudent approach would have been to continue shoving the door, pushing all the junk we had piled against it back inch by inch until it was completely open, then pour inside all at once to overwhelm us. But the men were no longer thinking straight. They were frustrated that a simple task like opening a door had taken the better part of an hour, and they were furious at our bombardment of bricks—even in the dark, we could see several had cuts on their faces.

So as soon as four or five of them were inside, they tried to rush us. "Charge!" shouted an officer, but his command disintegrated into a scream of pain as one of my bricks caught him full in the mouth. He crumpled to the floor, tripping two men behind him as they ran forward. Three others tried to jump the tangled barricade formed by the toppled gate, water tanks, and assorted furniture. But it ensnared them, making them easy targets for our bricks.

The pavilion door opened wider, and a steady stream of men poured in. But inside, they careened in all directions, stumbling over the debris of the barricade and their own wounded piling up on the floor. Bricks sailed at them from all directions; other women charged forward to fling handfuls of salt into the eyes of charging soldiers. The floor was littered with men crawling blindly in all directions, bellowing for help. Through it all, like a drummer keeping a backbeat, shouts echoed from women upstairs, relaying information from the lookouts in C Pavilion about what the soldiers outside were doing.

When the first few soldiers finally penetrated the barricade, our screams of pain mingled with theirs. They were armed with steel cables, iron bars, and wooden clubs, and they attacked with the fury of wounded animals. On one side of me, a guard battered a prisoner named Caridad de la Vega with a wooden stool, pounding her head and shoulders even after she collapsed in a dazed heap. A moment later the guard joined her on the floor, clawing his eyes after Luisa Pérez filled them with salt.

On the other side, Gladys sprawled in the rubble of the ruined gate, unconscious from a blow that no one had seen. Raquel Romero stood above her, firing one brick after another toward the door despite a long gash on the side of her head.

It was at that moment that we heard a staccato burst of gunfire from outside. The first volley was short, no more than half a dozen shots. It was followed, seconds later, by a much louder eruption that rose and fell for perhaps a minute and a half. The first shots interrupted our fighting, like a movie freeze frame, as guards and prisoners alike looked around in surprise. No bullets were striking inside the pavilion. I thought the soldiers outside must be firing in the air to scare us. But then we heard a shout from upstairs. *"Madre de Dios!* They're shooting each other there! C Pavilion says there are bodies all over the patio!"

We found out later that several soldiers, ordered to reinforce the men inside the pavilion, had refused. "We don't beat women," one of them said flatly. When an officer threatened them, a large number of other soldiers joined the mutineers. Troops on both sides drew their weapons, someone pulled a trigger, and the whole patio erupted into gunfire. The prison doctor told us he personally treated thirty-two wounded men—though as far as he knew, no one was killed.

The gunfire panicked the guards posted in the towers on the prison's perimeter. Because they were outside the compound formed by the pavilions, they couldn't see the patio and didn't know what was happening. They concluded that somehow we had seized some guns and were shooting it out with the soldiers. Two of them began firing their rifles through the windows of the D Pavilion dining room.

The surreal pause in the fighting inside abruptly dissolved into one of panic and terror by prisoners and guards alike. Ricocheting bullet fragments flew in every direction. Some people dove for the floor, while others sprinted for the door. The bullets cut a zigzag pattern across the interior wall, filling the air with a cloud of powdery dust.

The only person in the entire pavilion who reacted with a sense of purpose was a lieutenant who had been knocked to the floor by a brick several minutes earlier. He lay there motionless except for the blood leaking from a ragged gash in his scalp, which made a dark puddle around his head. But when the bullets began flying into the dining room, he lurched to his feet and drunkenly staggered toward the windows while wrestling his pistol from his holster. "Stop shooting, you fucking idiots, you'll kill us all!" he screamed, firing three wild shots of his own into the ceiling.

The shooting abruptly stopped. The lieutenant slumped to his knees and collapsed. Others who had taken cover on the floor began slowly climbing to their feet. I looked around, expecting the bullets to have taken a terrible toll, but miraculously no one had been hit. It was plain, though, that the fight was over. The soldiers were filing back out the door onto the patio.

"Somebody help me with him," said Onelia Valdés, Natacha's mother, as she dragged the lieutenant to his feet and steered him down the corridor. Other women carried a guard whose entire face was a swollen purple bruise.

I walked to the dining room window. Outside we could hear distant shouts as stretcher teams bustled back and forth from the prison infirmary carrying the victims of the shootout. No one was paying any attention to us at all. As I watched, a State Security car pulled up outside and a heavily bandaged officer climbed out. He was standing in the middle of the angle between the two wings of the pavilion.

"We don't want to hear another sound out of you shitty *gusanas* the rest of the night," he shouted. "We'll take away your visits whenever the fuck we want to. We don't have to ask permission for anything from a bunch of traitors."

"The only traitor I see around here is you, Fernando Comas," called a voice from a cell in the other wing. Looking across, I could see Beba at the window. "When we worked together against Batista, you said you hated dictators," she continued. "And now you're working for the secret police, sending our old friends to the *paredón*. Your whole life is a betrayal."

"Yeah, I've sent some *gusanos* to the wall, and I'll send more," the officer agreed. "If it were up to me, the Revolution wouldn't have prisons— we'd shoot you all."

I had heard enough. I picked up a big chunk of plasterboard blown from the wall by bullets, raised it over my head with both hands, and screamed, "Death to traitors!" I threw it against the bars of the window with all my strength. Just as the bricks had earlier, the plasterboard shattered on the bars and showered the officer with fragments.

"Whore!" he screamed, staggering backward and drawing a blunt-nosed .45 automatic from his hip. Less than thirty feet away, he fired his whole clip straight at me in a single burst. Bits of rock and mortar cascaded over my head and shoulders as the bullets hit the walls around me. "They killed Ana!" Beba shrieked, racing back into the pavilion.

I turned and examined the wall behind me. It was pockmarked with bullet holes to either side of where I had been standing. My hands shook a little as I ran my fingers over them, but when I returned to the window my voice was steady. "I sure wish they'd put you in charge of the firing squads," I called insolently. "That way, we wouldn't have anything to worry about." The officer, his face a study in disbelief, walked back to his car and drove off.

A few minutes later, Sinesia Drake came to the dining room looking for me. "Would you do us a favor and come talk to Beba?" she asked. "She's crying in her cell, saying you're dead, and asking who's going to tell your mother. She's afraid to come over here because she doesn't want to see your body."

As I followed Sinesia to the other wing, I was smiling for the first time in several hours. But my smile froze as we passed a cell where Onelia had the two soldiers laid out on beds. She was cleaning the lieutenant's wound with soap and water.

"Onelia, what are you doing?" I demanded. "That bastard came in here to beat the shit out of us. The only thing that stopped him was a brick. Why are you helping him?"

"Because he's bleeding," Onelia replied patiently. "And there's no one else here to do it."

"Let him bleed, let every fucking drop of his blood run out onto the floor," I spat. "If you'll get out of the way, I'll hold his feet up in the air so he'll bleed faster."

"Ana, Ana," she replied softly, shaking her head, "have you forgotten you wanted to be a doctor?"

I glared at her for a moment, then walked away.

Even before the canceled visit and the beating that followed it, Elda Hernández, Adelaida Martínez, and Mercedes Llauró were obsessed with escaping from Guanajay. Three women who lived together in the cell at the far end of D Lower, they talked about it among themselves all the time. They were convinced they could tunnel out of their cell, which would leave them outside the prison's central compound and a long way from any of the guard towers. The outer wall, only about seven feet high, could easily be scaled.

Their plan didn't go beyond the talking stage until the January battle with the guards gave them an unexpected advantage. Even though Matilde, the *llavera* abandoned inside the pavilion with us, had been released unharmed, the *llaveras* were furious. They refused to stay inside the pavilion anymore, which meant we passed most of the day unobserved.

Elda, Adelaida, and Mercedes stole several nails from the construction site next to the pavilion and went to work chipping a hole in the floor. They didn't tell anyone what they were doing, but we quickly noticed that they stopped coming out of their cell except for meals. Beba went down there one morning to see if everything was all right and found all of them on hands and knees, scraping diligently at the cement slab.

"Castro will die of old age before you break through that," Beba observed. "Don't you remember a few months ago when the prison sent some repairmen in here to work on the wiring? Their drill bits broke on the wall. If you're determined to escape, there must be an easier way."

Privately Beba thought they were crazy. So did I. López, the chief of the guards, had always hated us, and since the fight in January, he openly talked about killing one of us the first time he had an excuse. "If only you would try to escape," he said several times, naked longing in his eyes. "I have standing orders to shoot to kill anyone who tries to escape."

But Elda and the others wanted out desperately. In late January, they came up with a new plan.

A few hundred yards from the pavilion was an old building that the guards used for carpentry and other repairs. Because there was nothing inside except some lumber—the tools were kept in a locker elsewhere in the prison—the place was never locked.

"The first afternoon that we see it's not being used, we'll sneak in there and hide until after dark," Elda said. "Then we'll go over the chain-link fence." The fence was thirteen feet high and topped with six strands of barbed wire in a Y shape. It could be climbed, though not very quickly. But Elda and the others had picked a length of fence located between the carpentry shop and the prison's old church (now a warehouse) that was partially blocked from the view of the guntower with responsibility for surveillance on that side of the prison.

Once they were over the fence, the women would have to bolt about seventy-five yards to the perimeter wall and vault over it. If the single guard in the guntower was looking in another direction—or asleep, which we suspected was often the case—they could get away with it. If he wasn't, they'd likely be shot.

Elda and the others asked just one bit of help from us: We had to stymie the evening count. If the *llaveras* figured out someone was missing, the entire prison would go on alert before Elda and the others could try to sneak out.

On the afternoon of January 31, I was sitting outside against the pavilion wall, enjoying a cigarette in the afternoon sun. Beba sauntered over, plopped down beside me, and lit one of her own. "They're in the carpentry shop," she said in a low voice. "I saw them go in this afternoon." Despite my skepticism, a tiny current of excitement jolted through me. "We're going to do our part," I promised Beba. "This thing is not going to fail on our account."

We passed the word around the patio. When it was time for the six P.M. count before they locked us inside the pavilion for the night, everyone milled around even more restlessly than usual.

We were supposed to form into seven neat columns of ten women apiece for the count, but we never did. Someone was always remembering a pair of newly laundered slacks left drying in the sun, or cornering a *llavera* to demand a new pair of tennis shoes, or wandering over to another column to exchange gossip with the women from D Upper. The *llaveras* frequently got confused in their counting, but it never seemed to disturb them. The count, it seemed to me, was more of a tradition than an actual security measure. The fact was that Guanajay's administrators and guards didn't think a bunch of women were smart enough, or resourceful enough, or bold enough, to seriously attempt an escape.

We tricked the count easily enough that afternoon. After dinner we made a point of carrying on our classes and card games as usual, in case anyone was watching. But when the lights went out at midnight, the cells buzzed with whispered speculation. I spent the night in the corridor, as usual; even though I hadn't been able to read at night since our books were confiscated, I still liked the chance to be alone with my thoughts. A hundred times that night I thought I heard noises, the sounds of prisoners being marched back to the pavilion. But it was always a trick of the wind blowing the tiles on the roof, or the brick walls creaking as they cooled in the night air.

"Do you think they made it?" Beba asked me when she arose just before dawn.

"It's hard to say," I replied. "Maybe they've been caught, and the *llaveras* are just holding back the news to see if we have anything else planned. And maybe they haven't been caught, but were unable to get out, and they're still over in the carpentry shop. I think we just have to go on fooling the count as long as we can and hope for the best."

At the morning count before breakfast, Sinesia Drake and several others started a loud argument with the *llavera*, demanding extra water for laundry. The count was never completed. In the afternoon, Gladys accused the *llavera* of stealing something out of her last package. The *llavera* locked us up quickly just to make her shut up. Still there was no word.

We didn't really have a close call until the fifth day, when there was a visit scheduled. Midway through the afternoon, the *llavera* came to the pavilion. "Elda Hernández, your mother's here to see you," she called out.

"Elda, they're calling you for a visit," Sinesia Drake shouted toward the back of the pavilion, while looking at me with a question in her eyes. I waited a minute or two before getting to my feet. "I'm going to go back and see what's wrong," I told the *llavera*. "Maybe she's sick." I walked briskly down the corridor toward Elda's empty cell. A few moments later I was back.

"Elda says she doesn't want to see her mother, not today, not on the next visit, not ever," I told the *llavera* solemnly. I lowered my voice. "Her exact words were, 'That old woman can burn in hell.' "

"*Dios mío*," the *llavera* gasped, so enthralled by the breath of scandal that she forgot her revolutionary atheism. "Ana, what could her mother have done to make Elda say such a thing?"

"I only know a small part of it," I said confidentially. "And I can't even repeat that. But I'll tell you this—I don't know how that woman dares to show her face here after what she did." The *llavera* scuttled away, anxious to share this high-octane gossip with her colleagues.

We kept hoodwinking the count for two weeks. It became so routine that we almost forgot we were engaged in a hoax, until the guards burst into the pavilion late one night and conducted the most violent search in several months. They threw everything in our cells out into the corridor, shoving us roughly when we tried to intercede.

"I guess you all think you're pretty goddamn smart," shouted López, standing knee-deep in a lake of blouses and skirts in the corridor. "But you're going to pay a high price for this."

"I don't know what you're talking about, López," I replied calmly, although I had a pretty good idea.

"Don't bullshit me," he bellowed. "Your friends got political asylum in the Uruguayan embassy today. But don't think this is settled. You haven't heard the last of it."

Actually, we *had* heard the last of it from López. He was fired, and we never saw him again.

The prison's vengeance was swift and sure. We lost all privileges: no visits, no packages, no mail. We couldn't even go out onto the patio anymore—the pavilion was locked twenty-four hours a day.

But, perhaps because the guards never did figure out exactly how Elda's group got away, or when the escape took place, there was no improvement in security to go along with all the punishment. The counts were a little more rigorous for a couple of weeks, and then the *llaveras* lapsed back into their old ways. Women who were called out of the pavilion to visit the prison offices for one reason or another reported that no changes had been made in the section of fence that the escapees went over. We couldn't see it from our cells, but sometimes we thought we could hear it beckoning us like a siren.

No one heard its song more clearly than María Antonieta López. When the rest of us played cards or (our newest passion) charades, she never joined in. Sometimes I saw her craning her neck at a window in a futile attempt to look down the prison yard to the spot where Elda went over the fence.

I didn't know much about María Antonieta. She rarely got involved in the endless bull sessions in the D Lower corridor. The few times she did say something, it was always some escape fantasy. ("Say you had a friend with a helicopter . . .") She never talked about her family, although I knew she was married and had several grown children. In her fifties, she was a good deal older than most of us, and I think she understood better than we did how long a thirty-year sentence really was.

Her only close friend in the prison was her cellmate, Dora Victoria Reyes. They made an unlikely pair. María Antonieta had been a housewife in the countryside of Oriente province before her arrest. She was tall, dark, and muscular, her face a sensual mix of mulatto and Chinese that set off her straight red hair. Dora Victoria was short and blonde and had the sort of pale skin that you associate with someone who works in an office, which she did; she was a Camaguey lawyer before she went to prison. She was as chatty as María Antonieta was quiet; and her smart lawyer's mouth kept her in trouble with the guards all the time.

Outside, María Antonieta and Dora Victoria probably wouldn't have been able to keep a conversation alive for two minutes. Inside, they talked for hours. And what they talked about was escaping.

I first learned of the plan from Raquel Romero, who came to my cell to somberly explain that she had devised a complicated chain of subterfuges that would enable her to send her little boy Fernandito to live with his father.

"But Raquel, why?" I asked. "Here he lives with sixty women who love him and are totally devoted to him. Outside he'll be with a father who doesn't know him and doesn't know anything at all about babies." It was a stupid, selfish question—how many reasons did she need for not wanting to raise her child in prison?—but Fernandito and Natacha meant so much to all of us. They were our last links to the lives we led, or might have led, outside.

"Ana, I've lived in terror since those bastards fired their guns into the pavilion," she replied. "What if a bullet had hit Fernandito? And you know it's just a matter of time until they do it again. I can't trust my baby's life to blind luck. I'm sending him out, and then I'm going to try to get out of here myself."

The group was led by María Antonieta and Dora Victoria and included five others besides Raquel. Someone had three smuggled hacksaw blades, she told me. Using them on the iron bars of the cell windows was useless, but since the soldiers cut the lock out of the pavilion door with their blowtorches, it was fastened only with a padlock and a cheap steel chain.

"All we have to do is cut through one link and we're out," Raquel said. "Then we go over the fence the same way the others did. In the next few days we're going to ask who wants to join us and get their ideas, too."

"Don't ask anyone else," I urged. "Look, the reason Elda's group got away was that it was small and decisive. The more people you have, the more arguments you have, the more compromises you have, and the more potential there is for things to go wrong. To plan an escape, you don't want a democratic committee, you want a smart dictator."

Raquel thoughtfully pursed her lips. "Maybe you're right," she said. "I'll talk to María Antonieta."

They left five days later, on the night of June 30, during a hard rain. Between the sounds of the storm and the *click-click* of a domino game we purposely started, we thought we might mask the rasp of the hacksaw on the chain.

It took four torturous hours to cut through the chain. The blades, slick with sweat, were hard to control, and they got so hot from friction that they had to be changed every twenty minutes or so. I kept smiling as I played my domino tiles, trying to reassure Raquel, but inwardly I was so nervous I wanted to scream. I was worried less by the *llaveras*—their revolutionary fervor did not extend, I suspected, to walking out in the middle of a driving rainstorm just to check on us—than by some of the other prisoners.

There was an undercurrent of resentment in the pavilion over the escape attempt. We had been locked up for five months now because of the last escape. If eight more prisoners got away, the consequences for those of us staying behind would be disastrous. A number of women didn't see why they should pay the price for someone else's escape. All it would take was for someone to "accidentally" drop a bottle or a pan loud enough to alert a guard in one of the nearby towers, and the whole thing would be sabotaged.*

Just before midnight, a link gave way and the chain clattered to the floor. I gave Raquel a quick hug and then watched as she crept through the door and dropped into the tall grass beside the pavilion. The rain was

---

*The guards retaliated so savagely after an escape from the men's Isla de Pinos prison that the prisoners themselves formed a surveillance committee to prevent further breakouts.

still falling hard, but the security lights on the patio were appallingly bright. And even through the rain I thought I could hear the swishing of the grass as she crawled away. "Start the domino game again," I said urgently, and there was a halfhearted attempt.

One by one they plunged out into the rain. My friend Narcy Ibargollín, only nineteen and already a veteran of two years in prison, turned to me just before her turn came. "Ana, these white sneakers are going to give me away," she pled. "Trade me your blue ones. I'll give them back to you outside when the Americans come." The moment I jerked them from my feet Narcy was gone. I winced as I watched out a window. Narcy's mountainous breasts—we used to joke that she probably sold tickets to all the boys who wanted to dance with her in high school—kept her from hugging the ground effectively. She looked like some kind of strange amphibian animal humping along the ground. Breath held, I waited for the shout of a guard; but Narcy disappeared around the corner of the pavilion without any alarm being raised.

"Beba, take someone you trust and go watch the corridor nearest to the fence," I said. "Tell the women to cut off their lights in their cells—we don't need any extra light shining outside—but to leave on the ones in the corridor so it doesn't look strange. Gladys and I will watch the other corridor. Make it clear that anyone who makes any noise, I don't care how accidental it is, is going to wake up in the infirmary, if they wake up at all."

Beba darted off. Gladys, though, hung back. "Ana, why don't we go?" she said. "Why don't we leave, too? The door is still open. What's to stop us?"

"It wasn't our plan," I said softly, taking her hand. "They thought of it, they prepared it. If we went out now, and a guard saw us, the search parties would be out right away, and they'd be caught. Would you forgive yourself for that?"

"You think too much," Gladys sighed, and followed me down the corridor.

Six of the women, including Raquel and Narcy, found their way into foreign embassies where they got political asylum. They were soon on their way to Miami. The only two who didn't were María Antonieta and Dora Victoria, the odd couple who planned the escape. Instead of going into an embassy, they tried to organize a new underground resistance. They were recaptured a few months later and sent back to prison.

Inside the prison, things deteriorated. "You'll get your next visit when the Revolution breeds pigs that can fly," one of the *llaveras* informed us. There was a new round of searches, liberally punctuated with fists, as they looked for the hacksaw blades. But nothing really catastrophic happened— which, to me, was the most ominous thing of all.

· SEVEN ·

Protest!

THE WORD WENT out right after breakfast: a meeting in *Galera 3*, the largest of the dormitory-style cells in the crumbling Baracoa Prison. By ten A.M. all sixty-five of us were packed into a room built to hold a third that number. The guards eyed us curiously from their customary rooftop posts. Castro did not assign his best and brightest to ride herd on a bunch of women in a remote outpost like Baracoa; but even the dimmest of them knew that something must be afoot for us to crowd into a single cell in the stifling midday heat. Yet they made no attempt to enter the prison yard. The prison officials had warned them not to mingle with us, that counter-revolutionary thought was a communicable disease. And, anyway, what difference did it make what we were doing? No one was going to escape from Baracoa, isolated in the desolate mountains at Cuba's eastern tip. There was no place to go: Oriente province, with its unpopulated expanses of rugged peaks and dense jungle, was a tropical Siberia.

Actually, the guards had guessed wrong. Isabel Rodríguez, the young anesthesiologist who called the meeting, wanted to plan an escape—but not in the sense of going over the walls. "We've been here long enough," she announced. "I think it's time we did something to make them transfer us. What do the rest of you say?"

For the next hour, we argued back and forth. The debate centered not around our own living conditions, but the issue of visits. The families of the poorer prisoners couldn't afford the 450-mile trip from Havana to Baracoa. And those who could weren't permitted to travel by airplane— the Revolution's airliners would fly empty rather than suffer the presence of a *gusano*. Instead, they took their chances with wheezing trains that were often no match for Oriente's mountains. Passengers were frequently stranded for hours at a time under the merciless sun, without food, water, or toilets. The journey was an ordeal for anyone; for the elderly and infirm, it was downright hellish.

Once they reached Baracoa, the situation, if anything, was worse. Because visiting days were so rare (one every two or three months), when one was finally announced, our families would arrive en masse, overwhelming the town's one ramshackle little hotel. Hundreds of our relatives would wind up sleeping in the town park, where they begged passersby to take them in. The visits were so arduous and humiliating that many of us had quit telling our families when visiting days were scheduled.

Despite all these burdens, a number of the women—including me— argued against a protest. Anything strong enough to force the prison officials to transfer us back to Havana would also be strong enough to trigger harsh punishment, including the suspension of visiting privileges. We would be inviting a good deal of abuse without gaining anything.

But when the vote was taken, a large majority favored a protest, and the rest of us agreed to go along with it. Now we had to puzzle out how to go about it. We had staged protests before, of course, but never with so ambitious a goal.

"Look," I said, "the only way they're going to transfer us is if we make life intolerable for them. And the only way I can think of to do that is a *toque de lata* that goes on day and night without pause."

The room dissolved into a hum of conversation. We had never before tried a *toque*, the protests where we beat metal objects against the cell bars, for longer than a few hours. Usually we used it for a demand that was easily attainable, like more water to clean our cells, that didn't require a high-level policy decision. To attempt a twenty-four-hour-a-day *toque*, and to make the objective something that would require the consent of the Interior Ministry back in Havana, was for us the equivalent of jumping from slingshots to thermonuclear weapons.

"A round-the-clock *toque* will be a terrible thing for them," I said, raising my voice to quiet the din of conversation. "For one thing, the guards' barracks are so close to our cells that we'll keep them awake all night. For another, the way the prison is built, with the barracks on one side and the mountains on the other, the sound is going to carry right through town, which will embarrass the devil out of them.

"But remember that it's going to be terrible for us, too. The noise is going to be the worst right here in our cells. It's fun at first, banging on things like little kids, but later it will be torture. And a *toque* will be physically demanding, too. I don't just mean beating on plates and cups for hours at a time. It's possible that the guards will react violently. But if we start this, I think we have to see it through; otherwise they won't take our next protest seriously."

Despite my warnings, there was already a murmur of approval around the *galera*. Within minutes we drew up a schedule of ten shifts. I agreed to serve on all the late-night shifts—I knew that was when spirits were most likely to flag—and I also volunteered for the thankless task of waking up the women on the early-morning shift a few minutes early so that there would be no pause in the noise.

We were about to break up when Beba Canabal stood up. "I'm willing to go along with a *toque*," she said, "but it can't go on twenty-four hours a day. We have to take two or three breaks each day to try to explain to the townspeople what we're doing and why. A lot of them are going to be kept awake by the noise. We want to make sure that they understand we're not doing it just to be a bunch of annoying assholes. We've worked hard to make them more sympathetic to us, and we don't want to ruin it now. Remember how it was when we first came here."

"Beba's right, as usual," someone said, and the *galera* buzzed in agreement. I smiled as everyone settled back down to plan a propaganda campaign. If Beba wanted it, then of course she would get it. Barely twenty years old—yet already a veteran of more than two years in prison—she was a respected leader of our band of malcontents, even though nearly every woman in the *galera* was at least several years older. Everyone knew she was utterly fearless in any confrontation with the prison authorities, be it a debate or a fistfight.

There was a price, of course. As I studied Beba's pixie countenance, I saw lines that didn't belong on a face just a few weeks past its teens. I wondered if I had them, too. The transfer from Guanajay had been hard on all of us. I wondered if, when Beba said, *"Remember how it was,"* she was recalling that day in July.

It was just three weeks or so after the second escape from Guanajay that they had announced the transfer during breakfast. "The following women should pack, report to the prison offices, and be ready to leave in half an hour," the *llavera* said. She read about twenty names. Mine was one of the first. I wasn't surprised; I had been anticipating something since the last escape. The *llavera* refused to tell us where we were going, but everyone expected harsh conditions. It was a punishment tour, retaliation for our failure to rat on the escape plan.

I got up to pack and put on several spare sets of underwear. As I left the dining room, it looked like the trading pit at the old Havana Stock Exchange. Women were clustered everywhere, frantically trying to trade assignments. Several, including Beba, had offered to assume the identity of Onelia Valdés, Natacha's mother, who was on the list.

"Damn," Beba exclaimed when she found out someone had beaten her to it.

"Don't be so disappointed," I laughed. "I don't think this will be a luxury cruise."

"I think they're trying to break up our resistance by splitting up the people they consider the hardcore troublemakers," Beba replied, "and I don't think we should let them do it. We've got to stick together." She scurried to another table where she offered to take the place of a woman whose parents, we knew, were both gravely ill.

I packed hurriedly, trying not to think about the little treasures—a coffee pot, some oranges, a pair of blue jeans—that I would have to leave behind. When you have so little, every small object becomes precious, but there was no time to think about it. If I was late reporting to the offices, they were liable to make me leave everything. I stuffed as much as I could into my five small duffel bags and walked out, three strapped to my back and one under each arm.

As I marched briskly across the patio, I could sense trouble. I saw at least a dozen women whose names hadn't been on the transfer list but were, nonetheless, heading for the office with duffel bags. Encouraged by the fact that the transfer was being managed by the guards, who didn't know us on sight, instead of the *llaveras*, who did, a lot of prisoners were following Beba's lead and attempting to stow away on the transfer. The guards obviously knew some kind of trickery was afoot; I could see several arguments and shoving matches breaking out around the patio.

But nothing prepared me for the scene inside the office building. Scattered across the long, broad corridor inside were several knots of five or six guards apiece. At the center of each tight cluster, a prisoner was being battered mercilessly. It looked like a brawl from one of the cartoons they used to show at the movies when I was a kid.

Before I even had time to react, I saw Beba flying into the air from the center of one of the clusters like a human rocket. Her head hit the floor with a sickening crack, and she lay there in a lifeless heap. I stumbled to her side, duffel bags flapping, and felt her wrist for a pulse. To my astonishment—I had never seen anyone's head ram into a solid object with such force—it was still beating, although she was unconscious.

I looked around, wondering what to do. If I left her there, there was no guarantee she'd get any medical treatment. The guards might even beat her again when they ran out of other targets. Experimentally, I lifted her; her waifish body seemed to weigh nothing at all. Holding her up and clutching her to my right side, I rearranged my duffel bags to cover her. Her feet barely dangled out from under the bags. If I could walk along the wall to my right, keeping the guards to the left of me, there was a chance I could sneak her unnoticed through the chaos of the corridor and into one of the *jaulas* waiting outside to transport us.

I lumbered along slowly, like an overburdened and reluctant pack mule, picking my way through the patches of mayhem erupting around me. The guards seemed to be trying to root out impostors, but there was nothing systematic about it. The corridor was more like a large gauntlet that caught some women while others slipped through.

We were just a few feet from the iron gate that exited to the parking lot when several guards spotted me. For a moment I thought they were going to let me go—and then Beba's feet twitched as she stirred into consciousness. "What the hell is that?" a guard shouted. "Get her!" Two of them shoved me, sending me sprawling, and Beba tumbled free. Before I could untangle myself from the duffel bags, the guards were all over her. I tried to peel them away from the back, but there were too many of them; I just bounced off their tightly massed backs like a rubber ball.

As I prepared to lunge at them once more, someone behind me

shouted, "Ana! Help me!" I turned to see two guards kicking a woman on the floor. I couldn't see her face, but among the confused mass of arms and legs I saw a white plaster cast that told me she was Esther Castellanos, who had been shot in the leg during her capture. Suddenly her thick black wooden walking stick came sliding across the floor to me like a well-aimed shuffleboard shot. I picked it up and started swinging it like a baseball bat at the backs of the guards surrounding her. Hearing their screams of pain mingle with hers sent the adrenaline jolting through my veins, and I pounded at them like a madwoman. With every *thud!* of the stick an image of a broken bone flashed in my mind and I think I must have been wearing a terrible smile.

As the guards staggered away, swearing, I pulled Esther to her feet. "I'm okay," she said as she caught her breath. "Those *maricones*! If we ever had a fair fight, we'd kick their asses. But I'll never be able to move fast enough to make it to the *jaulas*. Go on ahead." I squeezed her hand as I gave back her walking stick. Then I headed for the door again, wondering if I could retrieve my duffel bags.

I was looking around for them when I saw Caridad, one of the *llaveras*. "Hey," she beckoned a guard, pointing to a prisoner trying to slip unmolested through the chaos in the room, "there goes another one." Immediately the guards were on the woman like a pack of wolves. "Oh, you bitch," I whispered. I summoned an empty-headed smile and I walked toward the *llavera*.

I kept any hint of menace from my face as I approached. "Caridad," I said amiably, "can I ask you something?"

"Sure," she said, returning my smile. "What is it?"

My only reply was my right fist, which shot up like a piston and caught her full in the mouth. She crumpled to the floor. I watched the blood streaming from her mouth with a sense of satisfaction at a job well done. Then I ran for the gate.

The scene outside was almost as confused. A *llavera* named Mercedes Crisóstomo was standing near the trucks, checking off names of prisoners assigned to the transfer as they arrived. But some women were simply sprinting for the trucks and leaping in. Several guards tried to tackle the interlopers, but they missed as many as they caught. Each *jaula*, built to hold seven or eight prisoners, was stuffed with twice that many.

"I'm on the list," I told the *llavera*. She nodded and pointed to the nearest *jaula*. But as I climbed in, I saw Beba, staggering dazedly out of the offices. Blood trickled down one of her cheeks, and her arms were black with bruises. She was completely defenseless, and two guards were already trotting toward her.

"Crisóstomo!" I called to the *llavera*. She turned to stare at me. "Call Beba's name, let her get into the *jaula*. If they beat her any more, they're going to kill her." She hesitated, looking from me to Beba, then shouted: "Beba Canabal, to the *jaula* on the right!" The guards pulled up. Crisóstomo took Beba's arm and helped her into the *jaula*, where she passed out on the floor.

The rest of the trip was like a prolonged existential nightmare, a series of long waits in the searing July sun punctuated by agonizingly slow travel to unknown destinations. No one would tell us where we were going. They took us to a military airport, loaded us aboard a plane, and flew us four hundred miles to a city some of the women recognized as Santiago de Cuba, on the island's southeast coast. Then we were trucked 120 miles along tortuous mountain roads, so narrow that the vehicles could barely maneuver around the clifftop curves. The journey took twenty-four hours in all. All the while we listened to the wheezing of a prisoner named Lydia Pino, who was suffering from a sharp asthma attack, and the moans of several injured women. Besides Beba, who was only intermittently conscious, the two most seriously wounded were Sinesia Drake and Gloria Solano, both of whom suffered long slash wounds in their buttocks from guards who prodded them with rifle-mounted bayo nets.

Only once did they stop to give us a little water and a scrap of meat. It was late at night, and as we sat on the ground, we could see lights twinkling from a settlement down below. "That's Guantánamo, the American naval base," a guard volunteered. We studied it silently. "It looks so close," Sinesia finally said. "I bet it's not more than three or four miles away." I shook my head. "It's a lot farther than the distance down the road," I replied.

It was nearly noon the next day when we saw a pretty little colonial town approaching. "I think that might be Baracoa," somebody shouted from the back of the truck. "There's a prison there, the first one the Spanish built in Cuba." As we rolled into the town, the narrow cobblestone streets slowed the trucks nearly to a crawl. People gaped at us from the sidewalks as we passed. "Down with Castro!" I shouted. "Down with Communism!" Other women took up the cry as a guard glared at us through the rear window of the truck's cab.

One old man, hearing our shouts, waved at us. *"Viva Cuba libre!"* he yelled, hurrying toward the truck, which was hardly moving at all. As he neared, a guard waved his rifle threateningly. "Oh, shit," wailed the old man, "you're prisoners! I thought we had won." He turned to walk away, shoulders slumping disconsolately.

The little town was indeed Baracoa, and the ancient prison was to be our new home. It was small, built to hold perhaps half our number of sixty-five, and we had to do some creative interior decorating to make the six *galeras* habitable for so many people.

In some ways, Baracoa marked a big improvement in our lives. The guards, though they openly despised us, were mostly *campesinos* who thought it was undignified to beat women without good reason, and we had few physical confrontations.

We also had food and medicine that our families in Havana hadn't seen in over a year. Oriente province's isolation meant that it was always the last place for Castro's decrees to take effect, and the economic measures that were sinking the rest of Cuba into poverty still hadn't been felt much in Baracoa. Store shelves were still full and the prison director permitted us to order anything we could pay for. (The prison food itself, though plentiful, was terrible. The staples were boiled green plantains, which caused crippling constipation, and cans of Russian mystery meat, so larded with grease that they gave nearly everyone fearful diarrhea and even caused some of us gallbladder problems.)

Another advantage of Baracoa—though it didn't seem like one at first—was that the prison was located right in the middle of town. We could hear radios from the houses next door, and sometimes even the conversations of lovers strolling the *malecón*, the boulevard running along the ocean, situated just beyond our walls.

Initially, all that meant was that we were in for some extra abuse. The peasant population of Oriente had strongly supported Castro when he was a guerrilla, and he was still popular. The townspeople of Baracoa clearly believed the government propaganda about us—that we were greedy *Ba-*

tistiana aristocrats, a collection of Cuban Marie Antoinettes who opposed the Revolution because we wanted our property back.

Just across the street from the prison's front entrance was an elementary school. Every afternoon when classes ended, the children gathered on a plaza outside the walls to shout, *"Paredón, Batistiana esbirras!"*—To the firing squad, Batistiana lackeys! It angered some of the women, but Beba (who suffered no lasting effects from her beating at Guanajay, at least not on her body) counseled turning the other cheek. "They're just kids, repeating what they hear from their parents," she said. "What we have to do is convince them that we're human beings, not ogres."

She started making little speeches to the children from a window in the prison dining room. They couldn't see her, but her voice carried well. Beba was a born propagandist—even before her arrest she had been expelled from our high school for making speeches that were too reverent about God, and not nearly reverent enough about Castro—and prison had not dulled her edge. Not only did the kids soon quit yelling insults, they started bringing their parents to listen to her.

Perhaps at first it was just for the sake of novelty—a hardscrabble little town like Baracoa had little in the way of entertainment—but it was clear that, over the months, the townspeople had developed a certain sympathy for us. Several dozen gathered in the plaza every day at noon and then again around six P.M. to listen to the disembodied voices of Beba and others floating over the dull gray prison ramparts, heaping ridicule on Castro and our jailers.

Their response initially heartened us; it was the first palpable blow, however minor, any of us had been able to throw at the Revolution since our arrest. But in October, during our fourth month in Baracoa, something happened that crushed the morale of most of the prisoners: the missile crisis.

We heard it all unfold on a radio that one of the prison's neighbors (she was, of all things, president of the local Committee for the Defense of the Revolution, one of Castro's neighborhood spy groups) thoughtfully placed in her window. It started on the evening of October 22, when President Kennedy went on American television to warn that U.S. spy planes had discovered Soviet missiles in Cuba capable of carrying nuclear warheads. The United States was going to see to it that the missiles were removed, Kennedy said, even at the risk of nuclear war. He announced that a naval quarantine of Cuba would begin in twenty-four hours.

The mood in the *galeras* was a schizophrenic mixture of excitement and fear. No one wanted a nuclear war, of course. But most of the women felt that Castro had finally gone too far, that the Americans would finally see that a madman running loose in the hemisphere was a threat to them, too. "This time they're coming, I'm sure of it," Gladys said, echoing a comment that was being heard throughout Cuba that night. "If the Americans are willing to go to war with the Soviets over this, they won't flinch from swatting a mosquito like Castro."

Optimism soared even further on October 24, when Soviet ships backed off and refused to challenge the quarantine. The threat of nuclear war was over, but the Americans would still have to act to get rid of the weapons that were already in Cuba, wouldn't they? But four days later the Russian premier Khrushchev announced the missiles in Cuba would be dismantled under United Nations supervision. I was neither surprised nor disheartened; I had given up on the Americans eighteen months earlier, after the Bay of Pigs invasion failed. But the other women plunged into a paralyzing depression. For the first time, many of them began to think they would actually have to serve out their prison sentences.

After that, things that seemed bearable in the short term—like Baracoa's suffocating heat, which reached 105 degrees nearly every day, and the hardships the distance imposed on our families—started to look unendurable. And at the December 21 meeting, we agreed to try to force a return to Havana.

We spent the afternoon preparing for the *toque*. Our first task was to tear the iron bars out of the ancient, splintered doors that opened from the *galeras* into the main yard. We wanted the bars as noisemakers, and we also wanted to preclude any attempt to lock us in our *galeras* once the protest began. The guards, watching from the roof, didn't like it, but they weren't overly concerned. It didn't matter to them if we could wander back and forth between the main yard and the *galeras* at will as long as we couldn't get out—and the bars in our windows, set in stone, were secure. And although it must have occurred to the guards that we could use the bars torn from the doors as weapons, they knew any fight would be a mismatch in their favor: They were armed with automatic rifles.

After we ripped apart the doors, we dismantled the only two iron bedframes in the prison. Then we collected every metal object we could find: plates, cups, ladles, pitchers, they all went into the stockpile. A few women who had tins of crackers—part of the precious ten pounds of gifts our families could send each month—emptied them and handed them over. At dinner we told the prison director what we were planning to do and why. She just snorted and walked away. Beba made a quick speech to the crowd assembled on the plaza (she told them, as we had agreed, that the *toque* would stop three times a day for her to speak to them), and at eight P.M. the first shift of six women started hammering the bars. The guards on the roof were smiling and joking with one another; they obviously thought that we would give up after a few hours. When the clamor hadn't diminished at midnight, they cut off our electricity.

Losing the light didn't bother us. We were, however, exhausted. That first night it was impossible for any of the prisoners to sleep; it was like we were trapped in a cowbell factory, with the *clang-clang-clang* echoing out of every corner. It sounded like sixty or seventy women banging away instead of six or seven.

Each prisoner on *toque* duty had at least four metal objects to "play" on her iron bar; a few of the more talented, like Fidelina Suárez, could use up to six. When my turn came, I soon realized how prescient my own warnings had been. After swinging the heavy iron bar in a steady, ceaseless rhythm for a couple of hours, every muscle in my body cried out for rest, and my brain begged for a moment of silence. When the shift ended, I sagged onto the thin mattress in my cell and lay there, eyes wide, wondering if I would ever sleep again.

Around noon on the second day, we discovered the guards had cut off our water. But we had anticipated this tactic and we were ready for it. On the roof above *Galera 5*, there was an antiquated iron cistern that collected rain during storms and functioned as an auxiliary water tank during the frequent interludes when the town's electric pumps failed. But the rusty old cistern leaked into the roof, producing a slow but steady drip inside *Galera 5*. When the guards cut the water off, we began using buckets to catch the drops that fell from the ceiling. Cachita López, María Cristina Oliva, and Gloria Solano took charge of changing the buckets and distributing water rations. The ration, a liter per person per day, wasn't much in Baracoa's daily 105-degree heat, but it kept us going.

On the third day, our meager breakfast of coffee and bread didn't arrive. When there was no lunch, either, we realized they were going to try to starve us out.

We had some supplies in reserve from the packages our families sent. But what really saved us was that a few of the guards continued to secretly pass us food. In some ways this was the most remarkable thing that happened during the *toque*. Our guards were drawn from the force that patrolled outside the U.S. naval base at Guantánamo Bay, about seventy miles southwest of Baracoa. Because so many Cubans tried to escape the Revolution by getting into the base, only Castro's most hard-core followers were permitted to stand guard there. Intelligence wasn't necessary, or even useful, but ruthlessness was. These guards had to be impervious to lavish bribes and heartrending entreaties. They had to be willing to shoot women and children without a second thought.

Ever since we arrived in Baracoa five months earlier, a few of the women had been trying to befriend the guards and plant some doubts about the Revolution among them. I always thought it was a wasted effort. Not only were these men among the most cold-blooded Communists in Cuba, but, as I mentioned earlier, their commanders deliberately kept them at a distance from us to avoid ideological contamination.

When the prison authorities cut off our meals, however, I realized that I had been dead wrong. Not many of the guards helped us—only four or five—but without them the *toque* might have collapsed. The guards were permitted to use the prison kitchen to prepare light meals and snacks while they were on duty. Those who sympathized with us would volunteer to do the cooking, and then pass us fried plantain patties and other tidbits through the barred window that connected the kitchen and our dining room. Occasionally (though it's debatable whether they were really doing us a favor), they even managed to slip us cans of the grease-caked Russian mystery meat.

It was sometime on the fourth day that I noticed that, unawares, I was adapting to the *toque*. The constant cacophony no longer gave me headaches and barely interrupted my sleep at night. Though I was still tired after my shift, I no longer felt like a death-march survivor. With a careful gaze, I inspected my fellow prisoners. They, too, looked better. The dark circles that had appeared under so many eyes during the first couple of days of the *toque* were fading.

The guards, on the other hand, were growing more irritable. They didn't understand how we were surviving without food or water (since our meals were suspended, they hadn't been inside the prison at all, and didn't know about the drip in *Galera 5*) and they sensed that the *toque* was stirring something among the townspeople of Baracoa. Every day the crowds gathering on the plaza to listen to Beba's impassioned oratory grew larger. The guards had begun barking threats, ordering them to disperse, but the townspeople ignored them—or, even worse, replied with catcalls and jeers.

It had never occurred to the guards that, in a contest with a bunch of treacherous *gusanas*, they would be anything but the heroes. Some of them could barely contain their smoldering anger. The most malevolent was a guard we called King Kong because he was huge, dark-skinned, and growled and bared his teeth like a gorilla when he was going to take a swing at one of us, which was often. When King Kong was on duty, he stalked along the roof, hurling fabulously profane obscenities at any prisoner in sight. Once he threw a bottle down into the main yard. When it shattered, one of the shards slashed a vein in the back of the knee of a prisoner named María Julia Martínez. She nearly bled to death before we got her patched up.

The only reason that King Kong and his fellow guards didn't vent their gathering fury more forcefully was their certainty that time was on their side. And, as the days of the *toque* became a week and then two, we also had our doubts. The drip inside *Galera 5* was slowing as the cistern emptied; our daily water ration was now just five ounces. Our clothes were filthy, and so were our bodies; though some of the women had used part of their water ration for sponge baths at the beginning of the protest, now every drop had to be consumed, to keep our bodies from shriveling in the barbarous heat.

And then there was the pestilential stench that enveloped every square inch of the prison. When the water was cut off, we immediately stopped using the toilets inside the *galeras*. Instead we used the primitive latrines called *patines* inside the prison's two empty punishment cells. The *patines* were really no more than holes in the floor that emptied into thick tubes which carried the waste away; they relied on gravity rather than water pressure. But with sixty-five women using them day and night, the tubes had backed up, and the odor grew more nauseating every day.

Still we continued the *toque*, stopping only for Beba's little speeches. On Christmas Eve, while the traditional dinner of roast suckling pig was being served in homes all over the island (or at least in those homes with the luck, perseverance, or clout to obtain a pig in Cuba's blighted economy), we hammered and pounded. On New Year's Eve, while other Cubans ate twelve grapes apiece to bring good luck in each month of 1963 (a once lighthearted rite that was acquiring a certain desperation as Castro began his fifth year in power), we pounded and hammered.

It was on the morning of the fifteenth day that Cachita, María Cristina, and Gloria—the water-rationing committee—went rushing through the *galeras*, summoning everyone to an urgent meeting. "You have to come, too," Gloria told the group of women who were hammering on the plates and cups. "That's how important it is." The *toque* made its first unscheduled pause in more than two weeks; the silence felt weird, like one of those dreams where you wake up in an empty town.

As soon as we walked into *Galera 5*, it was obvious what the meeting was about: The drip had stopped. "It quit last night," Gloria said dispiritedly. "We were hoping it would start again, but there hasn't been another drop. As of right now, we're out of water. What are we going to do? We can't go on without water."

Before anyone could say a single word, I shouted: "Let's say a rosary! Only God can save us now, by sending us rain."

Thirty years later, I cannot imagine what made me burst out that way. I was a good Catholic in those days, like most Cubans. But I was never one to flaunt my religion. Faith is a private commitment, not a public boast; you don't stand in front of a crowd and say, "God, help me jump over this mountain." In the best of circumstances, that's arrogant, and in *our* circumstances, it was dangerous. Nearly all the women were sustained, in some degree, by the belief that no matter how the prison made us suffer, God was with us. If we prayed for a rainstorm and it didn't come, what did that imply about whose side God was really on?

And, to make matters stranger, I always hated saying rosaries. I've always thought that prayer was a dialogue, a private conversation with God. The rosary—repeating the same tired call-and-response, over and over, by rote—seemed to me to be a primitive ritual rather than a genuine prayer.

Perhaps the primitive conditions of the prison had made my faith revert to the primitive as well. Perhaps we were all feeling a little primitive, because as soon as the words were out of my mouth, the rest of the women stormed into the main yard, fell to their knees, and chimed in. We delayed for a few minutes while Beba, ever the propagandist, shouted over the walls to the crowd already assembling in the plaza for her regular noontime tirade against the government. She invited them to join us, and then, under a blue sky marked by only the faintest wisps of clouds, we began to pray. I don't know how many thousands of times I had heard the words before, but never with the fervid, desperate urgency they held that day: *Hail Mary, full of grace, the Lord is with thee . . .*

The sixty-five voices in prayer, however, could not drown out the cackling taunts of King Kong, who was watching us from his post on the roof. "You've fucked yourselves," he bellowed. "You're really fucked. Because it hasn't rained in six months. At this time of the year in Baracoa, it won't rain for the devil himself." His invective continued nonstop, like a scatological weather report from a demented radio announcer.

I kept my eyes shut tight, afraid to look, afraid of the reproof in the clear blue sky, afraid of the jubilant look on King Kong's face. But about ten minutes into the rosary, I noticed a tentative note creep into King Kong's voice. "*Coño,* look at that," he exclaimed. "I shit on the Blessed Virgin! Hurry, bring me some scissors!" *Scissors?* I wondered as I continued chanting the prayer. *What does he need scissors for?* Then it flashed through my mind: the old peasant superstition that storms can be prevented by cutting off the tail of a funnel cloud with scissors. Was there really a cloud forming? I chanted with renewed vigor: *Holy Mary, Mother of God, pray for us sinners now and at the hour of our death . . .*

King Kong's voice was getting frantic. "On your mother's cunt, I want those scissors!" he barked. "Hurry, before it rains on these bitches!" As his voice dissolved into an incoherent shriek, we felt a surge of pressure, as though a mountain of air had settled on us. Our voices sounded smaller, lonelier, and our breath came harder. We finished the rosary and broke into a hymn: *O Queen of Heaven, Mary, Mary, O Mother of God, hear us . . .* King Kong, now sobbing imprecations on his own mother's cunt, began firing his rifle at the storm clouds. Even the shots sounded tiny, like firecrackers in the distance.

It was just as we finished the hymn that we heard the first thunderclaps. I opened my eyes to the most gloriously ferocious storm cloud I had ever seen in my life, a primeval black mass of billows and swells. In another moment it erupted. The rain flew into us with such force that it was like being caught in a river. I opened my mouth in a shout of joy, and nearly drowned.

King Kong and the other guards stood on the roof, silent in their stupefaction. In the yard below, we danced in elation, gleefully splashing around the yard. Someone ran into the *galeras* and brought back soap, and we started washing the clothes on one another's backs. Others formed a bucket brigade and poured pail after pail of water into the *patines*. Gladys Hernández and Carmen García had to alternate at the front of the line, holding their noses against the wretched odor. Even when the rain eased, buckets could quickly be filled at the drainpipes from the roof. When the *patines* were clean, we went to work on our own cells. By the time the storm ended two hours later, everything was clean and every available container was full of water. The minute the rain stopped, we started the *toque* up again.

Later, we didn't talk too much about the rosary. If the rainstorm was an answer to our prayers, we didn't want to overdraw our account with God; if it was nothing more than freak meteorology, we didn't want to know it. We just went about our daily chore of pounding our cups and plates.

A week later, as we started to run low on water once more, it rained again, this time without any appeal on our part for divine assistance. The second storm was not nearly as heavy as the first one, and this time the guards tried to keep us from collecting drinking water. First they stuffed the roof drainpipes with cloth. But as the water built up on the roof, it began creaking ominously. So they unplugged the drains—but first they poured diesel fuel into the water so that we couldn't drink it.

Our only reaction was to laugh aloud. We put our buckets out in the main yard to catch the rain falling directly from the sky for drinking water. We collected the water from the drainpipes, too, because the diesel fuel—which only amounted to traces in such a large amount of water—made it into a useful cleaning agent. Then we discovered that by soaking scraps of blankets in the fuel-tainted water, we could make torches that burned for hours. For the first time in three weeks, the prison didn't go dark at nightfall. To torment the guards, we used bits of cardboard to make playing cards and conducted a marathon poker game well into the night in the main yard while King Kong paced the roof in frustration.

The third storm followed five days later. The guards plugged the drains again and this time dumped detergent into the water before releasing it. We couldn't play cards all night, but we still used the water for washing clothes and cleaning our cells. That afternoon the guards looked resigned rather than furious.

We, too, were resigned. The initial exhilaration of our salvation-by-rainstorm had passed. Our lives seemed to have been drawn from the pages of an existential novel. We drank a little water, ate a little food, and hammered away with our iron bars for hours at a time. We had passed every test and we were confident that we could extend the *toque* indefinitely. And we feared that we might have to.

It was just after lunch on Thursday, January 17, that a guard walked into the main yard and told us to pack. We rushed to the front gate and peered through the bars; three *jaulas* were parked in front. We were being transferred! The group of women on *toque* duty put down their iron bars, the ear-shattering *clang-clang-clang* of metal striking metal was replaced with the expectant bustle of moving day. Within half an hour, the guards began calling us, three by three, in alphabetical order, into the prison offices.

I went to my cell to sort out which of my belongings I would take to the new prison, wherever it turned out to be. As little as I had—a few tin cups, some books and magazines, a couple changes of clothes—most of it would have to be left behind; we were only permitted to carry one small duffel bag apiece. As I separated things into two piles, Beba, Gloria, and María Cristina walked into the *galera*. "You know, I wasn't in favor of trying to force a transfer," I told them. "But now I hope I never see this goddamned place again."

"Ana," Beba replied with a sly smile, "maybe we can fix it so we don't have to."

They wanted to burn down the prison.

"Nobody's watching us," Beba pointed out. "And all this stuff we have to leave behind can be used as kindling. The walls are stone, but the roof is wood. Don't you want to teach King Kong one last lesson?"

The idea was so outlandish it made me laugh out loud, but Beba was right: Assuming that since we had fought so hard for this transfer all along, we wouldn't do anything to disrupt it, the guards had completely abandoned the inside of the prison. Even the men on the roof were gone. If we waited until almost all the prisoners were outside in the *jaulas* before lighting the fire, they might not notice anything until it was too late. And, if they kept calling us in alphabetical order, Gloria Solano and I would be the last two to leave.

Quietly, we went to work. We didn't tell the other prisoners; there was no time for a general meeting, especially since it would undoubtedly trigger a sharp debate. A lot of the women would say, "Are you kidding? They'll beat the *shit* out of us for that, and we're leaving the place anyway." And even if we could have gotten everyone to agree, the worst thing about a beating is anticipating it. I didn't want everybody moping around pondering the punishment to come.

So we kept our preparations surreptitious. Each time a *galera* emptied out, Gloria, María Cristina, and I slipped in to prepare it. (Because Beba's name came so early in the alphabet, she wasn't able to help much.) We split open the mattresses and stuffed them with pages of books and magazines dampened with what remained of the diesel fuel–tainted water. Then we added anything else we could find: letters, cigarettes, sugar, worn-out clothing. We broke apart the wooden bedframes and added them to the pyres. When there were only six prisoners left inside, Gloria and I scurried from cell to cell, lighting each mattress. They blazed more fiercely than I expected, and I wondered nervously whether the guards would discover them too soon—especially since dusk had fallen.

My anxiety increased when the final group of us was summoned to the office. Unaccountably, they broke alphabetic order and processed Gloria before me, making me wonder if something was up. It took every bit of my concentration to keep from glancing over my shoulder into the darkened prison yard.

Finally the lieutenant called me over and officiously flipped through the pages of my file, stamping things here and there. Every second felt like an eternity. At last he snapped the file shut and handed it to a captain who, evidently, was taking custody of us. "This is the last one," the lieutenant announced. "The prison is officially closed. Let's beat it." There was a tone to his voice which, later, made me wonder if the guards might not have detested Baracoa just as much as we did. But at the moment, the only thing I could think was: *Amen, let's go.*

All the prisoners were lounging around the office, waiting for the final paperwork to be processed. Now a group of guards, armed with automatic rifles, surrounded us and led us into the street toward the parked *jaulas.* And as I stepped out of the gate, I was so stunned that, for a moment, I even stopped worrying about the unseen fire blazing in the *galeras.* There in the street were several thousand people, nearly the entire population of Baracoa, waiting to see us leave.

The scene was so unreal, so mystical, that it seemed to have been staged for a movie—but no movie that I've ever seen. Baracoa had no streetlights, but the bright moonlight glanced off the fixed bayonets of a double column of guards struggling to maintain an open corridor from the prison gate to the *jaulas.* The line of glowing bayonets undulated from side to side, like a serpent of light, as the townspeople crowded against the guards to get closer to us. As we passed, I could see their gazes shift quizzically among us, trying to match our faces to the disembodied voices that had addressed them in the plaza for all these months.

Walking through the crowd was like drifting through a cloud of schizophrenia. Men, smiling, held their children aloft to see us; women, murmuring softly, reached through the line of guards to stroke our arms and shoulders. But every time their focus shifted to the guards, their faces hardened and their eyes glinted. Without saying a word, the people of Baracoa were making the greatest public show of defiance that I had witnessed since the day Castro came to power.

From the guards' faces, it was obvious that they longed to pound us with their rifle butts, to throw us down and kick us until we couldn't move. This was a defeat far worse than that of the *toque;* we had taken this town away from them. We arrived *gusanas,* and we were leaving as conquering heroes. In the face of this mass repudiation, the guards wanted to lash out. But they didn't dare.

Pressing our momentary advantage, I paused at the top of the *jaula's* entry stairs. *"Adios!"* I called. "We will never forget you, and we'll see you again—when Cuba is free!" No one spoke, but when I waved good-bye, thousands of hands waved back in silent answer. As I turned to enter the *jaula,* I stole a final glance at the prison. It was still dark—not even the moonlight seemed to penetrate it—and I wondered if the fire we had so carefully prepared had fizzled out.

The journey back to Havana was just as nightmarish as it had been in the other direction. They drove us all night, without food or water or bathroom breaks, to the airport at Guantánamo. There they left us inside the *jaulas* for the entire day. The steel-plated vehicles turned into infernos; some women vomited from the heat, others passed out. Only when we began desperately rocking the *jaulas*, trying to overturn them, did the guards let us out and load us onto an airplane to return to Guanajay, our old prison.

When the *jaulas* pulled inside the prison, they were opened one at a time. Each group of exhausted, dehydrated women had to pass through a double line of guards to reach the cellblock. They punched us, kicked us, and tore at our clothing; most of us were naked by the time we got to our cells, and all of us were bruised and bleeding.

Standing off to the side, cheering the guards on, was Manolo Martínez, looking as cadaverous as ever. As we fled the blows of the guards, we could hear his whinnying laugh and his shouts of "Cunts!" and "Whores!" echoing across the yard. Later, as he walked through the cellblock cursing us, a throbbing erection pressed against his tight pants.

We had dealt with Manolo before, of course, and most of the women assumed the beating was simply one more manifestation of his pathological sexual obsessions. They paid little mind to his garbled raving as he paced outside our cells. And if any of them saw me smile when he screamed, "I'll teach you bitches to burn down state property!" they probably thought I was amused by his complete lunacy.

· EIGHT ·

The Dark Ages

JUNE 13, 1963

"COME ON," THE guard growled. "It's your turn." Silently I rose from my bunk and stepped into the corridor between the two huge men in olive green. They pointed down the hall, and we walked. Behind me somewhere I could hear Manolo's malevolent cackle. A bad sign, that; wherever we were headed couldn't be pleasant.

They had been pulling us out of our cells, one by one, for the past twenty minutes or so. Each woman who was called walked down the corridor of Guanajay's D Lower pavilion into the dining room, escorted by two guards, and vanished. A few minutes later, another name was called. From my cell window I could see hundreds of soldiers milling around in the patio under the bright moon. Wherever they were planning to take us, or whatever they planned to do to us, they apparently expected trouble, and they were taking no chances.

I trudged along between the two guards, carrying my entire wardrobe—a pair of pajamas and a spare set of panties—under my arm, along with my contact lens case. As we entered the dining room, I glanced around expectantly for a hint of what was happening, but it was empty.

The guards didn't pause, but walked straight across the dining room to the door that led into the new wing, just finished after more than two years of construction. The door, usually padlocked, swung open easily, and we went in.

The corridor, lit only by a couple of ghostly lightbulbs at either end, was submerged in murky shadows. As we started down it, I had the disquieting sensation that it was stretching out beneath my feet, turning longer and narrower. The thud of the guards' boots echoed weirdly, and a musty odor of damp cement pervaded my nostrils. I knew I was less than seventy-five feet from the familiar territory of the D Pavilion dining room, but I felt like I had entered a prehistoric cave deep beneath the earth.

I forced myself to look away from the wan lightbulb at the far end of the corridor, which seemed to eerily recede as we approached it, and peeked to my side. Startled, I suddenly understood why the corridor was so dim. No light was entering through the cells—a thick steel plate had been welded over each door. Now an even more sinister image gripped my mind: that of a giant crypt. I took deep breaths, trying to stifle my rising panic.

"Here," one of the guards gestured, and we entered an open cell. Two more guards appeared from somewhere. "Strip," one of them ordered.

My fear abruptly turned to anger. In more than two years of prison, I had never appeared naked in front of them. But I knew it would be useless to fight these four burly men by myself; I would wind up naked *and* bleeding.

"I wouldn't do this in front of a *real* man," I spat as I started unbuttoning my blouse. "But since none of you have any balls, it's okay." They stiffened, and for a moment I thought one was going to punch me. But he dropped his hands back to his sides. As I undressed, one guard examined my pajamas while the others leered at me wolfishly.

"Put these on," the guard said, handing the pajamas back. His face contorted in a malignant smirk. "Welcome to the *tapiadas*." He spun on his heel and was out the door, followed by the rest. They left so swiftly that it took me a moment to realize they had taken not only my clothing but my contact lens case.

"Hey, I *need* that," I said, striding toward the door. But it slammed in my face, plunging me into a darkness blacker than I could ever have imagined. The sound of the steel deadbolt sliding into the wall revived, with overwhelming force, my thoughts of a crypt.

Tapiada, the guard had called it, a closed-in place. That was apt. I could feel the walls closing in around me, smothering me with darkness.

I whirled and put out my hands to ward them off. *They don't have the right to do this,* I thought. *They don't have the right to bury us alive. Nothing we did, nothing we even thought about doing, deserved this.* In desperation, my mind cried out to someone, anyone: *Please don't leave me here like this. I'll do anything, say anything, but don't leave me at the bottom of this tomb.* I could feel my mind rolling toward some edge, and I knew that over it lay a blackness even deeper than the one in the cell.

Hold on, I told myself, *hold on.* I tried to breathe deeply, couldn't remember how. *Step by step. Suck the air in. Hold it, hold it. Okay, let it out. Do it again. One breath at a time.* For a few minutes I had to concentrate with all my might just to make my lungs work. It drove everything else from my brain, including my panic.

I became conscious that I was still waving my arms, trying to fight off the walls, but they weren't touching anything. *Where is everything? What part of the cell am I standing in? Which way is the door? Why didn't I look around more carefully before they closed the cell?* With some effort, I held my hands still; after a few minutes, I forced myself to focus on my ears. What sounds could I hear? My heart, galloping like a herd of runaway horses. The buzzing of mosquitoes. And there! The thudding echo of bootheels. I turned and took several shuffling steps forward, my hands groping blindly, until I felt the smooth steel plate of the door. A shred of security—at least I knew where I was. I stayed there for a few minutes, letting the tide of panic recede.

One by one my senses returned. My bare feet hurt from the construction gravel still scattered across the floor. A gritty dust of powdered cement covered my skin. And mosquitoes were biting me everywhere.

Hesitantly I began moving along the wall, trying to map my cement-and-steel box. I hadn't taken more than a few steps when the door burst open. Even the sickly light of the corridor was enough to leave me half-blinded after the fathomless darkness of the cell. Three or four guards jumped into the cell, two of them grabbing my arms and twisting them behind my back while another held on to my neck.

They wrestled me out the door and down the corridor. As I stumbled along, I saw Mary Habach, a quiet, pretty prisoner, being dragged toward me by several guards. Her skirt was ripped and her blouse torn open, and one guard had her in a headlock so tight that she was gasping for breath. I tried to smile reassuringly as we passed, but she gave no sign. I realized that my smile probably looked like a grimace—I'm sure I presented the same picture to her that she did to me.

We went up a staircase to the second floor, where they shoved me into another cell and locked the door. But this door, like the others I passed on the second floor, didn't have a steel plate welded to it. The faint light from the corridor allowed me to inspect the cell. It was small, perhaps eight feet by ten feet. In one corner was a cement box with a hole in the top that was apparently a toilet; in the other, a small sink. There was no bed, not even a mattress, and the floor was littered with sand, gravel, and powdered cement.

In the wall opposite the door was a very peculiar piece of construction. It looked like a closed jalousie window in which the panes of glass had been replaced with sharply angled cement slats. There were nine slats; eight of them had inch-wide gaps at the bottom, which admitted a bit of air but no light. The ninth, at the top, was completely closed.

I studied the cell, committing it to memory, because I had a feeling the corridor lights would be turned off when they were finished transferring prisoners. I had just started clearing a place to sit on the floor when everything went so dark that I couldn't see my own hands in front of my face. A moment later, a heavy *clang!* signaled that the guards had left the pavilion, shutting the door behind them. I crawled to the front of the cell.

"Can anyone hear me?" I shouted, not even certain that there were other prisoners on my floor. "Yes!" answered a chorus of voices. There were several sobs, too.

"Listen, I know it looks bad, but everything's going to get better. We just have to get used to it," I said with a confidence I didn't really feel. "And we have some advantages here."

"Like what?" asked a dozen voices in unison.

"The pavilion door is closed with a padlock," I answered. "It makes a lot of noise as they unlock it. So we'll always have advance warning when they try surprise searches."

"Ana, they took everything away from me," said a voice down the hall. I recognized it—it was María Julia Martínez, the woman whose leg had been cut so badly at Baracoa. María Julia always got a lot of rough kidding because she had been Fidel Castro's next-door neighbor in the days of his budding political activism. Because he had spent all his time organizing strikes and demonstrations, he had never had enough money to feed his wife and son, and María Julia had often baked them a casserole out of pity. "If it weren't for you," the women would say to María Julia, "the son of a bitch would have had to get a real job, and we wouldn't be here right now." She took the jokes with a smile, but there was no trace of humor in her voice right now, just despair. "They even took my toothbrush. Did they leave you anything?"

"No," I admitted. "They even got the little piece of soap I hid in my pajama pockets."

"Then what good does it do to know in advance of the searches? We don't have anything to hide, anyway."

"I just think it's better to know," I said lamely. She was right—I was grasping at straws. I didn't know what else to do. The corridor lapsed back into silence and I sat there, wondering if dawn would ever come, and how I would know if it did. How long did they intend to keep us like this? A week? A month? A year? The rest of our lives? Mulling over the past six months, I searched for a clue.

Since we had returned to Guanajay from Baracoa in January, life had been a daily confrontation with the prison authorities—particularly Manolo Martínez, whose fascination with us had become obsessive. On the one hand, he viewed our destruction of the prison in Baracoa as a personal insult and a declaration of war; on the other hand, he was obviously delighted to have us back where he could see us. He was determined to break us, but felt a sneaking admiration every time we defied him.

He had tried everything: cutting our food rations, withholding our clothing and bed linens, confiscating our mail, suspending our visits, eliminating our patio time, transferring us from cell to cell every two or three days. Sometimes we responded to the sanctions with mini-*toques*; often we just ignored them.

Manolo's most creative effort involved installing four enormous overhead loudspeakers in D Pavilion, two in each corridor. Then he turned on music at ear-shattering levels: first *The Internationale*, the universal Communist anthem, followed by *The Guerrilla's Hymn*, a Castro favorite, and other various revolutionary songs. The bars, the walls, the floor, the ceiling, even our bodies vibrated to the crashing strains.

It thundered on twenty-four hours a day, obliterating all other sound in the pavilion. At first we tried to talk over it. But when I couldn't hear a word Fidelina Suárez said—even though she was standing right next to me, shouting directly into my ear with so much force that the veins stood out on her throat like quivering ropes—we gave up. We wrote each other notes on the rare occasions when we had paper, and devised a complicated sign language for the rest of the time. For the first few days we couldn't sleep, but once we got used to it, we actually slept more than usual, since there was nothing else to do.

They turned the music off only for the hour or so that it took the *llaveras* to deliver our food three times a day. Whenever it happened, we immediately began chanting, "We're hungry! We're hungry!" to protest the sparse meals and to show that the noise hadn't intimidated us. We kept shouting until the music resumed, and only then turned to our plates.

The racket was so loud that the guards couldn't sleep in their barracks at the other side of the prison. They tried turning it off around one A.M. for a few days, but we immediately began chanting again, which infuriated Manolo so much that he turned it back on. After about three weeks the guards were complaining so loudly that Manolo gave up and disconnected the speakers.

Nothing angered Manolo and the other officials more than our hostility toward their re-education plan. Re-educated prisoners had to write a political autobiography (*Cuéntame tu vida*, it was called, tell me your life) confessing the error of their ways, cataloging their counterrevolutionary acts, and making a list of all their accomplices—which had to include some still out on the street.* Once a prisoner's autobiography was accepted, she had to attend political re-education classes and accept a prison work assignment; in return, she got a reduced sentence, extra privileges, and occasional weekend passes to leave the prison.

The re-education program had actually been introduced in 1962, before we were transferred to Baracoa. We immediately sent a prisoner named Carmen García to infiltrate it. After telling surprised prison administrators that she wanted to make amends to the Revolution, Carmen was assigned to A Pavilion, where the other re-educated prisoners lived.

In a series of smuggled notes, she told us the program wasn't serious

---

*Some prisoners were given lists of people they didn't know and ordered to implicate them. The resulting "confessions" were used to extort the people on the list to become State Security informers.

at all; all the other women were old or sick or both. Only a few had volunteered. The rest were simply assigned to it so that the prison would have an excuse to dump them back onto the streets instead of caring for them. Carmen stayed two weeks, then got herself kicked out in a spectacular way. At a big reception in A Pavilion to celebrate the founding of the program, with several senior officials from the Interior Ministry in attendance, she overturned a long buffet table and raced around the room, smashing glasses and throwing cakes to the floor while she shouted, "Fuck re-education!" She was still covered with cake frosting when the guards dragged her back into D Pavilion.

After Carmen's report, we paid little attention to re-education. But by the time we returned from Baracoa the program was gaining momentum, with new pressures to join every day. We shunned anyone who joined and told ourselves that we were better off without them, that only the weak and treacherous would accept such a Faustian deal.

But one afternoon Onelia Valdés, Natacha's mother, called several of us to the dining room. She looked like she had been crying, but her eyes were dry as she spoke. "I know some of you are going to hate me for this, and I'm sorry," she said in a flat voice. "But I'm joining the re-education program." No one else spoke, and after a few moments she got up and left. Later we watched from our windows as she walked toward A Pavilion.

We knew Onelia was no coward, no traitor. She had fought beside us for two years. But her husband had divorced her while she was in prison and her mother was old and feeble. The only one holding her family together outside was her fourteen-year-old son, a pale, stunted boy whose shoulders drooped more every time he came to visit. And we also knew that Onelia was frightened by the violence that accompanied every transfer—not for herself but for Natacha.

Onelia was a brave woman, but the Revolution had her family by the throat. Her defection made us hate re-education all the more. Every time Manolo or some other official tried to talk to us about re-education, we heckled him until he stormed off in anger. Now, sitting in the darkness, I wondered what lesson about the Revolution Manolo thought we would learn from the *tapiadas*.

The night dragged on and on. My hands and feet were puffy from mosquito bites, my rear was scraped and sore from the gravel on the floor, and then, with timing so exquisitely bad that I would almost have been willing to believe that Manolo himself somehow caused it, my period started. I had no tampons or anything else to staunch the flow of blood. All I could do was to clench my thighs against the trickle. *In the morning they'll turn the water on, and I'll clean myself up at that little sink and wash out my pajamas,* I thought. *Imagine, I'll be able to bathe every day we're in here without standing in line for hours.* That luxuriant sink and its endless supply of cool water occupied my mind for hours, the reverie fattening and swelling until it was almost a sexual fantasy.

"Ana? Are you awake?" came a whisper from the cell to my left. It was Emelina Hernández.

"*I'm* awake," replied a voice from my right—Carmen Besada, known to everyone as Chirrí. "And I've got my damn period."

"Me too," piped in Isabel Molgado, somewhere down the corridor. "When are they going to turn the water on? It must be morning by now."

Despite my discomfort, a wry smile flitted across my face. About six months ago, we had noticed that everyone in D Pavilion was menstruating simultaneously. What a mess this place was going to be this morning.

As other voices joined the conversation, including some from downstairs (our shouts carried through the floor), I ticked off the names mentally and tried to puzzle out a rhyme or reason to the transfer. There were twenty of us, lodged one per cell. In many cases it was obvious why we were there. Gladys Hernández and I were chronic troublemakers. Caridad de la Vega had recently slapped a prison official during an argument. (Every time I thought about it, I cursed myself for missing it.) Olga Morgan had incensed the *llaveras* by proclaiming that her husband had been shot without a fair trial.* Sinesia Drake was perpetually in trouble because she violated the

---

*William Morgan was an American soldier of fortune who fought against Batista with a band of guerrillas in the Escambray Mountains. When the war was over, Castro gave him a job running a frog farm southwest of Havana. As the Revolution veered left, Morgan started reassembling his troops. But Castro struck first, ordering his arrest. Morgan continued to conspire even inside La Cabaña prison. Someone smuggled him a gun, and Morgan sent word that if Castro would visit him in prison, he would reveal everything he knew. Castro came, but refused to enter the cell, and Morgan couldn't get a shot at him. Instead, he went to the *paredón*. When he refused to kneel and beg for his life, a rifleman put a bullet through his knee, toppling Morgan to the ground. "See, we made you kneel," said the commander. Then he gave the order to fire.

• 128 •

official line that black people loved the Revolution. Olga Ramos was a last-minute addition to our ranks; she shouted "Assassin!" at Manolo as we were being transferred.

But what about Mary Habach? She rarely raised her voice to anyone. And Beba Canabal, the loudest of the loudmouths, hadn't been sent to the *tapiadas*. The ways of the Revolution were mysterious indeed.

The water didn't come. Neither did breakfast. When the *llaveras* brought lunch, a small bowl of cold *harina* and a six-ounce plastic cup of water, I gestured at the legs of my pajamas. The dark bloodstain stood out even in the faint light from the corridor bulbs. "That little cup isn't even enough water for me to drink, much less clean myself with," I said. "When are you going to turn on the water in the sinks?"

"Don't hold your breath," the *llavera* replied, and moved on.

The day passed, then another. And as miserable as the *tapiadas* were, we started getting used to them.

Our biggest complaint, at first, was the food and water—or, rather, the lack of it. For lunch we had a cold, sticky bowl of *harina*; for dinner, a few bites of rice and a mouthful of beans. The only time the meals were substantial was when the cooks had botched something so badly that no one else would eat it.

We learned about that the hard way when they brought us big, piping-hot bowls of beans. We were so hungry that we wolfed down half of them before realizing that someone had spilled a box of salt into the pot. We spent the rest of the night screaming for water.

Despite the meager portions, there were always a few women too ill or too finicky to eat—especially the *harina*, which was strangely acidic. We developed a way to pass leftovers (plus the few cigarettes we had managed to bring in with us) from cell to cell. We called it "The Train."

The Train's engine was an old tennis shoe that we tossed from cell to cell, extending our arms out as far as we could through the barred doors of our cells. At first we tied cigarettes to it with strands of Sylvia Perdomo's long, tough hair. But when we decided to hitch metal dinner plates containing leftovers to the shoe, we all contributed string and strips of torn pajamas to form a ragged rope so that Sylvia wouldn't have to go bald on our account.

The plate was lashed crosswise with the cloth—it looked like a pie cut in quarters—so that it wouldn't turn over. Then the shoe was tossed. It was soon routine to see a dirty gray tennis shoe flit by your cell followed by a hurtling metal plate full of wobbling *harina*. Even the women in the completely closed cells downstairs learned to use The Train, extending their arms out through the narrow slot in their doors through which meals were passed.

As time passed, we worried less about food and more about sanitation. We drank every drop of water they gave us. There was nothing left for bathing, for washing our hair, for brushing our teeth, for rinsing out our single set of clothing. We had no way to clean off our caked menstrual blood, nothing to wipe ourselves when the tainted water (the *llaveras* brought it to us in the same filthy buckets that were used in mopping the floor) triggered diarrhea.

The unventilated cells were like ovens during the day, and our sweat mixed with the concrete dust in the air and on the floor to form a grimy crust all over our bodies. I felt like I was wearing a light suit of body armor; sometimes, flexing a wrist or an elbow, I could actually hear it crackling.

Because we often had to eat with our hands—the *llaveras* sometimes brought us plastic utensils with meals, but frequently didn't bother—we tried desperately to keep them clean. Some women tore strips from their clothing to tie their hands to their necks at night, to keep them from scratching during their sleep in places they wouldn't touch while awake.

Did I say I was alone in my cell? That's not quite right. I was the only *human* occupant, true enough, but I never lacked for company, as unwelcome as most of it was.

The mosquitoes were there from the beginning. They bred, I think, in the toilet. It never worked, any more than the sink, but there was an inch or two of stagnant water at the bottom, just enough to breed the bloodsucking little creatures. They disappeared by day—the sweltering cell was too uncomfortable even for them—but they descended in a cloud as soon as the sun went down. When the corridor light went on as the *llaveras* brought dinner, I sometimes amused myself by clapping my hands in front of my face three times, then counting the number of mosquitoes I had smashed in my palms. Twenty-five was routine, and fifty not uncommon.

As much as I hated the mosquitoes, I preferred them to the next generation of insects. When the toilet had gone unflushed for about a week, it turned into a cockroach factory. I could hear them skittering fearlessly over the floor at all hours, making themselves at home in the cell in a way I never could.

I am not ordinarily squeamish about bugs. But thinking about the roaches crawling around in that foul toilet, collecting every kind of wretched tropical bacteria known to man, and then coming near me—I shuddered with repugnance. I did my best to avoid them, sleeping at the cell door, as far away from the toilet as I could go, but it was futile. When I awoke one morning with a crushed cockroach, two inches long, in my hands, I knew I needed Brunilda's help.

Brunilda was the name I had given to the frog that lived in the cement slats that covered the window of my cell. Her presence there—up on the second floor, far from any water—was an eternal mystery to me. Perhaps Brunilda, too, was a counterrevolutionary, expelled from some kind of frog collective for disdain of socialist fly-collection theories.

At any rate, she was there in the cell with me. I had listened to her plaintive croaks for days without trying to find her, but now I wanted to elevate our relationship from peaceful coexistence to active alliance. The next time I heard her on the cell floor, I got as close as I could without spooking her and sat down.

I sat there hours, nearly motionless, crooning her name, letting her get used to me. Eventually, as I knew she would, Brunilda hopped closer, attracted by the warmth of my body. When I was able to reach out and cup my hand around her without making her jump, I knew we were friends. After that I could usually attract her by leaving out a little of my food.

And what a friend she was! Brunilda mercilessly persecuted the cockroaches, gobbling down any that approached. She even made a dent in the mosquito population, though it would have taken an entire frog army to really get the mosquitoes under control. I murmured praise and encouragement every time I heard the soft *thhhhp!* of her tongue sucking in another quarry.

"Ana, are you all right?" Chirrí, in the cell beside mine, asked one evening. "Do you need a doctor?"

"I'm okay," I replied. "Why do you ask?"

"I think sometimes you're delirious," she said, her voice heavy with concern. "Sometimes I can hear you talking for hours to someone named Brunilda. Are you sure you don't have a fever?"

I bit my tongue to keep from laughing. I didn't dare tell anyone about Brunilda—Cuban women are notoriously phobic about frogs. Two or three others besides Brunilda were living somewhere on the corridor, and their nighttime croaking had driven the other prisoners to near hysteria. Just two days earlier, the *llaveras* had actually let me out for a few minutes to enter María Julia Martínez' cell and capture a fugitive frog. María Julia huddled in a corner the entire time, and the *llaveras* kept a respectful distance themselves.

Chirrí was even more frightened of frogs than María Julia was. One night when Brunilda's amphibian hormones were restless and she was croaking up a storm, Chirrí called to me.

"Ana, that frog sounds so close," she said. "Do you think it could get into the cells?"

"No, no, the corridor distorts the sound," I answered, stroking Brunilda in hopes she would quiet. "I don't think that frog is anywhere near us."

"Ana, don't tell anyone," Chirrí said, her voice dropping to a whisper. "But those frogs terrify me. I can't go to sleep because I have nightmares about them and I'm afraid I'll wake up screaming, and what will everyone think?" She paused. "Do you think you could tell me a story to help me stay awake?"

A lance of guilt pierced my heart. We sometimes forgot that Chirrí was just a kid, barely eighteen. Tiny, blonde, and beautiful, she should have been going to high school dances. Instead, because of some tangential involvement in a plot hatched by her father, she was squatting in a filthy cell, wallowing in menstrual blood and shit.

"Sure, I'll tell you a story," I replied softly, shooting a dirty look in Brunilda's direction. As it turned out, the story wasn't just for Chirrí but most of the corridor. The nighttime chatter faded as everyone listened to my epic tale of intrigue on a nuclear submarine. I was so pleased—the racket of ten conversations sometimes drove me crazy—that I deliberately prolonged the story and made it carry over to a second night.

After that, my stories were a regular nocturnal feature. They were always long—one took an entire week to tell—and they always had cataclysmic endings. One ended with a Communist takeover of the world;

another with an atomic war that left the Earth a smoking ruin. No one ever complained; I think everybody enjoyed hearing a story about people who were worse off than we were.

Frogs were not the only creatures that inspired loathing. Some women were unnerved by the large hairy spiders that, attracted by the mosquitoes, took up residence in the corners of our cells.* Xiomara Wong, ordinarily a very self-assured young woman—before prison, she had been a cabaret singer—lost her composure every afternoon as dusk approached. That was when, she was convinced, the spiders began prowling. She stammered helplessly as she called to other cells for reassurance.

"Olga!" I heard her cry out to Olga Morgan one night. "Olga! Are you still awake?"

"I'm here," Olga replied. "What's going on?"

"I th-th-think there's a spider in the cell with m-m-me. I he-he-heard it walking down the corridor, but now it's quiet. You kn-kn-know they always get quiet before they attack." Her voice trailed off in a strangled sob.

"No, Xiomi," Olga said soothingly, "it's not in your cell. It crawled into mine. And you don't have to worry, because I'm going to kill the son of a bitch."

"Bu-bu-but what about the other one? You know they a-a-always go around in pairs."

"That's what I'm waiting for," replied Olga. "As soon as the other one gets here, I'm going to kill both of them."

In the dark of her cell, Olga Morgan couldn't have seen a spider unless it was perched on her nose. Her words, nonetheless, had a calming effect. It might be another hour before the cycle started again.

Xiomara never slept a wink at night for fear of the spiders. As far as I could tell, there wasn't another thing in world she was afraid of. Whenever we fought with the guards, she was always right in the front, punching and scratching and biting. It wouldn't have surprised me to find out they built the *tapiadas* just for her.

In her mid-twenties, Xiomara was an arresting mixture of black and

---

*There was also widespread revulsion at a report that reached us from C Pavilion, where a prisoner named María Antonia Mier captured a live bat. She put a lit cigarette into its mouth, and it puffed away like a furry little chain-smoker.

Chinese blood, tan skin and almond eyes. I always wanted to ask about her family, to find out the story behind such an exotic mix of races and cultures, but I didn't dare. The Revolution had torn her family down the middle. Two of her brothers were State Security officers and—except for a single sister—none of her relatives ever visited her.

Xiomara never talked about it. But once, during a transfer, a State Security man walked into the pavilion. Before he could say a word, Xiomara pounced on him like a wild animal. She tried to gouge his eyes out with her fingers, and it even looked to me like she wanted to snap her jaws closed on his throat.

The State Security man, though he was much bigger, didn't hit her, just tried to pin her arms behind her back. Even when she was finally pulled off him, he didn't retaliate; he just hurried out of the pavilion. Xiomara's pitching, heaving body didn't go limp until the gate slammed behind him.

I always supposed the State Security man was one of Xiomara's brothers. I wondered how he could do that, how he could let himself be a gear in a machine that put his own flesh and blood in prison. And in the *tapiadas*, as I listened to Xiomara at night, I wondered if he was afraid of spiders.

The days became weeks, the weeks became a month. The filth and the heat and the sparse rations and the dirty water took a toll. Nearly everyone was ill, in varying degrees of seriousness, and the sharp odor of vomit mingled with the other squalid smells hanging heavily in the corridor air. Even when the women in D Pavilion volunteered to mop the corridor floors in the *tapiadas* and used the opportunity to smuggle us some vitamin pills, our collective health didn't improve much.

I had avoided the stomach problems that affected many of the women, but I had my own malady. Because the guards had confiscated my contact lens case when they took me to the *tapiada*, I had to wear the lenses for twenty-one consecutive days. I developed a low-grade infection that kept mucus running constantly from my eyes, even after I took the lenses out and put them in a smuggled case.

At night our conversations were listless. (The only exceptions were María Cristina Oliva and Gloria Solano, who had long, intimate talks about food. They invented all these strange dishes—say, beef smothered in shrimp—and then conferred in endless detail about how many minutes they had to be cooked at what temperature in what kind of pan. I wanted to kill them for it.) By day we no longer had the energy to talk at all; we lay inert in the baking heat of our cells, concentrating all our energy on breathing, on surviving until another sundown.

"Oh, God!" Chirrí wailed one afternoon, breaking the silence. "Is this why you kept us alive through all the beatings—so we could die in here by inches, all alone in the dark?"

She was greeted by a moment's silence. Then, outside, a mockingbird broke into a sweet, high trill. It sang to a sun we couldn't see, of a nest it would build, and babies it would nurse.

"I think you got your answer, Chirrí," I called hoarsely.

Three days later, they let us out.

We staggered like drunks as we walked down the corridor and through the dining room into D Pavilion. After fifty-nine days huddled in the darkened *tapiadas*, our equilibrium was gone, and even the dim light inside the pavilion cut our eyes like a knife.

Our appearance alarmed even the *llaveras*, who promised to keep the water on all afternoon so we could take long showers. When it was my turn, I plugged up the drain and splashed around like a child in a wading pool. Later I found out most of the others did the same thing.

On some parts of our bodies, the crust of blood, sweat, cement dust, and grime was so thick that it had to be scraped away with razor blades. And our hair was so matted with dirt that it was impossible to wash out. We spent the evening giving one another short, severe haircuts. From that day on, new prisoners were instantly recognizable—they were the only ones with long hair.

Manolo, in an unprecedented show of self-restraint, waited three days before coming to see us. Trailing in his wake were Roberto Fontanella, the head of the prison, and several Ministry flunkies.

"Good morning, ladies! It's good to see you again!" he said ebulliently, as if he were greeting us as we returned from vacation. We stared at him, silently. What he had done to us was inhuman. No one felt like a friendly chat.

Manolo's eyes hardened. "All right, if you want to be enemies, we can be enemies," he said. "You'd better get it through your heads that I give the orders around here. I can make your lives comfortable, or I can make them miserable. Since you want to be miserable, I'm going to transfer some of you." He pulled out a list, but before he could read any names, I interrupted.

"Fuck you, Manolo," I said evenly. "We're not going anywhere. If you think you're transferring anybody, you'd better call your little friends in olive green. And make sure they bring a doctor, because a lot of them are going to need one when it's all over."

Manolo's blue eyes bulged. He grasped Fontanella's arm. "You see how they are?" he blurted. "They always defy me! They don't care what I say. They're too crazy to be scared." His voice went higher. "It's killing me, Fontanella. I haven't been with a woman in months. I can't find one who pleases me. I'm dreaming of them every night now. I've got to break them before they break me!"

Fontanella didn't try to hide the distress on his face. "Manolo, let's talk about this in your office," he urged. "Come back there, and you can tell me all about it." He tried to take Manolo's elbow, but Manolo angrily shoved his hand away. "Don't touch me, goddamn it!" he shouted. He looked at us once more, then strode out of the room, trailed by Fontanella and his wide-eyed entourage.

He came back a few days later, at night, walking through the corridor and peering into the cells, hoping to catch one of us undressed. We were still mangy and ragged from the *tapiadas*, but there was no mistaking the lust in Manolo's eyes. *My God, he's getting crazier by the hour,* I thought. *Any day now, he'll come in here in a blue uniform and proclaim himself Napoleon.*

Manolo walked from cell to cell, imploring us. "Gladys? How have you been? Can we have a little talk? Isabel, you look so nice tonight. Oh, come on, don't be like that. Ana? Aren't any of you going to talk to me?"

By the time he reached the end of the corridor, no one had said a word to him, and he was shouting threats again. Still we kept silent. He left in a rage, slamming the gate, and walked furiously down the sidewalk in front of the pavilion. About halfway down it, he tripped on a rock, lost his balance, and stumbled several feet before righting himself. As he stood there, catching his breath, a voice—it sounded to me like Isabel Molgado's—sang out: "Manolo, you blockhead."

"That's it! Goddamn it, that's it!" he screamed. He waved at a passing group of guards. "You men come with me!" They raced into the pavilion, and Manolo went straight to Gloria Solano's cell.

"You think I'm a blockhead, do you, you cunt?" he shouted. "Well, we'll see what you think after a year in the *tapiada*!" He turned to two of the guards. "Take her away, and beat the shit out of her if she gives you any trouble!"

Gloria didn't resist, didn't say a word, as the guards led her away. But from the opposite end of the corridor came another singsong voice, almost certainly Xiomara's: "Manolo, you blockhead." Manolo ran to Gladys Hernández' cell, followed closely by the guards. "Take this bitch, too," he ordered. Before they even closed the cell door behind her, the words rang out again: "Manolo, you blockhead."

Manolo sprinted up and down the corridor like a human pinball, dispatching women to the *tapiada*. By now the chorus of "Manolo, you blockhead" was near constant. At the end of fifteen minutes, he was out of guards and had to send for reinforcements. He stood in the middle of the corridor while he waited, the cries of "blockhead" raining down on him like rotten tomatoes.

When a new detachment of guards arrived, Manolo resumed his frenzy, sending women to the *tapiadas* as quickly as their cells could be unlocked. But a few minutes later, a guard fearfully approached him.

"A thousand pardons for the interruption, *señor*, but I need to ask instructions," he said timidly. "All the *tapiada* cells are full, and we have six prisoners waiting. Where shall I put them?"

Manolo glared at him for a moment. "Bring the stupid bitches back, then," he ordered. "The six of them?" the guard asked. "All of them," Manolo answered impatiently. The guard saluted, turned, and walked several paces toward the *tapiadas*. Then he broke into a run.

Manolo looked up and down the corridor. "If any of you think of this as a victory, you would be sadly mistaken," he said. "You aren't getting out of your cells again until it's time for visits from your great-grandchildren."

He left the pavilion for the second time that night. This time he didn't stumble on the sidewalk. But as he passed my window, I could see the smile of a satisfied lover on his face. And, plain as day, I could read his mind: *They spoke to me after all.*

· NINE ·

The Longest Night

"ANA RODRÍGUEZ, COME with me to the office," the *llavera* we called Mirta the Big-Headed (to distinguish her from her colleague, Mirta the Big-Assed) shouted from the dining room. Sighing, I climbed heavily to my feet from the floor of D Lower, where a few of us were sitting, chatting about the clandestine talent show we had held the night before.

"Ana, you should change into a better uniform before you go to the office," chided Griselda Noguera. "That one is so faded it looks like you stole it from a museum." A beautiful and popular soap opera actress before the Revolution, Griselda somehow managed to keep looking stylish inside prison. She had even emerged from a recent two-month stay in the *tapiadas* with a certain élan, though the effect was marred somewhat by her inability, for several days, to walk in a straight line. (The guards, certain she was making fun of them, almost sent her right back inside.)

"The hell with that," I said irritably. "It's just another one of these stupid interrogations they do to justify their lives. I'm not dressing up just so they can ask if I've changed my mind about the Revolution in the last forty-eight hours."

Griselda didn't reply, and immediately I was shamed of snapping at her. For the past two days, I had been unaccountably depressed. After the talent show, Griselda had found me alone in my cell, sobbing. "Ana, you're never like this, you're always the strongest one," she said, putting an arm around my shoulders. "Tell me what's wrong." But I had nothing to tell her—it was a mystery to me, too.

I walked behind Mirta the Big-Headed across the patio, my aggravation subsiding a bit as I marveled once again at how she could hold that big watermelon-sized skull of hers upright. It was one of the Revolution's greatest achievements, an apparent suspension of the laws of biology and physics.

When we entered the office I flopped down in a chair and waited, wondering if I was going to get another beating after they were done questioning me. Probably. State Security interrogators had surprisingly little tolerance for sarcasm. The most recent one didn't get past the first question before slugging me. With my prison file right in front of him, he asked what my name was. "Cleopatra of the Nile," I replied earnestly, and it all went downhill from there.

But the poker-faced guard captain who approached me now didn't summon me to an interrogation. "Just wait here," he instructed. "A vehicle will be along to pick you up in a few minutes."

"Can I go back and pack my things?" I asked. Wherever they were taking me, I would still need clothes.

"No, just wait here," he repeated, and walked away.

I tried to guess what I might have done recently to make them mad enough to transfer me. I catalogued the usual assortment of crimes— talking back, complaining about the food, making fun of Castro—but, to my regret, I wasn't guilty of anything spectacular for the past couple of months. And whatever it was, why not just toss me in the *tapiadas*?

I hadn't come up with any answers when a *jaula* pulled up in front of the prison. As I got in, I was unpleasantly surprised to find that Leyda Dumpierre, one of the nastiest of the *llaveras*, was already inside with two male guards.

Leyda, who was so cross-eyed it made me dizzy to look at her, never missed an opportunity to make our lives miserable. A stupid woman (she had failed the third grade repeatedly in adult literacy classes) who owed her job to her older sister, an Interior Ministry bureaucrat, Leyda bullied us incessantly, trying to provoke a response so she could have someone sent to the *tapiadas*. She was often successful. *If this trip lasts more than ten minutes*, I thought, *we're going to get in a fistfight.*

But, as the *jaula* headed east, Leyda was quiet. So were the guards, and for once I could enjoy the scenery on one of these trips without nursing cuts and bruises. As we rolled through the pastures and fields of southern Havana province, I remembered family picnics and Sunday drives along these same roads. Around the village of San Antonio de los Baños, I watched carefully for signs the *jaula* was slowing. The Interior Ministry, I knew, confined several hundred prostitutes on work farms around there. *If that's where they're transferring me,* I promised myself, *they'll be sorry. I'm going to escape—I know this countryside so well, it'll be a snap to hide from them.*

But the *jaula* kept on going. My puzzlement was turning to apprehension as the landscape grew more familiar. But I refused to think, refused to focus. *It's just a transfer. They're probably taking me to some small jail where I can't be a bad influence on so many other prisoners.*

Then the *jaula* did slow as we approached a junction I knew well. A few miles down one unmarked road was the village of Santiago de las Vegas; down the other lay my town, Bejucal. The driver stopped, studying the junction in confusion. "My house is to the right," I said hoarsely, and the *jaula* veered toward Bejucal. I sat back and closed my eyes so I wouldn't see the look on Leyda's face.

The *jaula* stopped at my front door a few minutes later. Three and a half years had passed since I walked through that door with the State Security men. I never dreamed that the sight of it would cause me such pain. My sisters came running from inside. I could see their lips moving, the tears flowing from their eyes, but I couldn't hear anything. A numbness spread across my body.

The inside of the house was crowded, with two dozen or so neighbors and relatives milling around. But they were a blur. Only two things stood out in sharp focus: my mother, sitting in a chair on one side of the living room, and the gray wooden casket on the other.

It was only when my mother called me to her side that I started to hear again. Her voice, tinny and small, seemed to come from far away. Taking her hand, I settled on the floor beside her chair. It had been more than a year since we had been permitted to see one another; I was startled by the new lines in her face and the spreading gray in her hair. The tears flowed silently but steadily down her face, looking like they would never stop. "Oh, Ana, look what happened," she gasped in a strangled voice. "Look what happened."

My Aunt Mercedes emerged from the crowd to sit beside me. She and my mother were the two strongest women I had ever known, and I was sitting between the two of them as they both cried disconsolately. "What are we going to do without your father?" Aunt Mercedes asked me between sobs.

I didn't have the answer. In a house full of peppery feminine passion and intrigue, my father sometimes seemed to fade into the wallpaper. But it was an illusion; his quiet strength was the glue that held us together. Not just our family, but so many in our little town. He was the one everybody went to when there was no money to buy groceries at the end of the month, when the rent was a few pesos short, when the intractable Cuban bureaucracy was smothering someone in red tape. When, as a child, my exasperating arguments drove my mother to shout, "Because I say so!" my father was always willing to sit patiently and explain things one more time. As a child, he extricated me from one predicament after another, sometimes baffled by the willful little girl he had fathered, but always proud; and I knew it must have torn at his heart when I finally got myself into a jam from which he couldn't rescue me. What would we do without him? I didn't have any idea.

"What happened, Mercedes?" I asked quietly.

"There's been no way to get word to you," she replied, dabbing at her eyes with a handkerchief, "but your father's illness had been much worse for the past year." Though he neither smoked nor drank, my father for many years had suffered from cirrhosis of the liver. Sometimes it grew so acute that he was bedridden, but he always recovered.

"The last few days he hadn't been feeling well. And then yesterday he collapsed here in the living room. The doctor said a vein in his liver ruptured. He died a few hours later. He was conscious until the very end; he told your sister where to find his will, where he had hidden the property deeds, where he had buried some money." She paused, then added: "Have you noticed there are no flowers?" I nodded. "That was the last thing he said, that he wanted people to give the money to the nursing home down the street." Even at the end, he was solving other people's problems.

Leyda the *llavera* stirred uneasily from her post behind me. Looking around, I noticed the house was filling up. There were so many visitors that my sisters had removed most of the furniture from the living room, and still people could hardly move. I heard my name spoken softly here and there, and I realized word of my presence had spread through the town. The wake was turning into a quiet show of defiance.

"Leyda," I said quietly, "I want to go see the casket before it gets any more crowded." She nodded her approval, and we forged into the crowd. A path quickly opened for me, but closed just as quickly behind me. Leyda was immobilized in the crowd. I could hear her voice, accustomed to bellowing, straining to be polite as she said "pardon me, excuse me" over and over to no avail.

The coffin was sealed in glass against the exigencies of the tropical heat. I stood there, gazing down at my father's gray face. *I'm not going to cry, Papa,* I thought. *These people came to see a symbol of resistance, and I know you wouldn't want me to let them down.*

Leyda finally shoved her way to my side just as I was ready to go back and rejoin my mother. Once again we moved into the crowd, but the mood had gone from one of passive disobedience to open confrontation. People didn't even offer a pretense as they blocked Leyda's path. Her facade of civility finally cracked. "Let me through, or I'll take her back to prison right now!" she snapped.

"Go ahead and try," taunted someone in the crowd. "Let's see if you can." I braced myself—at Guanajay, those words would have provoked Leyda into using her fists. Instead, she surprised me. "You're asking too much of Ana," Leyda said in a voice that almost sounded compassionate even to my cynical ears. "She's suffering here. Let her go." The crowd, mollified, melted away. I hugged my mother and sisters again, and we left before anything else could get started.

Back at the pavilion I lapsed into a depression so deep it was almost like a coma. I lay on my bunk night and day, scarcely moving. Sometimes I thought about my father; other times I obsessed over trivia: the exact lyrics of old songs, lines from dimly remembered movies. Most of the time I didn't think at all, just lay there with my mind suspended in an empty twilight.

Other women crept in and out with food and clean clothing; I acknowledged it with a terse "thanks"—if that—and turned my back. For a time they congregated outside the cell, whispering, until I stormed out and screamed at them to get away. *Come on, what are you doing?* a tiny part of my brain reproached me, but I didn't care. All my life I had confronted my problems, from difficult textbooks to tyrannical governments. But how did you confront death? How did you reason with death, or cajole it, or threaten it?

It was ten days before the fog broke. I looked up for some reason and saw Gladys, my cellmate, sitting on her bunk. "Hello," she said, as if we hadn't seen each other for a long time. And, of course, we hadn't.

"I'm sorry for the way I've been," I told her. "But it's been impossible to break out of this. In the real world, when something like this happens, it hurts just as much. People grieve. But at some point, they have to go back to work, or to school. They have to cook dinner and take care of the kids. And the ordinary demands of everyday life force them to start healing.

"In here, though, there's nothing. My grief clings to me, like a cloud that won't let the sun shine through. I just can't shake it. I can't even cry, not a single tear for my own father."

"But Ana," Gladys said gently, "you do cry. Every night, in your sleep."

I just looked at her. There was nothing to say. I got up and, for the first time in ten days, walked outside.

A few days later, they began erecting scaffolding and rigging spotlights outside B Pavilion for what looked like a stage. Within hours, the prison's gossip hotline reported back the reason: a command performance of a play called *Liberty in Three Steps* for the re-educated prisoners in B Pavilion. Several senior Interior Ministry officials would be there, and they were even going to bus in some model re-educated prisoners from the men's prisons.

We knew all about this vile little melodrama. Written by several re-educated male prisoners, it was the linchpin of a government propaganda campaign to discredit political prisoners. It portrayed us as a bunch of criminal psychopaths who wanted to burn most of Cuba to the ground and give whatever was left to the Americans. The play had already been performed in several other prisons, and the Ministry planned to stage it in towns all over the country.

"We can't let them get away with this," said an indignant Gladys when we got the news.

"How are we going to stop them?" I asked. "They certainly aren't going to invite us." By now D Pavilion's reputation for bellicose resistance was firmly established. The prison authorities themselves had started it when we came back from Baracoa, when they decided to concentrate all the troublemakers under one roof where they could keep an eye on us more easily. Now it was beyond their control. Something like political alchemy went on in D Pavilion; docile women who had never raised a voice to a *llavera* would be transferred in with us, and suddenly they were picking fistfights with the guards.

"Let's do a *toque*, as loud as we can, when they start the performance," suggested Beba. "It probably won't be noisy enough to seriously disrupt the play way over there at B Pavilion, but it will embarrass them and make them mad as hell."

The prison kitchen worked overtime on the day of the play, preparing fancy hors d'oeuvres; the tantalizing scents only increased our resolve to spoil the show. Late in the afternoon the buses started arriving. Only a few cells upstairs had a view of the stage; we posted lookouts with instructions to shout a warning when the performance began, so we could launch our *toque*.

It was just after dark when we heard María Julia Martínez screaming hysterically upstairs. "Traitors! Traitors! Filthy traitors!"

"The show must be starting," said Gladys.

"Yeah, but what's wrong with María Julia?" asked Sinesia Drake. "She sounds like she's gone completely *loco*."

"María Julia?" I called from a downstairs window. "Are you okay?"

"My brothers are here," she sobbed. "Those traitors have joined re-education!"

The pain in her voice pierced my heart. María Julia's husband had gone to the *paredón*; now her brothers were cuddling up to his killers. "Traitors" didn't seem like a good enough word.

"Let's start the *toque*," I yelled. Instantly a hundred tin cups and dinner plates started banging together. We hammered away as hard as we could, hoping that María Julia's brothers and their friends could hear the note of rebuke inside the metallic cacophony.

The din we created was unbelievable. *It sounds like a thunderstorm*, I thought. Then I realized it *was* a thunderstorm. A wild cloudburst had erupted outside, drenching everything. Our *toque* dwindled away momentarily.

"María Julia, what's happening?" Beba called.

"It looks like everything is ruined," she called back, her voice still shaky. "They knocked over a lot of the food trying to get out of the rain, and all the scenery for the play is a big mess, too."

Spontaneously the sound of the *toque* swelled up again, this time with a lilting rumba beat. In the dining room several women put down the cups and plates they were beating to dance. Laughter echoed around the pavilion as we savored our victory.

"Ladies, we may have a problem developing," María Julia, still posted at her window, shouted. "A bunch of the Ministry people are walking this way with some of the guards, and they look like they want to beat the hell out of us."

We redoubled our rumba beat and the dancing continued. But now instead of joyous it was defiant. Let them see how the end of their party was the beginning of ours. Let them see how much pleasure we took from defeating them. It would rankle all the more.

Everyone who wasn't dancing clustered around the windows that looked onto the patio. Two or three dozen Ministry officials, obviously enraged, had gathered outside, where the rain had slowed to a drizzle. But the two hundred or so re-educated male prisoners bused in for the play were also massed nearby, and it looked like the two groups were exchanging words.

"What do you think is going on?" asked Gladys.

"It's amazing, but it looks to me like the re-educated men are defending us," I replied as I peered between the bars. Over the *toque*, I couldn't hear what any of them were saying, but the men in both groups looked stiff with tension. A fight seemed inevitable.

Then someone apparently gave an order, and the group of Ministry men broke up, most of them walking back toward B Pavilion. After a moment, the re-educated prisoners followed. Inside, our rumba beat flared anew; no beating tonight, a real cause for dancing.

I was just about to try a few steps myself when the pavilion door opened. I spun around quickly, sure they had returned to attack us, but it was a single uniformed man followed by a visibly reluctant *llavera*. The officer wasn't walking but dancing, with his hips extended so far forward that it looked like he was being towed by an invisible wire attached to his pelvis.

"*Dios mío*, it's Captain San Luís," shouted someone from the back of the pavilion. Now everyone stared. Eliseo Díaz Reyes—known as Captain San Luís, for the remote village where he grew up—was the infamous head of State Security for Pinar del Río province. Even within the Ministry, not exactly known for its compassion, the brutality of San Luís was legendary.

But this night a fight seemed the farthest thing from his mind. His slim hips and concave abdomen twitched in time to the rumba beat. His eyes were bright and dilated; he was certainly drunk or under the influence of drugs. "Who wants to dance with me?" San Luís called out. Getting no reply, he pranced toward Preciosa, drumming on a plate with a soup ladle. "I'm sure you'd like to dance, my pretty little one," he sighed, thrusting his pelvis so close it almost touched her.

Her real name was María Noelia Ramírez, but we called her Preciosa because her perfect alabaster skin and immaculate grooming made her look like a pretty porcelain doll. It was impossible to guess her age—and no one dared ask, for fear of those long, withering looks that were her specialty—but I thought Preciosa must be around sixty.

Preciosa viewed the Revolution with an amused contempt that *llaveras* sometimes mistook for softness, always to their regret later. San Luís was making that mistake now, misreading the faint smile on her lips for acquiescence. In reality, she was getting ready to brain him with her dinner plate. I leaned forward with real interest. San Luís bent backward even further at his waist, thrusting his pelvis forward like the prow of an obscene ship. My medical mind marveled at the flexibility of his backbone.

Preciosa was not the only prisoner on the verge of taking a swing at San Luís. Caridad de la Vega's face was reddening, and just as I saw Preciosa's grip tighten on her plate, Caridad grabbed the State Security man by the shoulder and shook him like a rag doll. "You vile, filthy drunk!" Caridad snarled as she jerked San Luís back and forth. "Have you no shame?"

San Luís gave her a quizzical look. "Doesn't anyone want to dance with me?" he asked in a slightly injured tone. His pelvis wobbled some more. Caridad took a deep breath, and Preciosa's smile frosted over. *Here it comes,* I thought, *here it comes.*

But the *llavera* must have thought so, too. Scampering across the room, she slipped in between San Luís and the two women. "Come on, captain," she begged, "we'll find another place to dance." She steered San Luís, still stutter-stepping to the rumba beat, across the dining room and through the door. We watched from the window as San Luís danced across the patio, the *llavera* trailing watchfully behind him.

"I guess no one wants to fight with us tonight," María Julia called from her window upstairs. There was a catch in her voice that might have been disappointment.

"Goddamn it, just look what those dirty bitches did to me!" We ran to the windows. It was unmistakably Manolo's voice outside in the twilight. He was pacing around outside the front of the pavilion, down near the *tapiadas*. His clothing was torn and disheveled, and even in the December dusk we could see the scratches on his face. "They cut me," he howled, "and they threw buckets of piss on me!" He stormed into the *tapiadas* without another word, while D Pavilion hummed with prurient conjecture. What was Manolo talking about? Had he finally tipped over the edge and lost his mind completely?

Half an hour later, we were even more confused. Some twenty women were transferred from the lower level of the *tapiadas* (where some of them had been for months) to the upper level. They shouted to us that Manolo had come racing into the cellblock, shouted to the *llaveras* to empty out all the *tapiadas* on the lower level, and then bolted back out of the building without any explanation.

We didn't get the final piece of the puzzle until just before dawn the next morning, when we were awakened by the rumble of half a dozen *jaulas*. There was another scramble to the windows, but the *jaulas* were parked at an angle that made them invisible to most of us. Then there was an excited cry from a corner cell: "It's common prisoners! They're practically naked, with everything flapping in the wind, and the guards are taking them into the *tapiadas*!"

In a few hours, we had the rest of the story. There had been some kind of a revolt at Guanabacoa. Several of the common criminals there had attacked Manolo, touching off a major battle with the guards. The worst culprits had been sent to join us at Guanajay.

The news ran through D Pavilion like an electric shock. Not since the early days, when the *Batistianas* were confined in the same pavilions as the common criminals, had the prison authorities tried to make the populations of common and political prisoners live side by side.

It wasn't that we were too proud to share cells with criminals. There *was* an important difference between the two groups—we were in jail for resisting the government, not for robbing or injuring innocent citizens. But we had made our peace with the *Batistianas* despite huge political, educational, and socioeconomic differences. If nothing divided us from the common prisoners but an intellectual distinction in status, it could have been overcome fairly easily.

The real problem was that we feared the common prisoners, with good reason. Most of them were out-and-out savages.

Cuba's paternalistic judicial system sent relatively few female criminals to prison. A woman who picked pockets, or forged checks, or hit her husband over the head with a frying pan, at worst might spend a couple of months in a local jail. It took a truly lurid crime for a woman to earn the kind of long sentence that would bring her to Guanajay or one of the other large prisons.

There was one woman who had killed her husband, chopped him up, and cooked him. (I never quite had the courage to ask if she'd actually gotten around to taking a bite.) Another, while pregnant, had extracted the fetus with forceps and fed it to her pigs. Not surprisingly, given their backgrounds, the common criminals settled almost all their disputes, no matter how minor, with violence. They bore the grisly scars to prove it.

The common criminals were capable of a more calculated kind of violence, too. Everyone knew the fate of a prisoner named Teresa. A nurse, she was in prison for killing her husband, an army officer. One morning her body, mutilated with more than a dozen stab wounds, was found in her cell. Some of the guards, friends of the murdered husband, had bribed a common prisoner to avenge him.

We knew that if we had to live with the common prisoners, they would push us, again and again, until we pushed back. And although we certainly had the willpower to fight with them, we lacked the skill.

I had discovered, to my amazement, that I had a real aptitude for fighting. I had no idea where it came from; until I entered prison, the only fight of my life was a scuffle with a cousin at age five. But right from the beginning I had an instinct for kicking guards and then jumping back out of reach, and the ability to stand up under the pain of a beating. I never even thought about this much; it just came naturally.

But I was one of a very few exceptions. The majority of us had never become good fighters. When we inflicted real damage on the guards, it was almost always because they were overconfident, assuming that a bunch of women posed no real threat. With the common prisoners, we wouldn't have that advantage.

And we might need it soon. For now, though they were nearby, we were still separated from the common prisoners: They were in the downstairs *tapiadas*, while the political prisoners in that wing were all upstairs. But for several months, the prison authorities had been demanding that we join a forced labor program, cultivating some fields outside the prison's residential compound but inside the perimeter fence. The re-educated prisoners in B Pavilion had accepted the assignment, but everyone in D Pavilion had refused. So far, the prison hadn't pressed the issue.

But what will we do, I wondered, if they tell us the price of refusal is that they transfer a few of us down onto the corridor with the common prisoners?

The first couple of weeks were edgy ones. The common prisoners were, for the most part, kept locked up in the lower *tapiadas*, so we had no direct contact with them. But the *llaveras* often left the dining room doors open, in effect connecting D Lower with the lower level of the *tapiadas* into one long corridor. Through cell-to-cell shouting, and occasional glimpses, we started to get to know one another.

Though most of them were now serving sentences for other crimes—mostly violent ones—nearly all the common prisoners had been introduced to prison because they were prostitutes who defied the Revolution's crackdown on their profession. (Many of them had worked at the same bordello, a notorious place known as Marina's House on the outskirts of Havana that catered to wealthy clients.) Castro always bragged about putting the prostitutes out of business, as though he were protecting the purity of Cuban womanhood, but the fact was that he had imprisoned prostitutes by the thousands because they were mini-capitalists, setting their own hours and prices and generally refusing to march to the Revolution's tune. And however you felt about prostitution as a profession, it was pretty difficult to see how Castro was "protecting" these women by locking them in places like Guanajay.

Some of them were pitiful, some loathsome, and some were an unsettling mixture of both qualities. I could never quite pin down my feelings about their leader, a woman in her mid-twenties known as Machete after the weapon she had used to kill a man. I once overheard her tell another prisoner how, as a child, her parents always kicked her. One day, when she was about eight, they stopped. For a couple of days she wasn't kicked a single time. She couldn't eat, couldn't sleep, couldn't stop crying. Finally she started calling her mother names until the woman lashed out savagely with her foot. Machete went to bed happy again that night.

On the other hand, some of the common prisoners, with the way they spent every waking moment threatening and extorting anyone weaker, barely seemed to me to qualify as human beings. The cruelest of them was known as Sappho, a half Chinese, half mulatto woman of thirty-five or so, with a body of spectacular curves and a face bisected by a jagged scar. Her name was a reminder of her current sexual inclinations; the scar, of her courting customs. Day and night, she announced the sexual favors she intended to claim from the prisoners in the cells around her the first time the *llaveras* left the doors unlocked, and the murderous consequences for anyone who resisted. To be within earshot of her cell was like living next to a backed-up toilet; the stench seemed to work into your very pores.

Sex was the favorite conversational topic not just of the hopelessly twisted Sappho, but of all the common prisoners. To them, sex had always been something that was bought and sold, and in prison it was their common currency—they exchanged it with one another the way we did cigarettes.

In some ways, their casual promiscuity was the most startling thing of all to us. Among ourselves, we rarely even talked about sex for the simple reason that so few of us had any real experience with it. Most young unmarried Cuban women in those days were virgins—not because we were extraordinarily virtuous, but because Cuban men believed that the most important quality in a bride was an intact hymen. It was a lesson our mothers drummed into us from the time we were old enough to walk: "Keep your head cool, even when your body is hot." Most of us had, and the indiscriminate sexuality of the common prisoners was utterly alien— and, often, repellent—to the majority of the political prisoners. But, as we would soon discover, there were much worse things than promiscuity.

It was late on a chill, blustery night in late January when we heard the single *jaula* pull up outside the *tapiadas*. We knew something strange was going on right away; even in a steady drizzle, the *jaula* was driving without headlights. The few prisoners in cells with windows offering a clear vantage point on the *tapiadas* peered out into the rain, but some of the prison's security lights were out, and they couldn't see anything. We heard the gate to the *tapiadas* open, and then a cell door; each, in turn, was closed again. The *jaula* left, its headlights still dimmed.

"What do you think that was all about?" Gladys asked me from her cell.

"I think they brought a new prisoner into the lower *tapiadas*," I replied.

"Well," mused Gladys, "if it was a common prisoner, it's the first time I've ever seen one transferred who wasn't kicking and screaming and biting and clawing and yelling about the guards' mothers."

A few political prisoners called down the corridor into the *tapiadas*, asking what had happened, but there was no reply. After a while, we gave up and went to bed. The mystery could wait until morning.

It was an hour later when the screams began. "Get your hands off of me!" a high, girlish voice squealed. "Don't touch me! Don't touch me!"

"What's going on?" I called, clutching the bars of my cell door, pressing my face against them in a futile effort to look down the corridor. "Who is that screaming?"

"It's coming from the *tapiadas*," Gladys answered. "I think it's from the far end, where Sappho's cell is."

"Let me go!" the voice screamed again, thin with terror. "No, no, let me go!"

Our end of the corridor was filled with shouts of confusion and alarm. "What are you doing down there?" Beba shouted. "Leave that girl alone, whoever she is." Other women were yelling from their cell windows, trying to get the attention of the guards in the guntowers on the prison perimeter.

There was the sound of a scuffle from the *tapiadas*, and then a shriek of pain. "Oh, God! Oh, Jesus, help me! They're raping me! Oh, mommmy, mommy!"

"Stop it! Stop it! Stop it!" Gladys screamed. Up and down the corridor, women were pounding things on cell bars and shouting threats. But the only reply was the girl's piercing sobs.

Frantically I ran to my window, intending to shout onto the patio. But I froze. Right outside was Leyda Dumpierre, strolling along with an umbrella as if she were walking in the park on a sunny day, instead of in a prison in the middle of a midnight rainstorm.

"Leyda," I gasped, "they've got a girl down in the *tapiadas*, and they're raping her. Go get her out of there!"

Leyda, toying with the giant ring of keys on her hip, gave me a wide, cynical smile. "Why, Ana, how sentimental you are!" she purred. "I would never have guessed."

"Leyda," I pled, "it's not even one of us. It's a *little girl*. I'm begging you, don't let this happen."

Slowly and deliberately, she turned her back and walked away. It was another half hour before the screams from the *tapiada* ceased.

By the next morning, we had much of the story. The victim was a thirteen-year-old girl from the Casa de Beneficiencia, a well-known Catholic orphanage in Havana that the government had seized after the Revolution. The "crime" that resulted in her confinement among the most vicious, predatory female criminals on the island was breaking a blackboard and a desk to protest an anti-Catholic lecture by the orphanage's new political commissar. (Among other things, he said the nuns who had raised the girl from infancy had intended to sell her into prostitution.) They put her in a cell with Sappho and three other women, who took turns holding her down and raping her. Afterward, they stole her soap, toothpaste, toilet paper, sheets, and mattress.

The darkened *jaula* arrived at the *tapiadas* again that night. Once again we heard a cell door open and close. This time we didn't go to bed; we waited, in fear and resignation. It was only a few minutes until the screams started, and they went on much longer, until just before dawn.

My fears were correct. A few days after the rapes, a Ministry official visited D Pavilion to discuss, once again, the subject of forced labor. What was the big deal about it? he asked. The male political prisoners had accepted it without a fuss eighteen months ago. Why were we so stubborn? Well, we would have to make our own decisions, but if we continued to be uncooperative the Ministry would have to . . . take steps. He left it at that. The next day, four political prisoners were transferred down to the lower *tapiadas* and placed, one per cell, in among the common criminals. The transfers were reversed three hours later with the explanation that a mistake had been made, but there was no mistake, just a message: Go to work, or fight for your lives, not in a group, but one at a time.

They had suspended all our privileges and were keeping us locked up twenty-four hours a day, bringing our meals to us in our cells. The real purpose, I suspected, was to keep us from meeting in a group to formulate a plan. It was impossible to have any intelligent discussion, much less reach a consensus, when we had to shout up and down the corridor. From the little snippets of conversation I could overhear from my cell, I knew most of the women were weakening.

I was, too. The screams of those girls echoed in my dreams every night. I could defend myself well enough in a single fight, or even several fights, I thought. But what if they put me in a cell with Sappho and her three cronies? What would happen the first time I went to sleep? And what about all the other political prisoners who wouldn't last even that long, who would be beaten senseless and raped within hours?

The prison authorities waited and watched. Near the end of June, they ordered the first three women (Marta Santanach, Nieves Abreu, and Felicia Olivia, none of them with a reputation for toughness) from D Pavilion to forced labor. It was an experiment, to see what we would do.

We did nothing.

Two weeks later, they ordered the rest of us to start tilling the fields behind the prison offices.

Our motto in D Pavilion had always been "Beaten, But Never Defeated." The guards could physically overwhelm us when they felt like paying the price, but we never willingly did anything that we thought compromised our rights as political prisoners or our dignity as human beings—until we agreed to forced labor. To work as slaves, to shore up that malicious and parasitic Revolution in even the tiniest way, was a total humiliation. The night before we started work was the quietest since I entered prison. We lay silently in our cells, desperate and depressed.

Four or five women had refused to accept forced labor. They were quickly packed off to the *tapiadas*. Xiomara Argüelles, who had less than a month of her sentence left, came up with a creative but painful solution that kept her out of the fields without giving them any excuse to extend her prison time. With a sharp blow against her cell door, she broke two bones in her right arm. "I fell out of bed," she explained to the *llaveras* who came running to see what we were yelling about.

But for the rest of us there was no escape. Bitterly and silently, we trooped down to the prison offices for a count, then walked half a mile or so out of the residential compound to the empty fields that lay alongside the perimeter fence. I hung my head the whole way, unable to look any of the other prisoners in their eyes. When we reached the field, they assigned each of us a garden plot, perhaps twenty-five yards wide and about the length of a city block. Our job was to weed it and water it once a day.

The first few days were mostly a blank to me. Aside from the overwhelming shame that drove practically every thought from my head, I was physically wasted. The broiling July sun, after four months locked inside my cell, threatened to cremate me on my feet. And the unfamiliar weight of the hoe blistered my hands and stretched the muscles in my shoulders until I thought they would tear.

We labored from eight A.M. until noon, paused to eat a bowl of *harina*, and then swung our hoes again until four-thirty, when we staggered back to the pavilion to collapse, comatose, until morning, when the cycle began again.

Various chunks of my plot were planted in carrots, radishes, pumpkins, and onions. But there was one small section with nothing at all. Sometime during the second week in the fields I approached one of the *llaveras*. "Why don't you let me plant some carrots of my own in that vacant area?" I asked. "It's just going to waste. And you know I could work better if I had something to eat besides a cold bowl of *harina*."

Ordinarily a *llavera* would have rejected any request like this out of hand. Why agree to anything that would give us the slightest comfort? But out here in the fields, the equation had subtly changed. There were forty prisoners, each carrying a hoe, and only five *llaveras*. There was no way we could stage a successful revolt—the guards in their impregnable towers would pick us off one by one with their rifles—but we could easily slaughter the unarmed *llaveras* if we felt sufficiently suicidal. I had made the point, none too subtly, a few days earlier when I was sharpening my hoe against a grindstone in the prison toolshed. "Hey, you shouldn't sharpen both sides," a *llavera* said. "That's not how you do it." I grinned at her coldly. "It is if you're planning to chop off a head," I explained. She moved quickly away.

So a sort of peaceful coexistence had evolved. The *llaveras* allowed us to take frequent breaks, including unescorted trips to the nearby warehouses and toolsheds to get water, and we did our work without giving them a hard time. By the end of the first week they barely supervised us at all, sticking to the shade near the prison wall where they could bitch among themselves about a duty that they found nearly as unpleasant as we did.

So when I asked about raising my own vegetables, the *llavera* merely shrugged. "Don't let it keep you from your job," she instructed me, "and don't shoot off your mouth about it to anyone from the Ministry." I nodded, and she walked away. I spent most of that afternoon digging up small carrots from the prison plot and transplanting them to my little patch. A few days later, they were big enough to eat. "You certainly have a green thumb," the *llavera* said as I munched on one. "I've never seen carrots grow so fast."

My theft of the carrots was the first act of what became a gargantuan war of sabotage against the prison's agriculture program. Still too mortified by our surrender on forced labor to talk much, nearly all of us began small private acts of resistance on our own. As we gloated over our little successes—chopping leaves from onions and cabbages to flavor our evening rice, swiping small beets and potatoes to eat late at night—we began confiding in one another again. Soon isolated acts of economic warfare intensified into a blitzkrieg of piracy and vandalism.

From sneaking a potato or two in our pockets, we escalated to stealing such quantities of vegetables that they had to be loaded into makeshift baskets fashioned from our hats. The women in D Upper lowered a rope to retrieve the baskets, emptied them, and returned them to us; then we could walk through the checkpoint at the compound gate at the end of the day without fear of a search.

One day we discovered the warehouse where most of the prison food was stored. It doubled as a repair shop for prison machinery, and the repairmen usually left it unlocked during the day as they lugged equipment back and forth. María Antonieta López—the woman who planned the second escape from Guanabacoa, but was recaptured a few months later—worked a plot of land that had a clear view of the warehouse. If she took her hat off, it was a signal that the coast was clear.

Three or four of us would take a water break and slip inside. Punching holes in the backs of cartons at random, we would take whatever we found—canned Russian mystery meat, milk, sugar, soap, bedsheets. Then we moved the gutted cartons to the back of the stacks. When the theft was eventually discovered, we were confident it would be chalked up to the guards, who were as hungry as everyone else in Cuba.

We slipped much of the booty through holes in the chain-link fence near D Pavilion, where other prisoners retrieved it and moved it inside. The rest we took back to the field, where we ate it if we could, and destroyed it if we couldn't.

We probably buried more food than we ate. In some distant future, archaeologists are going to dig around Guanajay and wonder what strange religious beliefs prompted Cubans of the mid–twentieth century to entomb vast quantities of canned Russian meat (which will probably be no less edible when they find it than it was when we buried it). I also buried most of my onion crop rather than let the prison harvest it. I spent an entire day digging a hole three feet deep and then dumping thousands of plump, firm onions into it. I was tentative at first—there was a guard watching me from one of the towers—but when he didn't complain I grew bolder and picked virtually every onion on the entire plot. Evidently some of the guards had their own disenchantments with the Revolution.

My most flagrant act of sabotage involved a pumpkin field near my plot. I came out to work one day and saw one of the prison foremen maneuvering a small tractor into position near the pumpkins.

"What are you doing there?" I asked.

"Getting ready to harvest them," he replied. "It's about time."

"Okay, you can have the half at the back," I said, gesturing to the far end of the pumpkin patch. "We'll take this half."

"What the hell are you talking about?" he said, confused. "Who told you that half of them were yours?"

"That's Communism, comrade," I explained patiently. "The workers own the fruits of their labor. Haven't you been listening in those classes they send you to?"

"But none of you prisoners worked on these pumpkins," he protested. "All the work was done before you started."

"This is our garbage dump they're planted on," I replied earnestly. "We produced every ounce of garbage that fertilized these pumpkins. So we're entitled to a share."

The foreman eyed me for a moment or two. "You're full of shit," he decided.

"If that's your attitude, you're not getting a goddamn thing from this field," I barked. Swinging my hoe like an axe, I tore into the pumpkins, splitting them open like firewood. The foreman was so astonished that he couldn't speak as I rampaged through the field, leaving a trail of gutted husks behind me. When I was finished, I swung the hoe hard against the wooden cart on the back of his tractor, tearing a hole in the bottom. Panic-stricken, he turned the ignition key and rumbled away as I brandished the hoe over my head.

Much of the mayhem we committed during forced labor was co-ordinated by a prisoner named Miriam Ortega, who often drew the task of carrying pitchers of lukewarm sugar water (the prison's idea of re-freshments) around the fields as we worked. Her flaming red hair shim-mering in the fierce sunlight, Miriam trekked back and forth across the sprawling fields, relaying messages and word of new schemes as she de-livered water.

Miriam had been transferred into D Pavilion about a year and half earlier after slapping a *llavera* without any apparent provocation. "I did it because it was boring over there in C Pavilion," she explained. "I wanted to come over here, where all the trouble is."

Despite the amount of time she had been among us, I had never had a chance to talk to her before. Miriam was always getting thrown in the *tapiadas*, locked up, or beat up. Although she was tiny—probably no more than eighty pounds—and not especially strong, Miriam was constantly getting into fights with guards and *llaveras*. The fact that they invariably beat the hell out of her (in one encounter with the guards, her right kidney was knocked a good six inches out of place, until it rested on her uterus) never deterred her in the slightest.

As I learned more about her during her visits with the sugar water, I was even more impressed. When she was first arrested, she managed to escape from State Security headquarters (the only person I ever heard of doing that) and fled to the Oriente Mountains, where she joined a guerrilla unit—one of just a handful of women to do so. She was eventually captured again and endured all kinds of torture, including beatings, fake executions, and being locked up in a mental ward. But she never gave up her secret, that the American CIA had trained her to use a scrambled radio transmitter to guide in aerial drops of weapons. No wonder she found C Pavilion dull.

*　　*　　*

It was during forced labor that our relations with the re-educated prisoners finally began to thaw. Without any formal truce—in fact, without any discussion at all—they began aiding us in our campaign of sabotage and theft.

The biggest help came from the re-educated prisoners who worked in the prison kitchen. Once or twice a week, a big load of potatoes was delivered to the rear entrance of the kitchen, which was near the same warehouse that we regularly looted. The potatoes usually sat there for several hours before the kitchen workers got around to bringing them inside.

As soon as the potatoes were delivered, the re-educated prisoners would signal María Antonieta from a side window. She in turn signaled us with her hat, and several of us would take a water break. We stuffed as many potatoes as we could into our blouses and pants and carried them back to the field to be smuggled or buried as circumstances permitted.

It was another re-educated prisoner in the kitchen who helped us with our most satisfying caper of all. She passed the word to María Antonieta whenever the top prison officials were scheduled to have steak for dinner. We took the meat from the warehouse and passed it through a hole in the fence. Not only did we get great dinners—for me, it was the first meat in three and a half years—but we touched off a terrible inquisition against the guards, who were the chief suspects in the theft.

Not every re-educated prisoner directly aided our sabotage. But many did, and many others could have ratted on us to the guards, and didn't. Their kindness in the face of our long-running hostility caused us to start rethinking our attitude. By now, a number of women had deserted our ranks for re-education, and we knew that their decision was usually prompted by difficult family circumstances rather than political revisionism. And, of course, we too had compromised with the authorities when we consented to forced labor rather than face transfers into the cells of the common criminals. It made us view the re-educated prisoners in a different light.

In the end, though, I wasn't certain that forced labor was a defeat. We stole so much food that I actually gained fifteen pounds. I had a new wardrobe of clothing fashioned from pilfered bedsheets. And I went to sleep each night content, knowing that I had ruined or purloined ten times as much as I produced. Finally the Revolution had instilled in me a work ethic. I actually woke up each morning smiling, eager to get the day's destruction and chaos under way.

Who ultimately won the battle of forced labor? That's hard to say. But I know this: The prison cried uncle. After about a year, without explanation, prison officials canceled the program. And they never tried to make us work again.

"Ladies! Ladies! Come on in here! I want to see all of you!" The voice made the book slip from my hands and tumble to the dining room floor, and I almost tipped over my chair. We hadn't seen him in more than a year, hadn't heard his whinnying laugh or seen his twitchy gait, but there was no mistaking that voice. Manolo was back.

Not since he jumped out of his car in front of the *tapiadas* fourteen months ago, his face bleeding and his clothes soaked with urine, had we laid eyes on Manolo. The *llaveras* wouldn't talk about him—went silent at the mere mention of his name—and we hadn't been able to find out a thing. Not even my friend Ilia Herrera, whose grandmother was vaguely related to Manolo's grandmother, though her family had asked plenty of questions. Opinion was mixed in the pavilion; some thought the final, slender thread of his sanity had broken, others suspected he had fallen to one of the Revolution's mysterious internal purges that sometimes sucked away officials without a trace.

But now he was here again, on a lazy Sunday afternoon in February, bellowing for us to come see him. He wasn't wearing his customary olive green fatigues, but fashionably cut gray slacks with a white dress shirt. Though still thin, he no longer looked like an animated collection of bones; wherever he had been, he had gained a few pounds. His hair was neatly trimmed and as I moved closer I could sniff a trace of cologne.

"Ladies! Come on! It's me! I want to see all of you!" he bellowed again, smiling like a happy papa home from the war. Behind him I could see Gilberto Ramos, the prison director, cringing in the doorway, tortured uncertainty all over his face. It looked like he hadn't expected this visit any more than we had.

Perhaps thirty or forty women had streamed into the room in varying degrees of perplexity. I could see some sneaking down the corridor in the opposite direction; Manolo's visits had often been the harbinger of unpleasant news, and for some women, prudence outweighed curiosity.

When most of the women were seated, Manolo turned to Ramos. "You can go back to the office now, Gilberto," he said firmly. "I'm here to see them, not you." He smiled at us again. "We're friends, despite everything I've done to them." Ramos hesitated, and Manolo's face twisted into an angry grimace. "Didn't you hear what I said?" he snapped. Then he inhaled sharply, composing himself. "Really, it's okay," he said more gently. "We'll be all right here."

Ramos, glancing back at us apprehensively, walked away from the door. Manolo waited a few moments, then nodded at me. "Ana, go to the window and make sure he's gone," he said. His voice was friendly, but with a note of urgency, as if he knew his time was short. "Ramos is gone," I reported, and Manolo relaxed, leaning against a table.

"Well, you probably wondered where I've been," he said. "Well, I went crazy, completely crazy." He paused, and I wondered if he expected us to exclaim, "Oh, no, Manolo, not you." If so, he was disappointed. After a moment's silence, he continued. "They put me in a psychiatric hospital. I've stayed there a long time, but finally they've let me out." He giggled. "They gave me a pass, and they told me I could go anywhere I wanted, anywhere at all, except here. They told me you were the ones who drove me crazy. They told me you were my enemies. But that's not true. I knew you would be happy to see me.

"You know," he continued conversationally, "I haven't been able to go to bed with a woman for a long time, because the only ones I wanted were in here. I could have women in the street—I'm an important man, you know there are plenty who would go to bed with me—but they're all shit. I want brave women. I want women like you."

We didn't even try to hide our amazement as we exchanged glances. If there was any doubt of Manolo's madness, he was resolving it with this speech. If any of it ever got back to the authorities, Manolo would be lucky to get off with a straitjacket. The *paredón* was the regime's cure for this kind of mental illness.

"No matter what I did to make you scared of me, you always made fun of me," he continued. "I remember all the times I came to the pavilion and you whispered, 'Nazi, Nazi,' as soon as I turned my back. I haven't been able to break you, and that's what I like about you—*no one* can break you. I told the doctors all the things I had done to you to make you give in, and how you just kept defying me. They said, 'Don't feel guilty, it was your job.' I said, 'Doctors, the problem is not that I feel guilty. The problem is that, locked up in this hospital, I can't see them.'"

He paused again, his expression one of a little boy seeking approval. Perhaps he mistook the incredulity on our faces for appreciation, because he smiled again. He looked at Gladys Chinea, who had always been one of his favorites, and asked his old question: "Gladys, if all of this disappeared, and the prison were gone, and we met each other in the street, would you go dancing with me?"

Gladys, speechless, could only stare at him. He turned to Mary Habach. "Mary, what about you? If we met in the street, would you go dancing with me?" She, too, was mute. He looked over to Vivian de Castro. "Vivian, would you go dancing with me?"

"Go to hell, Manolo," she sputtered. Manolo sighed. "See, I've ruined everything," he said sadly. "None of you would ever go dancing with me, would you? Not even out of pity." He sighed again. Then he brightened.

"Well, at least I can give you some presents," he said. "But we have to do it now. They're probably phoning around the Ministry right now, trying to find out what's going on. But if we do it quickly, by the time they find out I'm not Director of Prisons anymore, it will be too late." He looked again to Gladys Chinea. "Gladys, give me a list. Anything you want, anything at all."

Gladys, flustered, tried to think. "Well . . . soap, we could use soap. One bar each would be sixty bars."

"What, are you crazy?" Manolo snapped. "One bar each? I just told you—we can never do this again. *Three* bars each. And ask for mops, too. This place could use a cleaning."

Gladys, despite herself, broke into a smile. Manolo beamed. "See?" he bragged to us. "I've made her happy at last."

That broke the dam. Women all over the dining room called out suggestions: toothpaste, toilet paper, lightbulbs, all the little things that, to us, were large. Gladys made a long list and handed it to Manolo, who went to the door and beckoned a lurking *llavera*.

"Go get all these supplies at once," he ordered in his sternest to-the-*tapiadas* voice.

The *llavera* eyed the list doubtfully. "Well, it will take me about an hour," she said.

"An hour, nothing," Manolo barked. "I want it here in ten minutes, or you'll be in shit up to your eyebrows. Do you understand me? Get as many other *llaveras* to help as you have to, but just *do it*."

The *llavera* sprinted away. Manolo looked at his watch. Exactly nine minutes later, a parade of heavily laden *llaveras* lined up outside the door. "Just leave it on the steps, and get out," Manolo called. He waited in the dining room while we retrieved everything.

When the last mop was safely inside, Manolo gave us a final smile, this one strangely soft. "I'd better go now," he said. "The Ministry is probably already on the way over here with a net." We were silent. In a movie, the prisoners probably would have kissed him on the cheek, or cheered, or at least called good-bye. But it wasn't a movie; all the things Manolo had done to us, the beatings and the *tapiadas*, were real.

Still, I had a strange, undefinable feeling in my chest as I watched him march across the patio toward the prison offices. I couldn't identify it, and didn't try, except for one small part: a certainty that we would never see Manolo Martínez again.

· TEN ·

Escape

I ONLY INTENDED to get a drink, but the water bursting from the faucet of
the large patio sink looked so cool and inviting that I stuck my entire head
underneath it. I closed my eyes, letting the water blast the sweat and grime
from my face. When I opened them, as I raised my head from the sink,
Gladys Cavadilla was standing there.

"You must be dead tired," she said sympathetically. "That was a lot
of work."

"If you thought it was so much work, then why'd you make me do
it?" I asked brusquely. Cavadilla could never stand to have anyone mad at
her, a most peculiar character trait for an Interior Ministry lieutenant. She
was always trying to have it both ways, wanting to be our friend as well as
our jailer. It irritated me.

"Come on, Ana," she sighed. "You know those bunkbeds had to be
moved into the *galera*, because the prisoners who are arriving tonight have
to have someplace to sleep. And you know the beds had to be stacked on
top of each other, otherwise they wouldn't fit in the *galera*."

"Cavadilla, it's not that I object to the work itself. But when the rest
of the prison is empty, why do you want to cram thirty-six women into a
little *galera* built for nine or ten? Look in that room," I said, waving in
exasperation at *Galera 6*. The bunkbeds looked like skyscrapers, stacked

in towers of six apiece that reached nearly to the ceiling. Even so, there was barely room to walk between them. "Half the women will go crazy from vertigo, and the other half from claustrophobia."

"Ana, you know we have limited facilities—"

"Ahhhhh, save it," I interrupted, my aggravation giving way to weariness. "I need a cigarette." And before she could answer, I had nimbly lifted a pack right out of her breast pocket.

"Hey, you want to go in with the common criminals as a thief?" she said, laughing and lighting a match for me. "You can have one, but give me back the rest—I'm on duty all night, and that's the only pack I've got."

"Cavadilla, the only way you can get these back is if you run into me in Havana tonight, because I'm going to escape rather than be stuffed into that *galera* like a sardine," I said mockingly.

She laughed again. "You're forgetting this is Guanabacoa," she said. "Nobody has *ever* escaped from here, not in a hundred years."

"There's always a first time," I said. Then I laughed, too.

"Keep the cigarettes," Cavadilla said, chuckling as she turned to go back to the offices. "Nicotine deprivation has excited your brain." I smiled at her as she walked away. My talk about an escape had been an empty boast. But as I studied the patio, I wondered. . . .

It had been a year since the collapse of the forced labor program, a year in which the Interior Ministry had steadily increased the pressure on us. First, the Ministry had engineered what was euphemistically called the Social Security law, which permitted the government to indefinitely extend the sentence of any prisoner considered "a danger to the construction of a socialist society." Among its first victims was Beba Canabal. A few weeks before her scheduled release in November 1966, she had been told that six months had been added to her sentence. She was abruptly transferred to a prison in a remote section of Pinar del Río province on the west side of the island. Several other women due for release got the same treatment.

The rest of us talked about staging some kind of protest, but before we could act, the Ministry moved again, transferring a number of prisoners to a prison farm southwest of Havana. (The farm, run like a military camp, was called América Libre, Free America; the Ministry's ironists, I thought, probably had to work overtime to come up with all these names.)

In an exquisitely cruel touch, one of the prisoners transferred to the farm was Sara del Toro de Odio, whose family had owned the farm and used it as a summer retreat before it was seized by the Revolution. The move backfired on the Ministry, though. Some of Sara's former employees still worked at América Libre as groundskeepers and custodians, and far from despising their old boss, as the Revolution's theology would have had it, they were fond of her. The guards had to work overtime to keep them from smuggling her food and other contraband.

Most of the rest of us had been transferred back to Guanabacoa, the first prison I went to after my arrest in 1961. There they divided 120 women among three *galeras* that were intended to hold perhaps a third of that number, and kept us locked up nearly all the time.

The result was something like those overcrowding experiments with rats that I had read about in college. Our bunks were stacked six-high; the woman in the top bed needed five minutes—and sure hands and feet— just to climb into her bunk. And if she had to go to the bathroom in the middle of the night, she woke up at least five women on the way down.

On the other hand, that was still more convenient than going during the daytime. In *Galera 1*, where I lived, there were sixty women vying for three toilets during daylight. (Competition for the single shower was even worse.) Everything—using the toilet, washing your face, brushing your teeth—had to be arranged in shifts, with the inevitable arguments about who was out of turn.

Privacy in the bathroom was impossible, even though the women on the back two rows of bunks, which towered directly over the toilets, lay with their backs turned at all times. The worst thing of all to me was the constant din, with sixty women engaged in shouted conversations across the room during every waking moment. I could barely hear myself think.

To make life more bearable, we squeezed the towers of bunks even closer together to create a small empty space at the back of the *galera*, and we organized games there. Lots of them involved wordplay—which team could think of more words beginning with the letter *C* in five minutes, for instance. Another popular one was musical chairs. (Since we had no record player, somebody would be designated to sing.) But our version had little resemblance to the version played at children's birthday parties. When the music stopped, bodies went flying in all directions as women warred for possession of the chairs.

In early May, forty-five women—including Gladys, Miriam, and Isabel Molgado, among others—were transferred back to Guanajay and put in a pavilion with common prisoners. When word got back to us about what was happening there, we were appalled. The common prisoners used the pavilion dining room for daily nude dances that ended in orgies, with chains of four or five women apiece having sex with one another.

The disapproval of the political prisoners, if anything, seemed to spur the common prisoners to an even more aggressive brand of sexual depravity. They began propositioning even the old and infirm among the political prisoners.

Esperanza Oliva was a political prisoner in her sixties with the sunniest disposition of any prisoner I ever met. Even in the worst of times, when we were being starved or beaten or both, Esperanza always had a smile and a kind word for everyone she encountered. Everybody called her Abuela, grandmother.

One morning Esperanza was walking down the corridor when someone summoned her from the gate of the dining room. She turned to see a pretty teenaged prostitute, known as La Melancólica for her sporadic fits of catatonic depression.

"Abuela, come over here," La Melancólica called. "I want to show you something."

"What is it, child?" Esperanza asked as she approached the gate. "Closer, closer," La Melancólica urged. When Esperanza pressed against the bars, peering through, La Melancólica ripped open her own shirt and thrust a breast toward the old lady. "Feel my tit!" she cried.

That incident nearly touched off a riot at Guanajay. And when we learned of it at Guanabacoa, we were enraged. The Ministry's strategy was obvious: divide us into small groups, then break us down a few at a time. We had to retaliate with some kind of protest—otherwise we'd be scattered all over the island, a few here and a few there.

But what kind of protest? Within my *galera* alone there was one group that wanted to start an immediate *toque de lata*, another that wanted to launch a hunger strike, and a third wanted to wait until our next scheduled visit and then refuse to return to our cells. The other two *galeras* were full of women with different theories. We could communicate with them in a rudimentary way through a form of sign language, flashing hand signals back and forth between our windows, but it was impossible to hold a full-scale discussion that way.

Eventually, through a series of misunderstandings and miscommunications, *Galera 8* concluded that we weren't going to do anything, and launched a *toque* on its own. *Galera 5* joined in. The logical thing would have been for my *galera* to put its differences aside and add our voices (well, our spoons and dinner plates) to the *toque* as well, but too many of the women felt slighted. Instead of joining in, we sat around in a collective snit.

Our inaction made me nutty with anger. How could we leave the women at Guanajay twisting in the wind like this? They had shared with us every beating, every sneered insult, every filthy night in the *tapiadas*. They were our *family*. And now, out of some idiotic schoolgirl sense of false pride, we were turning our backs on them the same way that the rest of Cuba had turned its backs on us.

I pled, I cajoled, I argued with the other women. And when nothing worked, I decided to take things into my own hands. In the middle of the afternoon I walked to the gate at the front of the *galera* and called to a passing *llavera*. "Hey, asshole," I screamed. "Yeah, you, fatso, the one waddling around like a baby elephant. I just wanted to tell you—I shit on your mother."

I kept at it for hours, screaming mindless obscenities and insults at anyone who passed. Nothing I said was even slightly witty, and it certainly wasn't political. All I wanted to do was provoke a fight. I figured nothing would restore solidarity among us like the sight of the guards bursting through the gate swinging clubs. Besides that, I wanted a good excuse to hit someone in the mouth. I was sick of standing in lines for toilets, sick of bumping into somebody every time I turned around, sick of saying "excuse me" six times whenever I had to get out of bed, sick of the round-the-clock cacophony of sixty voices. I wanted to beat the shit out of someone.

But the prison authorities saw through it. They sensed that we were badly divided, and they pounced. One group of women was transferred to the América Libre prison farm, another to Guanabacoa's new *tapiadas*, and a third locked inside a *galera* on the other side of the prison. Through every announcement and transfer I stuck to my post at the gate, screaming crude insults like a foul-mouthed parrot, but not a single guard or *llavera* replied.

As the last group of women was led away, I looked around. The *galera* was empty. "That's right," jeered a *llavera*. "You're alone, and you're staying alone. Go ahead, yell at the mice if you want. We won't hear you." And she walked off.

I waited at the gate for a few minutes to see if there was a mistake. But no one came back. After a while, I walked back inside and flopped on the nearest bed. Holding my breath, I listened. It was quiet as a tomb. For the first time in days, I smiled.

The next day I wet down the *galera* floor and then slid all the stacked-up bunks to one side. That left me with a big empty space for—what? I decided to start exercising. All the muscles I had built up during the year of forced labor had gone slack during the months locked inside the crowded *galera* with no opportunity for exercise. This was a good time to get back in shape. For hours each day I did sit-ups, push-ups, and jumping jacks. To keep my vocal chords from withering away, I set aside an hour to sing, belting out hymns, show tunes, cabaret ballads, anything I could remember. Three times a day, a silent *llavera* delivered a plate of food; otherwise I saw no one.

It was on the fifth day of my isolation that a guard came to make a repair on the roof near my *galera*. He was there for a couple of hours, bustling around with different tools, and when he departed I saw that he had left behind a rope, forgotten in a nearby corner of the patio.

The next morning I washed all my clothing in the *galera* sink. "Look at all this stuff, it's not drying in here," I told the *llavera* who brought my lunch. "Can I leave it out on the patio? When you come back with my dinner, let me out for a minute and I can pick it up." She looked at me warily for a minute before agreeing. I spread the wet garments around on the flagstones of the patio, smiled at the *llavera*, and went back inside. That evening, when she let me out to retrieve it, I picked up the rope, too, hiding it underneath the pile of clothing.

The rope set off vague fantasies of escape, but mostly it was just a toy, something to vary my exercise routine. Using the bunks, I climbed to the window in the back of the *galera*, a good thirty feet off the floor. I tied the rope to one of the bars, let the other end tumble to the floor, and went back down. Then I practiced climbing up the wall with the rope. It was very difficult at first, and my knees took a hammering every time my feet slipped and I banged into the wall. But after a few days I was pretty good at it.

For six weeks I exercised, practiced with my rope, and drove the mice from the *galera* with my singing. On June 28, they told me my "punishment" was over; the next day I would move over to *Galera 6* and help assemble beds for the other women, who would arrive late in the afternoon. That night I wound the rope around my waist under my blouse, preparing for the transfer, and wondered what it would be like to have company again.

The next day, as I saw the way they planned to cram us into the *galera*, I knew exactly what it would be like: back in the rat overpopulation experiment. All day long, as I labored putting up the bunkbeds, my anger grew.

Now, as I smoked one of the cigarettes I pinched from Cavadilla's pocket, I assembled a blueprint of Guanabacoa in my mind.

To get out of the prison would require three separate escapes. First I would have to get out of the *galera*, which would be chained and padlocked after the evening count. Then I would have to get out of the main compound, presumably by climbing up onto the thirty-five-foot-tall roof atop the *galeras* and then lowering myself to the other side. And finally there was the perimeter wall, twenty feet tall and studded with four guntowers.

Because there was no way to study the perimeter wall from inside the compound, I decided not to worry about it until I reached it. I already had an idea about how to get out of the *galera*. And the rope underneath my blouse would enable me to climb down from the *galera* roof. That just left one obstacle—how to climb up onto that roof.

The first step was obvious enough. Around the interior of the patio was a small awning-type roof, two or three feet wide, designed to keep rain from blowing through the glassless windows of the *galeras*. It was only about eight feet off the ground; I was confident I could jump, grab hold of it, and lift myself atop.

But that still left me about twenty-two feet short of the main roof. *There's got to be a way,* I thought. *I just need to think.* Idly I gazed around the patio and noticed one remaining bunkbed, stacked two-high, that we hadn't been able to fit inside the *galera*. Casually I walked over and climbed up to the second bunk, pretending to inspect the frame while I actually looked over at the small awning roof.

I froze. There, folded and lying flat on the awning roof, invisible from the ground, was a ladder. *Somebody must have forgotten it the last time they whitewashed the walls,* I realized. It was a big one, probably twenty feet long.

My heart pounding, I forced myself to look away. Then, locking a bored expression on my face, I climbed back down from the bed. My idle crack about escape was on the verge of turning into a reality, if I could just accomplish one thing.

Cavadilla, to show us how bighearted she was, had told the *llaveras* to open up *Galera 7* so there would be twice as many showers available for the prisoners arriving from the transfer. Now I wandered in there to confirm my memory. Sure enough, the interior wall it shared with *Galera 6* (where we were going to be confined) did not go all the way to the ceiling—there was an open space of two feet or so at the top. At one time, it appeared to me, the two *galeras* had been one large room, and the prison authorities had split it in two with this makeshift wall.

I walked back onto the patio. It was nearly time for the evening count, and a pair of *llaveras* were starting to check the locks on all the doors. I waited until they rigged the chain on the door of *Galera 7*.

"Yeah, yeah, lock doors," I bellowed. "That's what you're really good at, isn't it? All that stuff about the Revolution serving the people, that's bullshit. You're just in charge of locking things. Why don't you just put a wall around the whole island and then lock the door? That would solve everything."

"What are you talking about, Ana?" asked Marta Goodrich nervously. The *llaveras* were always uneasy when we got belligerent. They knew how easily things could escalate.

"I'm talking about the fact that I don't even have a fucking pair of tennis shoes," I shouted. "I've asked and asked and asked, and you still make me go around barefoot. How can you keep women prisoners when you can't even supply them with shoes? Why don't you do something productive instead of running around acting like Nazi prison-camp guards all the time?"

"Damn, I forgot to bring the list for the count," Marta said, smacking her thigh. "I'll be right back." She hurried toward the safety of the offices, leaving the other *llavera*, the slow-witted Ildelina, to fend for herself.

"Well?" I shouted. "What are you going to do about my shoes, damn it?" Ildelina's broad face clouded, then brightened. "I know, Ana," she replied. "I'll go look in the office. Maybe I can find you a pair." She lumbered off, looking relieved. I waited until she was nearly across the patio. Then I closed the padlock on *Galera 7* without snapping it shut. It looked as though it were locked, but anyone could pop it open with a flick of a wrist.

I spent a tense half hour waiting for the count to begin. When the two *llaveras* returned they watched me uncertainly, waiting to see if I was about to turn loony again. *Let them wonder,* I thought, keeping a poker face.

"Line up for the count!" Marta shouted. As we shuffled into formation, she turned to Ildelina. "Did you finish locking up while I was in the office?" she asked.

"Of course," Ildelina—whose long-term memory, I suspected, was about ten minutes at the best of times—replied. "But I'll double-check." She started toward *Galera 7,* and I jumped out of my line.

"Hey! Hey! Where the fuck are my tennis shoes?" I screamed, waving my arms like windmills. Ildelina stopped and took a step or two back. "Tennis shoes," she repeated queasily.

"Yeah, my tennis shoes, you Nazi idiot! You told me you were going to get me some tennis shoes."

"Now, Ana," intervened Marta nervously. Even some of the other prisoners shot me strange looks. But I hurtled on. "You *promised* me! What do you think I am, stupid? Do you think I can't remember anything for five minutes? Where are they?"

Ildelina's brow furrowed as she labored mightily to construct a lie. "The shoes . . . They didn't have any in your size! That's right! They didn't have any in your size." She smiled in relief.

"Oh yeah?" I demanded. "Well, what *is* my size?"

"They don't have any shoes in any size, Ana," Marta interceded. "Now get back in line. Ildelina, help me get this damn count over with or we'll be here all night." The two of them started counting off prisoners. When they herded us into *Galera 6* for the night, *Galera 7*'s lock was still untested.

Inside, I lay on my bunk, waiting for darkness to fall, while I reviewed my plan: I would climb up to the gap in the wall that separated us from *Galera 7* and slip over to the other side. Then I would open the unlatched lock on the door and go out to the patio. There I would climb onto the low awning roof, prop up the ladder I had seen there, and climb to the main roof. I would lower myself from the roof with the rope hidden under my blouse. And then I would try to think of a way to get over the perimeter wall.

The *galera* was quiet that night. Everyone was tired from the transfer, and depressed about our new overcrowded quarters. After dinner, most of the women just lay around on their bunks, some of them in soft conversation with their neighbors. I kept to myself; I didn't want to tell anyone what I was going to do until the last minute—I didn't want anyone to start worrying what punishment the *galera* might suffer from the prison authorities in retaliation for an escape attempt.

About nine P.M. I got down from my bunk and walked to the bathroom, which was located along the common wall with *Galera 7*. I stepped onto one of the toilets, pulled myself to the top of the stall partition, and from there climbed onto the wall itself and looked through the gap. I saw that I would be able to climb down the other side in the same manner.

I turned my face back toward *Galera 6*. A few women were already watching me curiously. "Excuse me," I said loudly. "I have an announcement." Now every pair of eyes in the room was locked on me.

"I'm going to try to escape tonight," I said calmly. "I'm going to climb over this wall to *Galera 7*, where I'm pretty sure the lock is open. But after that I'm not counting on any help from anybody or anything. You know the odds are stacked against me. But if any of you would like to come along, you're welcome to join me." I didn't mention the rope or the ladder—if it turned out that *Galera 7* was indeed locked, I wanted all my tools still in place to try again some other time.

"I'm going with you," said Margarita Blanco promptly. "Put me on the list, too," added Ada Castellanos. I nodded, and waited for a moment to see if anyone else would speak. But the room was silent. I started back down the wall to make my final preparations.

"Does anybody have any jeans they can loan me?" I asked when I reached the floor. I gestured at my own pair, so tattered and shabby that even a wino would have turned away from them.

"I've got an extra pair," said Clara González, rummaging around in the duffel bag at the end of her bunk. She pulled out a pair that were nearly new, the denim still a rich blue. "Consider them a going-away gift."

I felt a twinge in my heart. Clara had three more years to serve, and she suspected the Ministry was already planning to extend her sentence under the new Social Security law. "Why don't you come with us?" I asked softly. "I have a good feeling about this." Clara shook her head. "I can't," she said, a mist in her eyes. "My father is so sick—this is no time for me to go into hiding." Then she smiled. "And besides, I don't want to sleep in the *tapiadas* tonight, which is where you're going to wind up."

Several women walked over to wish us well. The hardest moment was with Carmelina Casanova, an elderly prisoner who often talked of her fear of dying in prison. There was an infinite sadness in her eyes as she clasped my hand. I knew she wanted to go, and she knew she was too frail to try. Neither of us spoke.

Back up the bathroom partition I climbed. At the top I straddled the wall, letting first Ada and then Margarita use my legs to help themselves up and over. As I slipped over the wall, thirty-three drawn, silent faces watched me go.

The other two were standing silently in the darkness of *Galera 7*, waiting for my lead. I crept over and reached through the bars to the padlock on the door. With a single tug, it popped open. "Just a second," I whispered, quickly unbuttoning my blouse to unwind the rope wrapped around my waist. If either Ada or Margarita were startled, they didn't betray it.

It hadn't surprised me a bit that Margarita wanted to join me. Not only were we old friends—we had studied medicine together—but I also knew that no woman hated prison more than she did. It was all part of her complex, love-hate relationship with the Revolution.

Margarita and her brother had been raised, with little company but each other, by elderly parents on a remote farm in Villa Clara province in central Cuba. Both children came to Havana for college, where they shared an apartment and a disdain for Batista. But after Castro came to power, their paths diverged. Margarita turned against the Revolution, while her brother continued to support it. Even then their attachment for one another was so strong that they continued to live together until her arrest.

The confusion between Margarita's feelings for the Revolution and for her brother had never been sorted out; her soul was at war with itself. I could see it all the time when we talked about politics. Even after six years in prison—six years of experiencing the Revolution's cruelty up close and undiluted—she still thought that it had merely made a wrong turn, that some part of it could be saved. That was why prison was even more painful for her than for the rest of us; it was a perpetual reminder that the Revolution was fundamentally barbaric, and that her brother had gone down the wrong road.

So I had expected Margarita to join any escape attempt, even an ill-prepared one. Ada Castellanos was another matter. Chonchi, as we called her (she got the nickname, "Piglet," for her chubby appearance when she arrived in prison, although the prison diet had long since reduced her to skin and bones), was never predictable. She had a dizzy quality that was as endearing as it was exasperating.

If Chonchi was going to do laundry, you could always be sure she would offer to wash your things along with hers. But you could never be sure they would come back—likely as not, she'd give them away to somebody else on her way back to the cell. Nobody in the prison was more generous, or more social. All day long Chonchi was making tea, sharing chatter, showing newcomers the ropes. (Although, garrulous as she was, I noticed she almost never said anything about her family. There seemed to be some secret lurking there.)

Her unruly red hair, ruddy cheeks, and girlish freckles made Chonchi, who was about forty, look ten years younger. And along with her naive, slightly distracted air, they combined to offer the impression to some people that she was a bit on the dim side. Nothing could have been further from the truth. Her slightly screwball demeanor masked an observant eye and a shrewd mind.

The coiled rope in my hand, I inclined my head toward the door. They slipped out ahead of me, then waited while I put the chain back in place. Then I replaced the lock—and snapped it firmly closed. I had just burned all our bridges behind us.

The first thing I noticed outside the *galera* was that the extra bunkbed had been left on the patio. And in a real stroke of luck, it was close enough to the awning roof that we could use the bed as a stepladder. I gestured that we should crawl toward it; moments later, we climbed silently onto the awning roof.

In the darkness, the ladder was nearly invisible until we were right on top of it. When I lifted it into place, it easily reached the upper roof, and in a matter of seconds we were on top of the *galera*.

That was when I heard the drums. The sound was faint, but gathering volume. I recognized the primitive, compelling rhythm of a Santería rite. Scanning the horizon, I quickly spotted the source; though the neighborhood near the prison was mostly dark, the windows of a single house about one hundred yards away were brightly lit. Through them I could clearly see a crowd of dancers performing stylized, ritualistic steps as half a dozen men hammered away on large drums. This was the night that Santeros honored Ogun, their warrior god.

Santería is an ancient African religion that came to Cuba with the slaves the Spanish brought to work the sugar fields, and it is still the religion of the majority of Cuban blacks. Most people from the poor neighborhood around the prison were probably attending the ceremony, and those who weren't were locked inside their houses with the lights off to avoid attracting any wandering spirits stirred up by the ritual. The vague outlines of a plan began to take shape in my mind.

"What are we going to do now?" Chonchi whispered, the first words any of us had spoken since leaving the *galera*. "I've got an idea," I replied, "but give me a minute to think it through. Why don't you just enjoy the stars for a moment? How long has it been since you were outside under the night sky?" Margarita's deep black eyes, always so expressive, revealed a hint of skepticism—*This is not a tourist excursion,* they seemed to say— but Chonchi smiled with approval.

As they crouched behind a small wall running around the edge of the roof, I looped the rope loosely around the ladder and lowered it back to the dark corner of the awning where we found it. Then I jerked the rope free and pulled it back up. I wanted, as much as possible, to conceal the means of our escape. *Let them wonder if we had help from a guard,* I thought. *Let them simmer in their own paranoia.*

Crawling over to the outside edge of the roof, I knelt beside Chonchi and Margarita and surveyed the prison. Climbing down from the roof would be no problem—we could tie the rope to either of two nearby chimneys and lower ourselves to the ground. But from there we had to cross a brightly illuminated roadway, about thirty feet wide, and then get over the twenty-foot perimeter wall.

There was no way to scale the sheer wall. We either had to open the prison gate—an obvious impossibility—or climb the stairs into one of the four guntowers situated at the wall's corners. From there we could jump to the ground and pray that no one broke a leg or an ankle.

The two guntowers at the front of the prison were out of the question. Not only was there a guard in each of them, but there were two additional guards seated on stools below them, probably there to open the main gate should it be necessary. That was too many different sets of eyes to evade.

But the two guntowers at the back were a different case. I couldn't see guards in either of them. I suspected that the man assigned to the tower at the left was inside, asleep on the floor. If we walked in, we'd startle him awake and he would sound an alarm.

It was the tower to the right—the one closest to us—that had my full attention. Just below it, a guard sat on a stool. I was certain that he was not in his assigned spot; there was no gate to open in the back, no reason for a guard to be down on the roadway. I had sometimes heard guards complain that the towers attracted hordes of mosquitoes, and I was certain that the man on the stool had come down from the tower to get away from the insects. So the tower was empty.

And the guard, who was black, was visibly nervous, squirming in his seat, tapping his feet to the rhythm of the drums, and casting sidelong glances in the direction of the Santería house. *He's a Santero,* I thought, *and he doesn't like being outside on a night the spirits are moving around.*

I turned to Margarita and Chonchi, but their eyes were riveted on the Santería house. The old priest directing the ceremony was now visible through the window. His cottony white hair contrasted sharply with his obsidian skin. Using a gourd rattle as a baton, he conducted the drummers through a complex series of cadences. Behind him the dancers continued to writhe.

As I was about to whisper that it was time to go, the priest turned and looked directly at us. Chonchi gasped and ducked, but I locked eyes with him. It was impossible to read his expression at such a distance, but I knew he was wondering who we were. The relationship between the Revolution and Santería, though warm at first, had deteriorated badly in the past few years.* Castro was clamping restrictions on Santería's cere-

---

*Santería priests had been favorably impressed in the first few days after Castro came to power by something they saw as an extraordinarily good omen. During one of Castro's interminable speeches, a dove dropped out of the sky and settled on his left shoulder for a few seconds. The priests thought it was a symbol of divine protection. My own interpretation was that Castro's long-windedness had put the bird to sleep.

monies, trying to convert it from a religion to a bit of folklore that existed only inside museums. The Santeros were resisting fiercely. The ritual we were watching was probably illegal.

Keeping my eyes on the priest, I extended my hands straight out in front of my body and put my wrists together as if they were handcuffed. I hoped he would understand my signal: We were prisoners, not guards. I repeated the gesture three times. The third time, he nodded. Then he turned to the drummers and abruptly changed the tempo. The drumming turned louder, faster, angrier. The dancers whirled about the room in a furious blur.

"Follow me," I told Chonchi and Margarita. Quickly I knotted the rope to one of the metal chimneys and started my descent. But I barely got off the roof before I could hear the chimney buckling with a sickening metallic screech. Clinging to the rope with one hand, I frantically snatched at the edge of the roof with the other. Margarita and Chonchi grabbed me by the shoulders and dragged me back up.

Muttering curses—my hands were scraped and bloody—I untied the rope and looped it around the other chimney, much farther back on the roof. The added distance meant the rope would no longer reach all the way to the ground. As I started down again, I saw the old priest watching.

This chimney held, and luckily there was a small wooden awning over the back door to the prison kitchen, which was directly below us. I tested it, decided it would hold our weight, and signaled Margarita to come down. Chonchi followed a moment later. The drop from the awning to the ground was only seven or eight feet, but I gestured to the others to be careful; the area around the door was littered with pots and kettles that would go clattering into the roadway if we bumped them. I went first, landing lightly on my feet. Then I grabbed the legs of first Margarita and then Chonchi, helping to steady them as they descended.

Once on the ground, I understood why the security lights were kept so infernally bright. Our shadows looked like giant prehistoric animals, so enormous that I actually glanced behind us to see if we were really casting them. But there were no dinosaurs, just us. We pressed ourselves tightly against the wall of the kitchen to make them disappear.

"Okay, follow me, right behind, and do *exactly* what I do," I whispered. "We're spirits, called by the drums, and we're going to walk right past that guard and up into the tower. He'll be so scared he won't move a muscle."

It was a preposterous, harebrained scheme. If anyone had suggested it to me back at the *galera*, I would have howled with laughter. Sure, it was easy to see the guard was apprehensive, and *maybe* he would think we were spirits. But what if we scared him so much he screamed? Or, worse, picked up the rifle lying across his lap and fired at us? At this range, he'd never miss.

But none of those thoughts crossed my mind at the time. I was certain, absolutely *certain*, it would work. The possibility of failure simply didn't occur to me. And something of my confidence must have infected Margarita and Chonchi, because neither of them protested. Only Chonchi spoke.

"Ana, I've never been a ghost before," she said earnestly. "How do they act?"

"Keep your expression blank," I advised. "And, especially, don't show any fear. Spirits aren't afraid of anything. Keep a steady pace, but don't make any noise at all—the footsteps of the dead are soundless."

"Right," said Chonchi, looking as confident as if she'd just been briefed by an actual corpse.

The drumming was like thunder now, threatening and reckless, swallowing up even the hammering in my heart. I stepped away from the wall and started walking toward the guard. I had a second or two to let my face go slack and fix my gaze on a point in the distance. Then my shadow alerted him. He stared at me for a moment, and then ducked his head between his knees. I wanted to sprint for the tower, but I forced myself to keep the same pace, my arms dangling limp at my sides. My feet glided weightlessly across the asphalt as I approached the guard. As I passed him, no more than a few inches away, I could hear him hoarsely chattering a prayer.

With the guard behind me, I yearned to look back to see how Chonchi and Margarita were doing, but I didn't dare. I continued up the stairs, taking care not to stumble; I'd never heard of a clumsy ghost. As I approached the open doorway to the tower I felt my nerves coiling like steel springs. If I had miscalculated—if there was another guard inside, asleep on the floor—we would know it in a second or two. I stepped inside, and unleashed a deep breath of relief. The tower was empty.

But there was no time to dally. At any second, the guard might regain his nerve and start looking around. I looked out over the edge of the windowsill, and my stomach wrenched at the length of the drop. But there was no other way; we had left the rope behind, dangling from the kitchen chimney. I took a deep breath and let the tension go out of my body as I exhaled. *I sure hope my body remembers some of that high school gymnastics training,* I thought. And then I jumped, feet-first, into space.

The fall seemed to last forever. My eyes stayed open, and the white-washed prison wall went by in a long blur. Waiting for the ground, I had to remind myself to breathe. And then, all at once, it was there. My legs took over instinctively, bending like springs and then flipping me back up in the air. I started to lose my balance, but I hit the ground before my body got too far out of alignment, and I steadied myself with my hands.

Standing up straight, I wiggled my fingers and toes, slightly amazed that everything was in working order. The drums kept up their ferocious beat. I looked up and down the street, but there was no one in sight—except Chonchi, looking down from the tower. I made a catching gesture with my hands, and without a second's hesitation she launched herself over the edge. She fell like a stone, without turning or wobbling, directly into my arms. I expected to bend with her weight, but she felt like a feather; my knees barely flexed.

Margarita followed a few seconds later. She had seen me catch Chonchi, and she jumped with a serene expression, confident I would do the same for her. But Margarita started to twist in midair, rotating until she was almost completely horizontal. *Oh my God, we're both going to be killed,* I thought. At the last second I had to crouch in order to avoid catching her at an awkward angle. I thought my shoulders were being wrenched off, but she came to rest a few inches off the ground.

"Thanks," she said, straightening her clothes. "But I sure wish we had brought that ladder."

"Ghosts almost never carry them," I replied.

"We're going to be real ghosts if we don't get out of here," Chonchi observed. We started walking down the street, away from the prison. Our path took us past the Santería house, where the ceremony seemed to be nearing some kind of climax, the dancers moving with inhuman speed as the drums roared. The priest was still at the window. I bowed my head slightly as we walked by, and he returned the gesture, almost imperceptibly, and without moving a muscle in his face.

As the prison receded behind us, I pulled the crumpled pack from my pocket and lit one of the cigarettes I had snatched from Cavadilla that afternoon. *You lost the bet,* I silently taunted her, *fair and square.* Then I followed the advice I had given Chonchi and Margarita earlier, and lifted my eyes to drink in a view of the stars. For the first time in almost six and a half years, I was free.

· ELEVEN ·

The Street

IT WAS JUST past midnight as the taxi neared the Malecón, the seafront boulevard at Havana's northern tip. I nudged Margarita. "Time to get out the money," I murmured. She nodded, and started untying her tennis shoe.

For more than six years, since the day she entered prison, Margarita had been carrying a twenty-peso note for an emergency like this. How she had managed to hold on to it through all the transfers, searches, beatings, and stays in the *tapiadas* was a mystery of occult dimensions.

But when we saw the taxi cruising by, six or eight blocks away from the prison, Margarita knew her perseverance had paid off. "Flag him down, Ana, we can pay for it," she said excitedly.

Now, as she unlaced her shoe, I wondered if we could. When I entered prison, twenty pesos was a substantial amount of money, about the same as twenty American dollars. We could have ridden all over Havana for a couple of hours and still had money left over for ice cream.

But what was a peso worth these days? I had no idea. How expensive was gasoline? Hell, could you even *get* gasoline? My mother, on the infrequent occasions she was permitted to visit, complained that a lot of things were in short supply, but I wasn't sure exactly what they were. *We're like time-travelers,* I thought, *plucked from the distant past.* Now we were about to see the future.

Margarita interrupted my reverie with a nudge. "Ana, look," she whispered, a stricken look on her face. In each hand she held a worn, faded half of a twenty-peso bill. It had torn down the middle. As the cab slowed down, I took them from her.

"How much is it?" I asked the driver.

"Oh, let's call it twelve pesos," he said. I wondered briefly if he was cheating us, but it didn't matter. I bent over, as though fumbling in a pocket, and scraped a fingernail sharply across my pants. It made a dramatic tearing sound.

"Margarita, you idiot," I said coldly. "You're always screwing around. And now look what you've done to my money." I held the bills up where the driver could see. He took the pieces, fitting them together, and looked at us doubtfully. "I don't know if the bank will accept it," he said. "I certainly can't give you any change until I know. But give me your address, and I'll bring it tomorrow if the bank says it's okay."

"Oh, sure you will," I said, climbing out of the cab. "Sure you will. Well, just forget it. Margarita can pay me back—maybe it will teach her a lesson about acting like a jerk." Margarita, whose mouth had dropped open at my first outburst, was playing along now. She looked appropriately meek as she got out, with Chonchi following. The driver shrugged and sped away.

We stood there on the sidewalk, gaping like hick tourists from the countryside. Watching the late-night bustle of Havana, I felt an intoxicating rush of liberation. No walls here, no guards. I could pick out any of these streets, walk down whichever one I chose, slowly or quickly. I could change my mind for any reason at all, turn around, and go the other way. The possibilities made my head spin.

Without speaking, the three of us started walking slowly along the Malecón, absorbing the sights and sounds of the city. At first everything was a chaotic smear of light and noise, a deluge of strange sensations that were impossible to sort out. In the sealed, hermetic world of the prison, a single change in the environment—a new face, an extra strand of barbed wire, rice instead of beans at dinner—was a portentous event that could occupy us for days while we studied it, analyzed it, interpreted it. Now we were surrounded by strangers in a city we hadn't seen in years, buffeted by unfamiliar voices, snatches of music from the radios of passing cars, the sound of waves crashing against the foundation of the Malecón. It was too much. For the first few minutes I walked along like a zombie, barely comprehending the new universe around me.

After a while, though, bits of it started to snap into focus. And I was struck by how badly Havana had aged. The city had always seemed to be running on high octane, a place that throbbed with the energy of young love and bright neon.

But now it looked seedy and hard-bitten. The neon was all gone; all the buildings looked dirty and discolored. The young lovers who once strolled the Malecón had been replaced by packs of sullen kids who drifted along in solitary silence. Every time a police car pulled up—which was often—anger radiated from them like the heat rising from a summer sidewalk.

The police in one of those cars were staring directly at Chonchi, who was walking ten or fifteen feet in front of me. I realized she was weaving along in clumsy S-shaped curves, like a comedian playing a drunk. It was a common occurrence when prisoners came out of a long stay in the *tapiadas*—prolonged confinement in a small place made a lot of women temporarily lose part of their visual perspective—but Chonchi seemed to be dizzy merely from being outside the prison walls.

The policemen, I was sure, thought she was drunk. And even the most cursory questioning would reveal that we had no identification papers and no money. From there it would be a short trip to the police station, and eventually a much longer one back to Guanabacoa.

Speeding my pace, I caught Chonchi from behind and put a hand on her shoulder to steady her. "Thanks," she said gratefully. "I don't know what's wrong with me." A moment later, Margarita caught up and grabbed my other arm. "Don't walk so fast," she begged. "I feel like I'm seasick." Feeling a bit like the manager of two punch-drunk fighters, I steered us through Maceo Park, away from the stern gaze of the policemen. We went south through the park and entered the narrow, darkened streets of Old Havana, the city's ancient core.

All night we wandered the old part of the city. We kept to the back streets, out of the way of patrolling police, walking quickly enough to give the impression we had some purpose, slowly enough that we didn't keel over from exhaustion. We had made it out of prison on luck, daring, and momentum, but now our lack of a plan was beginning to tell. None of us had grown up in Havana, and although Margarita and I had attended medical school in the city, most of our student friends were either in prison or in exile. Nor was there any easy way for us to track down the few who might remain—political prisoners can't afford the luxury of keeping address books.

Near dawn, we did pass the apartment building where my Uncle Evaristo lived. I looked at it longingly as we walked by; we were hungry and thirsty and I had to go to the bathroom so badly I wanted to scream. I knew my uncle would welcome us without hesitation, offer us shelter as long as we wanted, give us anything he owned.

But I didn't say anything to Chonchi and Margarita. For all I knew, our escape had already been discovered and our relatives were under surveillance. And even if the authorities didn't know we were gone yet, I couldn't expose my uncle to the danger. He lived on the fifth floor of the building. The busybodies of the building's Committee for the Defense of the Revolution, Castro's neighborhood spy corps, would surely note a five A.M. visit by three ragamuffin women. Later, when the police came asking questions, my uncle would be in big trouble.

So we just kept on walking, crisscrossing Old Havana, waiting for an inspiration. We were relieved when dawn broke and the streets started to fill again, making us less conspicuous, but we soon wilted in the morning sun. Our freedom was starting to seem like some grotesque torture devised by our jailers: alone in the city with no money, nothing to eat or drink, nowhere to go, no one to turn to.

It was nearly noon when we paused at a corner that looked vaguely familiar to me. "Isn't the *arzobispado* around here someplace?" I asked Margarita, who knew Havana better than I did. "Maybe we could get some water there." The *arzobispado* housed the headquarters and staff of Havana's Catholic archbishop. *Surely any Catholic down on his or her luck could find a little charity there,* I thought.

"It's just a block or two from here," Margarita replied, her face breaking into a glorious smile. "And we can get a lot more than water there. I know the archbishop." My tired feet perked up a little at Margarita's enthusiasm as we rounded the corner and headed toward the *arzobispado*. At last we were moving with a purpose.

The heavy wooden doors of the *arzobispado* were propped open, seemingly an invitation to enter a stately colonial courtyard. The covered entryway, lined with lush green shrubbery, was deliciously cool. A couple of priests were tending to the plants, and I watched enviously as they poured streams of crystal-clear water onto the bushes.

"Can I help you?" one of the priests asked peremptorily.

"Yes, we'd like to see Monsignor Fernando Azcárate," Margarita said.

"He won't be back for two hours," the priest replied.

"Can we wait here?" Margarita asked. "We've come a long way."

"I suppose so," the priest said, not bothering to disguise his disapproval of our sweat-streaked clothing and sooty tennis shoes. He nodded at some hard wooden benches that, to me, looked as inviting as the softest mattress. Gratefully we sank down onto them. Before the priest could turn away, I asked: "Could we have a little water, please?"

"I suppose so," he said, shooting me a withering look. He deliberately returned to watering the plants for several minutes before walking inside the offices. He returned with a pitcher of water and a single glass. Slowly, measuring every drop, he filled it: once for me, once for Margarita, once for Chonchi. "May I have another glass?" I asked when Chonchi finished hers.

The priest looked at me as if I had asked for seconds on communion wine. "The pitcher is *empty*," he said frostily. Putting it aside, he resumed watering his plants.

"I guess there have been some new developments in theology while we've been inside," I observed to Margarita. "The pope must have decided that plants are morally superior to people."

"Oh, Ana, try to look at it from their point of view," sighed Chonchi. "They probably think we're crazy people who live in the street. That's what we look like. If we were dressed a little better, they'd treat us better."

I wasn't sure that was a good excuse, but I was too tired to argue. We sat there in silence, enjoying the luxury of a place we could rest without fear of the police.

The archbishop arrived two hours later. But Margarita's name didn't quite work the magic she expected; it was nearly an hour more before we were admitted to his office. And even then, Azcárate—a shriveled little man in his seventies—wouldn't look any of us in the eyes. He shuffled through papers as he extended his soft, manicured hand so that we could kiss his ring. Then he picked up a dagger-shaped letter-opener and began opening his mail. "What can I do for you, my daughters?" he asked in a bored voice.

"We just escaped from prison, Father, and we need help," Margarita blurted. "Don't you remember me?"

Finally we had the old archbishop's attention. His blue eyes seemed to shoot sparks. "Are you out of your minds?" he snapped. "Get out of here this minute. You're outlaws, you're fugitives from justice! Get out of here before I perform my duty as a citizen and turn you in."

Margarita, stunned, sat there with her mouth agape. My brain crackled with anger. "What a pity, Father, that Monsignor Pérez Serantes didn't feel that way," I retorted. "He would have saved all of us some great difficulties." Pérez Serantes, the archbishop of Santiago de Cuba, had personally intervened to save Fidel Castro's life when Batista was hunting him in the mid-1950s.*

The archbishop started to repeat his threat but Margarita, recovering her voice, interrupted him. "It's all right, Father, don't excite yourself," she hissed. "When we get picked up again, we won't exercise *our* duty as citizens to turn you in." She stood. "We're leaving. But don't you forget it—the only reason you're sitting in that chair, instead of rotting in a cell at La Cabaña, is that I never talked. Don't you forget it."

Now it was my turn to be stunned. Margarita had just revealed how she knew Azcárate—he had been a member of her underground anti-Castro group. And now he was repaying her loyalty by turning us out!

As we walked to the door, I turned to look at the archbishop once more. His eyes glowed with a scorching hatred that I had never expected to see on the face of a priest. But that wasn't what caught my eye. It was the little dagger-shaped letter-opener, still dangling from his fingers. How easy it would be to leap across that desk, snatch it, and put the tip against his soft white throat! Then we could force him to drive us to the office of the Spanish commercial attaché, the only diplomat in Havana who still granted political asylum to those who could get by the Cuban military

---

*Pérez Serantes perhaps felt the same way himself. Within eighteen months after Castro came to power, Pérez Serantes issued a pastoral letter calling Communist influence over the Revolution "the enemy within our gates" and urging Cubans to resist it. Castro eventually placed him under house arrest.

guards at his office door. With the archbishop as a hostage, I thought our chances of getting in were pretty good.

But I snapped out of my reverie. *I must be crazy, thinking of threatening a priest,* I thought as I continued out the door into the street.

It was another long night on the streets of Old Havana. We drifted from park to park, collapsing on their benches for an hour or two, then moving on before we attracted attention. I had to nudge Chonchi every few minutes while we were in parks; otherwise she went to sleep, an invitation to hostile questioning from the police.

Keeping Chonchi awake on a park bench, however, was easy compared with riding herd on her while we moved around. To my eternal dismay, she found a five-centavo piece on the sidewalk soon after we left the *arzobispado,* and Margarita and I had to stop her a number of times from entering stores to ask what she could buy with it. She might as well ask when people had stopped riding horses to work.

I did agree to stop in a café to ask if we could get a glass of water. It was useless. "The water's been cut off for two weeks," said the owner. "I can't even wash the dirty dishes, much less give you a drink." We tried in several other places, only to hear the same story. I believed it. As we walked the city, I noticed how smeary all the windows looked—evidently there was no water to wash them anymore.

Havana's fountains had been turned off for years. But every time we passed one, we checked to see if it held any stray rainwater, no matter how murky. After nightfall, we took turns urinating in a dark alley. A stray cat watched us impassively from the top of a nearby fence. *We're not much better off than you are,* I thought. *I wonder how long it will be before we're rummaging through garbage cans, too.*

Sometime before dawn, we headed farther south so that we'd be out of Old Havana by daybreak. We didn't want to start retracing our steps, stirring up curiosity.

As we trudged along, my thoughts returned to our encounter with the archbishop. As a Catholic, I had been taught that Santería was a low, primitive religion, witch-doctor stuff. Yet a Santería priest who didn't even know us had helped us escape, while a Catholic archbishop who had a personal debt to one of us and (at least theoretically) a spiritual link to all of us had turned his back.

If I could be sure it was just a case of a single man's hypocrisy—even though he was an archbishop—I would have been able to dismiss it. Any large institution, even a church, is bound to include some phonies.

But the church's relationship with the Revolution had been troubling me for a long time. The Vatican's embassy in Havana had been among the first to stop granting political asylum to political fugitives. And though many foreign ambassadors interceded whenever they could in an attempt to save political prisoners from execution, César Zacchi, the papal delegate in Havana, never would.

In fact, the church didn't even stand up for its own people. When Castro kicked hundreds of foreign priests and nuns out of Cuba, the church didn't so much as murmur in protest. When Castro jailed a priest named Miguel Angel Loredo on patently false charges that he was sheltering counterrevolutionary fugitives, church authorities advised him to admit his guilt and promise to accept exile from Cuba in return for his freedom. Loredo wouldn't do it, and he was still in prison.

But the church's policy of appeasement hadn't bought it peace with the Revolution. It was under attack on all fronts. Castro had renamed Holy Week as Playa Girón Week, after the beach where the Bay of Pigs invasion force was slaughtered. He had outlawed teaching children the Catholic catechism. And now a new law made it illegal for more than three "Catholic gentlemen" to assemble in the same place at the same time. That gave State Security the right, whenever it chose, to arrest entire church congregations as they gathered to celebrate Sunday mass.

As though my thoughts had stirred her up, Margarita stopped in the middle of the sidewalk. "The Iglesia de Reina church is about two blocks down the next street," she announced. "I have a friend there who might help us." From the way she said "friend," I knew this was someone else from her underground group.

We found the church, then wandered the area for another hour until the bells start chiming for the first Saturday morning mass. But when we approached I got another jolt. At every church I had ever attended, the doors were propped open before services, an open invitation to everyone to come inside and celebrate the mass. But one side of Iglesia de Reina's massive double doors was shut, and the other only half-open. It was guarded by a hatchet-faced old woman. Her eyes were beady and hostile as we neared the entrance.

"You can't come in here," she said before we could even speak. "You can't come in wearing blouses without sleeves." All three of us, it was true, had on sleeveless blouses.

"We're not here for mass," Margarita said, trying to placate her. "We just need to see Brother Mateo."

"To enter the church for any reason, you have to have sleeves on your blouse," the woman replied. She grabbed my arm and gave me a little shove backward.

My fists clenched. "Ana, let me handle this," Margarita begged. She turned back to the woman. "I'm going to see Father Millares," she said, trying to squeeze by. The woman planted a hand on her chest and pushed her back. "You have to have sleeves," she repeated.

We retreated from the door. "I guess we can wait and try to catch Mateo after the mass," Margarita said.

"And what if we miss him?" I asked. "And who is that old busybody bitch to keep us out? We tried it your way. Now we'll try it mine."

We waited at a distance until the woman stepped back inside the church to speak to someone. "Follow me," I said, and walked briskly to the door. I was inside before the old woman knew it. She turned around, sputtering, but I pushed her into a corner and put a threatening finger over her lips. "My friends and I have business in this church," I said in a low, menacing voice. "Now, if you know what's good for you, go sit down and listen to the mass. If you make any more trouble for us, you're going to be *very* sorry." Without waiting for her reply, I spun and walked toward the church offices, where Margarita and Chonchi were already asking for Brother Mateo.

Mateo, a handsome young man, came out moments later and hugged Margarita happily. He hustled us into a back room, where Margarita quickly sketched out our dilemma. "Margarita, you know I'll do anything and everything I can for you," he said when she was done. "But you also know I'm not the boss here. I'm going to get Father Millares to come talk to you. But I have to warn you—these are difficult times. The mother church is sending orders that a lot of us don't like."

When Mateo showed us into the church's immaculate white bathroom so we could clean ourselves up a little while he talked to Father Millares, I looked in a mirror for the first time in three years. (They were strictly prohibited inside the prison, though every once in a while a new prisoner managed to sneak one in.) Now I understood some of the strange looks I had drawn over the past two days.

My face, which had been doused in soot when the chimney buckled as I descended from the prison roof, was an ashen gray. Somewhere— probably as I slipped through the narrow space at the top of the wall between the two *galeras*—a net of spiderwebs had tangled in my hair, leaving it in uneven silver streaks. No wonder the guard at Guanabacoa had been so willing to believe I was a spirit: I was wearing ghost makeup. It took several drenchings from the faucet in the sink to wash it away.

Father Millares was a tall, slim man with intelligent eyes and an af- fable smile. He listened patiently to our story, though it was obvious Mateo had already briefed him. When Margarita finished, he sighed. "Bad luck certainly seems to follow you three," he observed. "And I'm not certain what we can do to help you change it."

Though his face was sympathetic, that answer—after our hateful re- ceptions from the archbishop and the old woman at the church door— goaded me to anger.

"Catholicism has certainly changed," I said acidly. "When I entered prison, I was still a daughter of the church. Now I find I'm nothing more than a bad omen. Why don't you just put up a sign outside that says, 'People with problems, keep out'?"

"I understand how you feel," the priest said. "But our orders are that preservation of the church is our top priority. We can't do that if we're in a war with the government."

"That's not the church I joined," I retorted. "The church I joined was founded in the catacombs of Rome and had to fight for its every breath. It survived only because a lot of brave men were willing to die on the cross for it. But I don't see any brave men now, only the weak and cowardly. I don't even understand what's left to preserve. Some buildings? A couple of automobiles? You've already lost everything that was important."

There was no anger in Father Millares' face, only resignation. "I agree with everything you say," he replied softly. "But we are not our own masters here. We took a vow of obedience when we put on these robes, and we must respect it. The mother church has ordered me to stay out of politics, so I can't help you." He paused, then added: "Truly, I am sorry." He got up to leave.

"Fine," I said coldly. "But the church has a debt to me that must be settled. I taught catechism classes for five years. I never asked for any money; I thought I'd get my reward in heaven. But if going to heaven means spending eternity with the spineless and the meek, then I'm not interested. So I'll take my payment in cold cash, right now."

The priest still showed no anger. "Let me see what I can do," he said, rising from his chair. He went into another office and returned a moment later with a thick wad of bills. "There's two hundred twenty-six pesos here," he said. "That's all I have at the moment. Take it, and when it runs out, send someone you trust and I'll give them some more. We don't have much, but we'll help all that we can."

Outside, we walked to a nearby park to plan our next move. I divided the pesos with Chonchi and Margarita so everyone would have some money in case we were separated. Margarita and I wracked our brains for names and addresses of anyone we knew in Havana, anyone who could hide us for a day or two. We had pressed our luck by spending two nights on the street; a third might be fatal. Finally I remembered Isabel Alonso, a friend from my first days in prison. Isabel had been released from prison a couple of years earlier. We had exchanged a few letters after her release, and I knew she lived in the Vedado district, on the northwest side of Havana.

"I think I can find her house," I told Margarita. "It's not ideal—they'll find her name in my file from the letters, and they'll check on her sooner or later—but I think they'll be investigating our families first. We could at least spend a night indoors."

Margarita nodded wearily. "We have to get some sleep, or we're going to collapse on a sidewalk somewhere and get arrested as drunks," she agreed. None of us had slept for more than a few minutes at a time since the last night we spent in prison, nearly seventy-two hours ago.

"Well, let's get started," I said. "Vedado is a long walk. Where's Chonchi?"

"She told me she was going to the little store on the corner to see if she could buy some food."

"And you let her go?" I asked, panicking. "Are you insane? She's going to go in there and ask for steak, or strawberries, or something else that hasn't been available for years. And who knows who's going to overhear it?" I scrambled to my feet, ready to drag her out of the store, but at that very instant Chonchi emerged, a broad smile on her face and a paper bag in her hands.

"Look, I bought us some lunch," she said brightly. From the bag she removed three small loaves of bread, three pats of butter, and two bottles of cola. I was speechless. My mother hadn't seen butter in the stores in years; bread was strictly rationed, and of course we had no ration books. I finally managed a single word: "How?"

"The lady in the store said I was about the luckiest woman on the face of the earth," Chonchi replied matter-of-factly as she buttered a piece of bread. "She said the last time she had bread was three years ago. But just five minutes before I walked in, somebody from one of the government ministries dropped off five loaves of bread and ten pats of butter. How about that?"

"How about that," I agreed. "Chonchi, since you're so good at doing the impossible, when we're finished, we'll send you to find cigarettes."

"Oh, I almost forgot," she said, fishing in the bottom of her paper bag. She pulled out an unopened pack. "I asked her if she had any extras she could sell without the ration book, and she sold me these. What do you think?"

I think God protects fools and little children, I replied mentally. But all I said was: "Thanks, Chonchi." It was the best lunch of my entire life.

We found Isabel Alonso that night after a long walk. She greeted us with hugs and kisses, gave us a bedroom in the house she shared with her mother, and hid us for a week. Though Isabel was in a precarious situation—she and her mother were trying to get exit visas to leave Cuba, and even the slightest suspicion of misbehavior would queer their chances—she threw herself into our plotting as though she were an escapee herself. She bought food for us on the black market, made contact with a few of our friends, mailed letters to our relatives telling them not to worry about us, and shuttled to Father Millares and a doctor friend of mine for infusions of cash.

She even watched the Mexican embassy—one of the few full-scale embassies from a non–Soviet bloc country that was still operating in Havana—for a couple of days, trying to discover a time when security was weak so that we could barge in and ask for political asylum. But she discovered that the ambassador routinely turned over asylum applicants to State Security. That scuttled our only real plan.

As comfortable as we were at Isabel's house, we knew our necks were in a noose there and we couldn't stay. We got the number of a pay telephone where we could call her at designated times, and at the end of a week we left—just in time. The very next day State Security officers, pretending to be public-health workers checking for insect infestations, searched Isabel's house.

We spent the next month scooting from house to house, like rats running a maze. It wasn't just the Catholic church that had been cowed by the Revolution—the entire country was living in fear. Every time we reached out to any of our old political contacts, it ended in disaster. I actually had to threaten to break the skull of one woman with a lamp. A former member of Margarita's underground group, she was about to call her apartment building's Committee for the Defense of the Revolution and turn us in on the spot.

The only people who helped us were personal friends, people we knew through our families rather than our politics. They shared food and lodging with us despite the grinding deprivation imposed by the Revolution's "scientific" economic policies. We stayed a week in one apartment where the husband worked at the government electric company all day, and then fished all night in an attempt to supplement the family's meager rations. He slept on the Malecón, a baited hook attached to a line tied to his big toe so that the tug of a fish would wake him up. He stopped at the apartment every morning, his skin mottled with mosquito bites, to change clothes and—if the water was on—shower before hurrying off to work again.

Under conditions like that, we didn't want to burden anyone with our presence for more than a few days. So as soon as we moved into one place, we'd start making plans to find another. We were like drowning women who spent all their energy treading water and had none left to swim for shore. We had no time to develop a master plan for getting out of Cuba; our few superficial inquiries about obtaining a boat—or even some inner tubes we could lash together into a raft—came to nothing.

We should have split up. Traveling alone, each of us would have been less conspicuous and would have posed less of a burden on people who wanted to help us. In fact, the night we escaped, I assumed that we would split up when we got to Havana.

But I hadn't expected the fear and the hostility we encountered on the street. Without even knowing it, I think, we had all slipped into a state of depression that made it difficult to break away from one another. And the longer we were together, the more entangled our lives became.

There were some nights when, lying uncomfortably on the floor of a threadbare apartment, hungry, unable to sleep, I wondered how much better off we were on the street than in prison. At least there we didn't live under the constant threat of betrayal, and our consciences weren't troubled by the risks we imposed on others.

Margarita, too, was feeling the strain. Nearly every one of her suggestions blew up in our faces. And then there was her frail hope that some tiny part of the Revolution was worth saving. At every turn she was assailed by new evidence that revolutionary Cuba was even worse than we had imagined it. Marxist economics had destroyed the country's wealth; Stalinist political controls had destroyed its spirit. The Revolution bred poverty and paranoia uncontrollably, the way a swamp breeds mosquitoes.

The only one really enjoying herself was Chonchi. She delighted in our small victories, like finding a store that had a few soft drinks for sale. And disappointments and hardships—even our forced marches back and forth across the city, which were much tougher on her because she was older—never seemed to bother her. When Margarita and I argued about politics (Margarita thought I was too hard on the church), Chonchi simply ignored us. Margarita tried to draw her into the debate once, but Chonchi just rolled her eyes. "You're always talking through a hatful of shit," she snorted, rolling over on the floor to sleep.

In early August, we set out once again. Margarita had remembered the phone number of a man named Pepín Sanchez who had been in her underground group. When she called him, he tersely directed her to an address near the Malecón and then quickly hung up. I didn't really want to go there—whenever we contacted one of Margarita's former resistance comrades, the reaction ranged from alarm to fury—but I didn't have a better idea. So off we went.

His apartment turned out to be a corner penthouse with an ocean view at the top of an elegant eleven-story building. I was immediately suspicious; it took big-time political connections to get a place like this.

My skepticism hardened into mistrust the minute I met Pepín. Though a tall, handsome man in his early thirties, Pepín had the furtive, oily air of a pimp (which, I learned later, was one of his avocations). He hastily pulled us into the apartment and closed the door.

"Be very quiet while you're here," he said. "The building manager is a member of the Committee for the Defense of the Revolution, and sometimes he listens at doors to see what information he can pick up." He gestured around at the apartment. "Make yourself at home," he said. "I'll go get us something to eat." He crept out the door like a cat burglar.

"That man is working for State Security," I warned Margarita.

"No, Ana, actually he's part of the advance guard for an invasion from Mars," Margarita shot back. "Sometimes his tentacles pop right through that phony skin." She shook her head. "You are completely out of your mind."

A look around the apartment did nothing to allay my suspicions. It had a large living room overlooking the ocean, complete with a wet bar; a spacious bedroom in the back; and two bathrooms. The walls were hung with a collection of antique swords, and a complete set of weightlifting equipment was stacked in one corner of the living room. One wall was dominated by a long bookcase piled high with leather-bound editions of classics like *Don Quixote* and *The Adventures of Huckleberry Finn*. The furniture, though a little too heavy and dark for my taste, was nonetheless expensive and well made.

In short, the apartment seemed to be a posh bachelor pad. But everything was covered with a thick layer of dust. And except for a small bag of rice tucked away in the corner of a cabinet, there wasn't a single scrap of food to be found. To my first two questions—what political connections enabled Pepín to rent such a place, and how did he afford it?—had to be added another: Why had he abandoned it?

Alas, my questions would have to wait. Because Pepín didn't return that night, or the next day, or the day after that.

It was on the afternoon of the second day, as I enjoyed the spectacular view out the apartment windows, that I noticed something odd. An ice-cream truck was parked down at one corner of the building. But ice-cream vendors had vanished from Havana's streets at least two years ago. And although children approached the truck from time to time, they all walked away empty-handed.

Curious, I looked down to the opposite corner. A couple cuddled together on a bench there, exchanging kisses and caresses. It was a sweet portrait of young love—so sweet that I distinctly remembered it from the day before. Going to the other window, I could see a third corner of the building. A beggar sat there. But he wasn't asking anyone for money, and he didn't carry a cardboard box with his clothing in it, as most panhandlers did. He just sat there, watching the building's entrance.

"Margarita," I said innocently, "I'm starving. Down the block I can see one of those little stands where they sell octopus and rice. You don't need a ration book for that. Why don't you go get us some? Chonchi and I will stay here in case Pepín comes."

When she left, I pulled Chonchi close. "We've blundered into some kind of trap here," I whispered. "Pepín is working for State Security. The building is under surveillance. And if they haven't already planted microphones here, they will soon. So from now on, don't say anything inside this apartment that you don't want State Security to hear. There's no use in discussing it with Margarita—she won't believe it—but if she starts talking, discourage her."

Chonchi contemplated the news for a moment or two. "Ana, I've been meaning to talk to you about something for a long time now, and I guess I should do it now," she whispered. "When we're arrested, and they ask me how we got down from the prison roof, what should I tell them?"

"Tell them I had Superman's cape hidden up there, and we flew down," I suggested. "Tell them they'll have to ask me where I got it."

Chonchi smiled. "I guess we're screwed, huh?" she said, just a trace of sadness in her voice. "I was hoping we could stay out awhile longer."

"Don't start packing your bags yet," I replied. "We can still have some fun with them."

Pepín finally returned on the third day. Margarita was asleep, so Chonchi and I were the only audience for his cock-and-bull story about how a friend of his, a captain in State Security, paid the rent as a favor. He waited nervously to see how we reacted. When I just nodded and smiled, he relaxed. "Tell me about your plans," he urged.

"Well, I don't like to talk about it much," I said, dropping into a dramatically low voice, "but I'm a captured CIA agent. Now I've gotten back in touch with them, and they're going to rescue us."

"How can they do that?" Pepín asked, his eyes wide.

"With a submarine," I explained. "They have trained dolphins that can lead them right through the anti-submarine defenses into Havana Bay. They've done it before, at least twice that I know of. But I can't talk about that, really I can't."

That was the start of a little game that was to last six weeks. I was fairly sure that the reason we hadn't been arrested the minute we showed up at the apartment was that State Security still hadn't figured out how we escaped from prison. The plan was to let us stay out a few days longer in hopes that Pepín could pry the information out of us.

Now I was dangling a much bigger fish in front of State Security: the chance of catching a CIA submarine right in Havana Bay. That, I thought, ought to win us a couple more weeks.

Pepín and his spymasters swallowed the bait and begged for more. Every few days he coaxed me into a new conversation about the CIA; after noting that I really shouldn't talk about it, I dropped some outlandish new morsel—my personal friendship with J. Edgar Hoover, my letter of commendation from Robert Kennedy, and so forth. I kept wondering if I'd gone too far, but Pepín always came back for more.

At one point, I said I had been smuggling coded letters out of Cuba in the Mexican embassy's diplomatic pouch, but I hadn't been able to send any in a while, and that was undoubtedly going to delay the rendezvous with the submarine. Pepín immediately offered to get the letters to the embassy for me.

After that I spent a fair amount of time each day writing nonsense letters to every friend and relative in the United States whose address I could remember. It was really rather difficult to make up so much gibberish. But every time I wearied of it, I thought of the Interior Ministry's cryptographers huddled over the letters, desperately trying to decode them, and I had a new burst of energy.

Aside from the letters, my life was rather pleasant. Now that I knew arrest was inevitable, I didn't have to worry about it. I could enjoy the large collection of books in the apartment; I read more in the next six weeks than I had in the previous six years. Meanwhile, Pepín kept the apartment supplied with food which, though not very good, was far better than anything we ate in prison.

Even though it was no longer necessary for us to scavenge, we continued to leave the apartment regularly. Sometimes we stopped at pay phones and called Isabel Alonso, who was still trying to find a way out of Cuba for us. (I also used the pay phone in an attempt to locate my old Communist friend from high school, Angel Pérez, who wound up in the Cuban air force, just as he predicted. I had a balmy fantasy that he would somehow fly me out of Cuba, for old times' sake. But I couldn't find him.) Other times we just wandered Havana, seeing the sights. We no longer had to worry about being picked up for not having papers.

It was probably these strolls that led to State Security's decision to jerk Chonchi back into prison. I think the plainclothes policemen who followed us every time we left the building worried that it would be too difficult to keep us all in sight if we suddenly split up and went in different directions. Or maybe State Security was just tired of feeding so many mouths.

Whatever the reason, when we had been in the apartment about a week, Pepín announced that it was too dangerous having three women there, that the landlord was asking questions. He had found a new place for Chonchi to stay. "I'll take you right now," he said.

Chonchi shot me an impassive glance. We both knew where she was going. "Walk me to the door," she said. As Pepín stepped into the hall, she hugged me hard and kissed my cheek. *"Hasta pronto,"* she murmured into my ear. "See you soon."

"Soon," I agreed. When she closed the door behind her, the apartment seemed chill and lonely.

In mid-September, Pepín visited the apartment several nights in a row, staying late to talk. His questions were more insistent than ever. When was the submarine coming? How would the CIA contact us? I parried his interrogation with one of my own: Where was Chonchi? Why couldn't she come to see us? The air was so thick with lies and evasions it was a wonder any of us could breathe.

On the night of September 16, the three of us were stripping the bed to launder the linens when a harsh voice shouted: "Hands over your heads!

You're under arrest!" I looked up to see a plainclothes State Security officer standing outside the window on the narrow ledge that ran around the penthouse. He was pointing a .45-caliber pistol at us.

My first thought was to snatch the pistol and take him hostage. But it wouldn't work; he was just a pawn that State Security would gladly sacrifice to catch two escaped counterrevolutionaries.

Still, the flamboyance of the arrest annoyed me. They knew we weren't armed; all they had to do was open the door and walk in. We were on the eleventh floor. Where were we going to run?

"Put down that gun, you asshole," I snapped.

"Shut up and put your hands up," he shouted again. "The whole building is surrounded."

"That's not going to help you much if I give you a shove," I replied. "In case you didn't notice, there's no railing behind you."

His face coloring, he lowered the pistol. A moment later the door opened and armed men poured into the room. A few minutes later they whisked all three of us downstairs and into the street. Pepín was arrested, too, in a lame attempt to preserve his cover as a State Security informant.

There were at least a dozen State Security cars arrayed around the entrance, their lights flashing like martial Christmas trees. Men in olive green carrying rifles, cartridge belts crisscrossed on their chests, scurried officiously in all directions. The street was empty of civilians, but upstairs I could see people looking out their apartment windows, undoubtedly wondering if Meyer Lansky himself had just been found in their building.

This is what you get, I thought, *for talking about CIA submarines.*

· TWELVE ·

Back Inside

SEPTEMBER 23, 1967

"PUT YOUR SHOES on," the guard said, stabbing his key into the lock of my cell door. "You're going for interrogation." He flicked his wrist expertly, and the lock clicked open. Silently I stepped out of the cell and followed him down one of the dim, labyrinthine halls of State Security headquarters. *I wonder how long it will take them to get tired of these sessions?* I mused. *I'm certainly sick of them.*

Every day for a week I had trudged down these hallways to meet a State Security interrogator for several hours of fruitless questions. They always took me to a different room—State Security apparently had enough interrogation chambers to run a small hotel—and it was always a different man asking the questions. That had less to do with a concerted strategy, I suspected, than it did with frustration. I knew I was driving the interrogators crazy.

Since the night of my capture, I had answered every question with a wisecrack or an absurdly obvious lie—starting right at the booking desk, where a dull-witted sergeant unquestioningly filled out a form that said my name was "Teresa Fernández," even though my long prison file with my real name was sitting right in front of him. Then I frustrated a dozen attempts to take my fingerprints, deliberately smudging them every time.

And when they tried to take a booking photo, I puffed out my cheeks, pulled my lip inside out, and stuck out my tongue.

It was the same every time they asked me questions, whether they blustered, bullied, or begged. I just turned everything into a joke. On the first day, after a couple of hours of verbal sparring, the interrogator appealed to my sense of compassion.

"Look, you need to get serious and help us get the story right, because innocent people are suffering," he said. "There are about a hundred people being held here right now on suspicion of helping in your escape. We both know that almost all of them are innocent. It's not fair, not fair at all. Help us establish who the guilty are so we can free all the others."

"What? A *hundred*?" I yelped. "You insult me, you insolent swine! What kind of a pipsqueak counterrevolutionary do you think I am? I don't want to hear another word about this until you have at least five hundred in jail. You're hurting my feelings."

"Perhaps I should clarify something for you," the interrogator replied. "The hundred include your entire family—your mother, your sisters, your aunts and uncles."

"You mean they're here?" I asked in a tone of childish wonder. "Right now? Great! When can I see them? I'll bet they've missed me the last three months." Behind my glib answer was the certainty that he was lying; I knew State Security, rather than jailing my relatives, would have wanted them on the street, under surveillance, in hopes that I would contact them.

What surprised me was that, no matter how angry I made the interrogators, no one hit me. In all my years in prison, I had never been so deliberately provocative. Every day I expected one of them to blow up, to beat me within an inch of my life, or even an inch past it.

And the truth is, I think, that I was asking for precisely that. I was seeking a way out—an end. I couldn't kill myself, but I was daring them to do it for me.

A corrosive anger had been eating me away from the inside since the first few days after our escape, and it was harder and harder for me to contain it. Being angry was nothing new, of course; rage was what had sustained me through six and a half years of prison. But I had always been able to keep that rage focused tightly on Castro and his uniformed bullies. What I saw on the street changed all that. I found myself despising not just Castro, but my countrymen, too.

We Cubans were no strangers to oppression. We suffered nearly four hundred years under the Spanish, the most tyrannical and bloodthirsty colonial rulers in recorded history. After independence from Spain, we were, more often than not, under the boot of some paramilitary gangster posing as a president—Batista was just the last of several.

But we had always fought back. The Spanish had rarely known a day of peace in Cuba, and even their attempts to put the whole country into an extermination camp had not been able to quiet our rebellious natures. The resistance to Batista started developing within hours of his 1952 coup, and it grew eventually to encompass most of the Cuban population.

When I went to prison in 1961, the majority of Cubans still supported Castro. But that was an error, not an act of obedience; most people still believed in the promises of the Revolution. And those of us who had glimpsed the skull beneath the skin had been willing to fight.

But during my months on the street, I had seen a strange, disturbing paradox. No one believed in the Revolution anymore. I didn't have to take a survey, or borrow a gypsy's crystal ball, to learn that. It was obvious from the sullen, suspicious faces that I passed on the sidewalk, the guarded, sidelong glances drawn by a simple request for a glass of water.

Yet no one was resisting, not even passively. About the boldest act of rebellion committed these days was to flee, to jump on an inner tube and try to float to Miami. Castro had achieved something that even the most savage of the *conquistadores* had only dreamed about: He had broken Cuba. The streets outside were like those of a foreign country to me.

After my capture, I tried to put it out of my mind. But it was impossible. The conversations of the other women in my cell made me want to scream. Newly arrested, hardly behind bars long enough to have been mistreated at all, they nonetheless confessed to anything and everything. They implicated anybody they could think of. I marveled over something I heard from one of them. "I wish I could answer them," she said plaintively, "but now they're asking about stuff that I really don't know anything about." As I listened to her lament over running out of things to confess, I thought of all the beatings we had absorbed in six and a half years. What had happened to my country in the time between my arrest and that of this whining little fool?

At times like that, I almost preferred the company of the State Security interrogators to that of my fellow prisoners. Now, as I headed for yet another session of cross-examination, I tried idly to guess at what today's questions might be directed. I had noticed that no one ever asked me how we actually got out of the prison that night; instead, the interrogators always seemed to zero in on who helped us in the street, particularly the money.

The guard whisked me into a small room and left again, closing the door behind him. An interrogator was waiting inside, sitting behind a desk, and he silently gestured for me to take a seat in front of him.

I recognized him as a man named Roldán; I had seen him around the building before, though he had never questioned me. He was a short man with a charming face, like that of a suave European of the movies. But it was marred by a self-smitten smile; I was sure he regretted the lack of a full-length mirror in the room, so he could enjoy the spectacle of his own preening. At once I was seized with an urge to slap him, and I think his uniform had only a little to do with it.

He rose behind his desk and started pacing back and forth theatrically, making a point of looking up into the air rather than at me. While I waited for him to realize that there were no Hollywood talent scouts present, I gazed around the small, chilly room.

The walls were well padded with soundproofing material, and I noted that I could no longer hear the echoes of footsteps from the hallway. As my eyes wandered here and there, I observed that his desk was covered with a thick sheet of glass. A crack zigzagged along the corner nearest me. I waited until the next time Roldán turned his back, and then my hand darted out to tug at the corner. A jagged chunk nearly a foot long pulled completely away. I quickly pushed it back into place and dropped my hands into my lap.

Roldán stopped pacing, and for a second I thought he must have seen me. But he had merely reached the point in his script where he was supposed to sit down and fix me with a long, searching stare. Stifling a yawn, I wished that he watched better movies. This one was getting dull fast.

"So," he finally said, "where on earth did you find that shithead with the red hair, the one who keeps babbling about Superman's cape?"

I was torn by conflicting impulses to punch him in the mouth and to collapse into laughter. The contempt that dripped from his voice when he spoke of Chonchi kindled a flame of fury deep within my gut. On the other hand, I could just see Chonchi's wide, innocent eyes as she assured a steaming interrogator: "I know it's strange, *señor*, and I've wondered myself how he could have flown away after he left his cape on the roof, but there it was, and . . ."

"Roldán," I asked, "were you guys all raised in test tubes? Because the way you talk about women, I can't believe any of you had mothers."

To my surprise, he actually looked abashed for a moment. But his embarrassment quickly gave way to anger that he had let me score a point. His lips went tight.

"Look, people like you are a waste of my time," he growled. "I just want to get something down on paper, anything, so I can quit dirtying my hands with you. So I want you to give me a plausible explanation, I don't care what it is, of where that money came from. Do we understand each other?"

"Oh, yes, I understand you *perfectly*," I said in a silken voice. "And the explanation is: soap. The way you people have wrecked the economy—I think you could create a sand shortage in the middle of the Sahara—a box of detergent is worth its weight in gold. Luckily I used to save soap for a rainy day, and—"

"You'll have to do better than that," Roldán interrupted through tightened lips.

"I was afraid you wouldn't believe it," I conceded. "But the truth is so embarrassing. You see, I noticed that there was no electricity, no water, no books to read, no movies to see, no music to listen to, nothing at all to do at night. So I became a prostitute. And people are so starved for entertainment that I was an instant success."

His lips rolled into a sneer. "Too bad I wasn't aware of this," he said. "I would have brought five pesos along today."

"Oh, I'm sorry, Roldán, I should have made myself more clear," I shot back. "I only slept with men—you know, guys with *balls*."

The sneer became a snarl. Angrily he reached for a drawer beside him where, I knew, interrogators usually stashed a pistol. Before he could pick it up I snatched the broken shard of glass from the desktop and jumped to my feet. I leaned across the desk, brandishing it a few inches from his throat. He froze, his face pale, as his eyes followed the sharp, glittering point of glass.

"Go ahead," I whispered, my voice coated with hatred. "Go ahead, Roldán. Show me how big your balls are, reach for that gun! But just think how fast the blood pumps out of a severed jugular vein. You might get a medal for shooting me, but they'll have to hang it on your tombstone."

Wordlessly, his eyes moved to the door.

"Forget the guard, he can't hear a fucking thing," I said. "And even if he could, it's the same as the gun in that drawer—he can't get in here fast enough to save your life. And the difference between us, Roldán, is that I don't give a shit if I live or die. Dying or going back to prison, it's pretty much the same thing, isn't it? I've got nothing left to lose. So go ahead, reach for the gun."

"Calm down," he said in a hoarse, croaking voice. "I swear to you on my mother that I'm not going to touch that gun. I'll shut the drawer, okay?"

"Pick up that gun by the barrel, slowly, and slide it across the desk to me," I ordered. Delicately he reached into the drawer and lifted the gun barrel with his thumb and forefinger, like it was a dead fish. He laid it on the desk and pushed it gingerly across.

I didn't touch the gun. Instead I stared at Roldán's bloodless, terrified face. *He thinks I'm going to kill him with his own gun,* I realized. The smell of his fear sent a roiling wave of nausea through the pit of my stomach. I replaced the fragment of glass on the desk, walked to the door, and stepped outside. "Let's go," I told the guard. "The interview is over."

They sent me back to Guanajay two days later.

The women greeted me with hugs and kisses. Strange as it was to be congratulated on returning to prison, I didn't mind. The streets had proven an alien landscape for me. I understood now why the Revolution was trying so hard to crush us inside the prison: We were the last resistance. Everyone else had broken or fled to Miami.

My glum mood began, slowly, to lift. The process was helped considerably by what the other women told of the aftermath of our escape. They had managed to confuse the count so badly that it was a full five days before the *llaveras* realized that Margarita, Chonchi, and I were gone. When they finally figured it out, it touched off an inquisition the likes of which the prison had never seen.

State Security was convinced that the first escapees in the history of Guanabacoa must have had inside help. (The only obvious clue about how we got out, the rope we left dangling from the kitchen chimney, disappeared without a trace. I suspect some workman noticed it, figured out what happened, and hid it to avoid repercussions.) Every guard and *llavera* at Guanabacoa had been called in for lengthy, grueling interrogations by State Security, some of them several times. The hundreds of doves that perched on the prison roof during the day were systematically shot by the guards and their bodies retrieved to see if any messages had been attached to their legs.

Gladys Cavadilla, the Interior Ministry lieutenant who playfully bet me her cigarettes that I couldn't escape, disappeared without a trace. It was rumored among the prisoners that she was in a mental hospital. Marta Goodrich, one of the *llaveras* who I tricked into leaving the *galera* door unlocked, was treated so brutally during her interrogation that she turned against the Revolution. She kept her job, but she stopped enforcing prison rules; no matter what we did, she wouldn't report it. Sometimes, if no other *llaveras* were around, she visited my cell for friendly conversations.

Every once in a while I was called in for odd, disjointed interrogations that convinced me State Security still believed my fabricated story about my connection to the CIA. The reverberations continued for years. In 1974, Cuban Air Force planes launched a mammoth bombing raid on Havana Bay itself, dropping several thousand pounds of explosives into the water. The only known casualty was a twenty-foot shark. The raid's objective was never revealed, but I always wondered if that unfortunate shark was mistaken for my fanciful CIA-trained dolphin, helping to sneak a gringo submarine into the bay.

I was assigned to what had been the upstairs floor of the *tapiadas*. But the angled cement slats that had covered the windows, blocking out the light, had been destroyed a couple of years ago, a victim of shoddy construction and the perpetual, patient vandalism of prisoners, who picked and poked at every little crack until it gave way. The cells were no longer darkened, claustrophobic boxes, and no one called them *tapiadas* anymore; they were just E Upper, an ordinary pavilion. The downstairs cells, where the cement slats had proven sturdier, were still *tapiadas*.

I shared a cell with Margarita, a lanky farm girl named Teresa Vidal (who, for some reason, was known only by her last name), and pretty, blonde Gloria Lasalle, who had just a few weeks left to serve. I settled back into the routine of prison life: standing in line for a quick afternoon shower;

drinking my fill of water during the two brief periods each day when the pipes were on; listening to the interminable shouted conversations that echoed up and down the corridor at night.

We were locked up around the clock. They didn't even let us out to go to the dining room. Our miserable meals of cold, plain macaroni and watery beans were usually delivered by a thin, fidgety guard named Bencomo, who shoved the aluminum plates through the bars of our cells. For some reason, we made him so nervous that he was always fumbling and juggling the plates.

And late one afternoon, when he brought Gloria Lasalle back from a visit to the prison doctor, he was so skittish he forgot to lock the cell door.

"If we can keep him from checking the lock after the evening count, we can escape," I whispered to the others.

"I don't see how," scoffed Teresa Vidal. "We have to get through the locked door at the end of the corridor, a locked door downstairs, a chain-link fence, and a wall."

"Just help me distract Bencomo during the count," I said. "Then you'll see." Vidal looked skeptical. Margarita, who had seen me produce a rope and a ladder like magic at Guanabacoa, didn't.

It was around six P.M. when Bencomo started moving from cell to cell, counting the prisoners and tugging each door to make sure it was properly locked. As soon as I heard him, I went to the cell door and shouted in an imperious voice: "Guard, present yourself at Cell 8 immediately!"

"Who the hell are you to give commands?" he yelled indignantly, as I knew he would. "I'll see you when I get to your cell."

"This is an *order*, Bencomo, not a request," I shouted back. "Get your lazy ass down here!"

"Shut up and sit down!" he screamed.

I kept at it, ordering him again and again to report to our cell. Every time, Bencomo got angrier. Chonchi, in a cell down the corridor, sensed something was up, and she started needling him too. By the time he reached our end, he was in a frothing rage. He deliberately walked on the other side of the corridor, keeping his eyes away from us so he couldn't see whatever it was that we wanted to show him. Then he walked back the same way. "I guess you see who's the boss here now," he called over his shoulder as he left the corridor and headed downstairs.

Vidal and Margarita looked at me questioningly, but I just shook my head. It wasn't until around ten P.M. that I opened the cell door and crept down the corridor to the cell of Esther Castellanos. "Ana!" she shouted happily when I came into view, but I shushed her. "Esther, our cell's open, but we'll need some help getting out," I whispered. "We're going to call the *llavera* to bring you a pill."

Esther's leg, badly shot up during her capture, had never healed properly, and the pain often became unbearable for her during the night. But I had noticed that when the *llaveras* entered the pavilion to bring her a painkiller, they almost never locked the door behind them for the two or three minutes they were inside. It provided us with a brief window of vulnerability.

Esther happily agreed, and I returned to the cell to explain to Margarita and Vidal. "We'll call a *llavera* to help Esther, but before she gets here, we'll leave the cell and hide in the showers," I told the others. "Then, when her back is turned while she's giving Esther the pill, we'll slip out the door, go downstairs, and out of the pavilion."

"What about the chain-link fence and the wall?" asked Vidal.

"We're just going to have to climb them as quickly and as quietly as we can," I said. "But look how hard it's raining outside—I think there's a good chance nobody will see us."

We whispered our good-byes to Gloria Lasalle, who preferred to stay and take her chances that the government would honor her release date. Her face, always pale, looked positively ghostly; she knew there was a good chance the prison authorities, blaming her for failing to raise the alarm, would extend her sentence. But she didn't try to stop us. As we started shouting for a *llavera* Gloria climbed into her bed and pretended to sleep. Moments later, we silently left the cell and stepped into the shower stalls.

It was ten minutes or so before we heard the loud, metallic *thump!* as the lock on the corridor door opened, followed by the mumbled cursing of an extremely wet *llavera*. Peeking out of the showers, I could see her down at Esther's cell. Moving on tiptoes, I quickly covered the few paces to the open door. Fighting the temptation to bolt down the stairs, I kept moving rapidly but quietly. As I reached the bottom I saw Margarita start down behind me.

When I pushed the door to the patio, it swung open easily—I was right, the *llavera* hadn't locked it. I grinned at Margarita as we stepped through it. But we hadn't gone more than a couple of steps when we heard a loud shriek from upstairs. Seconds later, Vidal burst through the door.

"She turned around just as I went through the upstairs door," Vidal gasped as we pressed ourselves against the pavilion wall. "Shit! Half a second more and she wouldn't have seen a thing."

"Let's go back upstairs, jump her, and tie her up," I suggested.

"It's too late, she's already screaming loud enough to wake the dead," Vidal replied. "And if we do anything to her, the punishment for the women in the pavilion will be ten times as bad. Let's just run for it."

Without replying, I dashed toward the narrow expanse of chain-link fence running between Pavilions E and C. The rain had slowed to a drizzle, but it helped muffle the sound of our footsteps, and it drew the night around us in a murky cloud. As Vidal scrambled up the fence, I saw the *llavera* explode out of the pavilion door. But instead of running toward a guntower and shouting a warning, the panicky *llavera* galloped across the patio toward the prison offices. *We still have a chance,* I thought as Vidal dropped to the ground on the other side.

Margarita was next. While she climbed, I nervously watched the guntower a couple of hundred feet to our right. I knew the guard inside had a searchlight, and any minute, when he heard three prisoners were loose, he would start sweeping the yard with it.

Margarita deftly climbed over the Y-shaped array of barbed wire atop the fence and plunged into the soft ground beside Vidal. Now it was my turn. Scaling the rigid chain-link fence was not difficult, but I got snarled between the two sets of barbed wire. The tight blue prison-uniform skirt I was wearing made it difficult to move freely, and the sharp barbs left long tracks along my legs as I struggled with the wire.

As I tried to tear my skirt free from the wire, the searchlight beam started moving toward me. I dropped down into the center of the Y and froze as the shaft of light flitted by, inches from my body. As soon as it passed, I jumped up and gave my leg a savage yank, freeing myself from the wire. Then I froze again as the tightly-strung wire gave off a loud, wavering tone like a giant guitar string.

The searchlight beam stopped, then began a herky-jerky return toward my place on the fence. I dropped to the ground and pressed myself into the soft muddy earth like a stone, silently beseeching the light to pass on by. It kept inching straight toward me, throwing every blade of grass along its path into sharp relief. I tensed, preparing to run the instant the light touched me, heading the opposite direction from where Margarita and Vidal were hiding to give them a chance to get away.

In the last fraction of a second before the beam hit me, a piercing screech erupted from a spot a few feet to my right. The beam instantly halted, then moved away from me in the direction of the sound. I didn't dare to move a muscle, but my eyeballs rotated with the light. There, caught in the beam, a scrawny black cat crouched in the grass, a defiant snarl on its face. The searchlight paused there for a few moments as if it were evaluating the cat. Then it abruptly went out.

Quickly we jumped to our feet and raced toward the perimeter wall, seventy-five yards away. There were few security lights here, outside the main prison compound, but we knew the searchlight could start up again at any moment. The rain had turned the ground into a muddy morass, and within a few steps my tennis shoes felt like cement blocks encasing my feet.

I boosted Vidal and Margarita over the seven-foot wall, then tried to vault it on my own. But my leaps were clumsy, and I couldn't seem to get a clean grip on the top of the wall. I couldn't understand why I was suddenly so awkward.

"It's your shoes," Vidal whispered, appearing atop the wall. "You must be carrying twenty pounds of mud. Take them off—we've got to get out of here." Kicking the shoes off, I jumped again in my bare feet, and reached the top easily. From there I leapt lightly to the ground. Exactly twenty days after my capture, I was free again.

With no plan but to hurry away from the prison, we struck off across a newly plowed field. The rain had stopped, but it was still so dark that we had to hold hands to keep from losing one another, and we had no idea in what direction we traveled. The silent, weary monotony of the muddy field was broken only occasionally. We passed a small lake, where the bullfrogs fell silent at our approach. A short time after that, a pig squealed in anger when we stumbled over it. And Vidal bumped into a horse, a colt, which led us about a mile and a half to a paved road. We paused there, exhausted by the effort of pulling our feet from the sucking mud with every step.

"Does anybody have any money?" Vidal asked. "Because we can't outwalk all the guards who are going to come searching for us. We need to get a ride into Havana." Both Margarita and I mumbled negative replies. "Well," Vidal continued, "I know a family that lives near here. I'm sure they'll give us a few pesos. Wait here for me." And before we could say a word, she vanished into the darkness.

"Vidal, wait a second," I hissed, starting to run after her. But I couldn't see her, and I was afraid to shout. I didn't dare take more than a few paces for fear of losing Margarita. Retracing my steps, I took her hand again.

"Look," she said. Back in the direction from which we had come, we could see a parade of distant headlights. The search had begun. "We can't stay here," Margarita said. "Vidal's going to be captured for sure." We left the road and plunged into the planted rows of a sugarcane field.

We slogged through the sodden cane for what seemed an eternity. With every step my body grew weaker. And the row of headlights that marked the highway didn't seem to recede a bit. Finally I stumbled to a halt.

"Let's break off some of this sugarcane and suck the juice from it," I suggested. "That should liven us up." Margaret nodded wearily. The tender cane gave way easily, too easily. It was too green to eat, and we knew it, but we were so tired our brains had disengaged from our hands. Sinking to the ground, we put the cane to our mouths and twisted it to and fro, letting the sweet juice run onto our tongues. We sat there quietly, savoring the taste.

The roar of the bullfrogs stopped.

Margarita and I looked at one another. A moment later, we heard a pig's frightened squeal.

"They're coming," Margarita whispered. "They're doing a *peine*, a comb." It was a technique the Cuban army had developed fighting anti-Castro guerrillas in the rugged mountains of Oriente; holding hands, the soldiers marched shoulder to shoulder across the scraggy terrain, flushing out any rebels hidden in the underbrush.

"If we can pass through the teeth of the *peine*, we're safe," I said. "They won't go back and search behind themselves. Then we can hide in the fields for a few days. We'll be safe." *Unless they bring out dogs to hunt for us*, I added mentally. We climbed to our feet and, still holding hands, broke into an awkward trot.

But within minutes I could feel the cramps. The green sugarcane was taking its posthumous revenge; spasm after spasm twisted through my gut, so powerful they almost lifted me off my feet. I couldn't see Margarita's face, but her painful grunts told me she, too, was in agony. Our trot slowed to a walk and then an uncertain stagger.

A shadow loomed up in the darkness, long and squat. "What the hell is that?" Margarita gasped. As we tottered closer, I could see it was the empty outer shell of a schoolbus, lying on the ground like a child's abandoned toy. Peering into the darkness, I could see the shadows of several others scattered haphazardly around the field. We had apparently blundered into some kind of a weird bus graveyard.

Soft vines had wound themselves about the shell of the bus, enveloping it completely except for the space where the door had been. I stooped to go inside and walked toward the back, where I squatted against the wall. Almost immediately I was shaken by an explosive, wrenching bout of diarrhea. The convulsions twisted every muscle in my body. When they were finished, I was so weak I could hardly stand up.

And why should I? I wondered. *If we get out of this, what will we do next? We haven't escaped prison—all of Cuba is a prison, a tropical gulag inside a sugarcane curtain.*

With a concerted effort, I fought down my despair and walked back outside, where I discovered Margarita had made similar use of one of the other buses. "I feel better, but I don't think I can run," she said. "It's all right, I don't think there's any need to hurry now," I replied. "Listen—I think they're all around us."

We could hear tires squealing, doors slamming, and shouted commands ahead of us as well as behind. Mingled in here and there were the disgruntled snorts of livestock expressing their disgust at this rude and unwarranted human intrusion. And then a single shot rang out.

"They just got Vidal," I whispered. The words were barely out of my mouth when we heard the muffled thuds of hundreds of boots moving across the ground.

"They're close," murmured Margarita.

We started walking again, but we made no effort to move fast. Only stealth would save us now. Yet somehow we managed to stay ahead of the men behind us. We walked about two miles before the moon peeked through for a moment and I realized that we were surrounded.

We were at the side of an open field, standing in the shadows of a tight, impenetrable line of thorny bushes planted by some *campesino* to form a natural fenceline for his cattle. The thorns blocked any escape to our left. A few hundred yards to the right we could hear the sounds of soldiers climbing out of trucks parked along the highway.

About a hundred yards ahead of us was another cane field. But between us and the shelter of the cane walked a long row of several dozen soldiers, hand in hand, making the *peine*. And meanwhile, we could hear the troops advancing behind us, so close we could make out their muttered curses as they stumbled in the muck of the field.

"We've got to crowd ourselves back as far as we can into the thorns," I told Margarita in a voice so faint I could barely hear it myself. "It's so dark that no one will see us. When the men behind us pass, we'll come out of the thorns and sneak into the line of the *peine* ourselves. But whatever you do, don't speak—your voice will give you away."

We crushed ourselves into the thorn fence, the spiny branches tearing gashes in our backs, and waited for the line of soldiers to pass. As I expected, the theory of the *peine* was a lot prettier than the practice. Holes in the line opened and closed constantly as men slipped in the mud or stumbled over rocks and stumps. Sometimes a falling soldier took down several other men with him, like a row of tumbling dominoes.

After they passed, I stepped out of the brush, Margarita right behind me. It was no more than thirty seconds until a gap opened in the line. I slipped right into it, taking the hands of the men on either side. I couldn't see Margarita, but I assumed she did the same.

On my left was a guard named Miguel, his gangly six-foot-five frame unmistakable even in the gloom of the night. He stumbled, righted himself, and made a noise of exasperation in his throat. "Goddamn, it's dark out here," he rasped. It seemed to call for some response, so, making my voice as deep and gruff as I could, I mumbled: "Yeah, kind of scary."

"What do you mean, 'kind of'?" said the man to my right. I recognized the voice of Arcadio, another guard. I had noticed, inside the prison, that he never took part when they sent the guards to beat us. "We're sitting ducks out here," he continued. "If they really have guns, they can probably kill a hundred of us before we even figure out where they're shooting from." *They think we're armed,* I realized in amazement. *My God, that CIA story I told them is never going to die.*

Our row was about to meet up with the line of troops advancing from the cane field. I saw a tree up ahead, silhouetted against the night sky, and

I took advantage of it to break the line and drop to the ground. I heard some stumbling and cursing off to my left, and a moment later Margarita joined me. We had beaten the *peine*. In a minute or two, the two lines would meet and the soldiers would get back into their trucks and go to search another field somewhere else.

And now that you've beaten it, what are you going to do? I wondered, lying on my back, resting my aching body while I futilely searched the sky for stars. *What's the plan? How will you get from that cane field up ahead to Havana? And from Havana, how will you get out of Cuba? How many nights will you spend walking the streets there, without food or water, without a prayer that anyone will help you?* I knew that the only way off the island was to get a gun and take hostages. But how many people would I have to hurt or even kill to do that? And where could I go? If I used force to leave Cuba, the rest of the world would judge me, not Castro, as the criminal. Kill a man, or a thousand, or even ten million, as Stalin did, while you're wearing a uniform, and the world blinks; that's "governing." But if I used a gun to try to escape, that would be "counterrevolutionary terrorism."

Suddenly I was weary, not just in my body, but in my soul. What was waiting for me beyond that cane field? The rest of the world neither knew nor cared what was happening here. At the United Nations, one humanitarian group or another was always reading clandestine letters smuggled from prisoners in South Africa and Rhodesia and Haiti and Nicaragua, anyplace where right-wing dictatorships had the people by the throat. But no one was ever interested in the letters that our families snuck out of prison for us. No one at the U.N. ever demanded an investigation of Cuban prisons, no one ever asked why Cuba had no elections, no one ever wondered why a tenth of Cuba's population had fled to Miami. No one cared about us. We had committed an unforgivable lapse: We were practicing anti-Communism out of season.

"Margarita," I whispered, "I'm not sure I want to go on with this."

She rolled over until our faces were just a few inches from one another. "What do you mean?" she asked. But beneath the confusion on her face was a knowing look. If anything, our time on the street in Havana had been tougher for her than for me. Time after time, her friends had turned their backs on us.

"I just can't see how we'll get out of Cuba without a bloodbath, and I don't think I'm ready for that," I said. "I think I want to surrender."

"But Ana," she said in a troubled voice, "how could we ever go back to prison and tell the others we gave up?"

"We'll just say we were captured," I said. She stared at me for a moment, then nodded.

Slinking across the field, we approached the highway. A single young soldier guarded the trucks parked there. Now that we had decided to give up, I wasn't even nervous as I snuck up behind him. I hit him hard in the backs of his knees, and as his legs buckled I snatched his rifle. Before he could even turn around I had it trained on him.

"Don't worry," I told him, smiling. "You're going to be a hero. I'm going to hand you back the gun, and you're going to fire a shot in the air to call the rest of them. When they get here, just tell them you caught us trying to sneak by."

His expression, at first fearful, was now mystified. He started to speak: "But—"

"But what?" I asked impatiently. "You want to tell them a woman took your gun away? Would that be better?"

Slowly, dazedly, he shook his head no. I handed him the rifle.

They sent us to the *tapiadas*, naturally, the downstairs cells that were still completely sealed from the light. And because they were convinced that Margarita and I could turn ourselves into smoke and escape through a keyhole, they posted a sentry at the corridor door around the clock. One of my few consolations was that Bencomo, the nincompoop guard whose error had led to our escape, was on sentry duty twenty hours a day as punishment. I cheerfully blackmailed him, demanding two packs of cigarettes a day.

The cigarettes were just about my only diversion in the *tapiadas*. Otherwise I was alone with my misery, trying to fight off the darkness, the heat, the mosquitoes, the filth. To make matters worse, some of the cells were occupied by common criminals, who screamed obscenities and threats to one another at all hours of the day and night. Their shrieks fed on one another, echoing through the closed cellblock, until they drowned out even my own thoughts. And sleep was impossible; I averaged less than an hour a day.

The worst offender was Dinorah Ferrer, better known as Kiss Me One Key, a garbled version of the English come-on line she used with sailors while working as a prostitute along the Havana waterfront: "Hey, Joe, give me one kiss." It must have worked pretty well; Dinorah's professional exploits were legendary. Before the Revolution, she had twice stowed away on freighters to the United States and serviced the crews all the way there and back without being detected by the officers, amassing a small fortune in the process.

A longtime street whore and a veteran of several stays in prison, Dinorah could have kept half the psychiatrists in Cuba employed for life. She had two distinct personalities. As Kiss Me One Key, though unlikely to be featured in any etiquette books, Dinorah was reasonably civil by the standards of the common criminals. And, unlike most of the rest of the prostitutes, she was both intelligent and articulate.

She considered prostitution an act of subversion against the government, a form of resistance to totalitarian regimentation. (She also dismissed sociological explanations of prostitution as so much bullshit. "Nobody ever forced me to do it, and my parents were perfectly normal people," she said. "I'm a whore because it's an easy way to make good money. I never went hungry until the Revolution came.") Outside the *tapiadas*, some of us had political discussions with her.

But without warning, Kiss Me could vanish, replaced by the other personality, Manolo the Merciless. Manolo was a butch lesbian who always kept a younger, weaker, and prettier prisoner as a girlfriend. And the most innocent contact with that girlfriend—saying hello as you passed her cell, or even making eye contact with her too long—could provoke barbaric retaliation from Manolo the Merciless, against both the girlfriend and the offending prisoner. Dinorah was always being locked up in the *tapiadas* for terrible injuries she inflicted as Manolo. Her specialty was slashing faces with makeshift knives; once, in a lucid moment, she bragged to me she had left major scars on the faces of more than one hundred women.

And it was Manolo who was most responsible for keeping me awake all the time. Her girlfriend of the moment, a young blue-eyed blonde named Iris Pérez, was confined in D Pavilion, catercornered across from the *tapiadas*. And Manolo constantly screamed lurid warnings to Iris about the consequences of unfaithfulness. "If I find one fingerprint on you when I get back, I'll slice your face off, you little bitch," she would bellow. "No, no, Manolito, you know I belong only to you," Iris would cry back in a wavering, fearful voice. This went on for hours at a time.

One night, as Manolo lovingly and loudly described to Iris what a machete could do to human flesh if swung at high speed, I had an inspiration. First I tore some long strips of cloth from my uniform and tied them to my tennis shoes. Then I waited for a moment of relative quiet and broke into loud, hysterical sobs. "Oh, God, no, stay away from me, please," I wailed.

"Ana! Ana! What's wrong?" came shouts from every corner of the corridor. No one had ever heard me carry on this way.

"I've never seen anything so terrible!" I wept. "There was a woman, right here in my cell, close enough for me to touch her. But someone had chopped her head off, and blood was bubbling from her neck. And even though she had no head, she spoke to me. 'Which one is Dinorah Ferrer?' she said. 'Point me to her cell.' I told her I didn't know Dinorah Ferrer, to go to another cell and leave me alone." (It had been years since anyone had called Dinorah by her real name, and I was gambling that she wouldn't remember that any of us actually knew it.)

When I finished my tale, the corridor, for once, was completely silent. Dangling my tennis shoes out the slot in the door through which our meals were passed, I manipulated them like marionettes, making a *slap-slap-slap* noise that even to my ears sounded ominously like the lurching, uncertain footsteps of a corpse. A chorus of sickly moans issued out of the other cells as the women pictured a bloody, decapitated cadaver approaching their doors.

"Goddamn it, everybody shut up!" screamed Manolo, a rising note of panic in her voice. "All of you bitches shut up and listen to me! From now on, nobody speaks to me! Not at all, not about anything! And don't speak my name, either, to me or anyone else. The cunt that says it, I'll kill her like a dog." She raised her voice toward D Pavilion. "Iris, you filthy whore, you've talked to somebody, and now I'm in trouble! Don't ever say another word to me, you cunt!"

"Manolito, Manolito, what are you talking about?" wailed Iris from the other pavilion, where she hadn't been able to hear my story and didn't have the faintest idea what was going on. "You know I would never do anything to you!"

"One more word, bitch, and I'll tear your tongue out with my bare hands the next time I lay eyes on you!" Manolo shrieked. The corridor went silent again. And a few minutes later, with a smile on my face, I fell asleep for the first time in days.

The *tapiadas* stayed quiet after that. There were whispered conversations between next-door cells. But on the rare occasions when someone raised her voice, my phantom tennis shoes started walking the corridor again, and everybody quieted down.

Unwittingly, my ghost story had played right into a panic sweeping the rest of the pavilions. I didn't know about it, but some of the common criminals did.

Months earlier, the Interior Ministry had designated D Upper as a cellblock exclusively for lesbians—who, like male homosexuals, were despised by the Revolution. The prison authorities were quick to spot the new pavilion's extortion potential. Troublesome prisoners were warned to shape up or they would be transferred to the lesbian cellblock and their families informed. It was a potent threat: In Cuba, revulsion for homosexuality was almost universal.

One of the prisoners who somehow ran afoul of the authorities was a woman named Alba Serrano, who was serving time for black market activities (that is, trying to buy food for her little boy). I had met her once or twice, a pleasant woman of twenty-five or so with curly black hair. Like the rest of the growing number of women jailed for buying on the black market, she had little in common with the hardened prostitutes and psychotic killers who composed most of the common-criminal population.

When Alba's relatives learned she was in the lesbian cellblock, they went wild. During their next visit, they lectured her: How could she do anything so unnatural? Didn't she understand she would burn in hell? How could she disgrace the family this way? Alba tried to explain it was just another one of the Revolution's dirty tricks, a cheap piece of blackmail, but her family was unconvinced. She left the visit in tears. And on October 30, 1967, abandoned and despairing, she hung herself in her cell. To spare the Revolution an autopsy, she left a piece of paper listing the cause of death: "I died of shame."

Deaths at Guanajay were rare—most prisoners in ill health were transferred to a hospital or released outright before they succumbed, so the prison wouldn't face any inquiries from international human-rights organizations—and no one knew what to do with Alba's body. It lay in her cell for a day and a half while the Interior Ministry wrangled with judicial authorities about jurisdiction.

But as word spread through the prison, it touched off a frenzy among the common prisoners. A suicide had to be buried at once; otherwise the corpse's ghost, denied entrance to heaven, would linger near the body. Fistfights, impromptu *toques de lata*, and generalized bouts of hysterical screaming and crying broke out across the prison. Eventually all the pavilions had to be locked down. To retaliate, the prison authorities started transferring common criminals to work farms. But to the authorities' surprise, the prisoners went willingly. They were convinced that Alba's angry ghost roamed the darkened corridors at night.

Perhaps they were correct; if ever a ghost was entitled to vengeance, it was Alba's. But it wasn't the prisoners who had anything to fear.

They released us from the *tapiadas* after three weeks, not because our punishment was over, but because they intended to punish the entire population of political prisoners. The prison authorities were in a foul mood from the escapes as well as the unrest following Alba's suicide, and they did everything they could to make our lives miserable.

They transferred most of us to Guanabacoa. Our rations, already sparse, were cut to a level one step removed from starvation. Breakfast was a small cup of warm sugar water containing a faint, wispy trace of coffee. Lunch and dinner were a few spoonfuls of plain, boiled spaghetti and a small piece of half-baked bread that fermented in our stomachs.

They also set up weekly disciplinary hearings, kangaroo courts where the tiniest infractions were inflated into sensational acts of counterrevolutionary terror. A prisoner, tasting her mushy, rancid bread, might say: "This must have been a reject from the Soviet bakery." A few days later, she would be called before the court (composed of a guard, a *llavera*, and a prison officeworker) and accused of standing on a chair in the dining room to shout: "Soviet bakeries are shit."

Almost everyone was convicted two or three times a week; the disciplinary hearings handed down so many punishments that there was a waiting list for Guanabacoa's new *tapiada* cells (even darker, smaller, and more poorly ventilated than the originals in Guanajay, though I could scarcely believe that was possible) and some of us had already lost mail and visits for the next seven or eight years.

It was a startlingly cold winter, and the *galeras* were so frigid that we slept six to a bed to keep warm. To thwart us, the *llaveras* started holding outdoor counts at five A.M., when the icy nighttime winds were still whipping across the patio. When we refused to go, they actually fired tear-gas canisters into the *galera* one morning.

And, of course, the periodic beatings continued. One of the worst was prompted when we made fun of a *llavera*'s shoes.

The brand name of those shoes was Illusion. Supposedly the finest handmade footwear in Cuba, they cost eighty pesos a pair (minimum wage was eighty-five pesos a month), and even at that exorbitant price, they were available only to dedicated Castro followers of the Revolution who had spent five or six years' worth of their Saturdays doing "voluntary" labor for the Revolution.

The *llavera* had been bragging for months that she was going to get a pair. Olga Morgan, the wife of the executed American adventurer, was the first prisoner to spot them. Pointing at them across the patio, she collapsed in helpless laughter. She barely got control of herself to sputter, "We're going to get it—they're going to beat us until their fists wear out!" As I studied the *llavera*'s feet, I could see what Olga meant. They looked like they were encased in asphalt speed bumps. The shapeless, oversized shoes were, without a doubt, the ugliest item of clothing I had ever laid eyes on, and I knew it would be impossible for anyone to keep a straight face in the *llavera*'s presence.

Olga's words were prophetic. The more we laughed, the angrier the *llaveras* got. Harsh words were exchanged. The guards were called. In the end there was a free-for-all that left two prisoners with broken arms, one with a broken shoulder, one with a broken finger, one with two dislocated bones, one missing several teeth, and everyone else with a large variety of cuts and bruises.

In April, we launched a hunger strike. The nominal cause was to demand medical care for Margarita, who was having severe stomach problems. But that was simply the last straw. We were fed up with our poor food, our cold *galeras*, our lack of medical attention. The prison had pushed us too far, to the point where we couldn't imagine how things could get worse.

The hunger strike gnawed at the prison authorities. It was a show of defiance beyond their control; they couldn't very well make us eat by beating us, and of course it was impossible to punish us by cutting our rations. About all they could do was to throw us into the *tapiadas*, which at least got us out of their sight, even if it didn't make us eat.

Eight of us were crammed into a little cell that was no more than six feet by four feet. It was so crowded that we had to take turns lying down to sleep, and whenever one of us needed to use the toilet (which was really not a toilet at all, but a primitive gravity-driven *patín* like the ones at Baracoa, which quickly backed up), everyone else had to shuffle around, like the different parts of a movable puzzle. We also shared the cell with a number of fearless rats that came and went through the *patín*, tracking excrement all over the cell floor, and hundreds of cockroaches that copulated ecstatically at all hours of the day and night.

On the thirteenth day, they emptied the *tapiadas* that held common prisoners, and started moving some of us out of the overstuffed cell. As they shuttled us from cell to cell, a guard took the little plastic cups we used to store drinking water, the only thing we were ingesting during the hunger strike. He promised to return them when we were all in place.

But watching through the dinner-plate slot in my door, I saw a guard gather the cups and head for the pavilion door. "Hey! The bastards are taking our cups!" I yelled. Immediately everyone else began shouting and banging on cell doors. Without the cups, we were lost.

A guard was walking Miriam Ortega to her new cell when the commotion broke out. Spinning away from him, she tried to tackle the guard who carried our cups. She caught him just beyond my cell door, as I angled for position to watch through the slot.

The guard, fat but surprisingly agile, sidestepped Miriam and caught her by the hair with one of his beefy hands. "Give back our cups, or I'm not going into my cell!" she hissed.

"You stupid piece of shit, you'll go where we tell you!" the guard roared. Dropping the cups from his free right hand, he pulled back his fist and launched a blow directly into her face.

But Miriam somehow turned her head slightly, deflecting part of the punch, and she snapped her jaws down tight onto his hand just below the thumb. His screech of pain was unearthly. He shot his right arm into the air trying to dislodge her, lifting Miriam completely off the ground, but her teeth held tight.

Miriam hung there like a punching bag, suspended in the air by her own teeth, as the other guards crowded around and showered her with kicks and punches. Her frail body, no more than eighty pounds after two weeks without food, absorbed blow after terrible blow, jiggling like a rag doll, but her teeth were still clenched. "Let go, you bitch!" the guard screamed, his voice a pure note of pain. My single eye, pressed at an angle on the slot in my cell door, was transfixed. It was as if all the cruel, vicious beatings I had witnessed in seven years of prison were distilled into this one hellish scene.

I almost sighed with relief when Miriam's body tumbled to the floor as the guard doubled over, his left hand squeezing tight around his right. Miriam lifted her face, and I could see blood running from the corners of her mouth. Her eyes gleamed with a glacial hatred. She spat a chunk of flesh onto the floor and wiped her mouth with the back of her hand. "Well, I finally ate today," she cackled. "I just had a mouthful of pork!"

A boot lashed out, catching her full in the face, and blood splashed everywhere. Then she was covered with guards, their arms and legs rising and falling like the pistons of a demented killing machine. The only sound was the horrid *splat* of heavy objects making contact with flesh.

My paralysis broke then. "Leave her alone, you Communist fuckers!" I screamed, banging on the steel plate welded across my door. "Leave her alone!" I hammered the plate with my hands and feet like it was the face of one of the guards, I screamed until I couldn't form words and only the sound of undiluted rage came from my throat.

I don't know when, exactly, I fainted, or how many hours I was unconscious. Sometime during my blackout my menstrual period had started, and my cutoff bluejeans were covered with a bloody crust that extended down my thighs to my knees. There was so much blood on the floor beneath me that for a moment I wondered if I had been beaten myself.

I crawled away from the filthy puddle and pulled myself up onto the cement slab extending out of the wall, what passed for a bed in the *tapiadas*. And there I lay, too weak and thirsty to move. Hours passed, then a day, then another, and another. My cracked lips ached. My swollen tongue filled my mouth. I dreamed only of water, at first when I was asleep, but then when I was awake. I could see a sparkling glass pitcher of water, rivulets of sweat trickling down its side, hovering in the corner of the ceiling. *That's absurd,* I thought, *a pitcher of water can't just hang there. Something would have to support it* . I squinted to make it go away, and this time I saw small, white, gossamer wings sprouting from its sides. When I listened closely I could hear them beating gently.

Oh, come on, I said to myself. *You can't take this seriously. Glass pitchers don't have wings.* The pitcher glided toward me, descending in a series of dips. The last one left it just out of my reach. *The hell with logic, I'm thirsty,* I thought, and lunged for it.

I came to on the cell floor, the prison doctor bending over me. "Don't worry, we're taking you to the hospital," he said softly, cradling my head.

"I'm not going anywhere until this is resolved," I said. The words came out from my cracked lips in a barely audible whisper. The doctor, shaking his head, left the cell.

A couple of hours later, an Interior Ministry officer in civilian clothes showed up. A look of nausea flashed across his face when he got his first whiff of the odor in the cell, but he suppressed it. "This is my day off," he said, rather proudly, "but I came over here to see what the problem is. Why won't you end this hunger strike?"

"Look at my legs," I instructed him. My menstruation had continued, and by now it looked like I was wearing shorts made of dried blood. "You don't even give us anything to clean ourselves during our period, and you wonder why we're on a hunger strike. Look around this cell, and then you won't have to ask stupid questions."

"But this is crazy," he answered. "You're not making conditions better by refusing to eat. You're just going to kill yourselves."

"That's right," I said. "We *are* going to kill ourselves. And what are you going to do then? How do you think you'll cover up the fact that fifteen women starved themselves to death in one of your prisons? The world has turned a blind eye to a lot of things in Cuba, Major, but if I were you, I wouldn't bet on getting away with that. Better get started on the cover story right away—it's going to have to be a masterpiece."

His face was expressionless as he left the cell. But a few hours later, a guard walked along the corridor with a bucket of water, passing it in to us in little cans. "The Ministry has sent this water so you can clean yourselves," he said as he handed each of us a thin sliver of soap. But instead of washing, I drank the water—three cans of it.

The next day, they transferred us out of the *tapiadas* and put us in a regular *galera*. We still refused to eat, but they gave us all the water we wanted for drinking and bathing.

On the twenty-fourth day of the strike, a delegation of Ministry officials arrived, led by Medardo Lemus, the new national director of prisons. "We've decided your living conditions have to be improved," he told us in an unctuously sincere voice. "There have been some grave errors committed here, errors of which I was not aware, and they are going to be corrected. We can talk about the specifics later, but for now, accept my word that changes are going to be made. Meanwhile, we're going to move all of you to the hospital, where they'll help you recover your health."

I wanted to spit in his face. Errors! The way they treated us was not an error, not an oversight, but a deliberate policy intended to break us the way the rest of Cuba was broken.

But I said nothing. We had won this battle; no need to rub their faces in it. It would just make them fight harder the next time.

· THIRTEEN ·

Re-Education

JULY 29, 1968

WE BRACED OURSELVES as the line of uniformed men tramped into the *galera*. Our brief, uneasy truce with the Interior Ministry was about to end. An escape attempt last night had ended in ridiculous failure—a warehouse roof near the wall had collapsed as several women tried to walk across it, with a crash loud enough to be heard in Miami—and we were about to learn what form official retribution would take. I tried to prepare myself for the worst (though, after seven and a half years, I knew my imagination was no match for theirs when it came to punishment). It must be grave indeed, because just about every top official in the whole Ministry had gathered before us.

"I told you before that we had made some errors in the way we've treated you," Medardo Lemus said, clasping his hands behind his back. "I'm not saying we're entirely responsible—the Revolution has been under constant attack by the gringos for the past several years, at times with the help of some of the prisoners in this room. Nonetheless, errors are errors, and it's time we corrected them.

"Within the next week, we're going to transfer you in small groups to the América Libre work farm. There you'll be able to get out in the sun and recover your health. But we've abolished the forced labor program there, so you don't have to work if you don't want to. You'll be permitted regular visits, and your packages from home will be larger. If you have any questions, I'll be happy to answer them now."

There were plenty of questions, but no one dared to ask the one that hovered at the edge of every tongue: What about the escape attempt? Weren't we going to be punished for it? Lemus didn't mention it once, didn't say a single word about it.

Each day ten or fifteen women departed for América Libre. Once they were gone, we heard nothing more from them. Was everything okay there? We had no idea, and our inclination was to expect the worst. I was part of the last group to leave; our transfer was scheduled for August 6. As the date approached, our speculation intensified. Surely something was afoot. What trick were they playing, what ambush had they laid for us? No one had any answers. But the constant worry took a toll on our sleep.

The night before the transfer, I didn't bother to close my eyes. I sat on my upper bunk playing solitaire with cards fashioned from tattered pieces of cardboard. Reina Peñate, in the bed next to mine, rolled from one side of the mattress to the other in a fruitless search for sleep. Pola Grau, in the bunk below Reina's, had dozed off, but her dreams were uneasy; every so often she mumbled a few indecipherable words in a troubled voice.*

Reina gave up her struggle to sleep and turned toward me. "Are you winning much?" she asked with a smile. "Or are you playing an honest game?"

"I only cheat when it's absolutely necessary," I said with injured dignity. "And it's not my fault. I'm the product of a society with impaired moral vision. Fidel Castro himself said so."

Down below, Pola mumbled in her sleep again. "What's she saying, anyway?" Reina asked. "I thought I heard my name."

Then Pola spoke again. "Somebody else sing something, for God's sake," she said, loudly and clearly. "Don't let Reina sing again—her voice makes me sick."

"*What?*" gasped Reina. "What did you say?"

"Reina's voice makes me sick," Pola obligingly repeated in her dream.

Reina jumped to the floor, grabbed Pola, and shook her hard. "Wake

---

*Pola's uncle, Ramón Grau San Martín, was Cuba's president from 1944 to 1948.

up, you damn hypocrite!" she bawled. "You pretend to be my friend, and then you stab me in the back. Wake up!"

"What's wrong? What's wrong?" Pola squawked, awake now but without a clue about what was happening. Across the room other women, jolted awake by the ruckus, were diving to the floor, believing the guards must be attacking us. Throughout the *galera* there were shouts of fear and confusion, except from a few of the bunks near us, where women who had witnessed the whole thing were doubled over in laughter.

I climbed down from my bunk and pulled the weeping Reina off of Pola. "What did I do?" Pola called to Reina as I led her to the front of the *galera*. "Backstabber! Backstabber!" was the only word Reina could muster through her tears.

Reina was about thirty-five. Well-educated (she had been an office worker at one of the American sugar companies before the Revolution) and even-tempered, she was one of our peacemakers, often moderating disputes between prisoners and smoothing over the little abrasions and irritants of prison life. She got along well with everyone (especially Pola Grau, her friend since childhood) except when it came to one thing: her singing.

Reina believed she was an undiscovered pop star, a diamond in the rough, and she always wanted to sing in the little plays and religious pageants we staged occasionally for our own entertainment. The truth, which no one had the heart to tell her, was that she was tone-deaf and sounded like a cat with its tail caught under a rocking chair. We used any excuse we could think of to keep her from singing, and now Pola had blurted out the truth in her sleep.

"I tell you, Ana, this has been the story of my life," Reina, still sniffling, told me as we sat at the front of the *galera*. "Since I was a little girl in grade school, I've wanted to be a singer, and no one has ever helped me. No one has ever recognized my talent.

"When I was eight years old, our church wanted volunteers for a children's choir. I didn't like the idea of a choir—it's a sin to hide a voice like mine in the middle of a crowd—but you've got to start somewhere. So I joined, and I spent weeks learning to sing the mass. And then, when we had the dress rehearsal, I was singing my heart out when the priest shouted, 'Stop the music, stop the music.' And he pointed at me from the altar and said: 'Get that child out of here! She's breaking my eardrums.' "

I wanted to laugh, but Reina's pretty face, wreathed in black curls, was so sad that I chewed on my knuckles to keep quiet.

"That priest, he gave me a complex, or jinxed me, or something. Because it's always been the same. I was married to an American, did you know that? He worked at the sugar refinery. He was such a gentle man, always good to me, and we had a happy marriage. We never fought about anything. One afternoon he came home from work, and I made him a drink, and brought it to him in his easy chair, and he gave me a big smile. He hugged me, and he said, 'Reina, you have the sweetest heart. If only your voice was as sweet as your heart, you'd be perfect.' After that, I could never look at him the same way again. We wound up getting a divorce.

"And now, when we have a pageant, Pola won't even let me sing the *fum-fum-fum* part in the background of the Christmas carols. She always gives me some alibi about how I'm needed to do something else. But tonight she gave away the real reason."

Reina sobbed once more, and I put my arm around her shoulders. *Pola's going to have to start wearing a gag in her sleep,* I thought.

The transfer took place the next day without incident. América Libre had been a summer retreat when it was a private farm, before the Revolution, and some of its graceful lines still showed through the barbed wire and concrete that had been added to turn it into a prison. The first floor of the vast main house had been converted into an office, and the second floor was the living quarters of Benilde Martínez, the prison director.

We lived in a building about twenty yards away from the main house that had once housed a small bowling alley and a ballroom. It was known as Central, and most of us were housed there in a single large room. Another building, a few hundred yards away, housed re-educated prisoners. And from the way Benilde Martínez and her deputies doted on them, it was obvious that the catch in this transfer was that the Ministry was going to redouble its efforts to push us into the re-education program.

Officially speaking, re-education no longer existed. It was now something called the Progressive Plan. Medardo Lemus and other Ministry officials insisted, in obfuscatory doubletalk that was cloudy even by the Revolution's standards, that the Progressive Plan was somehow different than the re-education program.

But to me it looked like the same old Orwellian stuff. You signed a confession of your sins against the Revolution, implicating others to prove your sincerity; with other prisoners, you went to "self-criticism" sessions where Ministry officials organized you into psychological paddle lines; and you performed slave labor to show your gratitude for the whole process.

There *were* a couple of new wrinkles to the Progressive Plan, which made it even more repulsive. One was mandatory participation in the idiotic Spoken Choruses. These consisted of groups of prisoners chanting in unison musty passages from Castro's speeches and letters. Perfect Communist art: It required neither talent nor imagination.

The other change was that prisoners who joined the Progressive Plan were paid for the labor they did. The promise of wages initially drew many common criminals, and a few political prisoners, into the plan. Their imprisonment was a financial drain on their families outside; here was a chance to help.

But the flip side of the wages was that prisoners in the Progressive Plan were billed for the costs of their imprisonment. They had to pay for food, for medicine, for uniforms, and for a host of "miscellaneous" charges that swallowed their earnings without a trace. Like the exploitative company stores on Cuba's old plantations, the Progressive Plan soon had most of its members hopelessly in debt, and the more they worked, the more they owed.

The Progressive Plan's fraudulence was soon apparent to even the dimmest prisoners. But the Ministry kept interest in it alive with an alluring insinuation. Medardo Lemus frequently called in prisoners to try to sell them on the plan. And, inevitably, in the middle of the conversation he would suddenly ask: "You have relatives in the United States, don't you?" The answer was almost always yes (at the rate Cubans were fleeing the island, there was hardly anyone in the country without some kin in the U.S.), and on the rare occasions that someone said no, Lemus quickly followed up: "Well, friends, then?" Then, just as abruptly, he changed the subject back to the Progressive Plan.

The day Carolina Peña came back from one of these chats with Lemus, she was elated. "Something's going on," she told me exuberantly. "I think Castro is bargaining a prisoner swap with the United States. And probably the Ministry wants to be able to say that everyone who gets released has been 'rehabilitated,' or something like that."

"Carolina, how can that possibly be?" I asked. "What prisoners does the United States have to trade?"

"Then maybe the United States will send money, or industrial parts, or something like that," she replied.

"But why would the United States do that? We aren't Americans. And when we fought Castro, we weren't working for the Americans. We did it for ourselves."

"Well," she said, her certainty unshaken, "why else would Lemus bring it up?"

The answer, I was sure, was that the Ministry was exploiting an ancient fantasy of the political prisoners. Ever since 1962, when President Kennedy ransomed the men captured at the Bay of Pigs with $53 million in food and drugs, rumors had periodically circulated that the Americans were negotiating another exchange, this one for political prisoners. Eventually the scuttlebutt had reached the ears of the prison authorities, who now were putting it to their own uses.

I never believed any of the stories about a prisoner exchange. And even if I had, it would have been impossible for me to sit in the self-criticism sessions, calling everyone "comrade" and pretending to have seen the light. My repugnance for the Revolution grew every day.

One afternoon I was sitting on a bench outside Central with a prisoner named Nenita Carames, making idle conversation, when we saw Antonio Abad passing by. Abad for several years was State Security's chief interrogator, and he had questioned nearly all of us at one time or another. But he had received several promotions in the past year, and we hadn't seen him around recently.

No State Security interrogator would ever win any popularity awards among us, but Nenita had a particular grudge against Abad because he had used an especially dirty trick against her. For months, while Nenita was being held alone and incommunicado at State Security headquarters, Abad tormented her with the story that her daughter Piluca was dating his son.

"They make a cute little couple, Nenita," Abad told her. "If you ever get out of here—not likely, seeing as how you're so uncooperative—you'll just love seeing them together. Ordinarily I wouldn't permit my son to go out with a member of a *gusana*'s family, but Piluca's thinking of joining the Party, so I've decided it's okay."

Abad told stories about the romance between his son and Piluca so often, and in such detail, that Nenita had little choice but to accept them as the truth, which drove her into a suicidal pit of despair. It was only when she was sent to prison that she learned it was all lies.

Now, seeing Abad walking slowly through the prison yard, Nenita jumped from the bench and followed him. "Abad, since you've always taken such an interest in my daughter, I wanted to give you the latest news," she said in a triumphal voice. "She got out of Cuba. And last month she was married in the United States. Maybe your son will see her there someday, when he gets sick enough of this place to leave."

Abad, without looking up, kept walking. "Hey, Abad, don't be such a spoilsport about it," I called. "You could at least say congratulations."

He stopped, turning to face us. To my surprise, his face was pale and drawn, and there were dark circles under his eyes. "A week ago today," he said, pronouncing the words slowly and carefully, as if he were in a trance, "my son killed himself with my own pistol."

Nenita and I stood there, frozen.

"It was time for his Obligatory Military Service, but he wouldn't go," Abad continued. "So I sent a squad to pick him up. When they got to the house, he ran up the stairs, locked himself in my room, and . . ." His voice broke off. "Afterward, there was nothing anyone could do."

"I'm sorry, so sorry," Nenita mumbled. There were tears in her eyes.

"Now," Abad added, his voice so low we could hardly hear it, "they've made me chief of State Security for all of Matanzas province."

"And you *accepted?*" I blurted out. He nodded, and started walking again. This time we didn't try to stop him. *It's men like that who keep the Revolution alive,* I thought as he disappeared into the prison offices.

It took us only about two months to be thoroughly sick of América Libre: the maddening sound of the Spoken Choruses, the repetitive talks about the Progressive Plan, and most of all, the silly attempts at instilling military discipline. Flor Chala Benítez, the prison's second-in-command, apparently thought she would be selected to run West Point after Castro took over the United States, and she was practicing on us.

Whenever she walked into Central, she shouted, "Attention!" We were supposed to jump up and stand at our bunks with our backs ramrod-stiff. (If anyone failed to do so, she hollered, "Flor Chala Benítez is here!" She always spoke of herself in the third person.) Beds had to be made up a certain way, with the sheets folded just so, and even the few items in our lockers had to be arranged in a particular order. She refused to let us into the dining room at mealtime until we lined up in a perfectly straight file. The extra visits and bigger packages we had been promised soon vanished in a flood of disciplinary reports as we failed to live up to Flor Chala's martial ideals.

So we did what we always did when times were tough: We organized a variety show.

We had been putting on shows for ourselves since the earliest days in Guanajay. Sometimes, especially when Pola Grau organized them, they were religious pageants. A few times Griselda Noguera, the former soap opera actress, directed small plays, drawing on her memory of the scripts.

But the most popular format was always the variety show. One person was appointed director, to coordinate everything, and the rest of us broke into small groups, each one in charge of producing a particular segment. Some did skits, some performed musical numbers, and there was always a "fashion show" featuring chic new outfits created from blankets and mosquito nets. Every clique went to great pains to keep its plans secret from everyone else, which made each segment a surprise to everybody except the few people who actually staged it.

Even more fun than watching, though, were the preparations. We couldn't ask the prison authorities for any help; the shows were strictly forbidden. Not, as you might suspect, because we made fun of Castro or the prison—political content was rare—but because anything we enjoyed was suspect and presumed counterrevolutionary.

So we had to go about the business of making costumes, scenery, props, and lighting from the few materials we had at hand, without alerting either the *llaveras* or each other about what we were doing. And since we would need our clothing and sheets and blankets and mosquito nets when the show was over, they had to be altered in ways that didn't destroy their effectiveness. To stage a show required us to be endlessly inventive, and it kept our minds off our troubles for months at a time.

We scheduled the show for September 20. As the date approached, América Libre fairly throbbed with conspiracy. We gathered about the yard in tiny groups of two or three that fell quiet at the approach of anyone, *llavera* and prisoner alike. We scoured the prison for stray scraps of cardboard and cloth. We asked our families to smuggle us dye pills, and overnight Central bloomed like a hothouse garden: Everything—sheets, blankets, pajamas, mosquito nets—turned various shades of blue, green, yellow, orange, and lilac.

Rather than joining any of the production groups, I took a job as a stagehand. It would be my responsibility to open and close the curtain—two blankets, dyed the color of green glass, suspended on a piece of twine run between two upper bunks. As part of my duties, I knew the plans for all the skits and songs.

The most elaborate was a production of a child's operetta called *La Juguetería*, a toy store where the merchandise comes to life each night after the lights are out. The lead character is a rather plain doll who's in love with a handsome lead soldier. The soldier, alas, has eyes only for a pretty ballerina doll. The plain doll despairs, but the rest of the toys remind her that they adore her. At the end, the plain doll learns that it's a big world, with more than one person to love.

The costumes for *La Juguetería* would be the fanciest ever attempted for one of our shows. The lead soldier, played by Japonesa, had a deep blue jacket with gold braids and a white belt. His helmet was fashioned from cardboard that gleamed with dozens of coats of methylene blue, a primitive antiseptic that we were allowed to keep in our lockers. Clara González, playing the pretty doll, wore a fluffy "chiffon" dress that was actually an intricate combination of dyed mosquito nets. Miriam Ortega, playing the role of a musical jack-in-the-box, had somehow obtained a bulbous clown nose made of red rubber and a small Mexican sombrero mounted with springy little antennae.

Though Miriam would play the jack-in-the-box onstage, her part would be sung by Caridad Roque, concealed backstage with our only musical accompanist, Lucrecia Sanchez on the guitar.*

I thought *La Juguetería* would be a big hit, not just for the clever costumes, but because its story would resonate with the audience. A lot of women who would be watching it had already been abandoned by husbands or boyfriends, and most of the others—at least secretly—feared it could happen to them. Most of the audience, I figured, would be in tears by the end of *La Juguetería*. And their tears of sadness might very well turn

---

*Caridad Roque was an actress who had appeared in a few small roles on Havana television before her arrest.

to tears of pain during the next number. Reina Peñate and Emma Rodríguez (whose voice was only marginally better) were going to come onstage singing a torch-song duet, *Miénteme*, lie to me. Nobody had ever walked out on one of our variety shows—it was a captive audience, after all, heh-heh—but Reina and Emma, I thought, might prove to be a precedent-setting act.

The *llaveras* had probably never seen such a clean, efficient count as the one on the night of the show. We made tight, orderly lines that would have made a German field marshal (or even Flor Chala) proud. We waited for a few minutes after the *llaveras* left, and hurriedly went to work pushing all the bunks to the side of the room and covering the fluorescent lights with dyed sheets to created colored lighting effects. We arranged things so the stage was adjacent to the bathroom, which could be used as a dressing room. The audience, sitting on the floor, would have its back to the main door of Central.

The fashion show was first, and then Japonesa, Miriam, and the others took their places onstage for *La Juguetería*. The story begins with the jack-in-the-box coming to life and waking the other toys; as the tempo of the music from his box picks up, the dance of the toys turns livelier and livelier. Looking around me, I could see the women in the audience were enchanted as the various clowns, dolls, and stuffed animals waltzed one another around the stage. They frowned in disapproval as the lead soldier spurned the plain doll. Then the final scene began, the jack-in-the-box singing his reassurances: *The broom and the dustpan love you, the lamp and the mop love you, the old clown loves you . . .*

Absorbed in the story, none of us saw the guards slip in behind us. Several dozen of them crowded into the room, and then, on a silent signal, they rushed the stage, wielding heavy electrical cables like bullwhips. They were on top of us before we knew it. Miriam was jerked from her cardboard music box, her bulbous red nose flying off into the air. Another guard tried to yank Clara González by her dress, but it pulled completely away, leaving her standing in the middle of the stage in bra and panties as the guard tumbled back into the audience.

Fists began to fly, but, weirdly, there were none of the shouted threats and curses that usually accompanied our fights. Both sides slugged it out in surreal silence, the thuds of landing blows the only sound.

Meanwhile, backstage, no one could see anything through the blankets hung from bunks we had used to create a backdrop. Caridad Roque finished singing, and Lucrecia the guitarist strummed the final chord of *La Juguetería*. Reina and Emma, in turn, took their cue to begin. Moving to opposite sides of the stage, they entered singing: *I've been living on your lies . . .* Their eyes closed as they bathed in the passion of the lyric; neither of them noticed that their audience was rolling around on the floor, kicking and biting at the uniformed invaders. Lucrecia, hearing their off-key wailing, struggled mightily to cover it with her guitar.

The fight spread backstage, and costumed women awaiting their cues started spilling around the sides of the backdrop, warding off blows from the guards. I saw Nieves Abreu, dressed as a black swan, running down an aisle between the bunks, pursued by three vengeful *llaveras*. Another *llavera* was dragging a kicking, squirming Miriam by the hair. The sound of the fight was louder now, with bunks being overturned and bodies slamming to the floor, but the only voices were those of Reina and Emma, screeching to a faithless lover to lie to them, lie to them just one more time.

A guard finally knocked Lucrecia off her chair backstage, ending the guitar accompaniment with a discordant twang that caused Reina and Emma to snap their eyes open. Stunned by the silent bedlam around them, they broke off their song in mid-verse. Seconds later, Emma jumped onto the back of a guard and began hammering him with her fists. But Reina looked around for a moment, closed her eyes again, and wailed: *It doesn't matter, life is a lie, lie to me more.* Her first starring role was not going to be interrupted by a mere riot. Two verses later, she brought the song to a stirring, if discordant, climax. Then, joyously, she took a few steps forward and slapped a *llavera* across the face.

It was two days later that Chonchi approached my bunk. I was lying flat on my back, staring at the ceiling, bubbles of anger bursting in my brain like sunspots.

"Still mad at those sons of bitches for breaking up our show?" Chonchi asked. I narrowed my eyes at her without answering. The question was either rhetorical, or really dumb. The whole *galera* was still sullen. All we had done was dress up and sing a few songs—that was no reason to beat us. Even by the seriously warped standards of Castro's prisons, the guards had gone way too far.

Chonchi ignored my show of irritation. "Would you like to get some revenge?" she asked, and smiled at the way my expression changed. "I have kind of an idea, but it would be easier to show you. Come to my bunk."

Most of the women were already lining up outside the dining room for lunch. The room was nearly deserted as we made our way to Chonchi's bunk. *How the hell does she sleep in that thing?* I wondered. The mattress sagged comically, like a swayback horse.

Chonchi pulled back the covers, slipped into the bed, and yanked the sheet and blanket back over herself until even her head was covered. "Do you see what I wanted to show you?" her muffled voice asked from beneath the bedclothes.

I did indeed. The cavity in the mattress was so big that Chonchi's body disappeared into it completely. With the covers pulled up, it looked like the bed was empty. Chonchi had found a way to hide herself in plain sight.

"Do you want to do it tonight?" she asked, burrowing back up into the daylight.

"No, not tonight," I replied. "Let's give everyone another night to brood about things. By tomorrow, the mood should be perfect."

"We're not telling anyone, are we?" Chonchi asked, smiling the same way she did when I told her about Superman's cape.

"Not a soul," I answered. "Not a single soul."

The evening count at América Libre was not very formal. Instead of lining us up, the *llaveras* usually just walked the room, counting us as we went about our business. The next night when I saw the *llaveras* enter, I nodded at Chonchi. In the blink of an eye she jumped into bed and rearranged the covers on top of herself. As before, the illusion was perfect.

I went on pretending to read one of the United Nations magazines the prison authorities had recently started allowing us to receive, while watching the *llaveras* out of the corner of my eye. Twice they walked through the room, and I could see them shaking their heads in consternation.

"Attention, everyone!" called one of the llaveras, a sergeant. "Get in your bunks so we can count!" A few prisoners wandered toward their beds, but the majority resolutely ignored her. The *llaveras* tried another count anyway, and again were frustrated. They knew someone was missing, but they couldn't figure out who.

"Attention, damn it!" the sergeant shouted again. "You're going to have to come outside and line up, so we can call you out by name." Perhaps as many as two dozen prisoners went outside. But the vast majority of women defied the order, continuing to leisurely brush their teeth, comb their hair, or gossip with their friends. No one understood what was bugging the *llaveras*. Except for me, nobody knew that Chonchi was hiding, and everyone just assumed the stupid *llaveras* couldn't count straight.

The *llaveras*, on the other hand, were starting to suspect that someone had broken out and we were deliberately thwarting the count, as we had after other escapes. Calling for help from the male guards, they angrily came back inside, walking the aisles between the bunks and ordering prisoners to stand in place. They stopped Olga Ramos, who was headed for the bathroom, and told her to stay put. Olga huffily spun on her heel and marched up to the sergeant.

"Would you kindly explain just what all this bullshit is about?" she demanded.

The smoldering sergeant, certain she was being mocked, cocked her fist and drove it deep into Olga's stomach. Miriam, standing nearby, jumped for the sergeant's throat. Guards swarmed over her. Within seconds, both Olga and Miriam were being dragged way. "We're keeping these two as hostages until you come outside for a recount," a male lieutenant shouted.

The room exploded into uncontrolled rage. Women leaped from their bunks to charge the guards. Others ripped away strips of aluminum from the big jalousie windows that lined the sides of the room and started smashing the glass. Teresa Vidal jumped through one of the windows and went after the guards carrying Olga and Miriam, quickly followed by a dozen others.

The guards inside fled Central in a panic as we threw chairs and buckets at them. Outside, they formed a cordon around the building, but they didn't dare try to come back in. We spilled outside, screaming threats and continuing to throw anything we could find. I felt a tap on my shoulder and turned to see a smiling Chonchi, who had crawled back out of her bed undetected to join the fight.

"I guess it worked pretty well," she giggled.

"Be quiet," I shushed her. "Look at these women—do you want them coming after us?" I was serious. I had never seen such universal rage. The panicky guards had already freed Olga and Miriam; now they were just standing back, dodging the scraps of broken furniture that were still being hurled at them.

"Go back inside now, or we'll call the firemen to turn their hoses on you!" the lieutenant cried out. "No!" we shouted back in near unison. Moments later, three flaming bunks were dragged out of the building and heaved toward the guards. "If the firemen come, we'll tear down this building brick by brick!" someone screamed.

I thought I heard something inside Central, and I walked back to take a look. The only person inside was Enriqueta Meoquí, an old woman nearly blind with cataracts. Queta, as we called her, spent nearly all her waking hours praying, asking God to send mice to play near her feet so she could get over her phobia of them. Actually, mice played at her feet all the time; she was just so blind she couldn't see them. The one time she did, she broke the spine of a prayer book trying to kill them with it.

But tonight all the screaming and sounds of breaking furniture had filled Queta with a cheery bloodlust. She was determined to get a piece of this fight, age and blindness be damned. As I walked in, she was groping around the floor for something to throw, and her hands found a bucket filled with water. Squealing in exultation, she flung it toward the windows.

Of course, all the windows were long since broken, and the guards were several hundred feet away from the building, but Queta was blissfully unaware of that. She paused, a mildly puzzled expression on her face, when there was no sound of breaking glass, but only for a moment; then she bent over, picked up a small wooden bench, and threw that. She kept up a steady hail of aluminum plates, pans, and assorted debris out that window.

A few minutes later, Pola Grau, soaking wet and clutching her shoulder in pain, walked into the room. "Queta, what are you doing?" she asked plaintively. "That pail you threw hit me in the shoulder."

Queta turned and placed her wrinkled hand on Pola's. Her blind eyes were shining with a warrior's ardor. "It's okay, Pola," she said solemnly, repeating a line from the Cuban national anthem, "to die for the Fatherland is to live!" Then she threw another plate.

No firemen ever came. After a couple hours of tense standoff, we went to bed, though hardly anyone slept. Lemus and several of his flunkies from the Ministry showed up the next day, somewhat embarrassed; after all, there was no missing prisoner—his stupid guards had touched off a riot with their inability to count. He promised us bigger packages and more visits. Chonchi and I listened with smug, knowing smiles.

As 1969 dawned, we knew there were changes ahead. Our group of prisoners had been together more or less continuously since mid-1961, when the Ministry started concentrating all the troublemakers in D Pavilion at Guanajay. Our numbers had waned slightly, due to escapes, transfers to jails in other provinces, and a few releases, but essentially the 165 political prisoners at América Libre were like a school class that had been together almost eight years.

But part of the class was about to graduate. Over the next eighteen months, a large number of women with comparatively short sentences of seven to ten years were scheduled for release.

The first was Margarita Blanco, my partner in both escapes. On February 13, when she completed her sentence (with an extra thirty-one days tacked on for our last escape), she was called to the prison offices and told to pack her things. But before she even had a chance to smile, the Ministry officials started ticking off a long list of conditions: She had to live in Havana (although her parents were hundreds of miles away, in Santa Clara province), she couldn't be away from her house for more than twenty-four hours without permission, she had to call State Security every day to check in.

We could hear her savage curses from the moment she left the office. No one dared speak to her as she slammed her few things into a canvas bag; she looked like she was ready to bite someone. She stalked out of Central without even saying good-bye. I didn't blame her; Margarita wasn't really being released at all—she was just going to a different prison, where the government wouldn't have to feed her.

In March they started releasing prisoners who were old, infirm, or ill. Queta was one of the first to go; Isabel Rodríguez, the young doctor who had patched up so many of us after battles with the guards, but couldn't cure her own persistent stomach problems, was another.

It was on December 31 that they released the first large batch of prisoners who had completed their sentences. Reina Peñate was released, prompting a sigh of relief from everyone who helped plan our variety shows. My friends Nelly Urtiaga and Ilia Herrera, who blocked me from escaping from the State Security car on that long-ago day when we were driven to prison together, were on the list. So was Isabel Molgado, whose *sotto voce* "Manolo, you blockhead," probably helped push Manolo Martínez from weirdness to madness. María Cristina Oliva, who helped me burn down the prison at Baracoa and later drove me half nuts in the *tapiadas* with her sensuous descriptions of imaginary meals, was also leaving.

They called us outside around noon to hear the announcement of the release. A charged current of exhilaration surged through the women whose names were called. Most of them were too keyed up to eat lunch after that; they hurried back to Central, packed their few belongings in canvas bags, stacked them outside, and sat down beside them. Unconsciously, they were already distancing themselves from the prison and from us. We had seen the reaction before; we respected it.

But as the sticky, sultry afternoon wore on, with no sign of a truck to take them away, the women began to get cranky and irritated. "With these people, everything's a bloody war," Isabel Molgado repeated, over and over. María Cristina, I could tell, was furious and wanted to slug someone, but she was trying to keep her anger off her face; any little thing could be the excuse they needed to extend her sentence. Dinner was served, and still the women didn't eat, but this time out of disgust rather than elation.

Finally, around ten P.M., a *llavera* appeared. Everyone tensed; would she tell us it had all been a joke? What would we do? "I'm sorry for the delay, but we had to get you clothing," she announced. "You can't wear your prison uniforms into the street. Ilia Herrera, please come forward and get your clothes."

They called them like that, one at a time, each after an interminable wait. I shook my head when I saw the new clothes; they were identical brown skirts and cream-colored blouses that looked even more like uniforms than the blue outfits we were wearing.

A truck pulled up outside, and—after more dithering—they started getting in. We crowded around, shouting good-byes. "We'll see you here at the fence," repeated both those who were leaving and those staying.

A war of conflicting emotions was being fought on every face. Though I think all of us staying behind were genuinely happy for those who were leaving, there was also an air of depression; we knew that, as our group grew smaller, resistance would be tougher. I think, if the guards hadn't been there, a lot of us would have been crying. The women who were leaving, too, felt contradictory tugs on their hearts. As delighted as they were to go, they knew no one outside would ever be able to understand what they had gone through here. Only we knew. In some ways, we were a more real family than they could ever have outside.

I floated on the edges of the crowd, feeling detached. I didn't want to rain on anyone's parade. But these women hadn't been in the street in years, and they couldn't possibly have the remotest idea of what it was really like out there. I did, and I knew that leaving the fences at América Libre wasn't going to make them free.

But when María Cristina, the last of the departing prisoners, climbed into the truck, a vibrant smile lit up her face. And that, in turn, lit up mine. Whatever was going to happen outside, she had earned that smile. All of us had.

Prisoners continued to trickle out of América Libre in 1970. A few had completed their sentences, but most were released a year or two or even three early. The early releases were necessary because Fidel Castro was trying to live up to an ignorant macho boast he had made seven years earlier.

At a time when the sugar harvest hovered around four million tons, Castro predicted that socialist economic planning would streamline production to the point that, by 1970, the Cuban sugar crop would be ten million tons. "We shall have the atomic sugar-bomb in our hands!" he crowed. With a crop that size, Cuba would dictate to the world market rather than the other way around.

Castro bragged again and again over the years about the ten million tons, stifling any questions in a flurry of ephemeral statistics. When the 1969 harvest brought in only five million, it should have been obvious that the goal was impossible—and undesirable. Castro had diverted so many resources to sugar that production prices were impossibly high; every ton that was sold from the 1969 crop meant a $90 *loss* to Cuba.

But the Maximum Leader would not be deterred, oh no. He more than doubled the cane-cutting season to nine months. His careful calculations, Castro announced, revealed that it would take a mere two hundred thousand workers, cutting cane eight hours a day, seven days a week, for nine months, to bring in the harvest. Then, just to be on the safe side, he ordered into the fields the army, university students, government bureaucrats, and anyone who had applied for an exit visa: "permanent volunteers," they were called.

The massive mobilization for sugar, of course, paralyzed vast sectors of the Cuban economy and set off a ripple effect of unforeseen shortages and bottlenecks that hobbled sugar production. As the crop fell further and further behind, Castro's measures became more and more drastic. We were one of those measures. By paring the number of political prisoners, Castro freed additional military units to work in the cane fields.*

A few years earlier, State Security would have lodged a vigorous and probably fatal objection to the releases, arguing that they would feed the counterrevolutionary fires. But these days there was simply no organized resistance to Castro at all; his enemies spent their time plotting to get out of Cuba, not to overthrow the government. In fact, if State Security had anything to fear, it was not counterrevolutionaries but budget-cutters, who wondered why it was necessary to keep funding such a huge secret police force. By permitting a few of us to be released, State Security could argue against cutbacks: Obviously, any of us who went into the streets would have to be watched carefully.

So the releases continued, even though we still rejected the Progressive Plan and all other forms of re-education. In February 1970, another group was freed, including Gladys Hernández and Chonchi Castellanos. In March 1971, Teresa Vidal went out with another group.

As I had expected, life outside proved only marginally more tolerable for most of the prisoners who were released. Though they weren't supposed to have contact with us, a few stopped by from time to time and talked to us from outside América Libre's chain-link fence. Most of them were under some form of parole that kept them from traveling, and they were followed whenever they left their houses. Jobs were virtually impossible to obtain

---

*Despite all Castro's efforts, the sugar crop was a failure; only 8.5 million tons of cane were harvested, and the milling yield was just 10.7 percent, the lowest in recorded Cuban history. Yet all the economic distortions Castro induced in an effort to fulfill his prediction continued to reverberate in the Cuban economy for years. One of the first casualties was the 1971 sugar crop, which fell to 5.9 million tons.

for former prisoners, but survival on the meager food provided by government ration books was also impossible.

Nearly all the former prisoners had given up any pretense of trying to rebuild their lives in Cuba. Instead, they were applying for exit visas, which the government was in no hurry to provide. Most of them were mordantly depressed. A notable exception was Chonchi. She spent her days visiting government butcher shops and, with a straight face, asking to buy a side of beef. "It's a lot of fun to see their faces," she reported one day through the fence. I could imagine.

I didn't think I wanted to be out in the streets under those conditions. Fortunately, it wasn't a dilemma I would have to address. Shortly after the release of the group including Vidal, Medardo Lemus came to see our group of political prisoners, which now numbered only about sixty-five. All of us were serving sentences of twenty or thirty years.

"Look around you," he said. "These are your traveling companions for the rest of your stay in prison. This group is frozen—we're not releasing anyone else early, and we're not going to permit new prisoners to get caught up in your clique. They're going directly into the re-education program now, without any choice in the matter. And that's the only way any of you are getting out, through re-education. We've been too soft with you, but that's going to change."

Books, which had recently been permitted inside the prison for the first time in years, were outlawed again, along with magazines and newspapers. Our packages were reduced in size and—along with our visits— trimmed to one every three months. And we were transferred from Central to the farm's old horse stables. Long, narrow, and cramped (the ceiling was six feet high at its tallest, and just five feet in the tiny bathroom), the stables were almost unlivable. We stayed outside even in the foulest weather, and entered them only to sleep at night.

But it wasn't until I came down with pneumonia that I really understood what Lemus meant when he said they wouldn't be "soft" with us anymore. Lázaro García, the national prison system's medical chief, prescribed three different medicines for me, only to be told none of them were available. In desperation, he wrote a prescription for six oranges a day. The fruit was readily available—there were orange trees planted all over América Libre—but we were forbidden to eat any of it, even when it was just lying on the ground spoiling.

The angry prison authorities reluctantly gave me the oranges. But they fired Dr. García.

It was a sunny day in May 1972 and we were sitting outside as usual, avoiding the suffocating heat of the stables, when several trucks of uniformed men pulled up outside the prison. Our curiosity as we watched them unload turned to anxiety as they went running into the stables.

"Who are those men?" Miriam asked one of our guards. "What are they doing in there?"

"Those are guards from La Cabaña," he explained. "And you'd better just stay away from them. It's got something to do with Boitel."

"What about Boitel?" I asked.

"He died today," the guard replied.

The news hit me like a blow. I knew Pedro Luís Boitel only slightly, but I had always admired him from afar. He exemplified the very best of my generation. As a student politician at the University of Havana, he fought Batista openly until he was forced into exile. When he returned, he was so popular that Castro first rigged the student-body elections at the university to defeat him, and then jailed him.

Boitel had been sickly all his life, and his health deteriorated rapidly in prison. Nonetheless, he was by far the most rebellious of all the male political prisoners. He was beaten so often and so badly that both his legs had to be amputated because of festering wounds. Even without his legs, he continued to lead hunger strikes. This most recent one had lasted fifty-three days. And now they had let him die.

I guess they were very proud of themselves, because they threw themselves a big party in the stables. When we were permitted back inside two hours later, the floor was a trampled mess of sugar, salt, and crushed crackers and cookies, every bit of food that had come in with our packages. Mixed in were the torn fragments of all the letters and photographs from our families. Our pajamas were torn to ribbons, our mosquito nets were slashed, and any container that would hold water had been perforated with bayonets.

When we asked Benilde Martínez, the prison director, what brought all this on, she replied blandly: "They were searching to see if you had any weapons, because they were afraid you'd stage a revolt to protest Boitel's death."

Of course, that was a fatuous lie; the only weapons we ever used against the guards were our feet and fists, and those usually only in self-defense. If the guards had anyone to fear, it was the common criminals. They got a reminder of that a few months later, when several male common prisoners stole knives from the kitchen at La Cabaña, killed a guard, and escaped.

Benilde called us together and read a long account of the escape from Granma, the official government newspaper. "The military unit the dead guard is from is enraged," she added gravely. "They want vengeance. They want to kill somebody." She repeated that a couple of times before dismissing us.

"What the hell does any of that have to do with us?" a bewildered Miriam asked as we walked away. "Does she think we masterminded the escape?"

"Oh, she was probably just reading the paper, got pissed off, and decided to give us a lecture," I said. "We're a handy punching bag. Probably half the stuff that happens to us is because some Ministry official argued with his wife at breakfast and comes to work mad."

"Yeah, but there was something funny about the way she talked," Miriam said. "It was almost like a warning, although against what, I have no idea."

Within a week the escaped prisoners were caught, tried, and executed, along with several people who helped hide them. We thought that was the end of the story, but we were wrong. A few days later, just after breakfast, the trucks rolled up again, and several dozen men in uniforms jumped out. They burst into the stables, where we were doing our morning cleaning, and started shoving us out into the yard. Several women went sprawling onto their faces. I started toward one of the most aggressive men, but an América Libre guard blocked my way. "Don't do it, Ana," he whispered urgently. "They're from La Cabaña, the unit of the murdered guard. And they're just looking for an excuse to kill someone."

We waited in the dining room until they were finished. When we returned to the stables, the scene was the same as before. Because we had less food this time—packages were smaller and less frequent these days—the guards had to search more thoroughly to find enough things to satisfy their hunger to destroy. Every tiny little thing we had was lying in a mangled heap in the middle of the floor. The new pajamas we had created at the sacrifice of our bedsheets were shredded to rags. In their frenzy, the guards even broke the prison's own aluminum dinner plates and iron ladles.

No one moved to clean up the mess. Instead, the women crouched around the pile of wreckage and studied it, as if it were an object dropped from outer space. A few picked up individual pieces to examine, peering carefully at each crack and tear, before dropping them back into the debris. A bitter silence filled the room.

I watched the scene from my bunk. *Their hatred for us just keeps growing,* I thought. *They know we had nothing to do with the death of that man, and yet they punish us for it anyway. We're a treat, the candy that parents give a crying child.*

For the death of their fellow guard, those men thought they were entitled to hate, and to lash out. I wondered what they thought about Boitel, who died because he thought that simple morality could overcome brute force, that reason would triumph over repression. Did they know what it was like to die of hunger: the cracked lips, the inflamed eyelids, the loosened teeth, the open sores, the skin gray and scaly from fungus? Could they imagine the sensation of the body devouring itself? Could they comprehend the loneliness of dying surrounded only by your enemies, those for whom your final breath would bring only pleasure?

For all these years I had been telling myself not to let hate get the upper hand in my soul. But now I suspected I had been wrong. A death like Boitel's *deserved* hatred. Castro and those who served him weren't mistaken or misguided, they were evil. What they did to Boitel, they were willing to do to the entire country—and, if they got the chance, the entire world. With sophistry and lies, they could flimflam the rest of the world about so many things like the kangaroo courts and the bullet-riddled *paredón*. But the way they treated us—weak, at their mercy, any potential to threaten them long since extinguished—was their true measure. Because we refused to think like them, they believed they had the right to torment us eternally. They punished us not only for things we did, but for things we might have done, or would have liked to have done. And now they were punishing us for things other people did.

I hopped down from my bunk, walked over to the heap in the center of the floor, scooped up a few things I recognized as mine, and dumped them in the garbage can. Then I walked outside to enjoy the sunshine. I felt a cold new current running through my veins. I thought about the murdered guard, and, for the first time, it made me happy.

Someone was coming. For days they had been pruning trees, trimming grass, raking brush, picking up trash. Then they even whitewashed the perimeter fence. The morning all the guards turned up wearing white leggings and dress helmets (except for two short and enormously fat men, Angelito and Ventura, who had been told to take the day off), we knew the visit was imminent.

The prison was atop a small hill, and we could see the Mercedes-Benz racing toward us when it was still a long way off, a cloud of dust trailing behind it. When it stopped at the offices, the guards snapped off smart military salutes while Medardo Lemus tripped over his own feet in his haste to step forward and open the passenger door. "It must be Fidel Castro himself," I observed to the rest of the women, who were observing as raptly as I was.

We were wrong. The man who emerged from the car was bald and pale. He brushed away Lemus' hand and reached back inside the car. A moment later, a voluptuous blonde woman climbed out. Lemus began leading them on a tour of the prison. He carefully positioned himself between the visitors and us, as though he were trying to block us from view.

They were much too far away for us to hear anything, but I noticed that whenever the man spoke to Lemus, the woman started talking a fraction of a second later.

"I think the woman's a translator," I said to the others. "So the man must be a foreigner. I'll bet he's a Russian, and Lemus is afraid we'll say something embarrassing, because he's doing his best to keep us out of sight."

"Why would a Russian give a damn about us?" inquired Berta Alemán. "I bet it's somebody from one of the Western European countries who wants to hear a lot of lies about human rights before he gives Castro some aid."

"Well, let's get him up here," said Japonesa. "We'll find out exactly who he is, and then we'll make trouble for that asshole Lemus. Because Ana's right about that—look at the way Lemus is trying to keep their attention away from us."

She darted into the stables. When she returned a few minutes later, we broke out laughing. Japonesa had smeared herself with burnt cork and donned a braided, African-style wig she had made for one of our variety shows. It was true—official visitors were invariably curious about black political prisoners. When Sinesia Drake was still with us, they flocked to her like flies to sugar. But she had finished her sentence, and we had no fashionable ethnic minorities with which to lure this stranger. So Japonesa would have to do.

Japonesa started dancing, an awkward semi-conga step, and sure enough, the visitors stopped to stare. Smiling broadly, she waved at the bald man. He turned to Lemus and said something, and they started walking toward us. Lemus wore an expression of pure panic that was almost farcical.

As they neared the fence around the stables, I could see the bald man squinting at Japonesa. His visage went from intense to startled to angry in rapid succession; he had recognized the disguise. He said something that made Lemus wince. But his pace didn't slow.

He barged through the gate and walked right into the stables like he owned them. Lemus and several other Ministry toadies scuttled along behind him, the blonde following indifferently. Inside he stopped here and there to scrutinize a bunk or a chair, sometimes probing a mattress with his fat little fingers. But he didn't speak until he reached the rear of the room and, without warning, threw open the door of Georgina Cid's locker.

Like everyone else's, it was virtually empty. An extra blouse and skirt were arranged on hangers, and in a neat row on the top shelf were one tiny jar of anti-fungus medicine, another holding three aspirin tablets, a small container of talcum powder, three extra buttons, and a sewing needle.

The bald man stared at Georgina's pathetic little pharmacy as though he were beholding the hidden cache of Montezuma's gold. Then he wheeled on Lemus and started barking. *Ahh, I was right,* I thought. *Russian.* The blonde calmly translated his words. "How is this possible?" he demanded. "How can they have so much medicine? Are you running a prison or a summer camp?"

Lemus, rubbing his hands obsequiously, was a portrait of desperation. "Really, I can't explain this," he said several times. "We almost never give them medical treatment. I can't imagine where she got those things."

"Bahhh," the Soviet growled, waving his hand in contempt. "Bahhh," the blonde dutifully repeated. There was a trace of a smile on her lips. I didn't think she liked Lemus.

The Russian stalked away, moving across the room, and then veered toward Berta Alemán's locker. But when he reached for it, she quickly stepped in front of it. "Who the hell are you to look in my locker?" she challenged him. "Even the guards don't think they can come in here and open our things as they please." She paused, then added disdainfully: "And at least they're Cubans."

Even before Berta's words were translated, there were flames in the Soviet's eyes. Again he turned to Lemus. "How can you permit this kind of defiance?" he bellowed. "Who runs this place? It's bad enough that you can't reform them, but you could at least teach them some respect!"

Lemus was frantic. "I swear to you, we've punished them a thousand times, every way you can possibly think of!" he babbled. "We've beaten them, we've starved them, we've done everything we could think of, every- thing! We've treated them like *shit!*" For a moment I almost laughed. It was like a scene from the blackest comedy ever written. *In a second, Lemus will promise to bring back branding irons and the guillotine,* I thought.

"There are no excuses for this," the Russian barked, overriding his protests. "No excuses at all! You've been coddling them, treating them like spoiled children instead of enemies of the state. There is a complete absence of revolutionary will in this institution."

"But sir," Lemus began, his voice now deteriorated into a childish whine. I couldn't stand it anymore.

"Have some respect!" I admonished the Soviet. The blonde repeated my words in Russian without missing a beat. "This isn't your country. You're the guest here, or perhaps I should say invader. I detest all these men here, but they're Cubans, and so are we. And no Cuban has to put up with this kind of insulting behavior."

The Soviet studied my face for a moment. Then, without replying, he turned to a knot of prisoners on his right. "Do you have relatives in the United States?" he asked one woman, his voice affable.

"Sure," she replied. "Are you going to let me out to visit them?"

"No," he laughed, "I just wondered if you hear from them. Does the American embargo include mail?" Several women spoke up in reply. The conversation turned into a trivial, but friendly, show-and-tell.

I edged around the group to Lemus. There was no sign of his customary swagger. Beads of sweat lined his forehead, and he tugged nervously at his collar.

"Remember all this, Lemus, remember it well," I said softly. "Because I'm certainly going to." Without giving him a chance to reply, I moved back into the crowd around the Russian.

· FOURTEEN ·

La Cabaña

July 13, 1974

CLIMBING OUT OF the ambulance, I felt the world start spinning. Surely those towering stone walls, so tall they challenged the sun itself, were going to topple over on us. I grabbed the roof of the vehicle, held it tight, and closed my eyes for a moment. The sensation passed, barely. When I opened my eyes, the guard pushing the rolling stretcher that carried Miriam was watching me closely. "I'm okay," I assured him. Miriam, too, seemed overwhelmed by the massive fortress we were entering. Her face was pale, her lips tight.

La Cabaña, located on a hill on a tongue of reefs protruding into Havana Bay, was celebrating its two-hundredth birthday in 1974. Its thick, high walls and narrow, sinuous streets were built for maximum protection from the cannons of marauding enemy ships. But right from the very start, the Spanish rulers of Cuba had recognized that the same qualities that made it such a good fort also made it an excellent place to lock up political deviants. Political prisoners had been confined in La Cabaña during every time of turmoil in the past two centuries, and this was one Cuban tradition that Fidel Castro was happy to uphold. He even improved upon it; the deep stone moats that wound through La Cabaña, now dry, made safe, efficient workplaces for the firing squads that Castro kept working day and night in the first years of the Revolution.

La Cabaña, surrounded by drill grounds and firing ranges, was still a military base. The Los Camilitos artillery school, where the sons of government functionaries trained as the army's future elite, was located there. But within Cuba, La Cabaña was known mostly as a prison.

Besides housing the maximum-security unit for several thousand male political prisoners, La Cabaña was also Cuba's largest prison for male common criminals. And there were also several *galeras* that held only homosexuals. The work farms where the homosexuals had formerly been locked up had started to attract international criticism, so Castro, with great fanfare, announced he was closing them. Then he quietly transferred the prisoners to La Cabaña.

La Cabaña had never held any women before. But now Miriam and I, after two weeks in a military hospital recovering from a long hunger strike, were going to join four others—Esther Campos, Sara Carranza, Berta Alemán, and María Amalia Fernández—who had already been locked up here for a week. *It's funny,* I thought as we walked along the ancient cobblestones. *This is probably the most dreaded place in Cuba. Who would ever believe that we chose to come here rather than a women's prison?*

Our road to La Cabaña began ten months earlier, when a rumor reached our ears in the stables at América Libre. On a farm south of Havana, the Interior Ministry was building a huge new women's prison that had already consumed ten thousand sacks of cement. It was to be called Nuevo Amanecer—New Dawn, another dry joke from the Ministry—and a pavilion for political prisoners had just been completed. That was the key element of the gossip: *a* pavilion, just one. They were planning to make us live with the re-educated prisoners.

Our relationship with the re-educated prisoners was much improved from the old days, but I knew it would be impossible for me to live in close quarters with them. As part of the Progressive Plan, they had to practice their revolutionary chanting, paint banners celebrating the anniversary of the October Revolution in the Soviet Union, and make a host of other public testimonials to the fact that their brains had been thoroughly laundered. That was okay with me, but I didn't want to live in the middle of it.

"But what difference does it make?" Pola Grau asked me during one of the many discussions in the stables after we heard the rumor. "We've been living with Communist propaganda for fourteen years. Why should this be any worse?"

"Because this is an attempt by the Ministry to divide and conquer," I responded. "The re-educated prisoners will be first-class citizens in that pavilion, able to freely express their political opinions. And we'll be second-class citizens who have to keep our mouths shut. They can put up banners saluting Marx and Lenin. Do you think we'll be allowed to put one up honoring the Hungarian freedom fighters or the Berlin airlift? The pavilion will belong to them, and we'll be like poor relatives, sleeping on the basement floor."

There were a lot of contentious conversations like that one. The majority of women sided with Pola, that there was little harm in setting up housekeeping with the re-educated prisoners. When the transfer was announced, only eight of us refused to go. We expected a beating and a trip to the *tapiadas*, but for once, geopolitical luck was running our way. Salvador Allende's teetering Marxist government in Chile finally went over the edge, falling victim to a military coup. Castro was nervous. There were rumors of CIA involvement. Was there more to come? Would the Americans start actively trying to oust him again?

Under the circumstances, nobody wanted to waste time and resources on a few renegade women. They offered us separate quarters if we would accept the transfer without a fight. We did.

We spent the first couple of months uneventfully in a small house on the prison grounds that had been converted from office space into a living unit. But in December they moved us to our permanent home—a small concrete cell adjacent to the prison's *tapiadas* for common criminals, a cell designed to hold a single guard.

We soon found out why that plan had been abandoned. Through the thin common wall, we listened around the clock as the *tapiada* prisoners—most of them with serious mental disturbances—screamed ghastly threats at their jailers, babbled their grisly fantasies, begged for mercy from their own bloodthirsty hallucinations. Worse yet, they threw all their vile garbage—used toilet paper, bloody sanitary pads, dressings from wounds—out onto the common patio. The stench was overwhelming.

After less than a month, we demanded a transfer out of the *tapiadita*, as we called our skimpy little cell. But the prison authorities stood firm; they had fulfilled their promise—we weren't housed with re-educated prisoners—and that was all we were going to get.

We were just starting to talk about how we could protest when Miriam fell while cleaning a water tank in the ceiling, breaking her right leg in two places. It was several weeks before she returned, wearing a white cast from her groin to her ankle. But she wanted to go ahead.

The *llavera*'s coffee brown face was contorted in rage. "Goddamn it, what are you prisoners doing out here?" she shouted. "You know you're not allowed to climb over that fence! You've really put yourself in the shit now."

Berta, Japonesa, and I stared back at the woman, continuing to insolently lounge against the tall chain-link fence that separated the *tapiadita* from the rest of the prison. "We told you that if you didn't move us out of that cell, we would get out of it ourselves," I reminded the *llavera*. "We told you it wasn't fit to live in. But you didn't pay any attention. So here we are."

Her jaw clenched furiously, like she was chewing the head off a snake. I could hardly keep from laughing. This woman was working herself into a frenzy, as I knew she would—as I knew they all would—over a protest that was really quite silly. Earlier in the morning we had forced open the shoddily constructed door of the *tapiadita*, climbed the chain-link fence, and dropped down into the main prison yard. We didn't try to go any farther, but the guard, as we expected, came running, spewing threats. Meanwhile, Miriam, immobilized by her cast, sat on the other side of the fence, yelling, "Me too! Me too!" whenever we said anything. *This is just like when I was little, riding in the backseat of the car, sticking my hand over the imaginary line that divided "my" half from my sister's, just to hear her scream,* I thought.

"Do you think we give a damn about your little problems?" the *llavera* was shouting now. "Do you think the Minister of the Interior is going to rebuild the prison to your specifications? Do you think he's going to drop everything to answer your letters? He has better things to do than to talk to you."

"I'm afraid you're mistaken," Berta replied sweetly. "He *has* to talk to us. He's in charge of this institution, and we have a complaint about it, and he must respond. That's the law. You aren't suggesting the Minister would break the *law*, are you?"

"That's it!" snapped the *llavera*. "I told you that you put yourself in the shit. This is an escape attempt. Now you're going to be punished—and I mean *punished*." She turned toward one of the guntowers to signal for more guards.

"Wait just a moment!" exclaimed Japonesa. The *llavera*, startled, as they always were, when such a big voice came from such a tiny woman, stopped in her tracks.

"I just want to tell you something," she lectured the *llavera* in grave tones. "If you're planning to beat me again, this time you're going to have to sign some papers first. The government newspapers are always talking about human rights abuses in Chile and Argentina. Well, a beating is a human-rights abuse. So you're not going to beat me unless you sign papers admitting that you're human-rights abusers. I'm warning you, I won't tolerate it."

The *llavera*, speechless, gaped at Japonesa. Twice she opened her mouth to speak, but no words came out. "All you political prisoners are fucking crazy," she finally mumbled. Then she turned and called for help.

Japonesa never did get her document, although we did get a sound beating. They threw the three of us into the same *tapiada* cells we were trying to get away from. After I scrubbed the cell with disinfectant—it was ankle-deep in shit from a backed-up toilet, and the previous occupant was a prostitute with syphilis—they carried Miriam in and sat her on the floor. After we were taken away, she had staggered up and down the little patio outside the *tapiadita*, dragging her cast behind her, screaming scandalous threats at everyone who walked by, until they agreed to put her into the *tapiadas* with us just to shut her up.

We launched an immediate hunger strike. Ordinarily it took a few days without food before we began to physically weaken, but we hadn't counted on the brutal heat of our cell. Located on the northern corner of the building, two of its walls were exposed to direct sunlight all day. The prefabricated cement worked like a stone oven, baking the air inside until it was like inhaling hot soup. Every one of our pores bled sweat until we felt like old, dried-out corn husks, so frail we might crumble in the breeze.

After the second day, Miriam was so weak she could no longer move her cast. I had to carry her to the *patín* and hold the cast away from her body while she urinated, so she wouldn't wet it, inviting an infection. After she finished and I moved her down again, I lay there on the floor, panting like a suffocating dog.

On the twelfth day, several guards came and loaded us into a car. "We're taking you to the military hospital," one of them said, loud enough that the women in the other cells would hear it. I thought it was odd— they usually waited until we were at death's door during a hunger strike before giving us medical care, and, weak as we were, that point was still a long way off—but I was too exhausted to argue.

But the car never left the prison grounds. It pulled around behind the prison offices, and the guards carried us up the back stairs to a room with boarded-up windows. "Wait here for an interview with the director, and then we'll take you to the hospital," a guard said, and they left.

I looked around the room dubiously. It was empty except for a bathtub, a sink, a toilet, and two cots. It didn't look like a waiting room; it looked like a cell, a secret one. Mindful of hidden microphones, I took out a pencil lead I'd hidden in my hair in anticipation of a trip to the *tapiadas*, and wrote Miriam a note on a scrap of paper I found on the floor: *No one knows we're here. They can just let us die, and no one will ever know.*

That point, I soon understood, might be much closer than I realized. There was no water in the sink or the toilet, and this room was nearly as sweltering as the *tapiadas*. No one came to see us that afternoon, or that night, or the next day either. I could barely summon the energy to keep my lungs moving. When Miriam had to urinate, I just dragged her to a fresh spot on the floor; I couldn't begin to lift that heavy cast.

It was on the fifteenth day of the hunger strike that Miriam went delirious. I awoke from a fitful sleep to hear her gasping: "Fire! Fire! The room's on fire!" It was so hot, and I was so disoriented, that for a moment I actually believed her and looked around the room in panic for an escape. When I realized she was hallucinating, I stumbled to the door and hammered it with my fists, croaking unintelligible noises. A *llavera* opened it almost immediately.

"Miriam's dying!" I rasped. "You've got to get her some water!" The *llavera* paused, her eyes uncertain, and I wondered how much she knew about what was going on here. Then, without saying anything, she closed the door and I heard the lock click shut. *Is she going to help us?* I wondered.

Or is this how it's going to end for us? For a long time, I had known I would die in prison, and in moments of boredom and depression I had imagined many final chapters: an overzealous beating, a trigger-happy guard, another case of pneumonia. But dying of thirst, in the middle of a building full of people—it was too bizarre. I rejected it.

A minute or two later, the faucets started hissing. The water was on.

They didn't cut it off again. But the Ministry's position was unchanged: To leave this room, we had to agree to return to the *tapiadita* or join the pavilion where the re-educated prisoners were. It wasn't until the thirty-second day of our hunger strike, when we were no more than clattering bags of bones, that Medardo Lemus arrived with a group of his Ministry flunkies.

"I'm not here to bargain," he said, glaring at us. "I just want to make sure you understand something: We're going to let you die, just the same way we did with Boitel. And then we'll take you over to that pavilion in a fucking pine box and leave you there anyway. Nobody blackmails the Ministry."

"You act so tough, Lemus, standing there with your bullyboys," I jeered. "Yeah, you're a mighty warrior when it comes to pushing around two starving women. But I remember a day you weren't quite so macho." I turned to Miriam, who was so weak she could barely hold her head up. "Do you remember that day, Miriam? The day we had a Russian visitor at América Libre?" She nodded. "I'm sure *you* remember it, Lemus, because I told you that afternoon that *I* would never forget it."

From the way his sneer had decomposed into a frown, I was pretty sure that the story of how the Russian had bullied Lemus was not often told in the halls of the Ministry.

"Look," he said, forcing his voice to a lighter tone, "this situation is getting out of hand. I think something can be worked out if we just all put our heads together and quit being so confrontational." He paused. "You know it was just bullshit when I said we'd let you die. But you make us very angry sometimes. Now, let's check both of you into the hospital, and get your health under control. After that, we'll come up with a solution that everyone can accept."

He opened the door, barked some orders, and then shooed his men down the stairs. As he walked away, he shot me a hateful glance over his shoulder.

"Do you think he's serious?" Miriam asked.

"I think they'll move us someplace for a few months, and then it will start all over again," I said. "But right now, a few months without a fight sounds pretty good to me."

The car came for us an hour later, and this time it really took us to the military hospital. After two weeks, Lemus asked if we would accept a transfer to La Cabaña, where we would join the other six women from the *tapiadita*. We started packing.

The *galera* was shaped like a tunnel, or a semicircle lying on its flat side. The front, where we entered, opened onto one of La Cabaña's serpentine streets. The back had a window looking onto one of the old dry moats, but we couldn't reach that; floor-to-ceiling bars blocked off the last twenty feet or so of the cell, forming a separate little room that, for reasons I never understood, we weren't allowed to use. There was a single shower on one side of the *galera*, one of the primitive latrines that we called a *patín* on the other.

The first thing I noticed, however, wasn't the cell's furnishings, but its occupants. There were only four women waiting for us—Japonesa and Mercedes Peña were missing.

"They asked for a transfer to a prison in Oriente province," Berta Alemán explained. "Both their families live there, and they think they'll be able to see their relatives more often."

Big mistake, I thought. Prisoners in Oriente's primitive jails lived an infamously rugged existence: less food, harsher punishments, compulsory work assignments, and no separation of the political prisoners and common criminals. *And I bet they'll be on report so often they won't get to see their families anyway.* I felt a pang of sorrow. It seemed that every time I closed my eyes, another couple of us disappeared. What would we do without Japonesa, building clandestine catchers' mitts and demanding the proper paperwork before submitting to a beating?

During our final days at América Libre, during an argument over re-education, Medardo Lemus had growled at us: "The problem with you is that you're all *plantada*, rooted in the past. Cuba and the Revolution have passed you by, and you need to wake up." After that, Ministry officials started referring to us often as *plantadas*. They intended it as an insult, but we accepted the name without complaint. It was true: We clung to the idea that each of us was entitled to live her own life and think her own thoughts without direction from the Revolution's apparatchiks.

But there was another meaning to *plantada*. It meant one who wouldn't bend. That was us, too.

Now, though, the *plantadas* were down to six.

Despite La Cabaña's fearsome reputation, we were reasonably content with the conditions there. The *galera* was spacious for six women, and because they served us the same portions they gave the men, we were eating more than we ever had in prison. The guards, though they had no compunction about carrying out orders, did not go looking for trouble from us. They had enough on their hands with the nearby homosexual *galeras*, where the prisoners settled every single dispute, no matter how small, with violence. We heard faint screams and the sounds of things breaking in those *galeras* at all hours, and, at least once a day, the mournful cry of an ambulance's siren as casualties were hauled away. A guard told us that the homosexual *galeras* averaged three murders a day.

Our only real complaint was the bold and pitiless rat population. A huge colony lived in the sewer pipes, and its members strolled into our cell from the *patín* whenever they felt the need for food or adventure. And explorers from other colonies routinely entered through the window over-looking the old moat. When the lights went out at night, you could hear them bustling through the *galera*, squeaking festive greetings to one another like our cell was the rat Tropicana.

The voracious rats devoured anything they could find—not just the food that came in packages from our families, but cardboard boxes, cloth bags, even our soap. I never heard Miriam scream the way she did one day after reaching into a sack for a bar of soap and pulling out a rat instead.

It was another incident involving Miriam that convinced me that we had to stand up to rat aggression. Everyone else had gone to sleep, but the sounds of the usual rodent festivities were keeping me awake. I gave up keeping my eyes closed and gazed around the *galera*. The dim moonlight streaming in through the window gave everything a dreamy, faded quality. The only thing that stood out clearly was Miriam's bright white cast, almost glowing, which attracted my eyes like a magnet.

But as I stared at it, part of the cast vanished, like the moon slipping behind a cloud. I pushed aside my gauzy mosquito net to get a better look, and a shrill cry escaped from my throat. The biggest rat I had ever seen, its feral teeth bared, was sniffing Miriam's foot. As I screamed and tried to untangle myself from the mosquito net, it tossed me an annoyed look and scampered out the window into the refuge of the moat.

The guards, alerted by my screams, turned on the lights. I had interrupted the rat before it bit Miriam's foot, but it had evidently been gnawing at her leg through the breathing hole in her cast; the plaster was dark with blood.

"Someone's going to have to stay awake and stand watch," I told the others. "I'll do the first one." The lights went off again, and a few minutes later the rat came back. He stayed behind the safety of the bars at the rear of the cell, taunting me, until I lunged for him; then he danced back out the window.

"That's some fucking rat," a guard said softly from the bars at the front of the cell. He had been standing there in the dark, watching the whole thing. "That's the Goliath of the rat world. You're going to need some technology to defeat that rat."

When he returned the next night, the guard had a long wooden plank, a shorter, thicker piece of wood, and a length of rope. I saw his plan immediately. I would rig the plank with the rope so I could drop it behind the rat after it came through the bars, blocking its retreat. Then I would corner the invader and club it to death with the smaller piece of wood.

"On some things," the guard explained, "we must stand together as a species." Then he left me, like Captain Ahab to my white whale.

It was well after midnight when the rat strutted into the *galera*, his ruby eyes brimming with disdain for me. I stood there innocently, not moving, willing him to crawl under the bars and enter our part of the cell. After carefully inspecting the room, he did. I waited one second . . . two . . . and let go of the rope. The plank crashed down behind him.

The rat didn't even turn around. He streaked straight for the *patín* and disappeared down it in the wink of an eye. But before I could even curse my own stupidity in failing to block the *patín*, furious squealing noises echoed from the pipe: A tragically inopportune lapse in rat solidarity had occurred. I waited beside the *patín*. When my adversary popped back out of the pipes a moment later, I walloped him with my club. Back down the *patín* he dashed. High-pitched rodent invective continued to issue out of the pipes for another half hour, but the rat did not reappear.

Three days later the *patín* backed up, discharging a nauseating stream of excrement mixed with millions of wriggling white pinworms. The pipes were so hopelessly blocked that the prison plumber had to break them open. Hours later, he reported everything was fixed. He had found the problem: two bloated rat corpses, locked together in a death grip.

We had other pursuits besides our holy war on the rats. We read a lot. Unlike the women's prisons, La Cabaña permitted prisoners to have books and magazines. When we felt mischievous, we used table scraps and cans of evaporated milk from our families to subvert a German shepherd dog from the prison's canine corps. He even started growling if any of the guards raised their voices around us.

At night we told ghost stories. Evenings were eerily beautiful at La Cabaña; everything was bathed in soft, silver moonlight that reflected from the cobblestones in the streets below, while a tangy breeze from the sea cooled and freshened the *galera*. It was the perfect setting for goose-pimply stories about buried treasure guarded by the vengeful spirits of peg-legged pirates.

Sometimes, to needle the guards, I would repeat the trick I had used in the *tapiadas* at Guanajay. Standing at the *galera*'s front door, within easy earshot of the guard on duty, I'd start describing a ghost I'd seen in the night, a scar-faced pirate with a patch over one eye and a hook where his right hand used to be, prowling down in the old moats. Within minutes, the guard would be skittishly asking questions. ("Did he seem to be, you know, *angry* about anything?") I knew I had really done my job well on the nights when a guard yelled, "Shut the fuck up in there!"

The ghost stories helped distract us from some of our problems. The most pressing was the tumor in Berta Alemán's breast. Berta was a housewife in her mid-forties from some little village in Matanzas province whose children—and now grandchildren—had grown up without her. She had been in prison since 1962, supposedly because she performed some minor tasks for anti-Castro guerrillas. But her real crime was that she was an outspoken Batista supporter who continued speaking her opinions even after the Revolution. She clashed with some of us when we were first thrown in with the *Batistianas* at Guanajay, but her implacable resistance to the prison authorities—she was on the front lines of every fight, and was usually one of the first to be tossed into the *tapiadas*—had won everyone over.

Berta had discovered the small, hard tumor shortly before she was arrested. For the past dozen years she had been appealing for medical treatment from the prison authorities, without results. Now it was growing again, and painful. Her dark eyes were animated when she talked. But in private moments, when she didn't know I was looking, they were full of worry.

It was also medical troubles that affected Sara Carranza, though not directly. Her aged mother was in poor health. Sara's sister had been caring for her, but the sister was about to leave Cuba. Her brother, a Communist labor leader, didn't want to be burdened with the problem. In the brave new Cuba—the one that had passed us *plantadas* by—the needs of one old lady could hardly be expected to prevail over those of the Revolution. The situation wore heavily on Sara's heart, though there was not a thing she could do about it.

One morning, shortly after breakfast, Roberto Luís, the prison director, stopped by our *galera*. "Sara, pack your things," he said. "You're being released."

"Yeah, in eighteen years," Sara retorted, thinking he was playing some sort of peculiar joke. "I think the packing can wait a year or two."

"No, you're being released now, as soon as we can get a car over here," Luís said. "Your brother arranged it. He's going to need help at home."

Sara looked like someone had just slapped her. "You mean I'm being released to be my brother's *maid*?" she asked.

"That's not what I said," Luís backtracked hurriedly. "But you know your mother is ill, and his duties will interfere."

"When I'm released, can I go anywhere I want to? Am I free to leave Cuba if I feel like it?"

"Well, no, there are some conditions, which we'll discuss with you over at the offices," Luís said. "But we're wasting time—"

"I'm not going," Sara interrupted. "So just cancel the car. I won't leave here with any strings attached, and I certainly won't leave to make it easier for my brother to be a good Communist. So this conversation is ended."

Luís left the *galera* shaking his head. I'm quite certain he had never seen a prisoner turn down release before. When he was gone, Sara lay silently on her bunk; a couple of us passed by and patted her shoulder. We understood what she had done, and at what cost.

Two hours later, Luís returned, a squad of guards (along with two or three *llaveras*) behind him. "The Ministry says the decision is already made, and your opinion doesn't enter into it one way or another," he said firmly.

"But it's *my* freedom," she protested.

"We're not asking you," he replied. "You're being released, right now."

Sara clapped her hands over her ears, like she was trying to blot out his words. If anything, she was even more surprised than before. She backed away, toward the rear of the *galera*, and Luís lost patience. With his head he gestured for the guards to grab her. Sara slapped at them impotently, trying to fend them off, but they seized her arms and legs and started dragging her out.

That was when we jumped them. The men were surprised; this was the first time the La Cabaña guards had ever used force on one of us, and they expected that the rest of us would stand meekly by. But Berta, Esther, María Amalia, and I were on them like the Furies, swinging fists, pulling hair, kicking at their balls.

Miriam rolled off her bed and crawled over to the melee, trying to restrain some of the guards by grabbing their legs. One of them turned, lifted her cast-encased leg in the air, and flung it into the stone floor as hard as he could. Miriam's scream split the air as the cast shattered. He did it again, and again. After the third time she didn't move.

I wanted to go to her, but I was surrounded. As I tried to dodge the powerful kicks of a guard, one of the *llaveras* lunged forward and ripped the front of my blouse apart with both hands, buttons flying through the air like popcorn. Another *llavera* behind me grabbed the blouse by the collar and tore it completely off. Seconds later, they repeated the same one-two maneuver, this time with my bra. Even in the confusion of the brawl, I was mortified at being half naked, but there was no time to retrieve my clothing—I just kept fighting.

Their numbers overwhelmed us, and after a few minutes it was no longer a fight but a beating. I clutched my breasts to protect them while blows rained down on my back and shoulders. Esther Campos was hit so many times in the midriff that her urine was bloody for weeks. Berta Alemán took a punch right on the spot over her tumor that left her breast red and inflamed. Miriam, when she awoke, was in agony; three days later, when the prison infirmary got around to X-raying her leg, it had two new fractures.

And Sara . . . Sara was gone, disappeared inside a cloud of olive green uniforms. We heard later that she refused to sign any release documents in the prison offices and was fingerprinted only when two guards grabbed her hands and forced them down onto the paper. She was pushed out of a prison truck in front of her house, where the block committee had special instructions to keep an eye on her.

Soon after Sara's release, a U.S. political delegation visited Cuba to "investigate" prison conditions. The investigation consisted of a Potemkin village tour of a couple of work farms and some carefully controlled "interviews" with prisoners (conducted in the benign presence of Interior Ministry officials). The Americans, duly impressed, pronounced Castro's prisons as therapeutic models for the whole world.

Miriam and I, standing at the front of the *galera*, listened to a report of the Americans' findings on a *llavera's* radio. "Too bad they didn't talk to us," Miriam said sardonically. "We could have showed them some of these human-rights medals"—she pointed at the bruises still lining my arms—"that the guards gave us when they took Sara away."

The *llavera* stiffened. "Are you suggesting that the Cuban government violates human rights?" she demanded.

"Have you been working on Mars?" I inquired. "You can't have been at La Cabaña long to ask a question like that."

"I've been here seven years," the *llavera* said, her tone heating up, "and I've never witnessed a human-rights violation."

"Then you must not know what human rights are. Let me just give you a short list: the right to choose your own government, the right to free speech, the right to an impartial jury trial—"

"That's it," the *llavera* snapped. "Your next visit is canceled. I'm putting you on report for insulting the Revolution."

I stared at her for a second, then started laughing. This was like something George Orwell cut out of *1984* as too silly to be believed.

"What are you laughing about?" the *llavera* growled. "Do you want me to put you on report again?"

"Excuse me, but you can't do that," I said, summoning a straight face. "Article 204, clause B of the Universal Declaration of Human Rights says: 'Every human being has the inalienable right to laugh at any time.' "

The *llavera* frowned as she contemplated this (purely imaginary) obstacle. "All right, then," she finally said. "I won't put you on report for laughing. But I *will* put you on report for thinking that the Cuban government violates human rights." *Solomon had nothing on these guys,* I thought as she walked away.

The blast was thunderous, the sound of a kettle drum played by giants. Its cymbal accompaniment was the sharp *pings* of shrapnel ricocheting off walls. I was standing at the window looking into the old moats—they let us use the space for exercise twice a week—when the explosion came, and I saw the thirty-foot wall that divided us from the men's *galeras* shimmy with the force of it, like it had turned liquid for a split second.

"Take cover!" screamed a guard from the front of the cell. He thought the prison was under attack. But after the deafening boom, everything was silent. Then we heard shouts, and, moments later, the wail of an ambulance.

"It was a couple of the SMO boys, playing with one of the old cannonballs that they keep piled around the antique cannons for show," a guard confided to us that afternoon. "I guess the cannonball was still loaded with gunpowder, and they accidentally set it off. Two of them lost their arms."

I didn't know much about antique weapons, but it seemed to me that, in those old guns, the powder was loaded into the barrel, not the cannonball. And even if I was wrong, what were the chances that a cannonball had been packed with gunpowder and then left undisturbed for a hundred years?

No matter, I thought. *If it involved the SMO boys, we'll know soon enough what the true story is.*

SMO was the Spanish abbreviation for Obligatory Military Service, the draft. Every boy in Cuba entered the army for three years at age fifteen. Originally the purpose was ideological indoctrination as much as anything else. But in the early 1970s, as Castro's military adventures in Africa expanded, he was in real need of warm bodies. The SMO boys were the cannon fodder he used when he played at being a world power.*

Most of them were trained at a base just outside La Cabaña, and they performed a number of small tasks on the periphery of the fortress, including guarding all the entrances and the exits.

None of their official duties brought them in contact with us. But on our second day at La Cabaña, a half dozen or so of them had showed up at our *galera*, crushing against the bars, snorting and cuffing one another like young bear cubs. "I *told* you they were women," whispered a tall, dark-haired boy, jabbing the blond kid next to him with an elbow. The blond boy didn't speak; he just kept staring at us, transfixed.

"Who are you, anyway?" the tall boy asked.

"We're political prisoners, the ones they call *plantadas*," Miriam answered. "But you boys better get out of here, right now. If the guards catch you here, you'll spend the next three years *under* La Cabaña."

"Oh, that's no problem," the tall boy bragged. "The guards let us do anything we want, because we control the prison entrance. If they get tough with us, we can start searching them when they leave, and then they won't be able to steal anything." The boys all giggled. So did we. Stealing was Cuba's national pastime these days, the only way a lot of families survived.

They stayed for a while, asking questions. Their attitude was mostly one of curiosity: What could we have done to get prison sentences of twenty or thirty years? What happened to our families? Why wouldn't we accept re-education?

But the next afternoon, a couple of the boys called to us from a grassy drill field across the old moat. "Hey, *plantadas!*" one of them yelled. "We'll stop by tomorrow! If you want us to take messages to your families, have them ready!" Then he hurled two tubes of toothpaste tied to a rock. With perfect aim, they flew through the bars of the window and skidded onto our floor.

We didn't dare pass messages to them that first time—for all we knew it was a trick by the prison authorities. But they came to see us

---

*A popular joke of the day: What's the biggest country in the world? Cuba, for sure. Its government is in Moscow, its people are in Miami, and its army is in Luanda.

almost every day, and it was soon obvious that they sincerely admired us.

They hated the government, feared being sent to Africa, and bitterly regretted that there was no organized resistance to Castro that they could join.

"All the young people despise the Revolution," one of them told us. "We see pictures our parents took of Havana in the old days, when people had cars and nice clothes, and there were bars and restaurants everywhere, and we think: Why can't it be that way for us? But it won't be, we know that. Outside, everything gets worse all the time. What do we have to look forward to, except dying in Angola among the snakes?"

The dream of every one of them, almost without exception, was to go to Miami. They talked about it incessantly, arguing the comparative merits of inner tubes, wooden rafts, and hijacked fishing boats. Everybody seemed to have an aunt or a cousin or a best friend who had made it to the United States and was going to help.

As I listened to them, I felt sad. That was the best thing our generation was able to bequeath them: the desire to leave Cuba. They were young, angry, and energetic, but we had left them no way to channel their hostility to Castro. How pathetic, that their only heroes could be five worn-out women in a forgotten prison cell.

The hostility of the SMO boys toward the Revolution did not surprise us (though the depth of it was startling). They were, after all, draftees drawn from the lower rungs of Cuban society. What truly shocked us was an encounter with the *Camilitos*, the young men training at the artillery school. They were the sons of the Revolution's gentry, being groomed to lead the army—and, eventually the country, for an olive green uniform was a prerequisite for most important government jobs.

One day, a few months after we arrived at La Cabaña, a formation of several dozen *Camilitos* marched down the narrow street in front of our *galera*. Drawn by the *whump-whump* of their boots echoing off the cobblestones and always anxious for any diversion, we pressed against the bars to watch the parade.

There was some minor screwup in the front ranks, and the officers halted the parade. The last few rows of boys were right under our cell. When the first one spotted us, he gaped for a few seconds, then hissed something to the soldier in front of him. As word traveled through the ranks, dozens of the *Camilitos* stared at us openly.

"Who are you?" one of them finally yelled. "*Plantadas*, political prisoners," Berta called back. Moments later, the march resumed, and they were soon out of sight.

We heard the *whump-whump* again the next afternoon, and again we clustered at the front of the cell to watch the parade pass. The first rows passed below us, and then—without any audible command—the boys stopped moving forward. They marched in place for a few seconds, their boots raising a fearful clatter, and then they started throwing things at us. We recoiled at first, but as the objects cascaded into the cell, we were not under fire. They were bombarding us with cigarettes, candy, soap, and small tubes of shampoo.

"What the hell's the matter with you men? Why have you stopped?" bellowed an officer from somewhere in the front. Instantly the column moved forward again, without a word having been exchanged between us.

The officers must have figured out what was going on, because the *Camilitos* never returned. But the SMO boys were regular visitors who never seemed to have any trouble getting access to our *galera*. We always worried about them, especially when they were denouncing the government; La Cabaña was such a complex maze of alleys and walls, and sound carried in such weird and unpredictable ways, that we never knew who might be listening. But none of them ever suffered any repercussions.

The SMO boys brought us presents, too. Usually they were things like candy or toothpaste. But occasionally one of them would say, "My mother thought you might like this" and shyly handed us a package of stockings or a simple blouse. At moments like that, there was a flirtatiousness about those boys, a reminder that they thought of us not only as prisoners, but as women. We could tell they tried to look their best when they visited, putting on freshly pressed uniforms or their best civilian clothes, and carefully arranging their hair just so.

Their puppy-dog coquetry always brought a smile to my lips. Miriam and I were old enough to be their mothers; Berta, María Amalia, and Esther, their grandmothers. And we looked it, too—the *tapiadas*, the beatings, the lousy prison diet, and the hunger strikes had bled us like vampires in the night. Once, an SMO boy smuggled a camera into the prison to take our pictures. "I'm going to escape to Miami soon," he explained, "and when I get there I'm going to tell the gringos all about you, so they can raise hell at the UN." We obligingly lined up for the photo. But later I told Miriam:

"Anybody who sees those pictures will say he took them in a nursing home rather than a prison."

In idle moments, I sometimes wondered what would happen if I could push a button and make Castro disappear. Could I pick up the pieces of my medical education? Was it too late for me to be a doctor? But I never even thought about a husband or babies. That part of life seemed so remote I couldn't imagine that it had ever concerned me.

Of course, that hadn't always been so. Once, years ago, a spiteful State Security interrogator asked if I had ever played with a baby. "Of course," I replied, mystified at the question.

"I'm glad to hear that," he responded. "I'm glad to hear that you've been around babies, that you know how beautiful it is to see one smile, to see its first uncertain steps, to hear it say 'Mama!' with your own ears. If you've played with a baby, then you must be able to imagine what it's like to hold that child and know that it's flesh of your flesh, blood of your blood. So go ahead and imagine it—that's all you'll ever do, because you'll be a withered, useless old hag by the time we let you out of here."

I made some smartass crack in reply, but his words stung me in a way that none of their threats and insults had ever done. I knew he was right—they had stolen a piece of my life, a piece that could never be replaced.

My only consolation was that it would have been so much worse to have had a child before going to prison. The story of every woman I met behind bars was heartbreaking, but nothing compared with those who had left children outside. Every day they were apart, they lost a little bit more of their sanity. Even the luckiest of them became an aloof figure to their sons and daughters, an irrelevance, if not a downright bother. And there were plenty of women who didn't rank among the luckiest.

The most difficult question anyone had ever asked me came from a prisoner named Ofelia Rodríguez, just after she got a letter informing her that her husband had fled Cuba with their three-year-old child. "I did all this for my son," she whispered. "I fought against Castro so that he could grow up in a free country. And now he'll grow up without me. What was the point?"

Ofelia's quandary was a common one. So was the plight of Fidelina Suárez, who had two children, a boy and a girl. Fidelina's husband, a policeman under Batista, got a thirty-year prison sentence immediately after Castro came to power. Fidelina, outraged, started working against the Revolution. She didn't think it was particularly risky; like so many people in those days, she assumed the United States would soon intervene. But that didn't happen, and Fidelina was soon serving her own thirty-year sentence.

Her mother-in-law had to raise the children. At first she regularly brought them to both prisons to visit both their parents. But as the political environment turned harsher, she got worried that the kids would repeat something they heard, or defend their parents too vigorously at school, and the state would seize them to make sure they got a revolutionary upbringing. It was not an idle fear; it happened all the time. You couldn't very well expect a six-year-old to chant "Viva Fidel!" during the day at school if he heard "Fuck Fidel!" all night at home.

So the mother-in-law started playing the role of a revolutionary—but she did it too well. The children turned into young Communists. They wouldn't come to see Fidelina anymore; the mother-in-law would show up on visiting days, embarrassed, and say there wasn't enough money to bring them, or they were busy. When no letters ever arrived from the children, the mother-in-law said it must be the prison's fault. Soon the mother-in-law's visits dwindled away, too, and that meant Fidelina lost touch with her husband, because prisoners were not allowed to correspond with one another.

So many nights I sat with an arm around Fidelina's shoulders as she cried. "I did all this for my son and daughter, and now I've lost them," she sobbed. "I've turned into their enemy. I'm fighting my own children."

A few days after the explosion at La Cabaña, an SMO boy confirmed that my suspicions about the official story were justified. The only part that was true was that two young draftees had inadvertently touched off the blast. "They were stealing gunpowder from the fortress arsenal, and something went wrong," the boy told us solemnly. A few of La Cabaña's old cannons were fired each night at nine P.M., a tradition left over from the days when Havana was a walled city and the shots signaled that the gates were closing for the night. The gunpowder was stored inside the fortress.

"Did they really have plans to use it?" I asked in amazement.

"I don't know," the boy replied. "No one has been able to talk to them—they're locked up tight."

State Security, though, seemed to think the theft was more than a lark. The gunpowder was moved to a regular military armory that was under heavy guard. A small amount was sent over to La Cabaña every evening, just enough to fire the cannons.

We had just finished breakfast, and Miriam was starting her walking exercises. Her leg had finally been removed from the cast a few weeks earlier, but it still had little strength. It was April 3, just short of nine months since we arrived at La Cabaña.

A guard walked briskly to the *galera* door. "Pack up," he said tersely. "You're being transferred."

"Where?" Esther asked.

"Back to Nuevo Amanecer, to the same cell you came from."

"Better come back later, with lots of help, because we don't intend to go anywhere," said Miriam. Expressionless, the guard walked away. "Damn it, why do they have to do this?" Miriam asked, watching him go. "Everybody's happy here."

"The human rights cavalry has finally arrived to rescue us from the Indians," I said. It was true: Some of the male prisoners had smuggled letters out of Cuba, complaining that it was inhuman to keep us in a brutal institution like La Cabaña. A few muted international protests had been raised.

The male prisoners undoubtedly meant well. But the fact was that we found La Cabaña anything but brutal. We ate better, got more mail and more visits, were allowed to have books and magazines. With the single exception of the beating when Sara Carranza was released, we hadn't been physically mistreated. I would have gladly traded any of the other prisons where we had been confined for this cell in La Cabaña, and I knew the others felt the same way.

Despite Miriam's bravado, we went ahead and packed. We knew there wasn't any chance we'd be able to stop the transfer; we just wanted to make it clear that it was being done over our objections. No one in the *galera* looked very happy as we dropped our things into canvas bags, but the sourest expression belonged to María Amalia. I started to ask if something was wrong, then bit my tongue. She had been prickly lately, quick to take offense. It seemed as the rest of us had become closer here, she had grown apart.

The guards entered an hour later. They grabbed Miriam first. She squirmed and shouted, but offered little real resistance—her leg was too weak. Assuming they would just put her in the *jaula* waiting outside, I went to Berta's aid instead, hoping to protect her right side, the one with the inflamed breast.

But I never reached her. Half a dozen guards pounced on me, dragging me to the rear of the *galera* to batter me with fists and boots. I tried to shrink my body into a tiny, hard ball, but the blows kept raining down. When I was in too much pain to do anything but go limp, they picked me up and carried me outside.

To my horror, Miriam was lying on the cobblestones, where the fat prison director, Emilio Bastos, was trying to crush her throat with his boot. Miriam was wrestling with his foot while launching flimsy kicks of her own that connected only with the air. Coming alive, I tore away from the grasp of the surprised guards carrying me and grabbed the fat man, throwing him off balance and away from Miriam.

Just as they grabbed me again and threw me into the *jaula*, I heard the sound of running footsteps. "Leave them alone, you sons of bitches, they're women!" someone screamed. Diving to the door, I looked out to see about fifteen SMO boys running up the street toward the *jaula*. At the front was the blond boy who stared at us so long the first day they visited, too shy to speak. About one hundred feet away, they were charging fast.

The cruel, staccato sound of machine-gun fire ripped the air from both sides of the *jaula*. Craning my neck, I saw two tripod-mounted weapons, one on either side of the street. *They sure planned for something,* I thought as the guns let loose another burst. *They must have known more about those visits from the SMO boys than we realized.* "Get back!" yelled one of the guards. "Or we'll stop shooting in the air!"

The young soldiers instinctively dropped to the ground when the first shots were fired. With the second burst, they started to scramble back down the street. "They're *women*, you fuckers!" one of them yelled, his voice trembling at the outrage. "They're *women*." His voice echoed in the air as the last of them rounded the corner.

Berta was the last of us to be lobbed into the *jaula*. As the truck started rolling down the street, I crawled over to where Miriam lay like a cast-off rag doll. "I can hardly breathe," she gasped. "It feels like I've been stabbed." I pulled her blouse up, but there was no blood. I started running my fingers along her ribs, sharply outlined against her scrawny body. Almost instantly I felt a fracture. Then another, and another . . . five in all.

"Listen to me," I said in a severe voice. "You've got broken ribs, a bunch of them. Lie still. Don't make any sudden moves, and for God's sake don't try to fight with them when they take us out of the *jaula*." I was terrified. A wrong move and she could easily puncture a lung or even her heart.

Berta looked only slightly better. Her face had a sallow, yellowish cast, and from the way she clutched her breast, I knew it had taken another blow—or several. "They certainly make sure those men are well trained when it comes to kicking," she said, offering me a sickly smile. "I'd say that, no matter how you look at it, those dogs won that round." I smiled and squeezed her hand.

Usually we yelled and screamed the entire way on a transfer that we opposed. But today we were silent, each woman lost in her own thoughts. It wasn't until Nuevo Amanecer was in sight that I spoke.

"You know they're going to put us in the *tapiadas* when we get there," I said. "Everyone has to make her own decision. But I'm going on a hunger strike until they find us a new place to live, away from the re-educated prisoners and away from the common criminals."

"I'm with you," Esther said immediately. Miriam waved a weak hand in agreement.

"Ana," Berta said, tears welling in her eyes, "as God is my witness, I don't have the strength for it this time. This time they've really hurt me."

"It's okay, Berta, I know," I said, squeezing her hand again. I didn't dare say more. I was afraid I would cry.

"Count me out," said María Amalia.

· FIFTEEN ·

School Days

MAY 29, 1975

"WHAT, EXACTLY, IS *this*?" the *llavera* asked in an appalled voice. Her thin, prissy lips were pressed in a tight white line.

"Come on, now, Victoria, we know you're a bright woman," Miriam cooed to her encouragingly. "You can figure it out. Look at it closer. Smell it. *Taste* it if you want to."

"Why are you doing this?" Victoria screamed. "Why are you throwing your own shit out here in the corridor?"

"Because the toilet doesn't work, and we've been telling you for four days, and nothing's happened," I said calmly. "And we decided that if we have to sit around in shit, the least you can do is walk through some of it."

"I won't bring your food anymore!" she threatened.

"Big deal," Miriam scoffed. "Like we could eat in here anyway. Why don't you come in and smell this place?"

To my surprise, Victoria took a key off the ring on her belt and opened the padlock on the cell door, then stepped into the darkened room. She grimaced in disgust at the stench that hung in the air. Groping for a switch, she tried to turn on the light, but there was no bulb. She stepped back into the corridor, shuddering.

"All right, all right," she muttered. "I'll get the water turned on. And I'll bring you a plunger to unstop the toilet."

"Victoria, we just ended a thirty-eight-day hunger strike," I said. "We're so exhausted we barely have the energy to *sit* on the toilet, much less fix it. So if you want us to stop leaving you little surprises in the corridor, you'll get a plumber in here to work on the toilet. And bring in a cleaning crew to get all the cement dust off the floor and the walls, too. Otherwise, you're going to see how passive resistance can make your life miserable. Remember what Mahatma Gandhi was able to do."

"Who's Mahatma Gandhi?" Victoria asked suspiciously. When we collapsed into helpless laughter, she stalked off. But the next day the water came on, a plumber visited, and a crew of common criminals mopped the floor. Our new cell was at least livable. A good thing, because I had the feeling we were going to be there a long, long time.

We called it *La Escuelita*, the little schoolhouse. The original idea behind the Nuevo Amanecer prison was to make it a place that Castro could show off to visiting dignitaries, with all kinds of educational and rehabilitational facilities. But the plans were overtaken by Castro's penchant for slapping people behind bars. By the time Nuevo Amanecer was finished in 1973, there were already two thousand prisoners waiting for six hundred spaces. Stuffing them all in left the cells hopelessly overcrowded, and the overextended plumbing and electrical systems failed all the time.

It was not, in short, the sort of place to take foreign visitors who still cherished any illusions about the Revolution. Accordingly, all the special programs—which were never more than window dressing—were dropped. Nuevo Amanecer's schoolhouse, located on the east edge of the prison near the perimeter fence, had never been used.

When the five of us returned from La Cabaña, Berta Alemán was immediately whisked away to the infirmary, María Amalia Fernández to the pavilion that held the political prisoners. Miriam, Esther Campos, and I were put in separate *tapiada* cells, where we immediately launched our hunger strike. For the next thirty-eight days, we ingested nothing but water.

Of the half dozen or so hunger strikes I had participated in during my twelve years in prison, this one was the most difficult. Miriam, with five broken ribs and a broken leg that had barely healed, really had no business refusing to eat. Neither did Esther, who had an array of nagging health problems and was actually too old for this kind of thing.

And though I was in better physical shape than either of them, chronic malnutrition (from the prison diet) and intestinal disorders (from the contaminated water supplies) had worn me down. At thirty-seven, I felt almost twice my age. During the single real fight we had with the guards during the strike, my heart raced like a locomotive, so fast that I actually feared a coronary attack was starting. We looked so skeletal, so wasted, that when Mother's Day rolled around and the *llaveras* offered to send cards inviting our families to visit, I asked them to send a card telling mine to stay home. I was afraid to let anyone see how I looked.

Why, exactly, the prison authorities finally gave in, I don't know. But in mid-May they offered to seal off one end of the schoolhouse and convert it into a cell for the three of us. When we accepted, they put us in the hospital while they did the alterations. Miriam and I were released after two weeks, Esther after four.

The cell they gave us was a single small classroom, walled off from the rest of the schoolhouse, twenty-one feet long and seven feet wide. Since the room contained three beds, a toilet, and shower, there was just barely enough space to walk around.

The front door opened into a hallway, the one where we had left our little surprises for Victoria the *llavera*. The back door (and three tiny windows) opened onto a small patio. It was enclosed on three sides by fifteen-foot-high walls that were topped with a five-foot-high chain-link fence, which was in turn topped by a two-foot-high Y-shaped double strand of barbed wire. And if we somehow climbed all that, we would run into a roof of tightly crisscrossed barbed wire, so densely strung that only the tiniest birds could get through it. The first time they let us out onto the patio, I suffered a crushing wave of claustrophobia.

The cell itself could be daunting at times. We couldn't look out our tiny windows during the day, because the sunlight bouncing off the brightly whitewashed walls fried our eyes to a crisp. So we had to face the dim, closed end of the room from sunrise to sunset, staring at each other.

Our isolation—from the rest of the prison, from the rest of the *world*—was total. Three times a day Victoria or one of the other *llaveras* arrived with plates of cold, greasy food; they rarely said more than, "Here, take this," before leaving. We had no other visitors, couldn't even see outside our own compound.

Sometimes, if a *llavera* was a few minutes late with our food, I would think to myself: *What if World War III broke out this morning? What if everyone out there is dead? How would we ever know?* I started having trouble visualizing the rest of the prison.

I resumed my old habit of staying up all night. I perched at one of the windows, catching the hint of a nighttime breeze on my face. I cast my mind like a net, trying to capture the thoughts of the world outside. The whole concept of "life" was turning dangerously amorphous in my brain, and I had to force myself to recall people walking in and out of doors, sitting at dining room tables, going to the office, watching television, doing things, thinking things. Once in a while, the wind carried blossoms from trees outside the walls into the cell. I studied them in painstaking detail, like Darwin on an undiscovered island.

Miriam and Esther usually woke up at seven-thirty. Breakfast—a piece of bread, a cup of watery warm coffee with sugar—arrived an hour later. After that I slept until noon, when lunch—a cold baked potato, a hard-boiled egg, and maybe some bread—arrived.

In the afternoons we played cards with a homemade deck and talked. Sometimes, reviewing our conversations later, I marveled at how utterly prison had consumed our lives. Our previous existences had been canceled and tossed down a memory hole. We talked about old fights with the guards, gossiped about how this prisoner or that one had changed over the years, remembered tales about women who had been released. For the first time, I talked a lot about the time I spent on the streets after my escape, how discouraged it left me.

Dinner was delivered at five-thirty—a few spoonfuls of rice, another egg, and sometimes bread. After that we'd walk around the cell as best we could for exercise, then talk some more. Usually one of us would try to remember a book or a movie we knew, and tell the story. At some point—usually early, because the later they stayed awake, the hungrier they got—either Miriam or Esther would give the lights-out signal: "Okay, we'll talk more tomorrow." Then I returned to my window, to start the cycle again.

Happy as we were to have the water turned on in our cell, a major drawback was soon obvious: The shower, located in the darkest part of the cell, was a fungus garden. No matter how much we cleaned it with disinfectant, the mold spread in the dark and damp corner. It was weird, multicolored stuff that I had never seen before, and its steady march across the shower walls and floor into the rest of the cell was scary. Now my isolation fantasies reversed: *What if the llaveras bring lunch one day and find we've been eaten by the fungus?*

We complained about it constantly to the *llaveras*, but they shrugged it off. "By now you ought to have gotten the idea that this is a *prison*," Victoria lectured us sternly. "Making it pretty is not a priority."

"Victoria, come in and look at this stuff," I begged her. "It's not a matter of being pretty. It's disgusting, like it's from Mars. Who knows what's in it?"

She wouldn't get very close. "I'll tell the people in the office you want to see them," she said doubtfully, backing away from the fungus as though it might spring on her. "That's all I can do." Still, no one came until we went on a seven-day hunger strike. By the time a couple of men from the office reluctantly visited, the mold had run completely amok; the shower looked like a malign version of the hanging gardens of Babylon. Within days the prison authorities carved a small window in the bathroom, right over the toilet, and the fungus promptly shriveled away.

The window, however tenuously, reconnected us to the world. From it we could see into the prison complex. There was little activity close by— we were stashed in an isolated corner of Nuevo Amanecer—but in the distance I could see small figures moving to and fro, going about their business. Our small universe had expanded, and there was life on nearby planets. I spent hours standing on the toilet, looking out into the world.

On an afternoon soon after the window was built, I watched a guard walking a few hundred feet away. His back was to me, so I couldn't see his face, but there was something familiar in his gait. He stopped, turned, and I felt an icy, terrifying jolt of recognition. "Miriam! Come look! It's—" But as he stepped closer I realized I was mistaken. "Forget it, it's nothing," I said as Miriam, on tiptoes, raised her face over the windowsill. For just one moment, I thought it was Arcadio.

Something had gone wrong for Arcadio. He had fought alongside Castro in the Sierra Maestra. But when the war was over and the other men were put in charge of ministries, or made officers in State Security, the only thing offered to Arcadio was a job as a prison guard. And he was never promoted. Year after numbing year, he sat in a guntower with his rifle. Sometimes I wondered: *Is it because he's not mean enough?* Because I had noticed that, when the guards came to beat us up or tear apart our cells, he was never there. I never saw him raise a hand to a prisoner.

He was a silent, taciturn man. The only time I ever heard him speak more than a few words was during my second escape, when I walked in line next to him, pretending to be a soldier myself, and he complained how dark it was. In fact, the only time he even changed expression was when he frolicked with Perico, the goat that grazed in the main yard at América Libre. As they playfully wrestled each other, Arcadio wore a broad smile.

On a sunny afternoon in May 1973, we were standing around at the gate to the dining room, waiting for dinner. Arcadio had just arrived for his regular mealtime assignment, manning a small, ground-level guardpost near the dining room. Perico, spotting his friend, bounded up to the guard-post. Arcadio drew back his hand and delivered a stinging slap to the goat's head. "Get out of here," he grunted. The stunned goat brayed loudly and trotted away.

"You people can be so mean," I berated him. "I thought that poor animal was your pal." Arcadio didn't reply, just looked at me with eyes that suddenly seemed very deep. Puzzled, I turned away. But my head snapped back when I heard the clicking bolt-action of his gun. His back was to me, the rifle butt resting on the ground, and his hand moved to the trigger. A shot rang out, and Arcadio's whole body jumped, like a terrible cartoon.

I heard the bullet ricochet off something, and then Caridad Cabrera was yelling to be careful, that it went right by her head. "Come on," I said to Arcadio, "stop that. Are you crazy?" Then his body slumped to a sitting position inside the guardpost, and as his weight shifted I saw an enormous hole, the size of a softball, with his heart pumping inside. "Hey!" I shouted. "He's hurt!" Several guards started running across the field toward us.

I thought the shot was an accident. But Arcadio slowly turned his head to stare at me, a gaze of anguish and sorrow, and lowered his chest to rest directly on the rifle barrel. The second shot knocked him to the ground just as three other men reached the wooden hut. When they picked him up, blood sprayed from his body like an open fire hydrant, splashing everything in sight.

The men started to run toward the infirmary with him. But they had only gone a few feet when a powerful spasm shook his body, twisting him to a sitting position in their arms. He drew a last, rasping breath, his face relaxed—it looked almost peaceful—and he fell limp. The guards continued running, but I could see it was all over.

At dinner, the dining room was hushed. Barely a word was spoken among the prisoners. As I walked back to the *galera*, though, I passed two *llaveras* standing by the bloody guardpost. "What a mess Arcadio made!" one of them complained. "You know, I never liked him. He was all bark and no bite." I kept quiet, but I marveled at those words. All bark and no bite! He pulled that trigger not once, but twice.

Some of the guards told us later that no suicide note was found, and no one had any explanation for what Arcadio had done. I believed them; they seemed sincerely mystified. And I had no idea, either. But I did know one thing: He picked a time and a place where he knew all the prisoners would be there watching, witnesses to an act of indecipherable eloquence.

The new window in our bathroom paid another unforeseen dividend. The nocturnal winds brought us news from outside, news you couldn't hear on the radio.

We knew there was a military training base near the prison—we sometimes heard volleys from the firing range—and we had always naturally assumed it was for the Cuban army. But now at night we could hear shouted commands, revolutionary chants, and sometimes even fragmentary conversations from the camp. And the more we listened, the more obvious it was that the base was training foreign guerrillas.

We frequently heard chants in memory of Farabundo Martí, Augusto Sandino, and Raúl Sendic, leftist revolutionary heroes of El Salvador, Nicaragua, and Uruguay, respectively. And the accents of the troops were a polyglot mixture from all over Latin America, including not only those three countries, but Chile, Argentina, Peru, Colombia, and Guatemala. Sometimes we heard Portuguese spoken, which made me suspect that guerrillas from Portugal's former colonies in Africa (including Angola and Mozambique) were probably in the camp as well.

"Well, when the Americans find out, that will be the end of Castro," Esther said one night as we listened to a group of Nicaraguans drill. "They're not going to let him start a war in every country in Latin America."

"Esther," I said tiredly, "you've been saying that once a week for the past thirteen years. The Americans gave up trying to do anything about Castro years ago. Now they've given up on Vietnam. They're not going to do anything about this, or anything else."

It touched off a long argument. Esther and Miriam thought I was too gloomy, too cynical. But when we were in the hospital, recovering from our last hunger strike, I had seen newspapers with photos of the fall of Saigon. The pictures of frantic, terrified Vietnamese clinging to the skids of the last helicopter leaving the roof of the U.S. embassy haunted me. Did the Americans turn out the lights as they left?

I remembered something else, too—a clipping that somebody smuggled into América Libre. It was a story from *Time* magazine about Uruguay's Tupamaro guerrillas (whose shouts we could hear through our new window). It called them "modern-day Robin Hoods, taking from the rich, giving to the poor."* Robin Hoods! The Tupamaros murdered so many Uruguayan policemen that the police actually went on strike demanding the right to wear civilian clothing rather than uniforms. The Tupamaros kidnapped an American diplomat and, when the Uruguayan government refused to give in to their demands, killed him in cold blood. These were the kind of people that many Americans saw as Robin Hoods.

If the guerrillas were Robin Hood, that made the rest of us, I supposed, the Sheriff of Nottingham. And everyone knew what happened to him.

Shortly after the turn of the year, they eased a few of the other restrictions on us. We were permitted to get copies of the Revolution's official newspaper, *Granma*, as well as magazines from Soviet-bloc countries. And our families were allowed to visit, the first time they'd seen us in nearly a year.

My mother and my sister Milagros couldn't disguise the shock and concern in their eyes when they walked into the visiting room—a sign, I knew, that the last hunger strike had left its tracks on my face. But their worries were soon eclipsed by the warmth of our embrace. In a rapid-fire,

---

*I noted the date: May 16, 1969.

stream-of-consciousness barrage of words, we tried to sum up the past eleven months to each other.

"Did you get the card telling you not to come last Mother's Day?" I asked. "I figured you would understand that we were in the middle of a protest."

"Card?" my mother asked, stumped. Milagros, too, looked blank. Then she shuddered. "No, we didn't get any card," she said. "And, my God, don't ever remind me of that day again. Just thinking of it makes me need some aspirin and a cold rag for my head."

"So you tried to visit me that day?" I said, my heart sinking. The humiliating searches and insults were hard enough for our relatives to endure when they got to see us; it made me ill to imagine them going through it for nothing.

"Go ahead, tell her," my mother cackled to Milagros. "We don't want her to think she's the only one having fun."

"Well, you've already guessed that we came, expecting to see you," my sister recounted. . . .

We saved our sugar rations for months, and we made you a wonderful cake with a huge pile of meringue frosting on top. But when we got to the front gate, the *llavera* said, "Sorry, you can't bring that in."

"Don't be ridiculous," I said. "We know the rules perfectly well. Cakes are permitted."

"Yes," she said pompously, "but meringue isn't." I was so angry I thought I would go blind on the spot. Of all the stupid, arbitrary rules they've ever imposed on us, that one was the worst. "Okay," I said, "no problem." And I jabbed my hand into that pile of frosting, scooped it all off.

"See?" I said, holding out my hand, this huge mound of meringue clinging to it like a cloud. "Now the cake can go in."

The *llavera* looked at me like I was a cockroach—you know how they hate it when you outsmart them—and she said, "Only *Señora* Rodríguez can go in. You have to stay outside." So Mama took the cake, and the rest of the things we brought for you, and went inside. I just stood there, looking like a fool with this big glob of frosting on my hand.

The next lady in line looked at me kind of apologetically. "Listen, I also have a cake with meringue, and I'll have to get rid of it," she said. "But I don't have any napkins or anything to clean myself up with. Since your hand is already a mess, would you mind doing it?" *Why not?* I thought, and I swiped my hand along the top. The new meringue stuck to the old, and all you could see at the end of my wrist was frosting, like I had been born with a really bizarre deformity.

A couple of minutes later, there's another lady with a meringue topping on a cake, and this time I scraped it off before she even finished asking. I was really enjoying myself now, because each time I did it, the *llavera* got angrier. By the time they admitted the last visitor, I had scraped off six cakes, and my hand looked like you could float to Miami on it.

My mother picked up the story:

When they let me inside, they didn't send me to the regular visiting room. They sent me to the office of the chief of the guards, that big, square-looking man, Reyes. He welcomed me like we were old friends, taking my hand, leading me to a big easy chair in his office. "You wait here, and I'll go get Ana," he said.

I didn't believe any of it. Since when are those people our friends? So when he left, I went to the window to watch. And he didn't go anywhere near any of the pavilions where prisoners live, he went into the sewing factory. A few minutes later he came out, and I knew he hadn't talked to you.

He came back to the office, and he had this tragic expression on his face, and he lamented: "Oh, *señora*, this is so painful for me to have to say, but your daughter refuses to come see you. She says she's on a protest."

That lie, that bald-faced lie, made me so angry I forgot to use my cane as I jumped up on my feet. "For such a big man, you sure don't have any guts," I yelled. "I saw where you went. To stand there and lie to an old woman like me on Mother's Day—you must not have a mother. You must not be human."

"You're right, I didn't see her," he yelled back at me. "And pretty soon I'll never have to see her again, because she's on a hunger strike, and we're going to let her die!"

"My daughter's not going to die!" I shouted. "She'll outlive you, you sneaky little son of a bitch!" And I walked out of his office.

Milagros resumed:

I was still standing outside, my right arm solid meringue up to the elbow, when I heard Mama's voice: "Sons of bitches! Sons of bitches! You're all sons of bitches!" A second later she came charging out of the prison, waving her cane in the air like a sword, with Reyes right behind her, screaming that the whole family belonged in jail. "Come on!" she said when she got to me. "We're going straight over to the Interior Ministry!"

I couldn't walk out on the street with this meringue on my arm—people would have run away from me screaming, thinking it was some new disease—so I asked the *llavera* if I could step into the prison offices to wash it off. She gave me that same smug, pompous look as when she told me that cakes were okay but meringue wasn't, and said: "Don't ask me to solve your problems."

I snapped again. "No problem," I said, and I shook my arm hard, like a dog drying off from a swim. Meringue flew everywhere—on the *llavera*'s uniform, in her hair, on her face. And we walked off. I half expected her to grab me from behind, but I think she was in a state of shock.

We got over to the Ministry, and Mama asked to see Medardo Lemus. They told us he had stepped out, but we could wait for him. We sat down in the lobby, and a few minutes later he came in. I saw the receptionist point us out, and Lemus came over, smiling. "How can I help you ladies?" he said.

"I have to talk to you about a prisoner," Mama explained.

"Well, that's my job," he said jovially. "What's the prisoner's name?"

"It's my daughter, Ana Rodríguez," Mama said. His face

went bright red, like someone had switched on a furnace inside. "I don't ever want to hear that woman's name again in my life!" he cried, and started walking away. Mama chased him across the lobby, chattering like a machine gun, and finally he told one of his deputies to talk to us. And he went running into the back like rabid dogs were chasing him.

Mama stepped into the deputy's office, and pretty soon there was a lot of screaming coming from in there. It sounded like a brawl. The receptionist arched her eyebrows at me and said, "That lady in there, did she come with you?" I couldn't even answer. I was just wondering if this day would ever end.

After a while, the door burst open, and Mama started out of the office. But the man said something else and she turned around and grabbed him by the collar with her right hand and started shaking him. Their faces were both so red, and they were yelling so much. I was sure Mama was going to have a heart attack, or get arrested, or both. How we got out the door is still a mystery to me.

By the time Milagros finished, tears of laughter were streaming down my face. I could imagine the expression on that Ministry man's face when my mother jerked his collar. The first thing we learned as children was to stay out of reach of her right arm when she was mad. All those years cutting cane had turned it into a lethal weapon.

Castro was always tinkering around with Cuban agriculture. He spent years on a genetic experiment that was supposed to breed a supercow, the F-1. (When one of the first of the new line died, Castro went into mourning. He had the cow stuffed and placed in a museum where "future generations could admire her magnificent udders.") But the result was disastrous; the supercows produced less milk than an ordinary Holstein. Another of his initiatives, raising a local plant called *gandul* as cattle feed, was even a bigger flop. Cattle wouldn't touch the stuff—as Cuban *campesinos* had known for centuries. They planted *gandul* to create natural fences that livestock wouldn't cross.

In early 1976, he was fooling around with Cuban chicken farms. No one seemed to know what happened, exactly, but suddenly there was a massive surplus of eggs. They flooded into stores across the island, and in the prison they became almost our sole diet: two fried eggs (cold and sodden by the time they reached us) for lunch, and two boiled eggs for dinner. On lucky days, there might be a bite or two of spaghetti or rice along with them.

Esther, Miriam, and I were no longer exactly picky eaters, and the boredom of an all-egg diet didn't bother us. But a few weeks after we started eating the eggs, we noticed that we all felt ill. Our joints turned swollen and achy, and our eyelids were red and inflamed. We asked to see the prison's new doctor, Carina Sessin.*

"Something's poisoning all three of you," she concluded after examining us. "You're being exposed to some kind of toxin, probably in your diet. I'm going to give you an antihistamine, which should bring down the inflammation."

"But what about the toxin?" I inquired. "If we keeping ingesting it, we're going to stay sick."

"That's right," she acknowledged.

"Well, what about these eggs?" I continued. "The health problems started at the same time as the eggs. Do you think it could have something to do with what they're feeding the chickens?"

"Could be," she shrugged. "But I'm not in charge of what they feed the chickens, and I'm not in charge of what they feed you. And if you expect sympathy from me, forget it. Because half the population of Cuba has these same symptoms." She went back to her television set.

We stopped eating eggs, and the symptoms promptly disappeared. But the *llaveras* wouldn't bring us anything to replace them. We asked for the eggs to be delivered raw, and we stacked them up after every meal. Soon we had hundreds, a gleaming white monument to Fidel Castro's prowess in agronomy.

When the egg crisis passed, we had another. The prison created a garbage dump right outside the fence, a few dozen feet from our cell.

---

*Carina was a rarity: a loyal Castro follower who was sent to jail. In a jealous rage, she had gunned down her husband and his lover. Ordinarily, her revolutionary credentials might have spared her official unpleasantness over this rash act, but her husband—who survived the attack—was Vice Minister of Fisheries and had a bit of clout himself. The compromise was that Carina was jailed, but she got her own cell, complete with a bathroom and television set, in the prison infirmary.

Predictably, we soon suffered a plague of flies of biblical proportions. We ate our meals wrapped inside our mosquito nets, and spent every waking moment killing the creatures, sometimes bagging three hundred in an hour. It took yet another hunger strike to get the dump moved.

Esther was furious as the *llavera* opened the cell door to let her in, then closed it behind her. She waited until the *llavera's* footsteps died away before launching a tirade.

"Damn those common prisoners!" she swore. "Damn every one of them."

"What's wrong?" I said. Esther had just returned from a trip to a civilian hospital in Havana for treatment of respiratory problems, and I knew some common criminals had been taken there at the same time. But we had been getting along with the common criminals rather well. Some of them stopped by our bathroom window from time to time to say hello. For the prison to build a separate high-security cell, complete with thirty-foot walls and a barbed wire roof over the patio, the common prisoners had concluded, must mean that we were greatly feared. They admired that.

"You should have seen it, Ana," Esther fumed. "They've all sliced their uniforms into tiny miniskirts, and cut the fronts so low their nipples are almost hanging out. And everywhere we went, they propositioned the men. Doctors, patients, people in the waiting room, seventy-year-old cripples and twelve-year-old boys, they don't care. It's always the same thing: 'Oh, hello, daddy . . .'" She lowered her voice to a salacious caricature of a sultry croon.

"So, what's the problem?" I asked.

"The *problem* is that I was wearing the same uniform that they were," she retorted. "The *problem* is that everyone we saw just assumed that the whole bunch of us were whores, including me." She kicked the bed. "I am not going back to the hospital in that uniform. Never again."

I wasn't sure what to make of her outburst. The isolation and cramped quarters of the schoolhouse cell were wearing on Esther. She was sometimes querulous, and occasionally not very lucid. (Some days she talked obsessively, for hours, about a French exposition she saw in Havana in 1928.)

But a few days later Miriam visited the hospital when her battered kidney acted up. She came back as exasperated as Esther: "We've got to get rid of these uniforms. If we have to wear a uniform at all, it should be completely different from the one the common criminals wear."

The problem of uniforms had been a vexing one ever since Castro started stuffing Cuba's prisons full of his enemies. Batista's political prisoners (who numbered a tiny fraction of Castro's) weren't required to wear uniforms like the rest of the inmates. But when Castro introduced new uniforms, there were no exceptions permitted.

Among women, the issue had gone mostly unnoticed for a long time. A gray uniform was introduced in 1962, replaced by a blue one in 1963, a yellow one in 1966, and another blue one in 1967. The only real protests were in 1967, when Miriam and a dozen or so other political prisoners refused to wear them. They were forced to live in bras and panties for several months, then threatened with incarceration among the common criminals, and they gave in.

Among the men, it was a different story. Thousands of them refused to put on the blue uniforms in 1967. Some of them wore nothing but underwear—and, at times, nothing at all—for years, enduring some terrible tortures along the way. Their protests had even raised some faint blips on the rest of the world's human-rights radar screen.

I had never given the uniforms much thought. Miriam's protest began while I was on the street during my first escape, and it ended shortly after I returned to Guanajay. And, unlike Miriam and Esther, I had never been out in public with common criminals. Whenever I was sent outside the prison for medical treatment, it was always to a military hospital where (whatever else might be said of the place) the potential for embarrassment was nil.

I could understand why Miriam and Esther were angry. But I also thought a protest about the uniforms had the potential to make us look ridiculous. We'd been wearing them, after all, for ten years. Were we going to claim we'd never noticed before that the common criminals had them, too?

"Let's try to talk to them about this first, before we threaten to hold our breath until our faces turn blue, okay?" I suggested. "We might even get somewhere with them on the issue of how the common prisoners act in public. It doesn't do the Ministry any credit if prisoners in their custody are out there flashing their crotches at the general public. Maybe they'll do something about it."

I was wrong, of course. Our complaints were directed to a new assistant prison director, a tall, horse-faced young woman named Ileana Hernández who had just recently gotten a psychology degree from the University of Havana. She was convinced that she could break us where others had failed—it would get her a gold star for revolutionary achievement, be her ticket into the big time. She wouldn't give any ground at all on the uniforms. I slowly realized that Ileana and her bosses were *gratified* by our complaint; they liked the idea of us being confused, in the public mind, with a bunch of vulgar, loudmouthed prostitutes. It marginalized us.

"I think you were right in the first place," I told Esther and Miriam after four useless months of jawing with the irascible Ileana. "I think we're going to have to do something dramatic."

Miriam started a complex negotiation with the common prisoners who sometimes stopped at our window. She managed to swap several packages of cigarettes for two rolls of silk thread, one red and one white, and a couple of needles, all stolen from the prison sewing factory.

One advantage of our secluded cell was clandestine activities could be carried on rather openly. We spent several days embroidering the words *Plantada Political Prisoner* in luminous four-inch block letters on the backs of one of our two sets of uniform blouses. The thread was surprisingly tough, and we put in several layers. No one could get rid of the lettered slogan without destroying the blouses.

Only once did we have to hurriedly hide them, when Ileana showed up unexpectedly at the cell.

"I just wondered why you've stopped complaining to me about the uniforms," she said.

"Because it's useless to talk to you," I answered bluntly. "We need to talk to someone at the Ministry level."

"The Ministry is on a vacation from you this summer," Ileana said. "Anything you have to say, say to me."

"A vacation?" I replied, raising my eyebrows. "Well, I hope they're taking it easy and enjoying themselves. There might be a lot of work when they get back."

Ileana stayed for a few more minutes, pressing us, but we just smiled enigmatically.

Three days later, our families visited. We put on the doctored uniforms and were careful to keep from turning our backs on the *llavera* who walked us to the offices. At the last second, as I slipped through the door, she saw the embroidered words. I could hear her gasp and then the clatter of her boots as she ran to spread the word.

The visit, needless to say, was a dud. Milagros was struck by killer diarrhea the moment she saw the embroidery and spent most of the time in the toilet. My mother could hardly keep from crying. All the while, we could see guards gathering outside like stormclouds. *Oh, this is going to be a bad one,* I thought.

When the visit ended, the guards didn't bother with the usual search. They led us back to the schoolhouse. But instead of taking us into the cell, they unlocked a gate that went directly into our patio. When we walked in, they closed the gate behind us, leaving us alone in the locked patio, with no access to our cell.

It was noon, the sun directly overhead. Its rays bounced off the white-washed walls, catching us in a merciless crossfire. Sitting against the wall, my face in my hands, I fancied I could hear my own eyeballs sizzling. The blue uniforms felt like hot coals heaped around us.

An hour passed, then another. Dizzying, hallucinatory images raced through my brain, breaking up before I could comprehend them. Thunder sounded inside my head. Remembering there was an industrial sink on the patio for our laundry, I staggered over to it and thrust my head under the faucet. Even the water seemed aflame. I had to beat back the urge to run to the gate and beg them to come in and get the beating over with.

Time ceased to exist. The heat was crushing us. I could no longer open my eyes for even a split second; everything shimmered in meaningless waves of light. The bell in the main dining room sounded for dinner. Could five and a half hours really have passed? Then there were other sounds, the indistinct babble of prisoners walking back to their cells. Six hours. The heat seared my lungs.

The grating sound of a key turning in a lock brought the three of us to our feet—too fast. I wanted to vomit. Bursts of hard white light went off someplace inside my head, drowning everything else out for a minute. Then I recovered to hear Ileana's voice.

"Hand over those uniforms!" she snapped. I opened my eyes a slit. She was inside the patio, with about thirty guards and *llaveras* clustered behind her. She looked furious, and no wonder: Her first big assignment and she had blown it. Miriam, Esther, and I instinctively took several steps back.

"Ileana, it doesn't look to me like you plan to employ strictly psychological techniques here," I said.

"Attack!" she screamed. A cloudburst of uniformed bodies were on top of us instantly. I tightly covered the buttons on my blouse with my arms, assuming they would attempt to tear it off, but they didn't even try at first. Instead, a *llavera* dragged her thick, jagged fingernails down my cheek and neck. I screamed and ducked as the flesh tore away beneath them. Somewhere behind me I could hear a woman shouting: "Be careful of Miriam! That bitch bites!"

I spun and flung myself at the *llavera* who clawed me, landing several hard punches to her head. But that left the front of my blouse unprotected. A huge guard gave the collar a swift, herculean yank, and the front of the blouse came free, along with my bra.

I stopped trying to fight, except for a few desultory kicks, and concentrated on holding my blouse closed. The side of my face felt like a blowtorch had been used on it, and drops of blood flew off it every time I dodged a punch. Blows glanced off me as the guards threw me from side to side, trying to pull the blouse away. Finally someone swiped lightly at me with a knife, opening a gash in the back of the blouse. In moments they had torn it to scraps. Two guards grabbed me and threw me into the cell, where Miriam and Esther had already been deposited.

When I could breathe again, I went to the bathroom to find the small mirror my mother had smuggled in recently. Two deep, bloody grooves wound across my right cheek down to my neck. *That bitch deliberately scarred me*, I thought. After fifteen years, they could still find new ways to make me hate them.

· SIXTEEN ·

Adios

JULY 2, 1977

"YOU MUST ALWAYS remember to be prepared," my father counseled. His voice was solemn, but his smile was soft and familiar. I smiled back warmly, pleased to see him so unexpectedly, and grateful for the sage advice. "So go ahead, take them." My smile didn't falter, but I was mildly perplexed as he pressed the sack into my hand. It brimmed over with chocolate coins wrapped in gold foil, the same kind he used to surprise me with as a little girl. They were spilling over the top, and I had to struggle to catch a few of them before they fell to the ground. "Why do we need so many, Papa?" I asked.

"So you'll have money when you go to America, Ana," he replied with the same amused chuckle that he used when my sisters or I asked if the moon was really made of green cheese. "They don't use ration cards there, you know."

I was still confused. There seemed to be plans afoot that nobody had mentioned to me. "When will I go to America?" I asked. My father pointed, and I saw Pola Grau standing at the head of a line of women, a worried expression on her face. Her hands were shuffling through a stack of paperwork; I could see official stamps scattered here and there through the pages.

"Pola's the first," he said. "That's when you'll know it's starting, when she goes. Castro is talking with the United States, and they'll make an arrangement about the prisoners. But it's going to take a long time, a very long time. And you'll be the last to leave. So try to be patient."

I awoke with a jolt. Sun streamed in through the windows of the little schoolhouse. Miriam and Esther were across the cell, murmuring to one another as they played cards. "We're getting out of here," I announced excitedly. "We're getting out. We've got to let our families know so they can start making plans."

Neither Miriam nor Esther said a word as I described my dream. I spoke with such certainty that they accepted it without protest. We agreed we had to tell our families to start hiding any keepsakes they wanted to take out of Cuba. When the government issued exit visas, it catalogued the recipient's property, and almost all of it was confiscated.

When we got word to our relatives, they were all sure I had finally cracked under the strain of prison. "I knew this is how it would end," my sister Milagros tearfully told my mother, "with Ana going completely crazy in there." But a few days later, they hid some things, just in case.

An unspoken truce existed between the prison authorities and us. We wore pajamas instead of uniforms, and the *llaveras* made no attempt to interfere. But our correspondence, packages, and family visits were suspended. It was a tolerable state of affairs, but our experience taught us that they would try again to impose their will. Warily we watched for the first sign of a new crackdown.

It was late August when a *llavera* came to our cell unexpectedly after lunch and told us to get dressed. We were going to the prison offices.

"What do you think they're going to do?" Esther asked as we put on clean pajamas.

"They're going to split us up," predicted Miriam grimly. "Probably we'll be put in with the common prisoners, each in a different place."

"If you're right, we've got to do everything we can to get back together," I said. "It's hard enough resisting them with just the three of us. Alone, I'm not sure how long any of us would last."

"You mean we should agree to wear the uniforms if they'll keep us together?" Esther said uncertainly.

"Damn, I hadn't even thought of the uniforms," I replied. "No, we can't give in on that. If they make us put on uniforms, we just take them off again. And we all launch hunger strikes until they reunite us."

"One thing at a time," insisted Miriam. "The first priority should be getting reunited. After that we can deal with the issue of the uniforms. I don't want to be in with the common prisoners, naked, by myself." A slight, involuntary shiver passed through her body.

"Miriam's right," Esther declared. "One thing at a time." I nodded my agreement. We walked out of the cell to face our fate.

They drove us to the offices and told us to wait in a small room. A few minutes later, a State Security lieutenant opened the door. "Miriam Ortega, come with me," she said. I heard their footsteps echo as they went up the stairs to the second floor, where the most senior officials had their offices. Esther and I went to different windows of the waiting room to watch outside. About forty-five minutes later, I saw a cluster of uniformed men walk out of the building and get into a truck. Was that Miriam in the middle? It was hard to tell.

"Ana Rodríguez, it's your turn," the lieutenant called from the door.

She escorted me upstairs to a large office. Inside were a colonel and a captain from State Security, and a man in civilian clothing holding a briefcase on his lap. Curious, I deliberately fumbled my cigarettes, letting the pack fall to the floor near him. As I leaned over to pick it up, I could see a small camera concealed beneath the briefcase.

I stepped back to the only remaining chair and started turning it so the man with the camera would have only a view of my left shoulder. "Put that damn thing back where it was," the colonel snapped.

Why do they want my picture so badly? I wondered. *They've already got mug shots from when I was arrested, and again when I was recaptured after my first escape. And if this is just a transfer, why have they sent two high-ranking officers to tell me about it?* Nothing made sense. I decided it was time for my crazy act.

I used it occasionally during interrogations when I couldn't figure out what State Security was up to. I would chain-smoke cigarettes in lightning succession, puffing away like a locomotive; jerk my head this way and that, like a hummingbird pumped full of caffeine; speed up my voice like a cartoon character; give my hands a slight palpitation. It was usually very effective in distracting interrogators, and sometimes made them slip up and give away their motive. Of course, State Security had its own techniques aimed at distracting prisoners. The most common was to ask dozens of detailed questions on irrelevant topics to divert your attention, and then casually slip in the real query while you were focusing your defenses elsewhere. I had sat in interrogation rooms for hours at a time as stern interrogators tried to pin down whether someone was my second cousin or my third.

I launched my act, lighting a cigarette with a trembling hand, then grinding the match into an ashtray on the colonel's desk with a spastic jab. The colonel reflexively grabbed at a small black object on the desktop that I hadn't really noticed before. It was a wireless tape recorder. *Hmmm,* I thought, *this gets stranger and stranger.*

The colonel picked up my file and tapped it on the desk. "Ana," he asked portentously, "what do you think of the Soviet Union's achievements in space?"

So that's it. We're going to be space chimpanzees, testing a new rocket, I thought. *Maybe we'll finally get some international support—from the animal-rights people.* I almost laughed, but squelched it into a cough at the last minute. Didn't want to spoil my nut act.

"Very impressive," I said in a flat monotone. "Very impressive." I belched smoke like a simmering volcano.

"Please, elaborate on that. We're interested in your opinion."

"The more we know about space, and the unlikelihood of survival on another planet, perhaps the less likely we'll be to blow this one up," I replied. The colonel's eyes narrowed as he tried to decide whether this was a subtle taunt. The captain, meanwhile, couldn't take his eyes off my hand, which was thumping against the arm of the chair like a wind-up toy.

We went on like that for half an hour. The colonel asked idiotic questions about space travel, while I bit my nails and sucked noisily at cigarettes. Then he abruptly shifted gears.

"How many kilograms of explosives did you have when you were arrested?" he asked, leafing through my file. "I can't find it in here."

I knew we had reached the real point of the interrogation, though I didn't have the faintest idea what it was.

"None, colonel, none at all," I replied. "The most incriminating thing you found in my room was a rat's skull. I guess your men mistook it for a State Security officer's head."

He ignored my gibe. "No, you had some explosives," he said, continuing to search the file. "I know I saw it in here a minute ago."

"If it's in there, it's because you people have forged documents," I replied. "Nobody ever said anything about explosives, not even at that phony trial you staged."

"You know perfectly well we haven't forged anything," he countered. "You know you are a convicted terrorist—"

He kept talking, but I wasn't listening. When I heard the word "terrorist," everything came together with a blinding flash of clarity.

"Forget the terrorist bullshit right now, Colonel," I interrupted. "The Americans will never believe it. And I don't know what you're negotiating with them, but I can tell you right now, any deal you strike with them better include exit visas for my family. I'm not leaving without them."

The colonel was not accustomed to interruptions from prisoners, and even less so to lectures. He smashed his fist down on the desk.

"You stupid cunt, you'll go wherever we tell you!" he shouted. "And when you're in Miami, you can send pretty postcards to your mother and sister, because they're staying right here. If you behave yourself over there, maybe we'll allow you to be buried beside them."

A serene smile spread over my face. I stubbed out my cigarette and let loose a long, hearty laugh. Then I leaned over toward the tape recorder. "The voice you just heard revealing a state secret was that of Colonel Fernández Blanco, making unauthorized disclosure of Fidel Castro's secret negotiations with the United States," I said in my best radio announcer's voice. "There are three witnesses here who will be happy to testify at the colonel's trial—Captain Lester Rodríguez, a State Security photographer, and political prisoner Ana Rodríguez."

I sat back in my chair. "I'm really sorry about this, colonel," I said. "You'll probably lose your job, at the very least. And after all the filthy, scummy things you had to do to earn that uniform." I clucked sympathetically.

"You're the worst fucking bitch that was ever born!" he shouted.

"No," I shot back as the captain hustled me away. "If that were so, I'd be sitting on the other side of the desk."

My instinctive hunch that Castro was negotiating with the Americans was right on target, though it would be years before I learned the full story.

In January 1977, Jimmy Carter had become president of the United States. Carter had the idea that the Cold War was at least as much the fault of the United States as the Soviet Union. He thought there was no problem in the world that couldn't be solved by extending a hand of friendship and offering to talk things over like gentlemen. Eventually, at great cost to the populations of Nicaragua, Iran, and Afghanistan, he would learn differently, but that was all in the future.

Cuba was one of the first targets of Carter's let's-be-friends strategy. His administration was packed with advisers from Stanford and Berkeley who believed that Castro was a social democrat who had been pushed into the arms of the Soviet Union by American intransigence. Even before Carter took office, his aides were hinting that they wanted to end the U.S. embargo of Cuba and open up a friendly relationship. And the first secret contacts with Castro began within a couple of weeks of Carter's inauguration.

What kept gumming up the works were Castro's attempts to play colonial superpower in Africa. He was sending troops or weapons or both to Angola, Ethiopia, Mozambique, Namibia, Somalia, Guinea, the Congo, and who knew where else. Even through Jimmy Carter's rose-colored glasses, this didn't seem like friendly behavior.

Castro had no intention of ending his military escapades in Africa. But he thought he might soothe the Americans another way. Carter was always talking about the importance of human rights. Well, why not offer to release Cuba's political prisoners?

But Castro was cooking the books. Releasing all his political prisoners would have amounted to at least twenty thousand, an embarrassingly high number even for Castro, considering the island's population was only about ten million. Instead, he contrived to minimize the numbers. One trick was "releasing" prisoners to house arrest. Another was reclassifying them as common criminals on the basis of something—say, punching a guard—they did while in prison.

Then there were "Batista supporters." Castro said he wouldn't release any of them at all, a stipulation that the United States accepted without complaint, as though supporters of the former dictator were subhuman. There *were* a lot of former Batista supporters in prison, but few who had committed serious crimes or were of any real political importance. Mostly they were guilty of backing the wrong side.

And finally Castro said he wouldn't release any "terrorists." That was a stroke of tactical genius. The Western world was under assault by hordes of thuggish assassins who cloaked their murderous attacks on civilians in the rhetoric of liberation: Italy's Red Brigades, Germany's Red Army Faction, the Popular Front for the Liberation of Palestine, the Japanese Red Army, and countless others.

The United States and its allies were loudly calling for the Soviet bloc to stop its support of these groups. They were hardly in a position to argue if Cuba said it wouldn't let convicted terrorists out of prison. But that gave Castro an enormous loophole. Anyone who participated even peripherally in armed resistance to his regime could be defined as a terrorist.

By the time Castro finished with all his bookkeeping legerdemain, he was able to tell the United States he had just three thousand prisoners to release. The Carter administration nodded credulously.

For several months after the abortive interview with State Security, nothing happened. But in March 1978, a Ministry official named Pacheco came to see us. He was, in his own way, a decent man, and had intervened on a couple of occasions to obtain small concessions for us that had ended hunger strikes. With him were two poker-faced State Security colonels.

"Look," Pacheco began earnestly, "what we've had here, for a long time, is a war: you in one trench, us in another, everybody fighting without quarter, taking no prisoners. Now imagine you see a white flag from my trench. 'Hey,' I yell. 'We're all countrymen here. Let's stop shedding one another's blood. Let's talk.' What would you say?"

"Ahh, Pacheco," I replied, "every schoolchild knows the correct answer to that: 'Here, nobody surrenders.' " Esther, Miriam, and I broke up laughing; it was Castro's favorite revolutionary slogan, the one he trotted out every time he announced a drop in the bread ration or a new cut in the electric supply. Pacheco started laughing, too, but caught himself when the two colonels fixed him with cold stares. "We'll talk again," he said hastily, and hurried away.

Despite my wisecrack, the significance of Pacheco's words was not lost on me: *"Imagine you see a white flag from my trench."* Could the Ministry really be considering surrender after all these years of trying to break us?

A few weeks later, we got the first tangible sign of a change in the Ministry's attitude. Our pajamas were declared our official uniform. That meant we would again be able to visit the hospital, our mail would resume, and our families could see us for the first time in nine months. Their first visit was scheduled for early May.

My mother and sister prepared for the visit like veteran drug smugglers. My mother stuffed two bags of coffee into the bottom of her bra. Milagros put on a double set of panties; hidden between them was a sealed package containing clandestine letters (most of them from former prisoners, who weren't allowed to write me openly) and a large cache of vitamins.

Prison rules prohibited visits from anyone but relatives with the same last name. But at the last minute my aunt Julieta Méndez, who hadn't seen me in years, decided to borrow an ID card from a friend named Rodríguez and come along. The three of them arrived early that morning, excited at the prospect of seeing me again, but prepared for the usual monotonous series of searches and delays.

To their surprise, a *llavera* ushered them inside, along with several of Esther's and Miriam's relatives. She led them to the prison offices. "Please, up these stairs," the *llavera* said. "I'll be right behind you."

Milagros, Aunt Julieta, and my mother all had the same thought simultaneously: They were going to undergo a strip search, a technique the Interior Ministry had abandoned years ago after we staged several hunger strikes to protest it. All three of them panicked.

"We're completely screwed," Aunt Julieta whispered to my sister as they started climbing the stairs. "We're going to be arrested." She knew her fake ID card would never pass a close inspection. Aunt Julieta repeated her prophecy of doom twice, but Milagros didn't reply. She was too busy fumbling inside her skirt, removing the bulky package of vitamins and rolled-up letters. She stuffed it in her mouth, the one spot she had never seen the *llaveras* search.

My mother, meanwhile, had gone into her old-lady routine. "At my age," she told the *llavera* in a quavering, querulous voice, "I don't climb stairs."

The *llavera* leaned into an office and pulled out a wooden chair. "Here, sit on this," she instructed my mother, "and the guard and I will carry you."

"What are you, a madwoman?" my mother screeched, waving her cane. "I'll fall off and break my neck. Is that what you want, to kill me? Is the Revolution executing old people now? Will you roast our sad old bones and give us away as rations?"

The *llavera* retreated, my mother's petulant complaints bursting around her like shells. "Just stay here with the guard," she said, hurrying up the stairs and out of earshot. My mother, biting her tongue to keep from smiling, sat down in the chair to wait, confident she had saved my coffee from the bloodhounds.

Upstairs, Aunt Julieta, Milagros, and the other families were surprised again. Instead of being ordered to take off their clothes, they were led into the office of the prison director and seated around a conference table. At its head was the director himself, a man named Acosta.

"I'm glad to see all you ladies," he gurgled. "I have the utmost respect for all of you. I know you've suffered, often unjustly, but you've always borne your troubles with great dignity. In fact, the only reason we're permitting this visit is our respect for you. These three prisoners continue to be obstinate and uncooperative. They're egotists. They don't care that their stubbornness diverts resources that could be put to work improving the life of other Cubans. And they don't even care about the suffering they cause you with their little tricks."

"That's not true," Esther's sister protested. "Esther loves us."

"I think I know my sister better than you do," chimed in Miriam's sister.

Aunt Julieta looked at Milagros expectantly. "Come on," she whispered loudly enough for the others to hear, "don't let him talk that way about Ana. Speak up!" But Milagros, who still had the package of letters and vitamins crammed in her mouth, couldn't say a word. She gave Acosta a reproachful look instead.

"These women demand different living conditions than everyone else," Acosta continued. "They won't wear the same uniform as everyone else. They even act like they're morally superior to the rest of the political prisoners. They're always looking for some excuse to make trouble, to disrupt the efforts of the Revolution to make a better Cuba. And they never acknowledge the Revolution's generosity toward them. How many times have they gone on hunger strikes? How many times could we have permitted them to die? That's what they really deserve, but in the end, we always come to their aid. So many times the Revolution has shown them forgiveness, and they respond only with hostility."

"It is possible that Esther is confused about the exact nature of the Revolution," interrupted her sister, choosing her words carefully, but unwilling to let Acosta go unchallenged. "But she is a person of good will and good intentions. She is never destructive for the sake of being destructive."

"Miriam does these things because she's convinced she's right," agreed her sister, "not because she wants to be a troublemaker."

"Speak up, Milagros!" Aunt Julieta urged her, not bothering to lower her voice. "Show some loyalty to your own sister!" The room was quiet; even Acosta was looking at Milagros. She waved her hand dismissively, and the director resumed his speech.

"Despite everything that has happened, we are still capable of forgiving these three women," Acosta said. "You know we've been releasing some other prisoners without forcing them to serve their full sentences. We could do the same for your relatives. But you have to make them understand that their freedom depends on their attitude. You must counsel them to start cooperating with us. If they want to leave here alive, they have to change."

Acosta stopped in surprise as loud sobbing broke out all around the table. The relatives of Esther and Miriam wept, knowing that if their freedom depended on their attitudes, they'd be in prison until their bones were dust.

Milagros was still silent. If she let herself cry, she'd strangle on the bag in her mouth. "Milagros, you are a scandal," declared Aunt Julieta, sniffling loudly. "Can't you even afford a few tears for your sister? Would you like to borrow some of mine?" What Milagros really wanted to do was bop Aunt Julieta on the head, but she didn't dare. Acosta was staring at them.

"So if you want these visits to continue, please talk to your relatives about ending this perpetual confrontation they've created," Acosta concluded. "And please don't tell them about this conversation. You know how they'll react. We're trying to calm them down, not make them crazier."

They filed silently out of the room. At the bottom of the stairs, my mother joined the procession as it headed toward the visiting area. "Your daughter is a disgrace," Aunt Julieta huffed to my mother. "If she dislikes Ana so much, why does she even bother to come here?"

Milagros glanced around and, seeing that the attention of the *llaveras* was elsewhere, coughed the package into her hand. She made sure Aunt Julieta saw it before slipping it back inside her dress. "Damn it, Julieta, didn't you think I might have a reason for keeping my mouth shut?" she complained.

"Well, child, how was I supposed to know it was in your mouth?" Aunt Julieta replied. "Why didn't you say something?"

"How could I say something when—Oh, never mind."

We knew, from the puffy eyes and solemn expressions on the faces of our visitors, that something had happened. It took about half an hour for us to pry it out of them.

It wasn't the first time the prison authorities had tried to work on us through our families. At La Cabaña, the *llaveras* had told them we could be released if only we'd start behaving ourselves and join the re-education program. But it wasn't an effective tactic. Our families knew us too well to even bring up the subject.

As I listened to Milagros and my mother describe what had happened, an emotional riptide pulled at my heart. How was it that they had come to know so much about strip searches and recounts? How had they become experts on the homemade technology of smuggling? This was not what they had planned for their lives. But for more than sixteen years they had been living my life, not their own.

Their world started spinning on a new axis the day I was arrested. Everything had changed. Friends stopped speaking to them, looked the other way when passing them in the street. Police showed up at the front door at all hours of the day and night, ransacking the house and store, stealing anything they liked by designating it as "evidence" and taking it away. Milagros was arrested—by one of our own cousins—and detained for three days around the time of the Bay of Pigs invasion; my father was jailed several times, sometimes for just a few hours, but sometimes for several days. Their only crime was being related to me.

My imprisonment reverberated through the family in so many unexpected ways. My sister Magda, four years younger than I, was engaged to her high school sweetheart, a boy who made fine furniture. But he was enchanted with the Revolution. After my arrest, they started arguing about me. One day Magda gave him an ultimatum—the Revolution, or me. He chose the Revolution.

And Milagros, so timid and quiet that as children Magda and I could steal her toys with impunity, hit a man one day at the store. He was an employee, a man who had worked for us for years, and she overheard him telling a customer: "I think every single one of those counterrevolutionaries should be shot, as fast as they can put them against the wall." Milagros lunged across the counter and delivered a vicious slap that sent him reeling into the wall. "If you ever set foot in this store again," she hissed, "I'll hit you so hard your eyeballs will pop out."

No one, I think, suffered more than Milagros. When my father died, all the burdens fell on her. Magda reluctantly moved to the United States, because before he died, my father made her promise to go. "The whole family can't be here fighting," he told her. "Someone has to go build a new life." So she left. Milagros had to run the store, care for my mother, and scrounge things for a sister in prison. She had never married, hadn't even had a boyfriend in years. What man in his right mind would want to get involved with the sister of a *gusana*?

Many times I urged Milagros to give it up, to take my mother and join Magda in New Jersey—especially after the Revolution confiscated our store and Milagros was reduced to acting as a commissar on our property.

"I would feel a lot better if you were out of the country," I told her. "Then I wouldn't have to worry that if I do something to make them mad, they might take it out on you."

"Don't be silly," she replied. "If we left, who would take care of you?"

"*You're* the one being silly," I argued. "The prison will take care of me. They put me here, they have to feed me and keep a roof over my head."

"If things were reversed," Milagros said quietly, "if I were in here and you were out there, would you leave?" For that I had no answer, except to look at her with pride. There was *plantada* blood in the veins of all the Rodríguez women.

What made me proudest of all was that no one in my family had ever complained to me, not once in all these years, about what my imprisonment had cost them. They rarely even told me of their troubles; most of what I knew came indirectly from other prisoners who heard gossip from their own relatives.

Not every prisoner was so lucky. On visiting days over the years, I had watched many times as sobbing relatives reproved other prisoners: "Why have you done this to us? Why have you ruined us? Why can't you do what the prison tells you?" On the other hand, there was María Cristina Oliva's mother, the toughest woman of all. Both her husband and her only daughter were political prisoners, and I guess she felt she had nothing to lose; she didn't take any shit from anybody. She once slapped someone from the Ministry who threatened to put her in jail. And if she came on visiting day and discovered that some of us were in the *tapiadas* in retaliation for a protest, she would turn to María Cristina and demand: "What's the matter with you? Why aren't you in there with them?"

In late August, the prison authorities started leaving the gate from our cell to the patio unlocked most of the day, giving us free access to the patio. We usually didn't go out until sundown, when the patio cooled off.

On the evening of September 6, as we strolled around the patio stretching our legs, we heard a loudspeaker crackle to life with the strains of one of the revolutionary anthems that customarily preceded a Castro speech. It was the first time we had ever heard the public-address system at Nuevo Amanecer; a speaker had obviously been hooked up specially for us. "Something's going on," Miriam said. "We'd better listen."

"They must be planning to leave us out later than usual tonight," Esther observed. "This guy can't clear his throat in less than two hours."

If we had any doubts that something was afoot, they disappeared during the first moments of the speech, when Castro referred to the Miami exiles as "the Cuban community abroad" rather than *gusanos*, his customary epithet. A few minutes later, he invited representatives of the exiles to come to Havana to discuss a rapprochement. One of the things they could discuss, he said, was permitting exiles to return on family visits. Another was the release of some political prisoners.

For the first time, the negotiations on our release were out in the open.* I had wildly conflicting feelings about the talks. On the one hand, I thought this might be the last chance for me to get out of prison alive; I knew I couldn't survive another sixteen years inside. Someday a guard would kick me one too many times during a fight, or a *llavera* would wait one day too long before calling a doctor, or the Ministry would let a hunger strike go on one day past our endurance. I didn't want my final sight on

---

*Although Castro pretended the release of prisoners was part of the talks with the exiles, years later Carter administration officials confirmed that the matter had already been decided in negotiations between the Cuban and U.S. governments. But both sides preferred to keep their contacts secret, so it was agreed that Castro would use the dialogue with the exiles as a cover for the release.

earth to be the inside of one of the bleak cells where I had spent the last decade and a half.

On the other hand, I didn't want to be a pawn in a game that helped Castro further solidify his power. And it sounded to me like that was exactly what was going on. During his speech, Castro—though not going so far as to admit his negotiations with the Americans—had pointedly noted he had "a certain détente" with the Carter government. The Revolution, he said, was "absolutely consolidated and irreversible. We know it. The government of the United States knows it."

Mostly I felt adrift, buffeted by two forces that neither understood nor cared why I went to prison: an object of manipulation. At least in our dealings with the prison authorities, we had a limited degree of control over our own fate. In the geopolitical chess match between Washington and Havana, we had none.

Even the Carter administration, which was nominally on our side, didn't really care about us. We were political cover. This way, when Carter came under attack from his political opponents for the way he pushed around American allies on the subject of human rights, he could say: *See, I'm tough on Communist governments, too.* But if Jimmy Carter really understood anything about Castro, if he really understood the intimate relationship between communism and barbed wire, he wouldn't have been doing anything that might extend Castro's reign so much as five minutes. Our lives were not worth the enslavement of an entire nation. If we had thought so, we could have gotten out of prison without any help, a long time ago.

"Can you believe the way Pola Grau talks?" Victoria the *llavera* asked as she put down the lukewarm cups of semi-coffee that were our only breakfast. "Who does she think she is?" Miriam, Esther, and I glanced at one another silently. The *llaveras* always assumed that we were wired in to some secret information network outside the prison, that we were aware of everything that was happening in the world. Actually, most of what we knew came from things they let slip. Now, what was this about Pola? We would have to delicately coax it out of Victoria, without letting on that we hadn't the faintest idea what she was talking about.

"Pola says a lot of silly things," I agreed. "But which one do you mean? You know, she's always shooting her mouth off, and I can't keep track."

"Well, the interview she gave on the Voice of America last night," Victoria said matter-of-factly. "She talked about all this suffering she endured in prison. But if you ask me, the three of you have suffered a lot more. I don't see what Pola Grau has to complain about at all."

I almost dropped my cup. If Pola was talking to the Voice of America, it must mean that she was not only out of prison, but out of Cuba. We knew Castro was talking with the Americans about releasing prisoners, but we didn't know he was actually *doing* it.

"Yeah, well, that's Pola," I concurred. "How long is it that she's been out now, exactly?"

"Well, this is December 1," Victoria said, her forehead wrinkling as she computed backward. "So, what, two weeks? But I think she just got to the United States a couple of days ago." She stepped out the cell door, locked it behind her, and went on her way. When we heard the outer gate slam shut, the three of us exploded into excited chatter.

"I never really believed it until now," Miriam said. "I know you heard it from the State Security man, Ana, and I know I heard Castro himself say it on the radio. But deep inside, I just always thought it was the same old bullshit we've been hearing for years about a release."

"The best news," broke in Esther, "is that she's in the United States. They must be giving exit visas as part of the deal—exit visas for the whole family. I don't think Pola would have left without her family, do you?"

"No," I agreed, "I can't imagine it. I think you're right." That had been one of our chief fears, that we would be released without visas, turned loose without ration books or jobs, trying to survive as non-persons in a tightly controlled Marxist society. Even less palatable was the idea of being sent into exile while our families remained behind as hostages who could be punished if we did or said anything that displeased Castro from afar.

"You know what's really crazy?" Miriam asked. "For Victoria to say, right in front of us, that she listens to the Voice of America. Imagine that—an Interior Ministry employee getting her news from an American propaganda station."

"That's right," chimed in Esther. "If any of the Ministry people heard her say that, she'd be seeing the *tapiadas* from the inside instead of the outside."

We continued for hours, reconstructing and deconstructing every word Victoria said, analyzing it up, down, and sideways. It wasn't until that night, when the others went to bed and I sat alone at the window, that I let myself think back to my father's visit in the dream. *Pola's the first,* he had said. *And you'll be the last.*

How did you know, Papa? I wondered, beaming my thoughts into the night air. *And what does it all mean?* Was everything predestined? And if it was, did that mean all our suffering had been meaningless? That even without all the beatings and hunger strikes, we would have arrived at this very same point in time and circumstances anyway? The questions troubled me, and no answers came back out of the night.

But I took solace in one other part of the dream, if a dream it was. *Are you happy?* I had asked my father. *Yes, Ana, I am,* he had replied. *Very happy.*

Acosta, the prison director, continued his campaign to win our families over to his side. They smiled and nodded during each meeting, swore they would never breathe a word to us, and then relayed the details as soon as they arrived in the visiting room. We had no intention of giving in, but neither did we protest his activities; our families wanted us to keep pretending we didn't know anything about his efforts.

To see if our families had really improved our attitudes, Acosta started dropping by our cell once a month or so, acting friendly. We were generally reserved. But when he stopped to see us in January 1979, his visit happened to come at the end of three consecutive days in which we found dead flies in our food. Since he was there anyway, I thought I might as well complain, even though it had never done any good.

"Acosta, the food is barely edible the way it's normally cooked, but you can't expect us to eat it with flies in it," I said. "Even the *llaveras* agree it's too disgusting for words. Just ask Victoria if you don't believe me."

"Of course I believe you," he said in a hearty voice. "Who could make something like that up? When I get back to the office, I'm going to speak with the head of the kitchen. It's intolerable."

He looked at us for a sign of approval, but our faces were impassive; we'd been told a million times over the years that something was going to be done as soon as the director got back to his offices, and rarely, if ever, had it happened. Acosta sensed our doubt.

"If you women haven't been able to eat in three days, you need a bigger meal than usual," he said. "We don't want you getting ill. I'm going to order them to cook you one of those chickens Margarita Gutierrez is raising over at the barracks."

Our eyes widened. The last time we had got chicken in a prison meal was in 1964. And one of Margarita Gutierrez' chickens would taste twice as good. She was an infamously depraved *llavera* whose specialty was biting prisoners in the most intimate spot she could get her teeth. She once bit Isabel Molgado's breast so savagely that it developed an infection that had to be treated in the hospital. Those chickens were like her babies; I only hoped she could be there to see me drive my teeth into one of them.

Perhaps the idea left me a little unhinged, because what I asked next was truly mad. "Acosta, why can't our families bring us coffee?" I asked. "If they want to give us part of their ration, what difference does it make to the Ministry?"

The rule against coffee had been on the books since the day I was arrested, and it was rigorously enforced. I might as well have asked if we could have weekend passes to Disneyland.

"You know, I don't know any reason for that rule, either," Acosta said. "Victoria!" He summoned the *llavera*, who immediately stepped into the cell. "When you call their families to give them the date of the next visit, tell them they can bring powdered coffee if they like."

When he left a few minutes later, we were too stunned to speak. "I think," Miriam finally said, "we're really getting out."

"Let's see if we get the chicken," I cautioned.

It arrived that night, just as promised. Victoria told us, with relish, that Margarita looked like a piece of her heart had been torn out as she watched a kitchen worker lead the chicken to its doom.

Later that week, Victoria called my Aunt Julieta to give her the date of our next visit. "And they've changed the rules," Victoria added. "So you can bring Ana some coffee this time, if you'd like."

Aunt Julieta promptly called my mother with the news. "What kind of a trick is this?" my mother fumed. "They just want me to put the coffee in Ana's normal package. Then, when they inspect it, they'll say, 'Are you crazy, *señora*? You've known for *years* you can't bring coffee in here. This is a willful act of defiance.' Then Ana won't have any coffee, and they'll probably suspend her visits for six months. I tell you, Julieta, those people play dirty. And it makes me mad that they think I'm so stupid."

The day of the visit, Victoria was at the door, inspecting packages.

She took a quick look through the one for me, and called my mother over. "Juana, didn't Julieta tell you about the coffee?" the *llavera* asked in dismay. "I called her myself to tell her you could bring some. Oh, Ana's going to be so disappointed!"

"You mean it's true?" my mother asked in disbelief. "It's really true? *Qué alivio tan grande!* Oh, what a relief!" She reached into her bra and, as half a dozen guards watched, pulled out two nylon stockings stuffed full of coffee. My sister went pale with fear. But Victoria started giggling, and by the time they reached the visiting room, she was roaring with laughter.

We were enjoying some of that coffee one morning a couple of weeks later when we heard a cry through our bathroom window: "*Plantadas! Plantadas!* We'd like to meet you." The three of us crowded around the window to see who was calling. A smiling blonde teenager stood a few feet away, and fanned out behind her were about two dozen other girls, not one of them over eighteen, wearing blue prison uniforms. They were all very pretty, with carefully groomed hair and freshly pressed uniforms. They looked like they had just stepped out of a magazine advertisement for the prison.

"Who are you?" I asked, not bothering to disguise the astonishment in my voice. They didn't look like any prisoners we had ever seen.

"We're *phaclanas*," the blonde girl answered. Her smile was so infectious that I returned it, despite my usual conviction that anything new in a prison environment should be considered dangerous until proven otherwise.

"What's a *phaclana*?" I asked. "That doesn't even sound like Spanish."

"It's not," the girl laughed. "It's Greek street slang for 'whore.' That's us, whores. They arrested about six hundred of us in August because Castro was hosting a big international youth festival and he was afraid we would embarrass him. We've been trying to meet you ever since we were arrested."

"Why would you want to meet us?" asked a puzzled Miriam. The expression on the girl's face was as if she'd just been asked why she thought the world was round.

"Because you're heroes," she replied. "You're the only ones they can't break."

"Where did you hear that?" asked Esther.

"Everybody knows it," the girl said with a trace of impatience. "We heard about you out on the street, before we were arrested. And when we got here, you're almost the only thing the common prisoners ever talk about. We would have come sooner, but it's not easy to get to this corner of the prison."

As if to prove her words, a *llavera* named Marina came rushing around a corner, red in the face, as though she'd been running a long way. "You girls get away from there!" she shouted. "You can't talk to them—do you want to be classified as counterrevolutionaries?"

"It would be an honor," the blonde girl replied coldly. "Unfortunately, we're just whores, born and bred by the Revolution."

"What do you mean by that?" the shocked *llavera* asked.

"Where do you think I learned that sex was something you could trade for advancement?" the girl said. "Out in the countryside, on one of the Revolution's agricultural labor mobilizations, where we were toys for the men in charge. It's a short step from doing it for a better work assignment to doing it for money."

Marina blanched. Her own daughter was on one of the mobilizations. Then she pulled herself together. "All of you, back to the pavilion, right now!" she shouted. "You'll be sleeping in the *tapiadas* tonight."

It was three weeks before we saw any of the *phaclanas* again. The blonde girl and two others called us to the window one night shortly after sundown.

"Sorry it took so long to return, but that bitch Marina was true to her word," the girl said. "I just got out of the *tapiadas* this morning."

"Isn't it a little risky to come back so soon?" I asked. "There's a gun-tower right behind us, and I'm sure the guard can see you."

"Forget the guard," she said, waving her hand dismissively. "We took care of him."

"You killed a guard?" I gasped.

"I don't think so," she laughed, "unless the girls have fucked him to death. There are a couple up there with him right now."

The *phaclanas*, she explained, had thoroughly corrupted the guards with offers of sex. Not only could they move around the prison with relative impunity, but they were able to obtain almost anything they wanted from outside—including marijuana, which they also shared with the guards.

It must have been true, because the *phaclanas* visited us frequently over the next several months. Every once in a while a *llavera* would catch them, but the guards in the tower never raised a peep.

Even so, we were always pleading with the girls to be careful. Nuevo Amanecer's new *tapiadas*, where they were sent if they were caught, were the ghastliest of all the Revolution's many cruel contributions to penology. Located in a large, windowless building that was barely ventilated, the cells were actually dug underground, so tightly sealed that sound scarcely escaped from them at all. It was like being walled up in a tomb. Prisoners held there never had any idea whether it was day or night, whether they were eating breakfast or dinner.

The experience was so nightmarish that common prisoners now regularly hid small surgical blades (stolen from the prison infirmary) under their tongues when going to the *tapiadas*, in case it was too much for them and they wanted to commit suicide. So many tried it that the *llaveras* stopped taking them to the hospital; instead, their wounds were sutured shut right there in the cell and the door quickly closed again.

The *tapiadas* were so grim that we probably should have told the girls to stop visiting us rather than take even a slight chance on winding up inside the underground cells. But, selfish though it may have been, we didn't want to lose their company. Not only did they keep us posted on developments within the prison, including the names of political prisoners who had been released, but their reports of life on the street were fascinating. Intelligent, articulate, and politically astute, they were a world apart from the old prostitutes we knew in Guanajay.

The *phaclanas* regarded themselves as rebels, striking their own small blows against the Revolution. Each *phaclana* was a one-woman propaganda squad: A foreigner who purchased sex got, as part of the package, a lecture about how life was in a drab, repressive Marxist state.

"A lot of them don't believe us at first," the blonde girl admitted. "Almost all of them are either visiting Havana for an official conference—in which case the government puts them in a hotel that has food and electricity and running water, unlike the rest of the city—or they're sailors, who just got off their ship for a few hours to get a girl and a beer, and they haven't seen much of the city.

"One thing that always impresses them is the ration books. Especially Western Europeans—they can't figure out where all this foreign aid they give Castro is going. Once I took a man down to the neighborhood store, and I showed him exactly how much food I could get in a month with the ration book. It was so little that he was sure I was lying. I had to get the lady who ran the store to confirm it."

The word *phaclana*, she told us, was something the girls had learned from an especially lusty shipload of Greek sailors. The girls adopted it to differentiate themselves from the government's own stable of prostitutes, maintained especially for visiting officials from other Communist countries.

Apparently the rest of the Marxist world didn't really believe Castro's boasts that he had eliminated gambling and prostitution from Cuba. When Russians, Czechs, and Bulgarians came to Havana, they expected to sample pre-revolutionary nightlife. To oblige them, the Cuban government operated a few small casinos and brothels. The *phaclanas* spoke contemptuously of these "union" prostitutes.

"The government gives them identification cards and regular health checkups," the blonde girl told us. "And in return, they have to work in government houses, where a concierge keeps track of how many customers each one has, and handles all the money. And the government keeps most of the money. Can you imagine? It's like having a pimp. And who wants a pimp? Even if it's Fidel Castro."

Twenty years ago, when Castro marched in from the Sierra Maestra, he spoke loudly and often of the corruption bred in Havana's gangster-ridden casinos, strip joints, and whorehouses. Prostitution, he said then, was a "social illness" and the Revolution would stamp it out just like it was smallpox or yellow fever. Now, outside our cell, a girl who hadn't even been born then was casually dismissing him as a pimp. *Truly,* I thought, *the Revolution has come full circle.*

OCTOBER 8, 1979

The face at the door loomed like a Shakespearean ghost, sent onstage to signal a change in the plot. Benilde Martínez, her thin, pinched face looking bonier than ever, stepped into our cell. She had run several of the prisons where we were confined, including Nuevo Amanacer when we first arrived, but then she disappeared into the upper rungs of the Interior Ministry. We hadn't seen her in six years.

"Get dressed in your best clothes," she said, not bothering with a greeting. "We're going to the offices to take photos for your travel documents."

We gaped at her. Travel documents? "Hurry up," she snapped. "We don't have all day. I'll fill out these release papers while you change."

The enormity of what she had said was just too much for us. We couldn't stop to think about it or it would sweep us away. We scurried to put on our cleanest, least ragged, pajamas. I could feel a smile spreading right down to my toes.

"What have you been doing the last few years, Benilde?" Miriam asked conversationally as she buttoned up her top. "We don't get much gossip out here." But Benilde didn't reply or even look up from the paperwork. It made my smile grow even further. "Poor Benilde," I cooed. "It seems as though the Maximum Leader has finally issued an order that she can't choke down. Don't worry, we won't tell anyone you had a lapse of revolutionary solidarity."

"Shut up and get dressed," she barked. "They told me I had to do this job, not that I had to like it." I laughed out loud. I thought of the old saying about Spaniards: *It's not enough for a Spaniard to know he's going to heaven; to be truly happy, he must also know that his neighbor is going to hell.* Half the fun of being free would be knowing how awful people like Benilde felt about it.

"Laugh all you want," Benilde sneered. "But it won't change the fact that you wasted your whole life in here. You should see how old you look."

"On the contrary, Benilde," I replied pleasantly, "I've never felt younger than I do at this moment."

Outside the sky was a pure cobalt blue, without even the trace of a cloud. The scorching ball of fire that had hung overhead all summer was gone, replaced by a friendly sun that bathed our faces with a gentle, sensuous warmth. *I could walk forever in this sun,* I thought.

We walked along the road that ran just inside the chain-link fence that lined the prison's perimeter. No one spoke; we were alone with our thoughts. Mine were incoherent fragments; every time I tried to piece them together, they tumbled apart once more. I didn't try very hard; I was content to just walk.

When we reached the dining room, the road curved sharply, and B Pavilion, one of the cellblocks for common prisoners, came into view. For a moment I thought the chain-link fence that surrounded the pavilion had been replaced with a solid blue wall. Then I realized the fence was covered with prisoners. Hundreds of them clung to it like a horde of insects.

"It's them!" someone cried, and the prisoners let out a collective roar. *"Viva las plantadas! Viva las plantadas!"* they screamed. Miriam, Esther, and I stopped dead in our tracks, pinned by the crushing surge of sound. Another, more distant wave followed it. It took me a moment to pinpoint it: It came from E Pavilion, which stood, surrounded by a high cement wall, next to B. Moments later, heads started popping over the top of the wall. Dozens of women were climbing it, dropping fifteen feet to the ground, and running to the chain-link fence. As they hurled themselves onto it, the fence began to sway dangerously. All the while, the chant—*Viva las plantadas!*—poured down around us like an avalanche of noise.

There was a roar from my own lungs, a roar of delighted laughter. The three of us waved with both hands, like movie stars. Suddenly a hand jerked my shoulder and spun me around. It was Benilde; she had been yelling at me, but I hadn't heard a word.

"Stop that waving!" she screamed, thrusting her face right in mine. "You'll cause a riot!"

I shrugged happily, and waved again. The booming cheers grew louder.

"Damn it, stop waving!" Benilde screamed again. "That fence is going to fall down." I could barely hear her. She turned and tried yelling at the prisoners hanging on the fence, but that was completely useless. Unleashing a string of curses, Benilde stamped her foot on the road like a berserk schoolmarm. "We should shoot every goddamn one of them!" she shrieked.

"That wouldn't do any good, Benilde," I shouted back. "You can shoot and shoot, until your fingers are tired from pulling the trigger, and you'll never be able to kill all the witnesses. Even if you killed them all, the stones of the prison themselves would cry out about what you've done."

By the time we walked away, the fence was swaying so precariously that I was certain I could have knocked it over with my little finger. But, somehow, it didn't fall. We disappeared into the offices, the *Vivas!* still pealing in our ears. Benilde, a vein in her forehead twitching furiously, deposited us in a room with a Ministry photographer.

"Which one of you is running for president?" he asked with a smile. "We almost had to cover our ears, that was so loud."

"How did they know we were coming?" wondered Miriam.

"You know some of the clerical work in here is done by common criminals," the photographer explained. "I think they heard Acosta in here this morning, giving orders, and they figured out you would be coming in. And from there it went on to the grapevine." He pointed at me. "You first—come smile for the camera." I sat down, remembering the night I was captured after my escape, when I made faces at the camera. I couldn't decide if it seemed like a long time ago, or just yesterday.

He took the pictures quickly, then told us to wait while they were developed, so he could redo them if anything was wrong. A silence descended on us once more. I wondered idly if my family knew yet. I tried to picture New Jersey, where my sister lived, on a map of the United States. I wondered what snow would be like.

A State Security lieutenant walked in about half an hour later. "The photos turned out fine," he said. "You can go into the other room, and they'll finish preparing your documents. Here, do you want to see your pictures?"

I peered carefully at the small black-and-white photograph he handed me. Benilde, for once, had been right. The girl who was coming home from the movies nineteen years ago, the one who was going to be a doctor and a wife and a mommy—where had she gone? It was a stranger's face that looked out at me from this photo. Her mouth was tight and wary, surrounded by deep lines of anger and grief. I recalled something I had read years ago, when I knew prisons only from gangster movies, something by Jose Martí, the man who freed Cuba from another cruel dictatorship. *The sorrow of prison,* he wrote, *leaves fingerprints that can never be erased.*

"We need that back," the lieutenant said genially. "It'll be a souvenir to remember you by." As I handed it to him, he saw something in my face. "Don't worry," he reassured me. "Black-and-white always accentuates the wrinkles. But they can be retouched."

· EPILOGUE ·

THE CHEERING THRONGS of prisoners as we walked to the office that day rattled the prison authorities. They delayed our release another five weeks. Hoping to avoid another scene like that one, they took us out of the prison before dawn on November 19. It didn't work. There were even more prisoners at the fence than the first time. They shouted *"Viva las plantadas!"* again, but this time, some of them were weeping, too. "Don't forget about us," one woman cried as our truck pulled away.

As my father predicted in my dream, Miriam, Esther, and I were the last three women freed as part of Castro's negotiations with the United States. A month later, Jimmy Carter's illusions about the reasonableness of Communist governments were shattered by the Soviet invasion of Afghanistan. The thaw in relations with Cuba slowed, then reversed into a deep freeze after Carter and the rest of the world got a close look at what Cubans really thought of the Revolution during the Mariel boatlift.

In April 1980, after the Peruvian embassy granted political asylum to six Cubans who broke into its grounds, Castro in a fit of pique had ordered all the guards removed from the embassy. To his embarrassment, ten thousand asylum-seekers crowded into the compound in a matter of days. Compounding his error, Castro announced that anyone who wanted to leave Cuba could do so. The result was the Mariel boatlift: a flotilla of yachts and other small craft shuttling back and forth between Havana and Key West. By the time Castro swallowed his pride and closed it down several weeks later, 120,000 people had fled Cuba.

It was no surprise to me. Although Esther flew to Miami almost immediately after our release, the visas for Miriam, me, and our families were mired in bureaucratic red tape, and we spent the next fifty-two days in Cuba. I spent a good bit of time traveling around the island. I wanted to see if anything had changed since the time I spent on the street in 1967. Was there any nascent movement to resist Castro? Was there any reason for me to stay?

I found plenty of people who despised the Revolution. But their idea was to flee it rather than fight it. Two decades of ruthless repression had done its job; most of the population was thoroughly cowed.

I decided to press on for my exit visa. It's one thing to risk your life for your country, but another thing entirely to commit suicide for it. I gave nearly nineteen years. I thought that was enough.

In January, we finally got our exit visas. Miriam and I suddenly found ourselves the most desirable two women in Cuba. Because our visas would cover husbands, too, we were deluged with marriage proposals. One man offered me $50,000 to marry him and take him with me. I was tempted to take up one of my instant suitors, not for the money, but just to help one more person escape, but in the end I didn't do it. I was sure that some of the offers came from State Security agents looking for an excuse to re-arrest me.

We flew to Costa Rica in mid-January aboard a chartered airliner full of former political prisoners—all of them, except for Miriam and I, men. As the plane passed over the island's edge, dozens of the men broke into tears. My eyes were dry. I was thinking of a statistic: In 1959, when Castro took over, Cuba had four prisons. As we flew away, there were two hundred.

We spent six weeks in Costa Rica while the U.S. government finished its paperwork. And on February 26, 1980—nineteen years to the day after my arrest—we arrived in Miami.

What became of some of the people who shared those nineteen years with me:

BERTA ALEMÁN, my companion in La Cabaña: When she dropped out of our little group of *plantadas* after we were transferred from La Cabaña, she was so ill from the tumor in her breast that I thought she had only weeks to live. About a month later, a *llavera* told me she had died. It was nearly twenty years before I discovered that was a lie: Happily, Berta survived, and lives in Miami.

ISABEL ALONSO, who helped shelter us during our first escape: She works at the Miami Fire Department.

MARGARITA BLANCO, who twice escaped with me: She lives in Miami with her three children. She's a medical researcher at the University of Miami.

ESTHER CAMPOS, one of my companions in the little schoolhouse: She lives in New Jersey.

BEBA CANABAL, former teenage propaganda ace: She lives in Miami with her husband, a Spanish businessman, and two daughters.

ADA CASTELLANOS (Chonchi), my companion on my first escape: She lives in Miami with several of her sisters.

DORA DELGADO (Japonesa), who started the baseball craze at Guanajay: She lives in Miami and works distributing food products to convenience stores. Since 1993, when Miami got its own major-league baseball team, her life has been heaven.

DINORAH FERRER (Kiss Me One Key, Manolito the Merciless), the prostitute with the split personality: Sometimes, after she finished serving her sentence, she came to the prison fence to model her new dresses for us. In 1971, police responding to a call found her bleeding to death from stab wounds. Before she died, she gave the name of her killer, a man with close connections to the army. His punishment: six months on a work farm.

MARÍA ANTONIETA LÓPEZ, DORA VICTORIA REYES, and NARCY IBARGOLLÍN, the engineers of the second successful escape from Guanajay: Narcy Ibargollín escaped from Cuba by seeking refuge in an embassy. She reached Miami, where she still lives, married and working in a medical office. She told me that many of the women in our *galera* were so angry about the punishment they received following the escape that, when they came to Miami years later, they still wouldn't talk to her. María Antonieta López and Dora Victoria Reyes, recaptured after the escape, were eventually released. María Antonieta dropped out of sight. Dora Victoria continued living in Cuba. In 1984, she obtained a visa to visit some family members in Miami. When she returned to Havana, she was arrested by State Security, and soon afterward died under circumstances that remain unexplained.

MANOLO MARTÍNEZ, the former national director of prisons: We never heard another word about him after his last bizarre visit to us in 1966. In 1994, a former Interior Ministry official who defected to Washington, D.C., was asked about Manolo's fate. "He disgraced himself, and he disappeared," the defector said. "That's all I know."

ISIS NIMO, the spy who got so many of us into trouble: It was impossible for her to continue working undercover after the wave of arrests in 1961, and the Interior Ministry gave her a desk job. But her only real skill, it seemed, was betrayal. After a while she was demoted to the Fishing Ministry, and then she lost that job, too. The last we heard of her, she had been confined on one of the prison farms for homosexuals.

MIRIAM ORTEGA, who joined me in so many protests: She runs a Miami nursing home. I see her frequently, but we almost never talk about our days in prison; "I don't remember" is her standard response whenever I bring it up. But as she read the parts of this book that include her, tears trickled down her cheeks.

ANGEL PÉREZ, my Communist friend from high school: He wound up in the Cuban air force, flying jets, as he predicted. But later he was purged and imprisoned as part of the so-called Microfaction, a Communist Party splinter group that wanted Castro to follow Moscow more closely. Angel wound up in Coral Gables, Florida, working as a waiter. I saw him years later and told him that, during my first escape, I tried to call him, hoping he could somehow fly me out of Cuba. "I would have done it in a minute," he said. When we argue about politics these days, I'm the leftist: Angel thinks the United States should invade Cuba.

RAQUEL ROMERO, Fernandito's mother: After her escape from prison, she took refuge in the Brazilian embassy and eventually made her way to Miami. Fernandito stayed in Havana, raised by a grandmother and aunts who were loyal to the Revolution. They told him Raquel was dead, and threw away all the letters she wrote to him. In the early 1980s, when Castro eased the rules for visits by Cuban exiles, she went to Havana and waited outside his house one afternoon. When he came walking along, she called him. "Fernando, I know you don't know me, but I'm your mother," she said. He ran away.

FIDELINA SUÁREZ, *toque de lata* specialist: "I did all this for my son and daughter, and now I've lost them," she sobbed after learning that her mother-in-law was raising the children as revolutionaries to keep them out of trouble. "I've turned into their enemy. I'm fighting my own children." The conflict with her mother-in-law destroyed her marriage. Now she lives in Miami, where she sells beauty products. The children live in Cuba, where they are ardent Castro supporters.

ONELIA VALDÉS, Natacha's mother: She still lives in Cuba. So does Natacha, who's a pediatrician now. Every so often one of us gets a postcard from Natacha: "Are all my aunties mad at me? Why haven't I heard from them recently?"

TERESA VIDAL, who came along on my second escape: She died of breast cancer in 1992, in Miami.

THE RODRÍGUEZ FAMILY: My mother lives with my sisters in New Jersey, where Magda is a computer specialist and Milagros is the bookkeeper for a floral warehouse. Says Milagros: "Sometimes I have to get up at three

A.M. to go to work, and it's cold and dark and there's snow and ice on the ground. And I think to myself—I'm so happy to be away from Cuba, I don't care." My aunt Julieta is there, too.

It took me some time to adjust to life outside prison. When I came to the United States, I had to consciously remind myself a dozen times a day that men in uniforms were not my enemies. If I saw a sign that said *Keep Off the Grass*, I immediately walked on it. When Magda took me to visit the big Macy's store in New York, I spotted the store detectives right away. My first impulse was to steal something, just to prove I could outsmart them. Fortunately, I stifled it.

I also felt, for quite a while, like a time-traveler who had bounced unexpectedly into the future. Cassette tapes, microwave ovens, Touch-Tone telephones: it was all brand-new to me. Even color television was a comparative novelty when I went to prison in 1962. And to this day, there are weird gaps in my grasp of history. Most of the space race and virtually the entire Vietnam War took place while I was in prison. The 1960s, the decade that, for better or worse, reshaped so much of the world's culture and politics, was only a rumor to me. To put it another way, I missed the Beatles completely.

I spent some time in New Jersey, but unlike Milagros, I could never quite get used to the snow. I moved to Coral Gables, Florida, a suburb of Miami, and started picking up the pieces of my life. It took years, shuffling between jobs, English courses, and medical school, but I finally got my medical degree. I expect to start a residency in pediatrics at a Miami hospital soon.

A dream deferred is twice as sweet when it's realized, and I'm living my life for the future, not the past. But I could never forget the years I spent in prison, nor forgive them; wounds heal, but scars remain. In all the years I was locked up, they never made me shed a tear, not once. But now, sometimes, I cry.

· INDEX ·